KYOTO CSEAS SERIES ON ASIAN STUDIES 4
Center for Southeast Asian Studies, Kyoto University

# CHINA AND THE SHAPING OF INDONESIA, 1949–1965

KYOTO CSEAS SERIES ON ASIAN STUDIES 4
Center for Southeast Asian Studies, Kyoto University

# CHINA AND THE SHAPING OF INDONESIA, 1949–1965

*Hong Liu*

NUS PRESS
*Singapore*

in association with

KYOTO UNIVERSITY PRESS
*Japan*

*The publication of this volume was partially funded by the Global COE Program of Kyoto University Foundation.*

© 2011 Hong Liu

All rights reserved. No part of this publication may be reproduced or transmitted in any form or by any means, electronic or mechanical, including photocopying, recording, or any information storage or retrieval system, without permission in writing from the publisher.

NUS Press  
National University of Singapore  
AS3-01-02, 3 Arts Link  
Singapore 117569  
www.nus.edu.sg/nuspress  

Kyoto University Press  
Yoshida-South Campus, Kyoto University  
69 Yoshida-Konoe-Cho, Sakyo-ku  
Kyoto 606-8315, Japan  
www.kyoto-up.or.jp  

ISBN 978-9971-69-381-7 (Paper)

ISBN 978-4-87698-353-7 (Paper)

**National Library Board, Singapore Cataloguing-in-Publication Data**

Liu, Hong.
 China and the shaping of Indonesia, 1949–1965 / Hong Liu. – Singapore: NUS Press in association with Kyoto University Press, c2011.
 p. cm. – (Kyoto CSEAS series on Asian studies; 4)
 Includes bibliographical references and index.
 ISBN: 978-9971-69-381-7 (pbk.)

 1. Indonesia – Civilization – Chinese influences – History – 20th century. 2. Indonesia – History – 1950–1966. 3. Indonesia – Politics and government – 1950–1966. 4. China – Foreign public opinion, Indonesian. 5. Public opinion – Indonesia. 6. China – Relations – Indonesia – 20th century. 7. Indonesia – Relations – China – 20th century. I. Title. II. Series: Kyoto CSEAS series on Asian studies; 4.

DS644
959.8035 — dc22                    OCN715921764

Cover: Sukarno and Mao, 1956 (*Presiden Sukarno Mengundjungi Tiongkok* [Jakarta: Kedutaan Besar Republik Rakjat Tiongkok di Indonesia, 1956])

Typeset by: Scientifik Graphics
Printed by: Mainland Press Pte Ltd

*In dedication to my mother, Lian Qingbo,
and to the memory of my late father, Liu Angbin*

# CONTENTS

| | |
|---|---|
| *Acknowledgements* | xi |
| *List of Figures* | xiii |

| Introduction: | China in Indonesia: What's in a Name? | 1 |
|---|---|---|
| | Déjà Vu *All Over Again?* "The China Fever" and Its Significant Precedent | 2 |
| | Approaches to China in Indonesia | 6 |
| | Nature and Characteristics of China Observers in Indonesia | 17 |
| | Structure of the Book | 22 |

## Part I: (Re)presenting China

| Chapter 1: | Changing Images of China in Pre-1949 Indonesia | 33 |
|---|---|---|
| | Historical Interactions and Perceptions of China in Pre-20th-century Indonesia | 34 |
| | Indonesian Nationalists and China, 1900–49 | 41 |
| | Perceived Parallelisms | 52 |
| | Conclusion | 57 |

| Chapter 2: | Discourses on Chinese Politics | 59 |
|---|---|---|
| | "New Democracy": Chinese Practices and Indonesian Perceptions | 60 |
| | China in the International Arena: "An Awakening Lion" or "A Threatening Red Dragon"? | 70 |
| | "Brother Mao": Images of Mao Zedong in Indonesia | 73 |
| | Conclusion | 76 |

| Chapter 3: | Social Dynamism and Economic Progress | 79 |
|---|---|---|
| | The Purposefulness and Orderliness of an Egalitarian Society | 80 |
| | New China's "Amazing" Economic Growth | 89 |
| | The People's Commune as an Epitome of Social and Economic Progress | 93 |

|  |  |  |
|---|---|---|
|  | *Making Sense of China's Socio-economic Progress: Politics or Chineseness?* | 96 |
|  | *Conclusion* | 104 |
| Chapter 4: | Of Culture, Religion and Intellectuals | 106 |
|  | *"New Culture" and Nation-building* | 107 |
|  | *Intellectuals in the PRC: "Engineers of Human Souls" or "Tools of Propaganda"?* | 112 |
|  | *A Question of Religious Freedom* | 119 |
|  | *Conclusion* | 124 |

## Part II: Constructing the China Metaphor

|  |  |  |
|---|---|---|
| Chapter 5: | Indonesian Dreams and the "Chinese Realities": The Sociopolitical and Intellectual Dimensions | 127 |
|  | *Political Instability and Cultural Antagonisms at Home* | 129 |
|  | *Disillusionment and Alienation of Intellectuals* | 136 |
|  | *Preconceptions about Indonesia and the Construction of China-images* | 144 |
|  | *Conclusion* | 153 |
| Chapter 6: | An "Inner China" and External PRC: The Ethnic and Diplomatic Dimensions | 154 |
|  | *Indonesian Chinese Society and the Construction of Images of the Ancestral Homeland* | 156 |
|  | *Brothers of Different Kinds: Indonesians' Paradoxical Views of the Chinese* | 168 |
|  | *Sino-Indonesian Diplomatic Relations and the Making of the China Metaphor* | 175 |
|  | *China Creates Its Own Images* | 185 |
|  | *Conclusion* | 200 |

## Part III: Shaping a New Trajectory

|  |  |  |
|---|---|---|
| Chapter 7: | Sukarno, the China Metaphor and Political Populism | 205 |
|  | *Sukarno and China before 1956* | 207 |
|  | *Mr Sukarno Goes to Beijing* | 213 |
|  | *Sukarno's Perception of China and Vision for Indonesia* | 223 |
|  | *Conclusion* | 230 |

| Chapter 8: | Pramoedya, the China Metaphor and Cultural Radicalism | 234 |
|---|---|---|
| | *Pramoedya before 1956: The Evolution of a Cultural Intellectual* | 236 |
| | *Pramoedya in China: The Politics of a Transnational Romance* | 242 |
| | *The Transformation of Pramoedya: The Critical Years, 1956–59* | 253 |
| | *Conclusion* | 259 |
| Conclusion: | China as an Alternative Modernity | 267 |
| Appendix: | Biographical Notes on Major China Observers in Indonesia, 1949–65 | 275 |
| *Bibliography* | | 292 |
| *Index* | | 316 |

# ACKNOWLEDGEMENTS

The research and preparation of this manuscript took me across three continents, on a journey in the course of which I accumulated a great debt of gratitude to many individuals. In the United States, William H. ("Bill") Frederick, Charles Alexander, Alonzo Hamby, Donald Jordan, Gary Hawes, Benedict Anderson, Hwa-wei Lee, Lian The-Mulliner, Kent Mulliner, Jeff Ferrier, Suharni Soemarmo, Kohar and Minar Rony, Tsing Yuan, Liren Zheng, Philip Kuhn, Adam McKeown, Michael Szonyi, and Min Zhou gave me invaluable help and support. So, in Asia, did Alan K.L. Chan, Wong Yoon Wah, Cheng Lim-keat, Lily Kong, Leo Suryadinata, Tony Reid, Lee Chee Hiang, Huang Jianli, Chen Chunsheng, Liu Zhiwei, Wang Hui, Li Bozhong, Li Minghuan, Fan Ke, Zhuang Guotu, Mizuno Kosuke, Shimizu Hiromu, Kaoru Sugihara, Carol Hau, Jojo Patricio Abinales, Junko Koizumi, Noboru Ishikawa, Yumi Kitamura, Masaaki Okamoto, Tomoko Shiroyama, Hideaki Shiroyama, Liao Chiyang, Wang Wei, Chen Laixing, Iijima Wataru, Naoto Kagotani, Matsuura Masataka, Kawashima Shin, Fujio Hara, I. Wibowo, James Chin Kong, Geoff Wade, and Koh Young Hun. So, in Europe, did Go Gien Tjwan, Mary Somers-Heidhues, Alistair Ulph, Steve Parker, Qi Luo, Michael Charney, Atsuko Naono, Ramses Amer, Xiaobing Wang, and Masako Ikegami. During the early and crucial period of research, Zhan Xiaojuan offered unflinching moral support and steady encouragement, for which I remain grateful.

I am immensely indebted, intellectually and personally, to Wang Gungwu, Gregor Benton, Bill Frederick, Takashi Shiraishi, Takeshi Hamashita, and Ezra F. Vogel, who provided expert advice and unwavering support at key stages of my research career, including while preparing to write this book.

I did research in the Archives of the Ministry of Foreign Affairs of the People's Republic of China (which started, from 2004 onward, declassifying its archives and making them available to the researchers), the Southeast Asian Collections of Alden Library at Ohio University, the Asian Collections of Kroch Library at Cornell University, the Asian Division of the Library of Congress, the British Library, the National Library of Indonesia, the Chinese Library of the National University of Singapore, the Library of the Center for Southeast Asian Studies of Kyoto University, the National Library of China, the library and archival collection of the Central Party School, Peking University Library, and the Library of the Nanyang Research Institute at Xiamen University. During my fieldwork in Southeast Asia, China, the Netherlands, and the United States, many individuals graciously shared with me their personal and professional experiences through many hours of oral-history interviews, which significantly enriched my understanding of Sino-Indonesian exchanges in the Sukarno era, and I owe them special thanks: Soeto Meisen, Chen Xiaru, Tong Djoe, Oey Tong Ping, Chen Wenxian, Huang Shuhai, Chen Lishui, Huang Aling, Huang You, Jiang Baolin, Lin Liushun, Shannu, Weng Xihui, and Zhang Ailing. Some of China's leading Indonesianists — who were born and educated in the archipelago before returning to the PRC in the 1960s — provided me with unique insights into the cultural and human dimensions of the changing Sino-Indonesian relationship: Zhou Nanjing, Liang Yingming, Ju Sanyuan, Liang Liji, and Huang Yuanhuan.

I would like to acknowledge the following funding agencies and institutions for their generous financial support for my archival, library and field research: the Henry Luce Foundation, the Japan Society for the Promotion of Science, the Lee Foundation, the Universities' China Committee in London, and the University of Manchester, where I had a precious opportunity to contribute to institution building in my capacity as the founding Director of the Centre for Chinese Studies and Professor of East Asian Studies between 2006 and 2010. I have spent most of my time over the past years meeting the new challenge of setting up a History Department at the School of Humanities and Social Sciences at Nanyang Technological University. A generous research grant from NTU (M58100049) enabled me to complete the final updating of this manuscript.

I am delighted that this book is to be published jointly by NUS Press and Kyoto University Press, two institutions to which I had the privilege of being formally affiliated for more than a decade. I thank Paul Kratoska, Yoko Hayami, Lena Qua, and Mario Ivan Lopez for facilitating the publication. I am grateful to the two anonymous referees for their thorough and constructive feedback, which helped improve the manuscript. Needless to say, I alone am responsible for the interpretations, ideas, and any remaining errors.

I dedicate this book to my mother, Lian Qingbo, and to the memory of my late father, Liu Angbin. They instilled in me a keen love of knowledge, but had to endure many years of my absence while I undertook study and research far from home. Last but not least, my wife Jessie and our daughter Sophie have been forbearing and understanding. Without them, this book would not have been completed.

# LIST OF FIGURES

1. Hatta Visiting the Sun Yat-sen Memorial Hall in Nanjing, 1957 — 49
2. Cover of Armijn Pane, *Tiongkok Zaman Baru. Sedjarahnja: Abad ke-19 — Sekarang* — 51
3. Cover of Arifin Bey, *Dari Sun Yat Sen ke Mao Tze Tung* — 66
4. Insertion of Sugardo's *Tiongkok Sekarang* — 67
5. Ali Sastroamidjojo having dinner with Mao and Zhou Enlai, Beijing, 1955 — 75
6. Poem of Situmorang and photo of him with Guo Monuo, Beijing, 1961 — 83
7. An Indonesian woman's writing about China: "We Come, We See, We Learn…" — 88
8. Cover of Sakirman's *Pembangunan Ekonomi Raksasa Tiongkok Rakjat* — 98
9. Cover of the *Kompas untuk Generasi Baru* magazine (1954), on Indonesian college students visiting China — 102
10. Barioen, Pane and Tabrani in Hangzhou, 1951 — 110
11. Indonesian visitors in Tiananmen Square, July 1965 — 112
12. Hatta in Xinjiang, 1957 — 121
13. Sudiro with students at Tsinghua University, Beijing, 1956 — 144
14. "Our Dilemma" — cover of *Ta Hsueh Tsa Chih* [College Student Magazine], 1951 — 159

15. Over 20,000 Chinese in Jakarta celebrating the establishment of Sino-Indonesian diplomatic relationship, May 1950 — 163

16. Zhou Enlai in Bandung, 1955 — 178

17. Sukarno dancing with Marshal Chen Yi, Jakarta, 1961 — 181

18. Sima Wensen in Surabaya, 1956 — 190

19. Calendar poster attached to and distributed with *Tiongkok Rakjat*, 1965: "A General sends his daughters to the countryside" — 193

20. Calendar poster attached to and distributed with *Tiongkok Rakjat*, 1965: "Preparing for the tilling of the land in winter" — 193

21. Sukarno was welcomed by Mao and the Chinese in Beijing, 1956 — 217

22. Sukarno and Mao Zedong, Beijing, 1956 — 222

23. Pramoedya speaking at the conference commemorating the 20th anniversary of Lu Xun's death, Beijing, 1956 — 246

24. Cover of Agam Wispi *et al.*, *Dinasti 650 Djuta* — 261

25. Cover of Chinese translation of Situmorang's *Collection of Poems*, translated by Chen Xiaru *et al.* — 262

26. Cover of the *Sastra* magazine (1964) which was closely associated with the "Manifesto" members — 265

# INTRODUCTION

# China in Indonesia: What's in a Name?

*What we have seen in the past ten days is very amazing and exciting. Amazing, because everywhere we saw people were energetically working for development. New factories, which had not existed before and had not even been thought about by the old regime, have emerged all over the place.*

Mohammad Hatta (1957)[1]

*In Indonesia, people only think of themselves; over there, everyone thinks of others. Here, people have to be greedy in order to survive; over there, the greedy instinct has been totally eradicated.*

Pramoedya Ananta Toer (1957)[2]

*While the outcomes in the field of economic construction are generally inspiring, the results are tragic in the fields of developing morality and protecting the basic rights of man.*

Arifin Bey (1953)[3]

*I went to the country where my ancestors were born, hoping to find a communist nirvana; what I encountered was more like a hell.*

Cheng Lim Fei (1959)[4]

---

[1] Mohammad Hatta, "Selamat Tinggal (Pidato pada Jamuan Makan yang Diadakan Duta Besar Indonesia di Peking, pada Tanggal 2 Oktober 1957)", in Hatta, *Kumpulan Pidato*, vol. 2 (Jakarta: Inti Idayu Press, 1983), p. 99.
[2] Pramoedya Ananta Toer, "Djiwa Revolusioner di Tiongkok Tetap Bergolak", *Sin Po*, 5 January 1957.
[3] Arifin Bey, *Dari Sun Yat Sen ke Mao Tze Tung* (Jakarta: Tintamas, 1953), p. 166.
[4] Cheng Lim Fei, "Saja Pernah Sekolah di Tiongkok", *Gadjah Mada* 9 (May 1959): 92.

This introduction chapter addresses three central issues intriguingly and intimately related to the studies of postcolonial evolution in Indonesia during the Sukarno era (1949–65): the significance of narratives and discourses about China, whose multifaceted presence and conflicting reception in Indonesia are vividly exemplified by the above quotations; major themes in the existing studies on China in Indonesia; and the nature and characteristics of China-image-makers. I argue that a transnational inquiry into the presentations, constructions, and domestic ramifications of perceptions of China can shed new insights into Indonesia's complex transformations and multidimensional Sino-Indonesian interactions. Furthermore, by focusing on the discursive formation of and interplay between knowledge and power and the unfolding of China as an alternative form of modernity in a non-Western society, this study intends to contribute to a comparative understanding of the changing image of China in the outside world, which has been almost exclusively built upon experiences in the West and Japan.

## *DÉJÀ VU* ALL OVER AGAIN? "THE CHINA FEVER" AND ITS SIGNIFICANT PRECEDENT

In November 2001, the Chinese prime minister, Zhu Rongji, paid an official visit to Indonesia — the trip caused quite a stir. All major newspapers in the nation published editorials and commentaries about his trip, the first visit by a PRC premier in more than a decade — after Zhu's predecessor Li Peng's trip to Jakarta in 1990, which resumed a diplomatic relationship that was frozen after the 30 September Movement in 1965. In an editorial entitled "We Can Directly Listen to the Successful Stories of China's Development",[5] *Kompas* stated that China's progress had been "spectacular and fascinating". With Zhu's visit, "we can now listen to the successful stories concerning China's development over the last 20 years". Hailing Zhu's visit as "very special", the editorial of *The Jakarta Post* pointed out that "Indonesia would do well to take advantage of and explore the opportunities presented by this occasion." It reminded readers of the fact that "this is a completely new, modern and very confident China that the rest of the world has to deal with". The editorial went on to say that Zhu had been "chiefly responsible for transforming China over the last 10 years

---

[5] "Kita Bisa Mendengar Langsun Kisah Sukses Pembangunan Cina", *Kompas*, 7 November 2001. On related and similar suggestions, see Charles Himawan, "Can China Help RI Eradicate Corruption?" *Jakarta Post*, 9 November 2001.

into its present state, and in doing so, he is also the man responsible for changing the global power equation".⁶

In the meantime, the past two decades have witnessed the rapid growth of economic relations between the two nations. By 2005, the year when the Sino-Indonesian strategic partnership was established, China became Indonesia's fourth-largest export market; bilateral trade jumped from $1.18 billion in 1990 to $43 billion in 2010.⁷ Sudrajat, Indonesian ambassador to Beijing, stated in 2008 that "China and Indonesia are almost in a 'honeymoon' state", while some commentators called it "a golden era of bilateral relations".⁸

This recent wave of China fever, however, is by no means unique in modern Indonesia. As this study seeks to demonstrate, during the Sukarno era, many prominent intellectual and political figures of various ideological persuasions, from the anti-Communist politician Mohammad Hatta to Pramoedya Ananta Toer, "one of the few Indonesians with a coherent and developed vision of the nation's history",⁹ regarded China as an inspiring model of social engineering and cultural regeneration in the nation-building process. Nevertheless, unlike the present time when the PRC is seen in a more detached and neutral manner,¹⁰ images of China during the Sukarno era were much more diverse and convoluted; they were widely represented through a variety of public and intellectual media. These representations, furthermore, were brought into policy domains and subsequently constituted a politically loaded site of contestation. For some, China was a

---

⁶ "Welcome Premier Zhu", *Jakarta Post*, 7 November 2001.
⁷ See the official website of the Ministry of Foreign Affairs of the People's Republic of China, <http://www.fmprc.gov.cn/eng/4360.html>; "China and Indonesia seal strategic pact", *International Herald Tribute*, 26 April 2005; "China Seeks to Boost Trade with ASEAN", *Business Times*, 27 April 2005; *Jakarta Post*, 31 March 2010; Wen Jiabao, "Strengthen Relations and Deepen Cooperation", *China Daily*, 3 May 2011.
⁸ "Indonesia, China Relations almost in Honeymoon State: Sudrajat", *Jakarta Post*, 14 April 2008; Zaki Amrullah, "From Pogroms to Partners – Indonesians' Views of China" (May 2010), <http://www.dw-world.de/dw/article/0,,5563991,00.html> [accessed 12 May 2010].
⁹ Adrian Vickers, *A History of Modern Indonesia* (Cambridge: Cambridge University Press, 2005), p. 3.
¹⁰ For instance, Jusuf Wanandi, a member of Board of Trustees of the influential Centre for Strategic and International Studies in Jakarta, suggested that "Southeast Asia should study the Chinese economy and its future development", but he also regarded China as "a market, an investor, and a development partner for East Asian economies". See his "China-RI Ties: Challenges and Opportunities", *Jakarta Post*, 7 November 2001.

totalitarian regime that their nation should not emulate, while for others it only served as a reminder of the existence of the local Chinese community — an "economically exploitative and socially separated ethnic minority". Indeed, even for the same individuals, China evoked changing images over different periods of time, ranging from Indonesia's foe to its friend.

China, in short, was anything but the mere name of a nation-state located to the north of the Indonesia archipelago. Rather, it represented an ambiguous and complex state (of mind) and a loaded site of contestation. The discovery of China became a pretext for and contextualization of the rediscovery of Indonesia itself, which in turn helped shape the country's trajectory. The affirmation of a revolutionary, efficient and seemingly prosperous China appeared to have highlighted to many Indonesians their nation's disappointing postcolonial transformation. The appeal of an imagined China, furthermore, revealed a deep sense of alienation in Indonesia. Through a process of discursive practice and intense debates, the conflicting China images were gradually transformed into what I call "the China metaphor", which mirrored the complex characteristics and ambivalent nature of Indonesian intellectuals and politicians. By way of its domestication and integration into their thought and policies, the narratives about China subsequently constituted a significant factor in Indonesia's postcolonial transformation. As such, the China metaphor acquired far-reaching significance beyond the original connotations of perceptions of the PRC.

China's physical and normative presence and its conflicting receptions, therefore, were important, because they touched upon one of the central issues embedded in the postcolonial transformation, namely, the intertwining of knowledge and power through a thick web of discursive and appropriation practices.[11] As will be established in the rest of this

---

[11] While my discussion of the conceptions of power and knowledge is influenced by Michel Foucault, who views power as constituted by certain structures or "discourses", this study considers the crucial contextualization of the power/knowledge equation and the specificities of the Indonesian notions of power. For some discussions of the Foucauldian conceptions of power and knowledge, see Michel Foucault, *Power/Knowledge: Selected Interviews and Other Writings, 1972–1977* (New York: Pantheon, 1980); and Nicholas B. Dirks, Geoff Eley and Sherry B. Ortner, "Introduction", in, *Culture/Power/History: A Reader in Contemporary Social Theory*, ed. Dirks, Eley, and Ortner (Princeton: Princeton University Press, 1994), pp. 3–45. For a penetrating analysis of Javanese ideas of power, see Benedict Anderson, "The Idea of Power in Javanese Culture", in *Culture and Politics in Indonesia*, ed. Claire Holt (Ithaca: Cornell University Press, 1972), pp. 1–70, esp. pp. 43–7, "Power and Knowledge".

introductory chapter, those responsible for articulating the China-images and moulding them onto the "China metaphor" were also the same people shaping the nation's political and cultural trajectories. The debates about China, as a consequence, became an integral part of the country's quest for a political format and cultural identity in a broadly conceived "Asian framework". Within this context, China served as a point of reference and an important yardstick against which differing political statements were formulated, expounded and heatedly debated. For instance, as will be detailed in Chapters 7 and 8, the political populism and cultural radicalism of the Guided Democracy period (1959–65) drew conceptual and practical inspirations from the China example, which in turn intensified the ongoing political polarization and ultimately contributed to the final showdown of events surrounding the 30 September Movement. The interplay between the search for new modes of sociopolitical engineering and the incorporation of China into these alternative modes, therefore, became a major dynamic in the tumultuous history of the Sukarno era.

This book explores the presentations, constructions and implications of the discourses about China within the context of a changing social and political milieu between 1949 and 1965. This period was a time of critical transition, in both Indonesia and China as well as in their relationships. The year 1949 witnessed the founding of both the People's Republic of China and the formal transfer of sovereignty from the Dutch to the Republic of Indonesia. The two nations established diplomatic relations in the following year, thus opening a variety of channels of interaction in the political, social and cultural arenas and facilitating the travel of ideas and practices across national boundaries. The 30 September Movement in 1965 ended the Sukarno era and propelled a rapid deterioration of diplomatic ties with the PRC. The year 1965 in China was a time when the final stage was set for a devastating decade-long period of internal turmoil, the so-called "Great Proletariat Cultural Revolution".

This study examines the following central questions: What were the substance and variations of Indonesians' perceptions of China? Who presented these perceptions and what were their sociopolitical characteristics? What were key explanatory factors (sociopolitical, intellectual, ethnic and diplomatic) that shaped the specific images of the PRC? How were conflicting perceptions of and narratives about China formulated and transformed into the China metaphor? How did the China metaphor reveal society's general mood and impinge upon the political and cultural thinking of the time? Was China constructed as an alternative form of modernity to the prevailing conceptions and practices originating from the West? And finally, does a transnational approach give us any new insights into the history of modern Asia and of regional transformation?

## APPROACHES TO CHINA IN INDONESIA

The existing literature dealing with China's presence in Indonesia and its receptions can be broadly divided into four categories, approaching the place of China from, respectively, the perspectives of *diplomatic relations, cultural exchanges, evolution of the Communist Party of Indonesia* and *the development of local Chinese communities*. This section examines the main themes emerging from this literature and pinpoints limitations that might have prevented most of these works from taking China's presence in Indonesia beyond the conventional diplomatic arena and forging a transnational perspective. I will also offer some suggestions as to the ways this book departs from existing paradigms based upon nation-state supremacy and a rigid compartmentalization of the subregions — a central pillar of Asian studies in the West (particularly North America) after the 1950s.

### Four Approaches and Research Foci
*Diplomatic Relationship*

Represented by the works of David Mozingo, Sheldon Simon and a few other authors,[12] this approach is mainly concerned with the evolution of Sino-Indonesian diplomatic relations in the international Cold War context, focusing specifically on *realpolitik* and the formation, implementation and ultimate outcomes of foreign policies. The central question in Mozingo's study, for example, is "why China's policy in Indonesia failed". To answer this question, he explores various constraints upon Chinese decision-making, especially how its Indonesian policy was subordinated to its policies toward the United States and the Soviet Union. While these studies depict China as an influential diplomatic factor having a noticeable impact upon Indonesia's foreign policy alternatives, little attention was given to the domestic ramifications of Indonesians' perceptions of China and their

---

[12] David Mozingo, *Chinese Policy toward Indonesia, 1949–1967* (Ithaca: Cornell University Press, 1976); Sheldon Simon, *The Broken Triangle: Peking, Djakarta, and the PKI* (Baltimore: Johns Hopkins University Press, 1969); Peter Hauswedell, "The Anti-Imperialist International United Front in Chinese and Indonesian Foreign Policy 1963–1965: A Study of Anti-Status Quo Politics" (Ph.D. dissertation, Cornell University, 1976).

corresponding impact upon foreign policies. In an important study dealing with Indonesia-China diplomatic relations between 1967 and 1990,[13] Rizal Sukma carefully analyses the domestic primacy in Indonesia's decision to suspend the diplomatic ties with China in 1967. The need to sustain the New Order government's political legitimacy and to counteract domestic challenges based upon the perceived Communist threat, he argues, prevented the restoration of diplomatic relations prior to 1990. While this study provides much new insight and information on the Indonesia-China relationship during the Suharto years, the Sukarno era is taken as a background to the later decades.[14]

## Cultural Exchanges

Represented primarily by studies of PRC scholars,[15] these works analyse China's role in the context of Sino-Indonesian cultural exchanges. This research focus is in essence an extension of the previous strand of scholarship, because both policy-makers and many PRC-based scholars tend to view cultural exchange as a function of and supplement to official diplomacy.[16] Here, China is portrayed as a benevolent power that brought, over centuries, various cultural amenities and enrichments, ranging from vocabulary

---

[13] Rizal Sukma, *Indonesia and China: The Politics of a Troubled Relationship* (London: Routledge, 1999); Rizal Sukma, "Indonesia's perceptions of China: the domestic bases of persistent ambiguity", in *The China Threat: Perceptions, Myths and Reality*, ed. Herbert Yee and Ian Storey (London: RoutledgeCurzon, 2002), pp. 181–204.

[14] There is a brief survey of the three periods of Sino-Indonesian relations during the Sukarno era: "The early years (1950–56): a time of suspicion", pp. 24–6; "The radicalization of Indonesia's foreign policy and Indonesia-China relations (1957–1965)", pp. 27–33; and "The breakdown of diplomatic relations (1965–1967)", pp. 33–7.

[15] See for example, Huang Aling, *Zhongguo Yinni Guanxishi Jianbian* [A short history of Sino-Indonesian relations] (Beijing: Zhongguo Guoji Guangbo Chubanshe, 1987); Kong Yuanzhi, *Zhongguo Yindunixiya Wenhua Jiaoliu* [Cultural exchanges between China and Indonesia] (Beijing: Peking University Press, 1999); Zhou Nanjing and Kong Yuanzhi, eds., *Sujianuo, Zhongguo, Yindunixiya Huaren* [Sukarno, China, and Indonesian Chinese] (Hong Kong: Hong Kong Social Sciences Publisher, 2003). See also the introduction in Claudine Salmon, *Literature in Malay by the Chinese of Indonesia: A Provisional Annotated Bibliography* (Paris: Éditions de la Maison des Sciences de l'Homme, 1981).

[16] Teng Yun, ed., *Dangdai Zhongwai Wenhua Jiaoliu Shiliao* [Primary materials on cultural exchanges between China and foreign countries in the contemporary era] (Beijing: Wenhua Yishu Chubanshe, 1990).

items in Bahasa Indonesia and the design motifs of batik to specific forms of literary expression. The positive contributions of the ethnic Chinese as a bridge in this cultural exchange are frequently emphasized. Because of the sensitive nature of Sino-Indonesian relations over the last three decades, quite understandably, these studies do not touch upon political motivations behind China's cultural diplomacy, its strategies, and diverse and complicated patterns of local responses.

## *The Evolution of the Communist Party of Indonesia (PKI)*

Represented by the studies of Ruth McVey, Cornelis Van Dijk and Antonie Dake,[17] this strand of research examines China's presence in connection with the evolution of the PKI, the third-largest Communist party in the world before its fatal destruction in 1965. One of the foci is on PKI leadership's attitudes toward the Chinese model as well as the impact of Sino-Soviet rifts in the early 1960s. These works provide detailed accounts about the PKI's ideological and organizational linkages with China, which are portrayed as an influential factor upon the party's policies and ideological stance. Understandably, these studies are not concerned with non-PKI politicians and intellectuals' changing attitudes toward China and their relevance to specific PKI views.

## *The Chinese Communities in Indonesia and Their Links (or Lack thereof) to the "Homeland"*

In the work dealing with the Chinese in Indonesia by Leo Suryadinata and a few other authors,[18] China is depicted as a remote, yet potentially influential factor in affecting the racial relationship between the *pribumi* (indigenous

---

[17] Ruth McVey, *The Development of the Indonesian Communist Party and Its Relations with the Soviet and the Chinese People's Republic* (Cambridge, MA: Center for International Studies, MIT, 1954); Cornelis Van Dijk, *The Indonesian Communist Party and Its Relations with the Soviet Union and the People's Republic of China* (The Hague: Interdoc, 1972); and Antonie Dake, *In the Spirit of the Red Banteng: Indonesian Communists between Moscow and Peking, 1959–1965* (The Hague: Mouton, 1973).

[18] Leo Suryadinata, *Pribumi Indonesians, the Chinese Minority and China*, 3rd ed. (Singapore: Heinemann Asia, 1992); Indira Ramanathan, *China and the Ethnic Chinese in Malaysia and Indonesia, 1949–1992* (London: Sangam Books, 1994); Zhuang Guotu, *Huaqiao Huaren yu Zhongguo de Guanxi* [Overseas Chinese and their relations with China] (Guangzhou: Guangdong Remin Chubanshe, 2001); and Benny G. Setiono, *Tionghoa dalam Pusaran Politik* (Jakarta: Elkasa, 2003).

people) and non-*pribumi* (referring mainly to the ethnic Chinese). This literature considers the Chinese minority's loyalty (or its absence) to the PRC as a notable factor in the making of Chinese identity and emphasizes its political implications for national integration. Perceptions of China are thus interpreted as one of the more important factors in the evolution of local Chinese communities. Although these studies provide well-documented accounts of correlations between Indonesians' views of the PRC and the government's policies toward the local Chinese, the complexity and multi-dimensionality of China's presence have not been fully scrutinized.[19] For example, why did Indonesians portray local Chinese and their compatriots in the mainland in significantly different fashions (denigrating the former while admiring the latter)? Why did many indigenous people still look at China favourably at the time of widespread anti-Chinese riots at home in the late 1950s and early 1960s?

The above-mentioned works, to be sure, are not centrally concerned with the questions of China's presence in Indonesia, and they are important in their own right. A few authors do take China beyond the conventional diplomatic/ethnic lens and credit its significant role in shaping the course of contemporary Indonesian history. In an article on the relations between Indonesian Communism and China, Ruth McVey identifies multiple meanings of China's presence and argues, "China has been not one thing to the Indonesians but three: a state, a revolution, and an ethnic minority".[20] China's images in Indonesian eyes, she contends, were at best ambivalent. As an example of a dynamic Asian socialist state, China had an appeal for many Indonesian radicals, but as the aspiring guardian and protector of the local Chinese community, its standing was more questionable. Anak Agung, the Indonesian minister of foreign affairs in 1955, claims that Sukarno's state visit to the PRC in 1956 was "a real milestone in Indonesia's political development both in the domestic field and in the conduct of its foreign policy".[21] George Kahin suggests that Sukarno borrowed and adapted some

---

[19] See Hong Liu, "Introduction: Toward a Multi-dimensional Exploration of the Chinese Overseas", in *The Chinese Overseas, Vol. 1: Conceptualizing and Historicizing Chinese International Migration*, ed. Hong Liu (London and New York: Routledge, 2006), pp. 1–30.
[20] Ruth McVey, "Indonesian Communism and China", in *China in Crisis*, ed. Tang Tsou (Chicago: University of Chicago Press, 1969), vol. 2, pp. 357–94.
[21] Ide Anak Agung Gde Agung, *Twenty Years Indonesian Foreign Policy, 1945–1965* (Yogyakarta: Duta Wacana University Press, 1990 [1972]), p. 251.

techniques of Chinese social and political mobilization in establishing the system of Guided Democracy.²² According to A. Teeuw, Pramoedya's first visit to China in 1956 represented a turning point in his intellectual and political career; primarily as a result of his experience in and perceptions of the PRC, "the dream of the poet was exchanged for the action of the social fighter".²³

However, partly because of a lack of reliable primary documents from the China side, these statements have not been substantiated; and the unsystematic comments about China's role in Indonesia are either frequently overlooked or simply dismissed.²⁴ Indeed, one finds very little reference to China perceptions (and their multiple meanings) in major biographies of Sukarno or Pramoedya.²⁵ Not coincidentally, standard and classic works on modern Indonesian history and politics, such as those by Herbert Feith and Daniel Lev,²⁶ also show a conspicuous neglect of the role of China in the country's political and intellectual evolution. In his otherwise excellent treatise concerning the external impact upon Indonesian political thinking, Feith refers only to Western influence and ignores the significance of other

---

²² George M. Kahin, "Indonesia", in *Major Governments of Asia*, ed. Kahin, 2nd ed. (Ithaca: Cornell University Press, 1963), p. 638. Kahin's observations were apparently based upon his extensive interviews with key political and intellectual leaders in the late 1950s. These hitherto unpublished interviews have been used extensively by Robert Elson in his examination of Indonesian political thinking in the late 1950s; see Robert Elson, *The Idea of Indonesia: A History* (Cambridge: Cambridge University Press, 2008), chapter 5.
²³ A. Teeuw, *Modern Indonesian Literature*, 2nd ed. (The Hague: Martinus Nijhoff, 1979), vol. 1, p. 167.
²⁴ See, for example, the criticisms of Kahin's view regarding the impact of China upon Sukarno, in Baladas Ghoshal, *Indonesian Politics 1955–59: The Emergence of Guided Democracy* (Calcutta: K.P. Bagchi, 1982), pp. 95–6.
²⁵ John D. Legge, *Sukarno: A Political Biography* (Sydney: Allen & Unwin, 1990 [1972]); C.L.M. Penders, *The Life and Times of Sukarno* (Kuala Lumpur: Oxford University Press, 1974); and Savitri Scherer, "From Culture to Politics: The Writings of Pramoedya Ananta Toer" (Ph.D. dissertation, Australian National University, 1981). Hong Liu, Goenawan Mohamad, and Sumit Kumar Mandal, *Pram dan Cina* (Jakarta: Komunitas Bambu, 2008) examines the central relevance of China in the evolution of Pramoedya's thought.
²⁶ Herbert Feith, *The Decline of Constitutional Democracy in Indonesia* (Ithaca: Cornell University Press, 1962); and Daniel Lev, *The Transition to Guided Democracy: Indonesian Politics, 1957–1959* (Ithaca: Cornell University Modern Indonesian Project, 1966).

Asian nations, such as China and Japan, in the evolution of the country's intellectual tradition.[27]

On a broader level and from a comparative perspective, in contrast to numerous studies documenting images of China in the West and Japan, there has not been a single monograph-length work pertaining to images of China in Indonesia. When this subject is discussed sporadically, China has merely been equated with Communism and ethnic minority — hence acquiring a fundamentally negative reception in a nationalistic Indonesia. This study argues that greater attention is needed to unveil the ambivalence and complexity of China in Indonesia. By treating China as something more than a Communist state and the ethnic Chinese homeland, and placing its changing and multifaceted constructions in postcolonial Southeast Asia, this book intends to go beyond the conventional approach framed by the primacy of the nation-state, diplomacy, ethnicity and the East-West binary.

## Beyond Methodological Nationalism

The preceding cursory review of studies on various aspects of Sino-Indonesian interactions shows that China in Indonesia has been investigated in subordination to, and for the purpose of illustrating, other scholarly or thematic concerns. In other words, the discourses about China and their implications have not been examined in their own right, nor are they analysed within the larger context of nation-building endeavours in Asia. This neglect is by no means accidental; it reflects two major limitations in the studies of post-revolutionary Indonesian history and Sino-Indonesian interactions: the predominance of analytical paradigms derived largely from Western experiences and the supremacy of the nation-state framework that is simultaneously reinforced by a rigid subdivision of the Asian region. The latter can be seen as an example of "methodological nationalism" — "the assumption that nation/state/society is the natural social and political form of the modern world" — that has dominated much of social science thinking in the past century.[28]

As a number of scholars have convincingly argued, the dominant framework for evaluating Indonesian political and intellectual history has

---

[27] Herbert Feith, "Introduction", in *Indonesian Political Thinking, 1945–1965*, ed. Herbert Feith and Lance Castles (Ithaca: Cornell University Press, 1970), pp. 1–24.
[28] Andreas Wimmer and Nina Glick Schiller, "Methodological Nationalism and Beyond: Nation-state Building, Migration and the Social Sciences", *Global Networks: A Journal of Transnational Affairs* 2, 4 (2002): 301–34.

essentially been based on Western paradigms, with a strong liberal predisposition. Within this framework, the failure of Western-style parliamentary democracy and its reasons, for instance, constituted the paramount concern in the study of the country's post-independence transformation.[29] Simon Philpott even goes so far as to argue that the liberal basis of American social science has profoundly shaped the understanding of Indonesian culture, tradition, ethnicity and modernity, and that "the genealogy of contemporary Indonesian politics studies is Orientalist" in the sense that it accepts "a basic and irreducible separation between Orient and Occident, East and West".[30] One consequence of the dominance of this paradigm, I think, has been a tendency to ignore and/or oversimplify possible influences from non-Western sources on Indonesia's domestic development. When China is brought into overall configurations of Indonesian modern history and culture, it has habitually and expediently been equated with Communism or reduced to issues pertaining to the local Chinese community. It is a truism that the international climate of the 1950s and 1960s, when the Cold War was at its height, reinforced the propensity to perceive the presence of China simply as an extension of Communist ideology. Scholars tend conveniently to dismiss China's (real and potential) influences upon non-Communist Indonesians, many of whom actually saw China primarily as a nationalistic state sharing similar aspirations in attaining a just and prosperous society.

This neglect is reinforced by the supremacy of the nation-state and of (rigid) subregional divisions in Asian studies, which gives little heed to transnational interactions beyond the realms of diplomacy. As mentioned, the major underpinning of existing literature has been the notion of

---

[29] The most provocative critique of using Western yardsticks to judge Indonesian history is Harry Benda, "Democracy in Indonesia", *Journal of Asian Studies* 23 (1964): 449–56. See also Benedict Anderson's insightful observations in "Perspective and Method in American Research on Indonesia", in *Interpreting Indonesian Politics: Thirteen Contributions to the Debate*, ed. Benedict Anderson and Audrey Kahin (Ithaca: Cornell Modern Indonesia Project, 1982), pp. 69–83. Other reassessments of Indonesian democracy can be found in David Bourchier and John Legge, eds., *Democracy in Indonesia: 1950s and 1990s* (Clayton: Centre of Southeast Asia Studies, Monash University, 1994); and Anders Uhlin, *Indonesia and the "Third Wave of Democratization": The Indonesian Pro-Democracy Movement in a Changing World* (Richmond, Surrey: Curzon Press, 1998).

[30] Simon Philpott, *Rethinking Indonesia: Postcolonial Theory, Authoritarianism and Identity* (New York: St. Martin's Press, 2000), pp. 3–4.

*realpolitik* and ideological confrontation, with the nation-state constituting the key unit of analysis, often at the expense of transnational sociocultural forces and their local adaptations. It has been pointed out that the historiography of modern Indonesia has been characterized by national and Indonesia-centric perspectives and the *de facto* dominance of political and militarized history.[31] This inclination, of course, displays a larger problem in approaching modern Asian history and politics. Since its inception in the post-World War II era, Asian studies has been divided, somewhat artificially, into four sub-areas: East (further divided into "China and Inner Asia" and "Northeast Asia"), South, Southeast and Central Asia. These fixed geographical, temporal and ideological boundaries further reinforce the nation-state framework. Although this subregional structure has its irreplaceable analytical utility, it overlooks cross-regional/transnational intersections and their domestic ramifications. Accordingly, when China and Southeast Asia are studied together, the overriding framework has been that of diplomatic relations.[32] As Ruth McVey perceptively points out, "too often the interest of Southeast Asian specialists stops at the borders of the nation-state [or the Southeast Asian region, for that matter] where their research is centered, and they neither consider broader patterns nor make use of the comparative contrasts and differing methodological approaches offered by work on other parts of the region."[33] Thongchai Winichakul has

---

[31] See, for example, Rommel Curaming, "Towards Reinventing Indonesian Nationalist Historiography", *Kyoto Review of Southeast Asia* (March 2003), <http://kyotoreview.cseas.kyoto-u.ac.jp/issue/issue2/index.html> [accessed 23 April 2007].

[32] Some efforts to redress this imbalance can be found in Wang Gungwu, *Community and Nation: China, Southeast Asia and Australia* (St. Leonard, NSW: Allen & Unwin for Asian Studies Association of Australia, 1992); Anthony Reid, ed., *Sojourners and Settlers: Histories of Southeast Asia and the Chinese* (Sydney: Allen & Unwin, 1996); Arif Dirlik, *The Postcolonial Aura: Third World Criticism in the Age of Global Capitalism* (Boulder, CO: Westview Press, 1997).

[33] Ruth McVey, "Globalization, Marginalization, and the Study of Southeast Asia", in *Southeast Asian Studies: Reorientations: The Frank H. Golay Memorial Lectures 2 and 3* (Ithaca: Cornell University Southeast Asian Program, 1998), pp. 38–64, at p. 53. For some critiques of Asian studies and its ignorance on transnational themes, see Ravi Arvind Palat, "Fragmented Visions. Excavating the Future of Area Studies in a Post-American World", *Review* 19, 3 (1996): 269–315; Hong Liu, "Sino-Southeast Asian Studies: Toward an Alternative Paradigm", *Asian Studies Review* 24, 3 (2001): 259–83; Masao Miyoshi and H.D. Harootunian, eds., *Learning Places: The Afterlives of Area Studies* (Durham: Duke University Press, 2002); David Kang, "Getting Asia Wrong: The Need for New Analytical Frameworks", *International Security* 27, 4 (2003): 57–85;

also argued that "the old national story has served its purpose, to establish a nation-state; it has perhaps run its course". He suggests that it is time for other narratives of non- and trans-national subjects to emerge and blossom.[34]

With respect to Sino-Indonesian interactions, the nation-state framework has at least three drawbacks. First, historicity finds no place in this narrative. China and Indonesia had a long history of extensive flows of peoples, ideas and goods well before the coming of the Dutch in the 16th century.[35] It was at the turn of the 20th century that Chinese intellectuals began to construct a new regional order of Asia. In this endeavour, the *Nanyang* ("South Ocean", the Chinese term for Southeast Asia) constituted an indispensable component of this radically reimagined region through transnational circulation of magazines pertaining to China, Southeast Asia and Japan.[36] During the pre-World War II decades, the Chinese revolution entered into the debates of the Indonesian nationalists, many of whom considered it an inspiring example in their own struggle for independence.

---

Peter Katzenstein, *A World of Regions: Asia and Europe in American Imperium* (Ithaca: Cornell University Press, 2005); and Prasenjit Duara, "Asia Redux: Conceptualizing a Region for Our Times", *Journal of Asian Studies* 69, 4 (2010): 963–84.

[34] Thongchai Winichakul, "Writing at the Interstices: Southeast Asian Historians and Postnational Histories in Southeast Asia", in *New Terrains in Southeast Asian History*, ed. Abu Talib Ahmad and Tan Liok Ee (Athens: Ohio University Press, 2003), pp. 3–29.

[35] On the significance of intra-Asian trade in the historical context, see Giovanni Arrighi, Takeshi Hamashita and Mark Selden, "Introduction: The Rise of East Asia in Regional and World History Perspective", in *The Resurgence of East Asia: 500, 150 and 50 Year Perspectives*, ed. Arrighi, Hamashita and Selden (London: Routledge, 2003), pp. 1–16; Kaoru Sugihara, ed., *Japan, China, and the Growth of the Asian International Economy, 1850–1949* (Oxford: Oxford University Press, 2005); and Takeshi Hamashita, *China, East Asia and the Global Economy: Regional and Historical Perspectives*, ed. Linda Grove and Mark Selden (London: Routledge, 2008). The extensive and diverse nature of Sino-Southeast Asian interactions is also reflected in the six-volume anthology, Geoff Wade, ed., *China and Southeast Asia* (London: Routledge, 2009).

[36] This point is elaborated in detail in Hong Liu, "China's Rediscovery of Nanyang and the Imagination of a Transnational Asia in the early 20th Century", paper presented at the Conference on Asianisms in Historical Perspective (Hokkaido University, 30–31 January 2010). For some relevant discussion, see also Rebecca Karl, *Staging the World: Chinese Nationalism at the Turn of the Twentieth Century* (Durham: Duke University Press, 2002); Hong Liu, "Beyond Orientalism and the East-West Divide: China and Southeast Asia in the Double Mirror", *Stockholm Journal of East Asian Studies* 13 (2003): 45–65.

As this study will demonstrate, this historical experience found its contemporary resonance after 1949.[37] A transnational and cross-regional perspective, therefore, is necessary in forging an understanding of Indonesian domestic evolution. Indeed, as a study suggests, "From a long-term perspective, the most salient features of the region [Southeast Asia] have to do with intercivilizational encounters and their local ramifications.... Southeast Asian traditions took shape in active interaction with dominant external models, and it is a flexible combination of imported and local patterns that is most characteristic of the region, rather than any persisting indigenous infrastructure."[38]

Second, the conventional structure of Asian studies tends to ignore the flexible patterns of intersections in non-diplomatic arenas. It is my belief that dynamic and multifaceted flows of ideas and cultures across national borders need to be more forcefully brought into our discussions. As this study seeks to demonstrate, these intersections existed not only in the visible geographical and political sites with tangible impact, where the state-centred diplomacy and its manoeuvres prevailed, but also, more importantly for this study, in the invisible realm of the contacts and fusions of ideas, in which both state and societal actors were involved and intertwined.

Third, as the nation-state narrative is framed within a fixed territory and its (indigenous) ethnicity, it tends to separate ethnicity from the nation, thus (potentially) ghettoizing the Chinese in Indonesia. According to Anthony Smith, ethnic communities are "defined as named human populations with shared ancestry myths, histories, and cultures, having an association with *a specific territory and a sense of solidarity*".[39] However, the ethnic Chinese in Indonesia throughout most of the 20th century did not have an exclusive, fixed territory or geographical site to themselves. As such, they are often excluded from the Indonesian nation-state narratives and have commonly been treated as a disconnected analytical category, instead of as an embedded component of the nation's postcolonial evolution.

---

[37] A study of the core importance of ideas and ideologies in much of the 20th century has highlighted the continuity of political thinking of the nationalists in the pre-independence and revolutionary periods and of the leaders of the postcolonial era in Southeast Asia. See Clive Christie, *Ideology and Revolution in Southeast Asia, 1900–1980: Political Ideas of the Anti-Colonial Era* (Richmond, Surrey: Curzon Press, 2001).
[38] Johann Arnason, "The Southeast Asian Labyrinth: Historical and Comparative Perspectives", *Thesis Eleven* 50 (1997): 99–122.
[39] Montserrat Guibernau and John Rex, eds., *The Ethnicity Reader: Nationalism, Multiculturalism and Migration* (Oxford: Polity Press, 1997), p. 27 (emphasis added).

## A Transnational Inquiry

This book departs from the predominant paradigms in China and Southeast Asian studies by focusing on the multifaceted intersections between these two cultural-political domains. My treatment of these issues is informed by the new approaches to redefining Asia as a flexible geographic construct that are also fruitfully aided by the emerging cultural/literary studies theories that interrogate the complex constitutions of knowledge and narratives, and that regard culture as a symbolic, linguistic and representational system.[40] This study is concerned with the encounters between non-Western peoples who had engaged in extensive networks in the past.[41] Central to this transnational and network perspective is the notion that, while the nation-state is important for an understanding of Sino-Indonesian interactions and continues to be relevant to this inquiry, greater attention should be given to the making of and contestations over knowledge about a multifaceted China that had close bearings upon power relations, domestically and diplomatically.

Furthermore, transnational networks and flows of ideas are not rigidly structured, but constantly in motion. In this sense, China does not merely refer to the People's Republic that has been commonly represented as a Communist state or an abstract form of the nation-state. Instead, we may heed the good advice of Lucian Pye: "China is not just another nation-state in the family of nations", but rather "a civilization pretending to be a state".[42] As the following chapters will demonstrate, there has been a variety of Chinas emerging in the political and cultural discourses in Sukarno's Indonesia, and the multidimensionality of China-imaginations thus constitutes a defining feature in the transnational enquiry. In the discursive

---

[40] Victoria Bonnell and Lynn Hunt, "Introduction", in *Beyond the Cultural Turn: New Directions in the Study of Society and Culture*, ed. Bonnell and Hunt (Berkeley: University of California Press, 1999), pp. 1–34.

[41] For more detailed discussions on the applications and limitations of networks to the Asian context, see Hong Liu, "Network Building between State and Society in the Asian Context", in *State and Civil Society in the Context of Transition: Understanding Non-Traditional Security in East Asia*, ed. Zhang Yuling (Beijing: World Affairs Press, 2005), pp. 8–35. In a fascinating study on Asianism in the late 19th century, Carol Hau and Takashi Shiraishi have employed network theory to investigate the circulation of ideas across national borders. See their "Daydreaming about Rizal and Tetcho: On Asianism as Network and Fantasy", *Philippine Studies* 57, 3 (2009): 329–88.

[42] Lucian Pye, "China: Erratic State, Frustrated Society", *Foreign Affairs* 69, 4 (1980): 56–74.

process of mingling knowledge and power, interpretations of China became an integrated component of modern Indonesian culture. Here, as Clifford Geertz reminds us, "culture is not cults and customs, but the *structures of meaning* through which men give shape to their experience".[43]

This study, therefore, attempts to interrogate the structures of meaning about China and how they intersected with power and were constituted as metaphorical conceptions. "Metaphor" in this book is used in a broad sense; instead seeing it just as "a device of the poetic imagination and the rhetorical flourishing" or "a matter of language, that is, of mere words", I concur with the argument that "the essence of metaphor is understanding and experiencing one kind of thing in terms of another".[44] Or, as Geertz eloquently puts it, "In metaphor, one has, of course, a stratification of meaning, in which an incongruity of sense on one level produces an influx of significance on another."[45]

## NATURE AND CHARACTERISTICS OF CHINA OBSERVERS IN INDONESIA

In his classic study of American images of China and India, Harold R. Isaacs argues, "All images are shaped by the way they are seen, a matter of setting, timing, angle, lighting, distance."[46] While the following chapters will detail the setting, timing and angle, we shall first look at the question of who created China's images in Sukarno's Indonesia. The images of China did not project themselves automatically onto the Indonesian scene; instead, they were construed, constructed and reconstructed by China-image-makers — those Indonesians who, individually or collectively, articulated and formulated their perceptions of China and presented them to the public. Some of them also attempted to appropriate certain images and perceptions into their own sociopolitical thought and policy-making process. Who, then, were the China-image-makers in Sukarno's Indonesia?

---

[43] Clifford Geertz, "The Politics of Meaning", in his *The Interpretation of Cultures* (New York: Basic Books, 1973), p. 312 (emphasis added).
[44] George Lakoff and Mark Johnson, "Metaphors We Live By", in *Cultural Metaphors: Readings, Research Translations, and Commentary*, ed. Martin J. Gannon (Thousand Oaks, CA: Sage Publications, 2001), pp. 3–5.
[45] Clifford Geertz, "Ideology as a Cultural System", in his *The Interpretation of Cultures*, p. 210.
[46] Harold Isaacs, *Images of Asia: American Views of China and India* (New York: Harper & Row, 1972 [1958]), p. 390.

Unlike countries such as the United States, where a relatively large number of professional "China-watchers" perform the function of interpreting things Chinese for the concerned elite and mass public,[47] no such professional group existed in Indonesia during the period under consideration. (The Institute of Sinology at the University of Indonesia, for example, was primarily concerned with China's remote past, a legacy of the Dutch Oriental scholarship.[48]) Indonesians had to rely on a broadly defined intellectual class in constructing and presenting images of China. Intellectuals in this study are loosely defined as "all persons with an advanced modern education and the intellectual concerns and skills ordinarily associated with it", and those who perform the broad intellectual function of being deeply involved in thinking, speaking and writing about their nation and society.[49] More specifically, intellectuals are "that section of the educated class which had aspirations to political power *either directly by seeking to be society's political rulers or indirectly by directing its conscience and decisions*".[50] In view of this intellectual spectrum, and judged from the Indonesian context, this study divides the nation's China-image-makers into two groups: political intellectuals and cultural intellectuals.

"Political intellectuals" are those individuals who, despite assuming administrative or political responsibilities in the government or other political bodies, still maintained certain broad intellectual concerns for the

---

[47] It is generally agreed that professional China-watchers in the USA consist of four main types: academic China specialists, government China specialists, private sector China specialists, and journalist China specialists. See David Shambaugh, ed., *American Studies of Contemporary China* (Armonk, NY: M.E. Sharpe, 1993). On recent changes in international China-watchers, see Robert Ash, David Shambaugh, Seiichiro Takagi, eds., *China Watching: Perspectives from Europe, Japan and the United States* (London: Routledge, 2006).

[48] See Thio In Lok, "Interview dengan Prof. Dr. Tjan Tju Som: Perjakinan Sinologi dahulu dan sekarang", *Star Weekly* 372 (February 1953), pp. 23–4, 95. Concerning the role of China specialists in the making of foreign policy, see the brief discussion in Panitya Penulisan Sedjarah Departemen Luar Negeri, *Dua Puluh Lima Tahun Departemen Luar Negeri, 1945–1970* (Jakarta: Jajasan Kesedjahteraan Karyawan Deplu, 1971), p. 53.

[49] Edward Shils, "Intellectuals in the Political Development of the New States", in his *The Intellectuals and the Power and Other Essays* (Chicago: University of Chicago Press, 1970), p. 389.

[50] Lewis S. Feuer, "What is an Intellectual?" in *The Intelligentsia and the Intellectuals: Theory, Method and Case Studies*, ed. Alexander Gella (Beverly Hills: Sage Publications, 1976), p. 49 (emphasis added).

nation's social and political development. As creators and articulators of ideologies, their primary domain of activity is the "political market-place". The double identity of power and knowledge formation was, to some extent, a continuation of the characteristics of the Indonesian nationalist movement during the pre-World War II era, when most would-be political leaders had been intellectuals in one way or another.[51] It also reflected a common characteristic of postcolonial transformations in most new nations, whereby no clear boundaries existed between politics and intellectualism.

This study investigates the attitudes toward China and their public representation by such prominent political intellectuals as Sukarno, Mohammad Hatta, Tan Malaka (whose ideas had a powerful impact on the younger generation, despite his death in 1949), Sutan Sjahrir and, to a lesser extent, Ali Sastroamidjojo, Roeslan Abdulgani, Subandrio, Sartono, Wilopo, Liem Koen Hian, Siauw Giok Tjhan, as well as certain PKI leaders including Aidit, Njoto, Sakirman and Jusuf Adjitorop.[52] For the purpose of illustrating a political climate that facilitated a widespread attention to China, this study also includes some political functionaries (such as Sumarno, mayor of Greater Jakarta in the late 1950s) who may be considered semi- or quasi-intellectuals. Although they were all institutionally embedded in the state/bureaucratic/party apparatuses, their views of China were presented and contested in the public domain for wider consumption instead of remaining merely in policy circles. Knowledge about China, therefore, became intimately intertwined with power.

"Cultural intellectuals" in Indonesia fit the conventional definition of the term "intellectual". According to Max Weber, they are "a group of men who by virtue of their peculiarity have special access to certain achievements considered to be 'cultural values,' and who, therefore, usurp the leadership of a cultural community".[53] Absent from direct responsibilities either

---

[51] On the evolution of Indonesian intellectual class prior to 1949, see George Kahin, *Nationalism and Revolution in Indonesia* (Ithaca: Cornell University Press, 1952); Robert Van Niel, *The Emergence of the Modern Indonesian Elite* (The Hague: Van Hoeve, 1960); John D. Legge, *Intellectuals and Nationalism in Indonesia: A Study of the Following Recruited by Sutan Sjahrir in Occupation Jakarta* (Ithaca: Cornell Modern Indonesia Project Publications, 1988); and Yudi Latif, *Indonesian Muslim Intelligentsia and Power* (Singapore: Institute of Southeast Asian Studies, 2008).

[52] The appendix of this book, "Biographical Notes on Major China Observers in Indonesia", has more details about the political and cultural intellectuals under examination and their linkages with China, institutionally, metaphorically or otherwise.

[53] H.H. Gerth and C. Wright Mills, eds., *From Max Weber: Essays in Sociology* (London: Routledge & Kegan Paul, 1961), p. 176.

within the government or political parties, they functioned principally as interpreters of the world, producers of ideas and depositories of cultural values. They shared with political intellectuals some fundamental concerns, such as the question of building a viable national identity in a heterogeneous and multi-ethnic society. As outsiders of the establishment, however, they exhibited a greater degree of detachment from power, though they could be either "the critics of the power" or "the associates of power".[54]

The cultural intellectuals under discussion in this book include the writers Pramoedya Ananta Toer, Armijn Pane, Trisno Sumardjo, Sitor Situmorang and Ramadhan K.H.; the journalists Adinegoro, Arifin Bey, Melik Sayuti, Satya Graha, Kwee Keng Beng, Asa Bafagih and Sugardo; the educators Barioen A.S. and Prijono, as well as literary critics and poets associated with the left-leaning "Institute of People's Culture" (Lekra), such as Buyung Saleh and Anantaguna. I also examine attitudes toward China held by university students, who played a critical role in the political mobilization process during the closing years of the Sukarno regime.

The distinctions between political and cultural intellectuals, it should be pointed out, were much more complex than the above, somewhat simplified account suggests. Apart from the commonality that, throughout the post-independence era, intellectuals played "a dominant role in all political groups ... and in the leadership of the state",[55] it is worth underlining that the foremost concern of political intellectuals was governance and power; their construction of China-images was essentially supplementary and subordinated to this ultimate agenda. Cultural intellectuals, on the other hand, looked at more deep-rooted issues emerging from the process of nation-building; many came to regard politics as one of the means of tackling these essentially cultural or moral problems. It was against this backdrop that China entered into their thought and imagination. As will be demonstrated later, there were both implicit and explicit differences between these two groups of intellectuals with respect to their perceptions and representations of China.

Another commonality between these two types of intellectuals is their close association with the mass media. As exemplified in the biographical profiles of the selected China observers in the appendix of this book, over half of them had some sort of formal affiliation with the media (mainly

---

[54] This distinction is drawn from Richard Hofstadter, *Anti-Intellectualism in American Life* (New York: Knopf, 1964), p. 429.
[55] Latif, *Indonesian Muslim Intelligentsia and Power*, p. 252.

in journalism), either before 1949 or in the postcolonial era (or both). Their professional experience as reporters and editors of newspapers and mass-circulated magazines provided them with a keen understanding of the sentiments and needs of a changing society; it also furnished them with essential tools in presenting their views in a manner that could be easily comprehended by laymen. Hence, though the number of political and cultural intellectuals examined in this book is relatively small, their influence upon society and in shaping public opinion went far beyond their numerical count.

The public intellectuals enjoyed rising influence in a changing society like Indonesia. The post-independence years saw the rapid growth of the adult literacy rate, from 7.4 per cent in 1930 to 46.7 per cent in 1961. For males between ten and nineteen, the rate was over 76 per cent. This was a result of expanding education. Between 1950 and 1958, the number of (secular) lower and upper secondary schools increased from 954 to 4,608, while the total number of students jumped from 138,668 to 754,089. The number of universities increased from four in 1950 to well over 135 higher-education institutions by 1960, and total enrolment grew from about 6,000 to 60,000 or 70,000 in the same period.[56] Correspondingly, the daily circulation of newspapers increased from 500,000 in 1950 to 930,000 in 1956, and that of periodicals trebled to over 3.3 million in the same period.[57]

The articulations and representations of China-images were principally undertaken in the public sphere, through such media as commentaries and interviews in newspapers and popular magazines as well as public speeches. It was at this conjuncture that contestations about the multiple meanings of China — and their domestic (ir)relevance — constituted an integral component of Indonesian cultural politics. Here one is reminded of a central characteristic of power accumulation in the Indonesian context. As Benedict Anderson has argued: "Where illiteracy is the rule, writing has an enormous power-creating potential.... *Literacy is simply an external sign of the possession of knowledge*", which, according to him, "becomes the key to Power".[58] It was in this larger political and cultural context that

---

[56] Ibid., p. 256.

[57] M.C. Ricklefs, *A History of Modern Indonesia since c. 1200*, 3rd ed. (Basingstoke: Palgrave, 2001), pp. 290–1. Concerning the circulation and functions of major newspapers in the 1950s, see also Rosihan Anwar, "Persuratkabaran Indonesia Sekarang", *Konfrontasi* 3 (1954): 19–30.

[58] Anderson, "The Idea of Power in Javanese Culture", pp. 43, 46–7.

discourses about China gained wider significance. It is true, in this sense, that "metaphor is pervasive in everyday life, not just in language but in thought and action".[59]

## STRUCTURE OF THE BOOK

This book is divided into three main sections, dealing respectively with the (re)presentations, constructions and implications of the China metaphor in Indonesia between 1949 and 1965. The first section, "(Re)presenting China", documents in detail Indonesians' somewhat favourable and sometimes ambivalent attitudes toward China's sociopolitical transformations and cultural evolution. It argues that these perceptions were consistently characterized by an inclination to interpret China as a nationalistic and populist experiment and to separate China from Communism. The attraction to and fascination with that country's seemingly powerful administration, orderly social system and rapid economic growth were typically mixed with disdain for its denial of religious freedom, lack of human rights and social regimentation.

This section starts with a brief discussion of the historical evolution of China's presence in pre-1949 Indonesia, with an emphasis on the nationalists' views of the modern Chinese revolution. This chapter also examines the patterns of imagining China and their historical legacy for the years between 1949 and 1965. Chapter 2 is mainly concerned with Indonesians' conflicting interpretations of three central aspects of Chinese politics in the 1950s: the New Democracy, China's foreign policy behaviour, and Mao Zedong, considered an embodiment of the new China. The subsequent chapter shifts to Indonesian representations of China's experiments in generating social and economic changes. It finds that the consistent admiration for China's impressive economic achievements was accompanied by conflicting explanations for reasons behind the progress. Chapter 4 examines Indonesians' changing views of cultural development in China. In addition to discussing their ambivalent attitudes toward intellectuals' role in nation-building and the relationship between the arts and power, it also investigates their uneasy treatises on the question of religious freedom (or the lack of it) in China.

The purpose of the second section, "Constructing the China Metaphor", is to take a step back and answer the question of why China was

---

[59] Lakoff and Johnson, "Metaphors We Live By", p. 3.

represented in the ways described in the previous section and, more importantly, how the discoveries of China became a troubling process of self-rediscovery and discursive formation in Indonesia *per se*. It in essence examines the representations by interrogating both the contextualization and image-makers themselves. This exploration is indispensable, because views of China can only be understood in the larger context of Indonesians' self-perceptions and their search for alternative modernities at a time of tortuous sociopolitical transition.

Chapter 5 analyses the sociopolitical and intellectual environments in the shaping of Indonesians' representations of China. After a brief account of the nation's tumultuous political change, I explore the intriguing connections between intellectuals' alienation from their own society and their idealization of China. Their quest for an external utopia (in this case, an imagined China) was not only shaped by situations at home, but also guided by their own predispositions about Indonesian society. By creating a China in their own image, Indonesians transformed their China narratives into the China metaphor, a mirror that revealed more about the complex and ambiguous nature of political and cultural intellectuals than about Chinese realities. Chapter 6 examines relationships between ethnicity, cultural diplomacy and China-image-making. The existence in Indonesia of nearly 2.5 million ethnic Chinese presented a unique and fluid context in moulding China-images. For one thing, Indonesians' perceptions of China were clouded, to say the very least, by their mixed views of the local Chinese. This chapter also considers the PRC's well-orchestrated efforts in contributing to the (trans)formation of China perceptions and investigates the various strategies it employed, in both China and Indonesia, in shaping its hopeful images.

The third and final section of this study, "Shaping a New Trajectory", probes the process of translating specific "knowledge" and discourses about China into Indonesian political and cultural processes. Although it is very difficult to bridge empirically the gap between perceptions and their execution, there are some subtle yet unmistakable linkages. As Indonesians' views of China formed an integral part of the quest for national and cultural identities, domestic agendas always figured prominently in the minds of China observers who were simultaneously leading politicians and intellectuals of the time. They had a penchant for comparing and contrasting conditions at home with examples from China, leading to rejections, modifications or reaffirmations of views about their own society. When their revised political and cultural thinking was translated into practice, the China metaphor created significant and tangible impact beyond the realm of perception-formation and image-making.

This section will examine, among other things, how interpretations of the Chinese experience became a driving force behind political populism and cultural radicalism. Chapter 7 focuses on connections between views of China and political populism in Indonesia.[60] By centring on the perceptions of China of President Sukarno, arguably the single most important person in postcolonial Indonesia, I will demonstrate why and how political intellectuals blended their knowledge about China with new visions for Indonesia and translated them into implementation. Chapter 8 analyses the cultural left-leaning trend and how it was engineered and reinforced by the Chinese model. It focuses on Pramoedya Ananta Toer, a prominent cultural intellectual and one of the foremost writers of the 20th century. I will explore linkages between his perceptions of China and the transformation of his cultural and political views. I argue that the cultural radicalization process reached its height in the "cultural polemics" of 1963 and 1964, in which China's cultural and literary theories constituted one of the key issues under heated contestation.

The concluding chapter, "China as an Alternative Modernity", recapitulates the main findings of this study by highlighting the three master narratives on China as well as the complex interplay between knowledge and power that was an integral part of Indonesians' rediscovery of their own identity. This chapter also briefly considers the relevance of the Indonesian story by placing it in the context of China's rising soft power in Southeast Asia at the turn of the 21st century.

---

[60] There are different definitions of populism: it is generally defined as "a political movement that emphasizes the interests, cultural traits, and spontaneous feelings of the common people, as opposed to those of a privileged elite". *Britannica Concise Encyclopedia* (Chicago: Encyclopaedia Britannica, 2002), cited in Marc F. Plattner, "Populism, Pluralism, and Liberal Democracy", *Journal of Democracy* 21, 1 (2010): 81–92. For an interpretation of contemporary Indonesian populism as exemplified by Sukarno's daughter, see Daniel Ziv, "Populist Perceptions and Perceptions of Populism in Indonesia: The Case of Megawati Soekarnoputri", *South East Asia Research* 9, 1 (2001): 73–88. Mizuno Kosuke and Pasuk Phongpaichit, eds., *Populism in Asia* (Singapore and Kyoto: NUS Press and Kyoto University Press, 2009) provides an innovative and comparative perspective in examining populism in contemporary Asia.

With respect to research data, various forms of written and spoken commentary about China by Indonesians constitute the core of primary materials used in this study. They appeared in newspapers, popular magazines, pamphlets, travelogues, memoirs, textbooks, public speeches and parliamentary debates. Indonesia enjoyed a high degree of press freedom during most of the 1950s, and the expression and dissemination of dissenting views were largely uninhibited. Information and views on China presented through these diversified mass media were not censored for the most part. They were effective in reaching the general public and, especially, "the political public", who had an important impact upon the political process.[61] Memoirs and autobiographies in Indonesia are not merely about their authors' recollections of the past; they are also an arena in which to think out politics and nationalism, and were frequently forward-looking.[62] As such, they serve as illuminating sources for an understanding of Indonesian self-perceptions and attitudes toward foreign countries such as China.

It should be noted here, however, that these data offered perspectives that were principally Javanese, Jakarta-centred and male-dominated. This unavoidable pitfall reflected in part the elitist thrust of political and cultural discourse throughout the years under study. This was also partly a product of demographic reality. In 1961, 61 per cent of the population lived in Java, with Jakarta alone, as the centre of politics, commerce and culture, having a population of 2.9 million.[63] The possible remedy for this inadequacy, I think, is to be more inclusive by encompassing authors with wider regional backgrounds or class representations. Because most of the writings about China, including those by Muslim intellectuals, appeared in secular and vernacular venues aimed at the general and educated public, I have not divided these writings according to their authors' religious backgrounds,

---

[61] On the definition and importance of the "political public", see Feith, *The Decline of Constitutional Democracy in Indonesia*, pp. 108–13. According to him, the clearest indication of membership in the political public was "regular newspaper reading" (p. 110). "Most of the nationally significant political action", Feith suggests, "took place within the political public".

[62] Susan Rodgers, *Telling Lives, Telling History: Autobiography and Historical Imagination in Modern Indonesia* (Berkeley: University of California Press, 1995), Part One.

[63] Ricklefs, *A History of Modern Indonesia*, p. 290.

focusing instead on Indonesians' China perceptions in the context of their search for a secular future.⁶⁴

This book makes extensive use of Chinese-language materials that have seldom been utilized before in both Indonesian and China studies. They not only include official and restricted or internal (*neibu*⁶⁵) materials regarding Indonesia and its relationships with China, but also recently published memoirs by Chinese diplomats and those involved in Sino-Indonesian exchanges. Between the end of 2004 and November 2008, the Archives of the PRC Ministry of Foreign Affairs declassified, in three phases, a significant amount of materials for the period between 1949 and 1965, which contain rich data pertaining to the inner workings of China's diplomatic and cultural strategies in Indonesia; these have been used extensively in this book. Furthermore, as Indonesians' trips to the PRC played an important part in shaping the (re)discovery of China, I have attempted to identify and analyse their speeches and reflections about the PRC (sometimes in Chinese translation, when the original Indonesian versions were not available). In addition to distilling those messages that might have been written to display politeness to the hospitable hosts, I have, whenever possible, compared these writings with the Indonesian versions in order to ensure accuracy and objectivity. Finally, this study employs materials and perspectives through my own personal interviews with some individuals who were directly involved in Sino-Indonesian exchanges between 1949 and 1965.⁶⁶

This study attempts to engage a dialogue with three different, yet somewhat related, fields and subfields in modern Asian history and politics.

---

[64] More specific examinations on Indonesian Muslims' vision for the country's future can be found in Latif, *Indonesian Muslim Intelligentsia and Power*.

[65] On the nature and usefulness of these *neibu* materials, see David Shambaugh, *Beautiful Imperialist: China Perceives America, 1972–1990* (Princeton: Princeton University Press, 1991), pp. 15, 39; see also his "A Bibliographical Essay on New Sources for the Study of China's Foreign Relations and National Security", in *Chinese Foreign Policy: Theory and Practice*, ed. Thomas W. Robinson and David Shambaugh (Oxford: Clarendon Press, 1994), pp. 603–18.

[66] The interviewees include Soeto Meisen, Sukarno's personal assistant on China affairs and Chinese interpreter; Huang Shuhai, a Ministry of Foreign Affairs official and Zhou Enlai's Indonesian interpreter during the 1950s; Chen Xiaru, an Indonesian interpreter affiliated with the Chinese Writers Union who was host to a number of Indonesian cultural delegations; Chen Lisui, assistant to and chief interpreter of Chinese ambassadors to Indonesia between 1950 and 1961; and Chen Wenxian, who worked in the cultural division of the Chinese embassy in the 1950s.

First, this book hopes to contribute to a better understanding of a critical phase in Indonesia's postcolonial transformation, a much neglected area of study. Ann Laura Stoler has pointed out, the 1950s — described by Henk Schulte Nordholt as a "more or less a forgotten decade"[67] — has been "more cosmopolitan, 'modern' and politically progressive" than it has been usually portrayed; with a vibrant intellectual and political environment, the 1950s was a time that "held promise, because there existed venues for popular participation on the ground".[68] Her view is echoed by Robert Elson, who suggests that "the political history of modern Indonesia is a cascade of related and unrelated themes and plots, a whirling kaleidoscope of people, emotion, interests, skullduggery, nobility and violence not lending itself readily to interpretation". With some notable exceptions, he argues, "much of the modern period remains seriously understudied ... few have bothered to dip into the exceptional riches of the newspapers of the 1950s or to test the memories of those few participants of the period who still survive".[69] Anthony Reid has also pointed out that the 1950s and 1960s have been considered as a "more dangerous territory of many dark shadows" and that the "heavy national imprint" on national unity has prevented the flowering of local, social or alternative history.[70]

The discourses on China, I think, consisted of central themes that both were related to national unity *and* went beyond the nation-state paradigm, helping to shape a vibrant and cosmopolitan Indonesia of the 1950s and 1960s. Within a carefully formulated transnational framework grounded in the geocultures of the archipelago, this book seeks to establish empirically

---

[67] Henk Schulte Nordholt, "Introduction", in *Indonesian Transitions*, ed. Nordholt (Yogyakarta: Pustaka Pelajar, 2006), pp. 1–21. An international team of researchers led by Jennifer Lindsay of the Australian National University has been working on a major research project, "Indonesia's Cultural History, 1950–1965: In Search of a Lost Legacy", which will undoubtedly shed new light on postcolonial Indonesian cultural history.

[68] Ann Laura Stoler, "Untold Stories: On the Other Side of 1965 Lay a Vibrant Indonesia Worth Remembering", *Inside Indonesia*. October/December 2001, pp. 6–7. See also Vedi Hadiz, "The Left and Indonesia's 1960s: The Politics of Remembering and Forgetting", *Inter-Asia Cultural Studies* 7, 4 (2006): 554–69.

[69] R.E. Elson, "Brief Reflections on Indonesian Political History", in *Indonesia Today: Challenges of History*, ed. Grayson Lloyd and Shannon Smith (Singapore: Institute of Southeast Asian Studies, 2001), pp. 69–71.

[70] Anthony Reid, "Writing the History of Independent Indonesia", in *Nation-Building: Five Southeast Asian Histories*, ed. Wang Gungwu (Singapore: Institute of Southeast Asian Studies, 2005), pp. 69–91, at p. 75.

the contents and variations of Indonesians' representations of China and, more importantly, to place them against a shifting backdrop of Indonesia's search for national identity and alternative modernities. In so doing, this study will shed new light on the nature and characteristics of intellectuals and politicians who were also China-image-makers. This transnational perspective, I hope, will facilitate a multidimensional comprehension of the dynamics and trajectory of modern Indonesian history.[71]

Second, although this study is not a diplomatic history, a close examination of China's changing role in the making of its own images and corresponding receptions in Indonesia during the height of the Cold War confrontation will enrich our knowledge of the Sino-Indonesian relationship, which has been characterized by recurring cycles of amity and enmity over the past six decades or so. It will not only contribute to the growing literature on the history of the Cold War in Asia,[72] but also reveal the historicity of China's contemporary rise as a major Asian power and its lure as a viable model of development. This transnational inquiry may in turn help forge a better understanding of the complex interactions between two major Asian nations.[73] Moreover, by deliberately grounding this

---

[71] It should be emphasized that the acknowledgement of Chinese elements in Indonesian political and cultural thought does not necessarily diminish the creativity of Indonesian intellectuals. As W.F. Wertheim has convincingly demonstrated, the ability to preserve the valuable assets of the past and selectively adapt new (foreign) elements has been one key trait of Indonesia's cultural dynamism. See his *Indonesian Society in Transition* (The Hague: W. Van Hoeve, 1964), pp. 280–323. See also the provocative discussions on cross-cultural interactions in the Malay archipelago and their implications for the making of pluralism and multiculturalism in Indonesia, in Robert Hefner, "Introduction: Multiculturalism and Citizenship in Malaysia, Singapore, and Indonesia", in *The Politics of Multiculturalism: Pluralism and Citizenship in Malaysia, Singapore, and Indonesia*, ed. Robert Hefner (Honolulu: University of Hawaii Press, 2001), pp. 1–58.

[72] See for example, Christopher E. Goscha and Christian Ostermann, eds., *Connecting Histories: Decolonization and the Cold War in Southeast Asia, 1945–1962* (Stanford: Stanford University Press, 2009); Zheng Yangwen, Hong Liu, and Michael Szonyi, eds., *The Cold War in Asia: The Battle for Hearts and Minds* (Boston and Leiden: Brill, 2010); and Tsuyoshi Hasegawa, ed., *The Cold War in East Asia, 1945–1991* (Stanford: Stanford University Press, 2011).

[73] During the period under study, China and Indonesia were respectively the first and fifth-largest countries in the world in terms of population. The total population of China was 669 million in 1958 and 97 million in Indonesia in 1961. See Widjojo Nitisastro, *Population Trends in Indonesia* (Ithaca: Cornell University Press, 1970), p. 168.

study in a cross-regional domain, this study of Sino-Indonesian interactions challenges the rigid compartmentalization of Asian studies, and may offer a case for approaching the Asian region as a dynamically constructed and intimately networked entity that calls for new paradigms other than conventional ones.[74]

Finally, this study is situated within a larger and more established genre of intellectual and scholarly tradition, namely, the interpretation of China's changing images by the outside world. Over many centuries, the simultaneously mysterious and enchanting Middle Kingdom has been the domain of intense scholarly scrutiny and literary imagination.[75] Yet this literature focuses almost exclusively on the views of China in the West and Japan, with little attention being drawn to images of China in non-Western societies.[76] In the meantime, while some existing studies have revealed

---

[74] I have explored this issue in more detail in my "Sino-Southeast Asian Studies".

[75] The works are too numerous to name; see, for example, Raymond S. Dawson, *The Chinese Chameleon: An Analysis of European Conceptions of Chinese Civilization* (London and New York: Oxford University Press, 1967); Julie Ching and Willard Oxtoby, eds., *Discovering China: European Interpretations in the Enlightenment* (Rochester: University of Rochester Press, 1992); Xin Jianfei, *Shijie de Zhongguoguan: Jin Lianqiannian Shijie dui Zhongguo de Renshi Shigang* [The world's perceptions of China: A history of the knowledge about China over the past two thousand years] (Hong Kong: Sanlian Shudian, 1991); Paul Hollander, *Political Pilgrims: Travels of Western Intellectuals to the Soviet Union, China, and Cuba* (Lanham, MD: University Press of America, 1990 [1981]); Steven W. Mosher, *China Misperceived: American Illusions and Chinese Reality* (New York: Basic Books, 1990); Jonathan Spence, *The Chan's Great Continent: China in Western Minds* (New York: W.W. Norton, 1998); Joshua Fogel, *The Literature of Travel in the Japanese Rediscovery of China, 1862–1945* (Stanford: Stanford University Press, 1996); D.R. Howland, *Borders of Chinese Civilization: Geography and History at Empire's End* (Durham, NC: Duke University Press, 1996); Stefan Tanaka, *Japan's Orient: Rendering Pasts into History* (Berkeley: University of California Press, 1993); Richard Madsen, *China and the American Dream: A Moral Inquiry* (Berkeley: University of California Press, 1995); and Colin Mackerras, *Western Images of China* (Hong Kong: Oxford University Press, 1989).

[76] One of the few studies dealing with some related issues is Sandra Gillespie, *South-South Transfer: A Study of Sino-African Exchange* (New York: Routledge, 2001), which examines Sino-African student exchanges since 1949; see also B.K. Kumar, *China Through Indian Eyes: A Select Bibliography, 1911–1977* (Delhi: Concept Publishing, 1978). China's venture into Africa has received increasing attention; see, for example, Chris Alden, *China in Africa* (London: Zed Books, 2007). Stephanie McCrummen commented that, "The idea of China as a symbol of potential prosperity is taking hold,

close connections between attitudes toward China and the characteristics of China observers themselves, few have attempted to document and analyse any significant effects of these China perceptions upon their respective societies and politics.[77] It is hoped, therefore, that this study will contribute to a comparative understanding of China's changing images in the globe and their domestic ramifications.

---

seeping into the consciousness of ordinary Africans and occupying a place that the United States, and to some extent European countries, once claimed". McCrummen, "Struggling Chadians Dream of a Better Life — in China", *Washington Post*, 6 October 2007.

[77] With some notable exceptions (such as the works by Hollander, Madsen and Fogel cited in note 75), when the impact of perceptions of China is discussed, it is normally within the foreign policy arena. See, for example, John K. Fairbank, *China Perceived: Images and Polices in Chinese-American Relations* (New York: Knopf, 1974); Leonard A. Kusnitz, *Public Opinion and Foreign Policy: America's China Policy, 1949–1979* (Westport, CT: Greenwood Press, 1984); and Christopher Jespersen, *American Images of China, 1931–1949* (Stanford: Stanford University Press, 1996), which analyses how America's China-images in the mass media (especially under Henry Luce's media empire) influenced the nation's China policies. For a preliminary attempt to compare the Indonesian and American perceptions of China and their political implications, see Hong Liu, "Intellectual Representations and Socio-Political Implications: Comparative China-Imagining in Postcolonial Indonesia and Contemporary United States", *Asian Thought and Society* 26, 76 (2001): 29–50.

# PART I
(Re)presenting China

CHAPTER 1

# Changing Images of China in Pre-1949 Indonesia

*Ever since then [1918], nationalism has been implanted in my heart, through the influence of the Three People's Principles.*

Sukarno (1945)[1]

*This great event in the Chinese mainland [the 1911 Revolution] gave rise to a spirit of nationalism in the Indonesian Chinese. This situation in turn moved the hearts of the Indonesian people and helped to speed up the emergence of the first people's movement.*

Mohammad Hatta (1930)[2]

*We regard China's past as an indicator of her present and future. It is impossible to grasp the meaning of contemporary Asian developments without some knowledge of China's history.*

F.J.E. Tan (1956)[3]

---

[1] Sukarno, "The Birth of Pantja Sila" (1945), in *Pantja Sila: The Basis of the State of the Republic of Indonesia* (Jakarta: Department of Information, 1964), p. 27.
[2] Mohammad Hatta, "Objectives and Policy of the National Movement in Indonesia" (1930), in his *Portrait of a Patriot: Selected Writings by Mohammad Hatta* (The Hague: Mouton, 1972), p. 107.
[3] F.J.E. Tan, "The Early Foreign Maritime Trade of China from the Former Han to the Ming Dynasty (206 B.C.–1644 A.D.)", *Ekonomi dan Keuangan Indonesia* 9 (June 1956): 347.

> *The triumph of the PRC indirectly strengthens the Indonesian people's revolutionary struggle, because they have learned from the victory of the Chinese people that imperialist forces could in fact be defeated.*
>
> I.S. Yusuf (1950)[4]

Narratives and discourses of China in post-independence Indonesia were juxtaposed within two contexts: the historical legacy of Indonesia's longstanding interactions with China and the formations of China-images, especially by modern nationalists who remained intellectually and politically active during the Sukarno era and the significant sociopolitical transformations taking place between 1949 and 1965. While chapters 5 and 6 will look at the contemporaneous contextualization in shaping Indonesian perceptions of the PRC, this chapter examines, in a cursory manner, the substance and impact of Indonesian views of China prior to 1949, with a focus on the first half of the 20th century.

The terms "China" and "Indonesia" are employed loosely in this chapter. For the sake of convenience, they include the geographical, social, political and cultural realms that cover the present-day territories of the two countries. As historical constructs, both nations were being reshaped in the late 19th and early 20th centuries; substantial changes took place with regard to the form and substance of these nation-states as well as the ideas behind them.[5] The examples employed in this chapter are selected primarily for the purpose of illustrating the historicity of China in postcolonial Indonesia; as such, a certain degree of generalization and, perhaps, oversimplification is unavoidable.

## HISTORICAL INTERACTIONS AND PERCEPTIONS OF CHINA IN PRE-20TH-CENTURY INDONESIA

Indonesians were no strangers to China's physical and cognitive presence in their land. The two countries had a long history of economic, cultural and political exchange, dating back to the beginning of the Christian era.

---

[4] Yusuf, "Zhongguo Renmin Geming Shengli dui Yinni Renmin Geming Douzheng de Yingxiang" [Impact of the Chinese people's revolutionary victory upon Indonesian people's revolutionary struggle], *Seng Hwo Pao* (Jakarta), 4 July 1950.

[5] There are a number of important works on the making of the modern nation-states of both China and Indonesia; see, for example, Prasenjit Duara, *Rescuing History from the Nation: Questioning Narratives of Modern China* (Chicago: University of Chicago Press, 1995) and Robert Elson, *The Idea of Indonesia: A History* (Cambridge: Cambridge University Press, 2008).

This relationship was the backdrop against which images of China were formulated at different levels of society. Sino-Indonesian interactions in the pre-20th century can be broadly divided into two periods: the pre-colonial era (before 1600) and the colonial era (1600–1900).[6]

## China in Pre-Colonial Indonesia (Before 1600)

According to Chinese historical records, trading ties between China and Indonesia can be traced to the Later Han dynasty (AD 23–220). In 131, the king of a West Java kingdom sent envoys to Luoyang, the capital city of Later Han, and paid tribute to the emperor.[7] During subsequent centuries, China engaged in both direct and indirect trade with various kingdoms in the Indonesian archipelago, which was located on the crossroads of China's maritime links with the West and the Middle East. The Buddhist kingdom of Srivijaya was a favourable place for Chinese monks to study Buddhist classics and a transit point on their long journey to and from India. During the Tang dynasty, one-third of Chinese monks stopped at Srivijaya on their pilgrimages to India.[8]

The relationship between China and Indonesia reached its height during the Ming dynasty. In the 1420s alone, 15 tribute missions from Java to China were recorded and the Chinese emperors seemed to give them favourable treatment.[9] During the historic overseas expeditions between

---

[6] Because of the scarcity of indigenous primary materials, I have had to rely heavily on Chinese sources and Western travellers' accounts for this very brief discussion of China's historical images, which cannot do justice to their complexity and multi-dimensionality.

[7] Wen Guangyi *et al.*, *Yindunixiya Huaqiao Shi* [A history of Indonesian Chinese] (Beijing: Haiyang Chubanshe, 1986), pp. 3–4; Li Xueming and Huang Kunzhan, *Yinni Huaqiao Shi* [A history of the Chinese in Indonesia] (Guangzhou: Guangdong Gaodeng Jiaoyu Chubanshe, 1987), p. 12; and Huang Aling, *Zhongguo Yinni Guangxishi Jianbian* [A short history of Sino-Indonesian relations] (Beijing: Zhongguo Guoji Guangbo Chubanshe, 1987), p. 3. For an authoritative study on the Sino-Southeast Asian historical relationship, see Han Zhenhua, *Zhongwai Guanxi Lishi Yanjiu* [A historical study of China's relations with foreign countries] (Hong Kong: Centre of Asian Studies, Hong Kong University, 1999).

[8] Wen Guangyi, *Yindunixiya*, p. 14.

[9] Wang Gungwu, "China and Southeast Asia, 1402–1424", in his *Community and Nation: China, Southeast Asia, and Australia* (Sydney: Allen & Unwin, 1992), pp. 108–30; Anthony Reid, "The Rise and Fall of Sino-Javanese Shipping", in *Looking in Odd Mirrors: The Java Sea*, ed. V.J.H. Houben, H.M.J. Maier and W. van der Molen (Leiden: Vakgroep Talen en Culturen van Zuidoost-Azie en Oceanie, 1992), pp. 192–3.

1405 and 1433 led by Zheng He, a Muslim admiral of the Ming court, large-scale fleets and sailors stopped in the Indonesian territories for four lengthy periods, and some of Zheng's crew members stayed behind and never returned home.[10]

During this period, China was a major external power affecting domestic political and cultural developments in the Malay archipelago.[11] The Zheng He voyages, for example, were regarded as a major factor in the spread of Islam in Indonesia, and some even suggested that "Chinese Muslims who stayed in Malacca influenced the growth of Islam".[12] Indonesians' views of China, therefore, were formulated and presented in this broad framework of Sino-Indonesian exchange and the archipelago's sociopolitical transformations. By and large, China appeared to enjoy favourable receptions, evidenced in part by the examples that both Chinese immigrants and official

---

[10] On the Zheng He voyages and their implications for ties between Southeast Asia and China, see Louise Levathes, *When China Ruled the Seas: The Treasure Fleet of the Dragon Throne, 1405–1433* (New York: Simon and Schuster, 1994); Hong Liu, ed., *Haiyang Yazhou yu Huaren Shijie zhi Hudong, 1405–2005* [Maritime Asia and interactions with the Chinese world, 1405–2005] (Singapore: Chinese Heritage Centre, 2007), especially the first part, "Zheng He and the Overseas Chinese".

[11] Concerning China's influence on the domestic development of the indigenous nations, see Slametmuljana, *A Story of Majapahit* (Singapore: Singapore University Press, 1976); G. Coedès, *The Indianized States of Southeast Asia* (Honolulu: University Press of Hawaii, 1968 [1964]); and Lin Jinzhi, "Ming Dai Zhongguo yu Yindunixiya de Maoyi Jiqi Zuoyong", [Sino-Indonesian trade during the Ming dynasty and its influence], *Nanyang Yanjiu* 4 (1992): 17–27.

[12] Slametmuljana, *A Story of Majapahit*, p. 217; and S.Q. Fatimi, *Islam Comes to Malaysia* (Singapore: Malaysian Sociological Research Institute, 1963), pp. 8–36. On the role of Zheng He in facilitating the spread of Islam in Java, see *Chinese Muslims in Java in the 15th and 16th Centuries: The Malay Annals of Semarang and Cirebon*, trans. H.J. de Graaf and Th.G.Th. Pigeaud, ed. M.C. Ricklefs (Melbourne: Monash Papers on Southeast Asia, 1984). The thesis that the Chinese played an important part in the early process of Islamization in the Indonesian archipelago has been a subject of scholarly debate and political contestation; see Syed Naguib Al-Attas, *Preliminary Statement on a General Theory of the Islamization of the Malay-Indonesian Archipelago* (Kuala Lumpur: Dewan Bahasa dan Pustaka, 1969). This thesis has found more favourable reception in the post-Suharto years. According to Professor Abdullah Dahana of the University of Indonesia, "This country has a long historical record of relations with China. The spread of Islam here was closely related to China's trade and political history. There is more to China than business". *Jakarta Post*, 27 January 2007.

envoys were generally well received by the public and court elite. According to *The Chronicle of the Song Dynasty*, "the Chinese traders in Java were treated courteously; they were put in superb guest houses and served with delicate and clean foods".[13] An interpreter travelling with Zheng He reported that the Indonesians "liked the Chinese in particular", while official annals detailed splendid receptions rendered to Chinese missions.[14] Husein Umar, a well-known Muslim preacher in Jakarta, commented that local people of the time easily accepted the new religion (Islam) because of the need to trade with the Chinese: "While teaching the new religion, the Chinese traders bartered silk and other luxury goods with local commodities."[15] The Chinese contributed to the development of social and cultural life, including batik, ceramics, paintings, popular literature, traditional gamelan music and the theatre. These influences were particularly prominent in port cities where Chinese merchants settled and married local women; motifs with Chinese characteristics can be seen at many mosques in the West Java town of Banten as well as at Demak, Kudud and Jepara in East Java.[16]

To the Javanese court elite, China represented a politically and economically powerful kingdom. Their knowledge about China was obtained principally through the so-called tributary missions to the Middle Kingdom, in which Indonesian kings dispatched envoys with exotic presents to pay homage to the Chinese emperors, who gave them seals, royal insignia or other tokens of recognition in return. As Wang Gungwu has demonstrated, by engaging in this seemingly unequal tributary relationship, the Southeast Asian kingdoms had their own agendas to pursue.[17] Economically, it was the only legal channel, throughout much of the time between the Song and

---

[13] Quoted in Li and Huang, *Yin Ni*, p. 45.
[14] Ibid., p. 53; Zheng Hesheng and Zheng Yijun, eds., *Zheng He Xia Xi Yang Zhiliao Huibian* [A collection of primary materials regarding Zheng He's overseas expeditions] (Jinan: Qilu Shushe, 1983), vol. 2, pt. 2, pp. 1349–53. This three-volume document, based upon official and private records, contains the most useful materials regarding Sino-Southeast Asian relations between 1300 and 1500.
[15] Andi Asrun, "Chinese Culture Colours Local Muslim Life", *Malaysiakini*, 8 January 2002.
[16] Ibid.; Adrian Vickers, *A History of Modern Indonesia* (Cambridge: Cambridge University Press, 2005), pp. 68–9; Asvi Warman Adam, "The Chinese in the Collective Memory of the Indonesian Nation", *Kyoto Review of Southeast Asia* (March 2004), <http://kyotoreview.cseas.kyoto-u.ac.jp/issue/issue2/index.html> [accessed 15 October 2008].
[17] Wang Gungwu, *The Nanhai Trade* (Singapore: Times Academic Press, 1998 [1958]).

Qing dynasties, by which Sino-Indonesian trade could be conducted. This trading relation was indispensable, particularly because Chinese coins were used as currency in many parts of Java.[18] Studies have shown that, by defrauding customs and receiving large quantities of presents from the Chinese courts, Indonesians were able to make profits.[19] The tributary relationship, argues O.W. Wolters, "was a mutually advantageous one" to China and Srivijaya. In the same vein, Anthony Reid suggests that it "proved extremely lucrative to rulers as well as to those who arranged the mission".[20]

Politically, the tributary mission was regarded as a "token of the esteem and reverence"[21] that could enhance local rulers' influence. Throughout most of the pre-colonial period, China "occupied a very exalted place in the estimation of the greater part of Asia, its higher civilization, the splendor of its courts, the richness and extent of its territory, easily account for this feeling and veneration".[22] Modern Indonesian writer Armijn Pane pointed out that a close relationship with this powerful empire would strengthen the position of certain indigenous kings in domestic power struggles; this contemplation prompted some former vassals of the Majapahit empire to seek protection from China.[23] Even the Majapahit kingdom requested confirmation of official recognition from the Ming dynasty in 1450, because "it intended to use China's prestige to strengthen its domestic position".[24]

To the masses, knowledge of the remote empire was based upon encounters with Chinese traders and immigrants. In the meantime, China

---

[18] Reid, "Rise and Fall", p. 194; Li and Huang, *Yinnii*, p. 53; and Robert S. Wicks, *Money, Markets, and Trade in Early Southeast Asia: The Development of Indigenous Monetary Systems to AD 1400* (Ithaca: Cornell University Southeast Asian Program, 1992), pp. 231–300.

[19] Li Jinming, *Ming Dai Haiwai Maoyishi* [A history of maritime trade in the Ming dynasty] (Beijing: Zhongguo Shehui Kexue Chubanshe, 1990), pp. 11–68.

[20] O.W. Wolters, *The Fall of Srivijaya in Malay History* (Ithaca: Cornell University Press, 1970), p. 20; Anthony Reid, *Southeast Asia in the Age of Commerce, 1450–1680* (New Haven: Yale University Press, 1993), vol. 2, p. 234.

[21] W.J. Cator, *The Economic Position of the Chinese in the Netherlands Indies* (Chicago: University of Chicago Press, 1936), p. 2.

[22] W.P. Groeneveldt, *Historical Notes on Indonesia and Malaya: Compiled from Chinese Sources* (Jakarta: Bhratara, 1960 [1880]), p. 4.

[23] Armijn Pane, "Indonesia di Asia Selatan: Sedjarah Indonesia sampai c. 1600", *Indonesia* 1/2 (1951): 13–4; see also Slametmuljana, *Story*, pp. 184–7.

[24] Bujung Saleh, "Orang² Tionghoa di Indonesia sebelum Kompeni (VOC)", *Sin Min*, 31 December 1956.

entered the Indonesian scene through importations of its cultural symbols, including vocabularies and artistic forms of popular entertainments such as music and plays.²⁵

It should be noted that images of China were changing over time, reflecting both the change of China *per se* and shifting situations in Indonesia. For instance, in the late 13th century, when the Majapahit empire became strong, admiration and respect for China was replaced by contempt; its king not only ignored the Yuan emperor's demand to pay tribute, but humiliated and expelled its envoy.²⁶

## China in Colonial Indonesia, 1600–1900

With the establishment of the Dutch East Indies Company (VOC) and the gradual colonization of the archipelago after 1600, China came to be perceived in a very different light. For one thing, official economic and political ties were largely cut off and the court elites ceased to be the major articulators of China-images. During the latter part of this period (after the early 19th century), China also faced tremendous domestic turbulence and the mounting threats of Western imperialism, which further prevented it from acting as a self-proclaimed "protector" of its former "vassals". Within this altered environment, the ethnic Chinese (*Huaqiao*) constituted a major channel through which China's presence was indirectly felt. Indonesians' views of China came increasingly to be linked to their attitudes toward the local Chinese.

Before and during the VOC's early years, the Chinese functioned as financiers to the courts as well as intermediaries between domestic producers and foreign traders. Upon arriving in Batavia in 1685, Father Guy

---

²⁵ Concerning cultural exchanges between China and Indonesia in the pre-colonial period, see Claudine Salmon, "The Contribution of the Chinese to the Development of Southeast Asia: A New Appraisal", *Journal of Southeast Asian Studies* 12, 1 (1981): 260–75; Zhou Nanjing, "Lishishang Zhongguo he Yindunixiya de Wenhua Jiaoliu" [Cultural exchanges between China and Indonesia in the historical period], in *Zhongwai Wenhua Jiaoliushi* [A history of cultural exchanges between China and foreign countries], ed. Zhou Yilian (Zhengzhou: Henan Renmin Chubanshe, 1987), pp. 190–238; and Pramoedya Ananta Toer, *Hoakiau di Indonesia* (Jakarta: Bintang, 1960). This exchange was a two-way street; China also imported some cultural elements from Indonesia. See, for example, Nio Joe Lan, "Perhubungan Kebudajaan Indonesia-Tiongkok", *Mimbar Indonesia* 8, 49 (1954): 5–6.

²⁶ This action led to a failed invasion of Java by the military sent by Kublai Khan in 1293. See Groeneveldt, *Notes*, pp. 21–34.

Tachard (c. 1650–1712) observed: "Since the Chinese are industrious and clever, they are of the greatest value at Batavia and without their help it would be difficult to live at all comfortably. They cultivated the land; there are scarcely any artisans excepting Chinese; in a word they are nearly everything."[27] With the advent of Dutch colonialism and the deployment of the "divide and rule" policies, the Chinese gradually became overseers, opium retailers, tollgate keepers, moneylenders and rural tax collectors. They were, therefore, directly linked to the oppressive Dutch economic regime and were seen as competitors of the indigenous people, even though there was a "progressive civic face of Chinese entrepreneurial activities".[28] The local Chinese constituted objects of suspicion and hatred during the Dipanagara War (1825–30); they were even labelled as "evils" by the Javanese rebels.[29] Westerners' accounts captured the increasing hostility toward the Chinese. In 1800, a Dutch report went so far as to assert that the Chinese "like blood-suckers, took as much as they could get".[30] In the late 19th century, an American traveller observed: "The native hatred of the Chinese is an inheritance of those past centuries when the Dutch farmed out the revenue to Chinese, who gradually extended their boundaries, and by increasing exactions and by secret levies oppressed the people with a tyranny and rapacity the Dutch could not approach."[31]

Within this radically altered landscape, China's image gradually became more negative, and it was mentioned primarily in reference to "the exploitative Chinese". Thomas Raffles, whose view might reflect that of his local informants, stated that "the Chinese are only itinerants and not children of the soil, and [they] follow the almost universal practice of remitting the fruits of their industry to China, instead of spending them

---

[27] Quoted in Victor Purcell, *The Chinese in Southeast Asia*, 2nd ed. (London: Oxford University Press, 1965), p. 402.
[28] Vickers, *A History of Modern Indonesia*, p. 67. See also Salmon, "The Contribution of the Chinese to the Development of Southeast Asia", and Anthony Reid, ed., *Sojourners and Settlers: Histories of Southeast Asia and the Chinese* (Sydney: Allen & Unwin, 1996).
[29] Peter Carey, "Changing Javanese Perceptions of the Chinese Communities in Central Java, 1755–1825", *Indonesia* 37 (1984): 1–48; Li and Huang, *Yinni*, pp. 203–4; Philip A. Kuhn, *Chinese among Others: Emigration in Modern Times* (Lanham, MD: Rowman and Littlefield, 2008), pp. 154–7.
[30] Quoted in Cator, *Economic Position*, p. 21.
[31] Eliza Scidmore, *Java: The Garden of the East* (Singapore: Oxford University Press, 1984 [1899]), p. 39.

where they were acquired".[32] According to a report by the Dutch Council of Batavia, China was a country that produced and sent the Chinese who "are refuse of their nation", and who came "half naked and poor in the extreme".[33]

This cursory and inevitably simplified overview, to be sure, cannot do justice to the rich terrains of Sino-Indonesian exchanges and the evolution of the local Chinese communities, including their significant contributions to Indonesia's economic and cultural development. While China was largely well received during the pre-colonial era and seen as a symbol of a rich civilization and a powerful polity, the colonial period witnessed the start of the association of the local Chinese with an increasingly negative image of their ancestral homeland. The Sino-Indonesian exchange, in other words, was formed primarily at the state level during the pre-colonial period, through such venues as exchanges with the court elite, who sought to capitalize their ties with China. In the colonial era, the ethnic Chinese became the main venue of exchanges, and they came to be seen as a symbol of a declining China. The emerging economic competition between the Chinese and indigenous entrepreneurs and the "divide-and-rule" policy further contributed to the deteriorating image of the local Chinese — and those of China.

## INDONESIAN NATIONALISTS AND CHINA, 1900–49

The beginning of the 20th century witnessed a series of deep-seated political changes in both Indonesia and China, which in turn affected the substance and characteristics of China-images. Without a doubt, the most important development was the rise of nationalism in both countries, with the Chinese revolution taking place a step ahead in terms of timing. In this new environment, China evoked a different image in the eyes and minds of the Indonesian nationalists who were fighting for the same goal of independence. China no longer represented a powerful state or a great civilization;

---

[32] Thomas Raffles, *The History of Java* (Kuala Lumpur: Oxford University Press, 1965 [1817]), vol. 1, p. 224.
[33] Cited in Raffles, *The History of Java*, p. 226n. These, of course, were not necessarily the realities of the Chinese community. For a much more positive discussion of Sino-Southeast Asian trade and the Chinese immigrant community in the region during modern times, see Nie Dening, *Jinxiandai Zhongguo yu Dongnanya Jimao Guanxi Shi Yanjiu* [A study of economic and trade relations between China and Southeast Asia in modern times] (Xiamen: Xiamen Daxue Chubanshe, 2001).

instead, it was increasingly associated with revolution against both Western imperialism and social injustice. For the first time in the history of China's presence in Indonesia, it acquired an ideological and inspirational appeal. It was within this context that the nationalists, who constituted the core of political and cultural intellectuals in the Sukarno era, emerged to become major perceivers of China. Thanks to their profound and lasting influence,[34] their views of China had enduring significance for the society at large, thus validating closer scrutiny.

## Sources of Indonesian Knowledge of China

Indonesian nationalists' knowledge of China was primarily based upon two sources: writings about the Chinese revolution and their personal contacts with those ethnic Chinese sympathetic to the nationalist cause in the Dutch East Indies. Their understanding of China was partly precipitated by Chinese intellectuals' changing attitudes toward the *Nanyang* in general.

By the end of the 19th century, the Chinese civilization had faced unprecedented challenges resulting from Western intrusions. This became a key motive behind the constitutional reforms led by Kang Youwei and the nationalist movement led by Sun Yat-sen. It was a time of high imperialism in Southeast Asia. This shared fear of political annihilation constituted a backdrop against which intellectuals from both areas formulated anti-Western strategies. These strategies coalesced into non-state-centred, trans-regional discourses on Asia — "a radically politicized cultural regional concept".[35] Many Chinese intellectuals began to view *Nanyang* in a new light. Unlike the state-centred narratives of various dynasties that had displayed hegemonic and superior attitudes toward the southern neighbours, these intellectuals were more sympathetic to the fate of *Nanyang* and even attempted to forge collective alliances in the struggle against Western imperialism. In the radical construct of Chinese intellectuals,

---

[34] Many members of Indonesian foreign policy elite acknowledged in the 1970s that the most influential writings upon their initial impressions of the outside world were those by nationalists such as Tan Malaka (1897–1949), Sutan Sjahrir (1909–66), Sukarno (1901–70) and Mohammad Hatta (1902–80); see Franklin Weinstein, *Indonesian Foreign Policy and the Dilemma of Dependence: From Sukarno to Soeharto* (Ithaca: Cornell University Press, 1976), p. 59.

[35] Rebecca E. Karl, "Creating Asia: China in the World at the Beginning of the Twentieth Century", *American Historical Review* 103, 4 (1998): 1096–119; Hong Liu, "Beyond Orientalism and the East-West Divide: China and Southeast Asia in the Double Mirror", *Stockholm Journal of East Asian Studies* 13 (2003): 45–65.

Southeast Asians were no longer "barbarous Southerners"; instead, they were *"tongzhong"* — "same race" — with the Chinese. A shared sense of global "lostness" and a profound concern for the survival of Chinese civilization was thus linked to "same race/kind discourse". At the turn of the 20th century, Chinese intellectuals repeatedly referred to the Filipinos as *"tongzhong* pioneers of the yellow race" in the global struggle against the "white race". Similarly, Chinese reformists of the late 19th century evoked the example of King Chulalongkorn of Thailand to validate their activities; reformist newspapers provided extensive coverage of the king's reform efforts and explicitly highlighted their analogousness with China.[36] From the Southeast Asian nationalists' viewpoints, China served as an essential yardstick of reference and a potentially inspiring model of anti-Westernism. The work of Liang Qichao, who formulated a global space in which Asia became an entity and site for new modernity projects,[37] was widely read and discussed by the Vietnamese scholar-gentry. Vietnamese intellectuals first came across Western ideas by way of China; the 1911 Revolution and the Republic set up by Sun Yat-sen served as a model for Phan Boi Chau, the father of early nationalist politics.[38]

As a result of the new political awareness in both China and Southeast Asia, the ethnic Chinese gained a new role as the intermediaries of flows of ideas between China and their emigrating nations and subsequently became an important factor in shaping China-images. It was no coincidence that the closing years of the 19th century saw the emergence of *Huaqiao* (Chinese sojourners) as a sociopolitical discourse, and that various factions of transnationalists from the mainland put contending visions of the country's future before the Chinese overseas.[39] They helped forge an

---

[36] Karl, "Creating Asia"; Yu Dingban and Yu Changshen, *Jindai Zhongguo yu Dongnanya Guanxi Shi* [A history of Sino-Southeast Asian relations in modern times] (Guangzhou: Zhongsan Daxue Chubashe, 1999), pp. 365–73.

[37] Tang Xiaobing, *Global Space and the Nationalist Discourse of Modernity: The Historical Thinking of Liang Qichao* (Stanford: Stanford University Press, 1996).

[38] David Marr, *Vietnamese Anticolonialism, 1885–1925* (Berkeley: University of California Press, 1971).

[39] Prasenjit Duara, "Transnationalism and the Predicament of Sovereignty: China, 1900–1945", *American Historical Review* 102, 4 (1997): 1030–51; Hong Liu, "Introduction: Toward a Multi-dimensional Exploration of the Chinese Overseas", in *The Chinese Overseas*, ed. Liu (London: Routledge, 2006), vol. 1, pp. 1–30; Huang Jianli, "Conceptualizing Chinese Migration and Chinese Overseas: The Contribution of Wang Gungwu", *Journal of Chinese Overseas* 6, 1 (2010): 1–21.

imaginary Sino-Southeast Asian synergy, in which ethnic forces were politicized. Often, by way of the ethnic Chinese communities, Western ideals were transmitted to Southeast Asia.[40] Ethnic Chinese authors played an important role in the development of modern Indonesian literature. Over the course of 90 years (1870–1960), this ethnic group gave rise to more than 800 authors of 3,005 books, while in the 50-year period from 1918 to 1967, non-Chinese authors of modern Indonesian literature numbered only 175 and produced around 400 books (not including translations).[41] In the Malay world, many Chinese publications (in both Chinese and Malay) were concerned with politics in the Asian context. In the novels of Pramoedya Ananta Toer, "the heroes and heroines are not only a mixed-nationality batch, but of many types of cultural and political persuasions". It is hardly surprising that in his acclaimed *Buru Quartet*, a Chinese woman in exile in the Indies becomes a leading nationalist propagandist at the turn of the century.[42]

The reconfigurations of China's position in Asia had direct bearings upon Indonesian perceptions of that country. During the first half of the 20th century, the emerging "printing nationalism" began to play an increasingly important role in facilitating the transnational flows of ideas. There were large numbers of publications about China available in the Dutch East Indies, many with distinctively radical orientations and focusing on the Chinese revolution and revolutionaries. Works by and about Sun Yat-sen (in both Indonesian and English), for example, were discussed extensively among the nationalists, as were the writings of Mao Zedong, Chiang Kai-shek and reports by sympathetic Western journalists.[43] Günther Stein's *The Challenge of Red China*, for instance, was translated by Liem

---

[40] Marr, *Vietnamese Anticolonialism*, p. 100.
[41] Claudine Salmon, *Literature in Malay by the Chinese of Indonesia: A Provisional Annotated Bibliography* (Paris: Éditions de la Maison des Sciences de l'Homme, 1981), pp. 50–60.
[42] Benedict Anderson, *The Spectre of Comparisons: Nationalism, Southeast Asia, and the World* (London: Verso, 1998), p. 293; Hong Liu, "Pramoedya Ananta Toer and China: The Transformation of a Cultural Intellectual", *Indonesia* 61 (1996): 119–43.
[43] Salmon, *Literature in Malay by the Chinese of Indonesia*, pp. 66–7, 75–6; Kwee Kek Beng, *Doea Poeloe Lima Tahoen Sebagai Wartawan, 1922–1947* (Batavia: Kuo, 1948), pp. 32–43; Wu Wenhua and Gan Meifeng, "Benshiji Sanshi dao Wushi Niandai Huawen Tushu zai Yinni" [Chinese publications in Indonesia from the 1930s to the 1950s], *Dongnanya Zongheng* 3 (1993): 41–6.

Koen Hian and published as *Chungking dan Yenan* in 1949.⁴⁴ The single most important piece of writing influencing the Indonesian nationalists' understanding of China was Edgar Snow's *Red Star Over China*. Translated in 1938 by Siauw Giok Tjhan, it was published in a serial form in the *Sin Tit Po*, until the Dutch deemed it as "dangerous" and subsequently banned it.⁴⁵ Indonesian leaders later recalled that this book was "a kind of handbook" for them. George Kahin, who conducted extensive interviews with the nationalists during the Indonesian Revolution (1945–49), confirmed that the army used it as a text on the guerrilla warfare of the time.⁴⁶

Another source of Indonesian nationalists' knowledge of China derived from their contacts with local Chinese who were supportive of their cause. During the first three decades of the 20th century, a China-oriented *Sin Po* group emerged in the Chinese community.⁴⁷ Together with individuals associated with the newspapers *Sin Tit Po* and *Mata Hari*, this group was sympathetic to Indonesian nationalism. These newspapers provided not only extensive coverage on events in China, but also a forum of communications among the nationalists. The *Sin Po*, for instance, is thought to be among the first Malay-language newspapers in the East Indies to use the terms "Indonesia" and "Indonesian", rather than "the Dutch East Indies" and "the native", to name the country and its people. It was also this newspaper that first published the *Indonesian Raya*, the future national anthem of the republic.⁴⁸

---

⁴⁴ Leo Suryadinata, "Liem Koen Hian: A Peranakan Who Searched for Political Identity", in his *Peranakan's Search for National Identity: Biographical Studies of Seven Indonesian Chinese* (Singapore: Times Academic Press, 1993), p. 75.

⁴⁵ Mary Somers, "Peranakan Chinese Politics in Indonesia" (Ph.D. dissertation, Cornell University, 1965), p. 100; Siauw Tiong Djin, "Siauw Giok Tjhan: The Making of a Peranakan Leader", in *Indonesian Political Biography: In Search of Cross-Cultural Understanding*, ed. Angus McIntyre (Clayton: Centre of Southeast Asian Studies, Monash University, 1993), pp. 123–60. On Siauw's career and political views, see Siauw Tiong Djin, "Siauw Giok Tjhan: Perjuangan Seorang Patriot Membangun Nasion Indonesia dan Masyarakat Bhineka Tunggal Ika" (Ph.D. dissertation, Monash University, 1998).

⁴⁶ Cited in Weinstein, *Indonesian Foreign Policy*, p. 59; personal correspondence with Mary Somers-Heidhues, a former student of Kahin, 18 January 1994.

⁴⁷ Mary Somers, "Peranakan Chinese Politics", pp. 9–103; Leo Suryadinata, *Peranakan Chinese Politics in Java*, rev. ed. (Singapore: Singapore University Press, 1981).

⁴⁸ Hong Yuanyuan [Ang Goan Jan], *Hong Yuanyuan Zizhuan* [An autobiography of Hong Yuanyuan] (Beijing: Zhongguo Huaqiao Chuban Gongsi, 1989), pp. 44–5. This unpublished memoir by a major Chinese nationalist was translated by Liang Yingming, a professor of Southeast Asian Studies at Peking University.

The supportive attitude of these local Chinese won the nationalists' trust and friendship. For example, Sukarno held regular discussions in Bandung with his Chinese friends regarding the strategies of the nationalist movement. China's revolutionary and progressive image, presented to him partly through these intermediaries, might account for his intention to establish close contacts with the revolutionaries in China.[49]

## Substance and Variations of China-images

For the Indonesian nationalists in the pre-war decades, China evoked three images: a declining state and civilization, an exciting revolution and a populist project.

The first image of China was associated with a weakening and humiliated state that was characterized by internal disunity and pervasive control by Western imperialism. This theme ran through the writings of Tan Malaka, perhaps the most knowledgeable person about China among the Indonesian nationalists.[50] He spent a total of 12 years (1923–25, 1927–37) in China in his capacity as the Comintern's agent for Southeast Asia (based in Canton) and as a revolutionary in exile. He wrote extensively about his China experience. In his close reading and analysis of Tan's writing on Shanghai, Abidin Kusno argues: "When Tan Malaka wrote about Shanghai, therefore, he was deeply concerned over the nature of the Indonesian revolution: his Indonesians lacked aim, organisation and determination…. It is my opinion that the geographical imagining shaping Tan Malaka's anticolonialism and (Indonesian) revolution can be attributed, in large part, to his experience of the colonial geography of Shanghai."[51] Similarly, Rudolf Mrazek has demonstrated that Tan Malaka's China experience affected the evolution of his thinking,[52] and that his perceptions of China significantly influenced Indonesians' understanding of that country.

---

[49] Kwee Kek Beng, *Doea Poeloe Lima*, p. 35; Hong Yuanyuan, *Hong Yuanyuan*, p. 79.
[50] Tan Malaka's thinking had an important impact upon China's official perceptions of the Indonesian society too, as evidenced in the writings about Indonesia by Wang Renshu [Ba Ren], China's first ambassador to Jakarta. Interview with Chen Lishui, Wang's personal assistant in the early 1950s, Beijing. See also Zhou Nanjing, ed., *Baren yu Yindunixiya* [Ba Ren and Indonesia] (Hong Kong: Nandao Chubanshe, 2001).
[51] Abidin Kusno, "From City to City: Tan Malaka, Shanghai, and the Politics of Geographical Imagining", *Singapore Journal of Tropical Geography* 24, 3 (2003): 327–39.
[52] Mrazek, "Tan Malaka: A Political Personality's Structure of Experience", *Indonesia* 14 (1972): 1–48; William H. Frederick and Soeri Soeroto, *Pemahaman Sejarah Indonesia* (Jakarta: LP3ES, 1982), pp. 328–59.

In his autobiography, *From Jail to Jail*, which was written in 1947 and serialized in the Indonesian newspapers the next year, Tan Malaka depicted China as a disunited state being torn apart by Western imperialism and as a society full of economic and political contradictions: "China, with its comprador capitalism, was a *semi-colony*. In both politics and economics, China was only half in control."[53] Referring to the Western powers' prevalent influence in China, he wrote,

> This *unequal treaty*, which throttled the Chinese economy by granting *customs control* over almost all the principal ports and giving legal protection to all foreigners, whether ordinary traders or scoundrels, brought peace and plenty to the foreigners and poverty and discord to the Chinese.[54]

The most visible and illuminating symbol of China's humiliation, according to him, was the signs in front of parks in Shanghai, which read: "Chinese and dogs are not allowed".[55] To Tan Malaka, this weakened China presented a stark contrast to its glorious past and tremendous potentials:

> It [China] has the largest population on earth; its territory is nearly as large as that of the U.S., the richest and strongest country in the world; it has strong nationalism and unity against the outside world; and its people are diligent, courageous, and clever and have an ancient culture stretching back for four thousand years. In spite of fulfilling all the supposed conditions of independence, for the last one hundred years China has remained only an object for the politics of foreign imperialism.[56]

To Sukarno, China was similarly a victim of Western imperialism. "At present, power over China is the competitive goal of these three imperialistic materialists [Great Britain, the United States and Japan]", he remarked in 1930, "Whoever holds the environs of China will control the affairs of the

---

[53] Tan Malaka, *From Jail to Jail*, trans. and ed. Helen Jarvis (Athens: Ohio University Southeast Asian Series, 1991), vol. 2, p. 15 (emphasis is original).
[54] Ibid., p. 6 (emphasis is original).
[55] Ibid., p. 14. This was such a powerful metaphor of the old China that many post-independence Indonesian writers repeatedly referred to it. See, for example, Sugardo, "Bukan lagi Djamannja Tjina dibajar untuk Menjanji", *Mimbar Indonesia* 7, 27 (1953): 9–10. On the historicity and myth of this sign, see Robert Bickers and Jeffrey Wasserstorm, "Shanghai's 'Dogs and Chinese Not Admitted' Sign: Legend, History, and Contemporary Symbol", *The China Quarterly* 142 (1995): 444–66.
[56] Tan Malaka, *From Jail to Jail*, vol. 3, p. 165.

entire Eastern world. For that reason, the materialists will fight to the death over China."[57]

This image of foreign oppression and internal disarray was evoked in the post-1949 writings about China. The journalist Arifin Bey, for instance, made frequent mention of signs of a weakening China such as treaty ports and extraterritoriality.[58] Adinegoro, a journalist who visited China in the 1930s, described it as a "semi-colony" and a society torn apart by "internal polarization".[59] This prevailing image of a feeble nation was summed up aptly by an Indonesian nationalist, who commented that the old China was like "a loaf of bread sliced up by the imperialists".[60]

The second image of China was a revolutionary one. Being the most powerful symbol of the Chinese revolution, aiming to expel foreign imperialism and eradicate internal injustice, Sun Yat-sen was at the centre of this radical imagining. Sukarno described him as "a very great nationalist leader" and "the father of the Chinese masses".[61] Tan Malaka, who had held face-to-face discussions with Sun Yat-sen on Asian revolutionary strategies, was impressed by his "sincerity, unselfishness, and his closeness to his people". Despite disagreeing with Sun Yat-sen on strategic matters, he was convinced that "Dr. Sun's writings are far more informative than those of the Mahatma [Gandhi] on politics and economics or on concrete actions."[62] To Mohammad Hatta, the revolutionary image of China was inseparable from the person of Sun Yat-sen:

> When I was young, I read a great deal about the exciting revolution under the great Chinese leader, Dr. Sun Yat-sen. His significant influence also ignited the Indonesian revolutionary spirit. The name of Dr. Sun Yat-sen was known to the Indonesian youth fighting for independence.[63]

---

[57] Sukarno, *Indonesia Accuses*, ed. and trans. Roger K. Paget (Kuala Lumpur: Oxford University Press, 1975), p. 17.
[58] Arifin Bey, *Dari Sun Yat Sen ke Mao Tze Tung* (Jakarta: Tintamas, 1953), pp. 10–1.
[59] Adinegoro, *Tiongkok: Pusaran Asia* (Jakarta: Djambatan, 1951), pp. 73, 106.
[60] Cited from Weinstein, *Indonesian Foreign Policy*, p. 89.
[61] Sukarno, *Nationalism, Islam and Marxism* (Ithaca: Cornell University Modern Indonesian Project, 1984 [1926]), p. 43; Sukarno, *Indonesia Accuses*, p. 55.
[62] Tan Malaka, *From Jail to Jail*, vol. 1, p. 102.
[63] Mohammad Hatta, "Pidato pada Rapat Umum yang Diselenggarkan oleh Lembaga Persahabatan Tiongkok-Indonesia di Peking (24 September 1957)", in *Kumpulan Pidato*, ed. I. Wangsa Widjaja and Meutia F. Swasono (Jakarta: Inti Idayu Press, 1983), vol. 2, p. 97.

Hatta Visiting the Sun Yat-sen Memorial Hall in Nanjing, 1957 (By permission of the Xinhua News Agency, ID: 12469656).

The revolutionary image of China was so pervasive that it even attracted the attention of the Sarikat Islam, a political and religious movement that acquired an increasingly anti-Communist and anti-Sinic undertone after the mid-1920s. Hadji Agus Salim, one of its founding members, acknowledged in 1928 that the establishment of the Sarikat Islam in 1912 "was on the example of what had happened in China".[64]

---

[64] "Report of the Meeting of the Partai Sarikat Islam held on 26 January 1928 at Yogjakarta, to Commemorate its Fifteen years of Existence", in *Indonesia: Selected Documents on Colonialism and Nationalism, 1830–1942*, ed. and trans. L.M. Penders (St. Lucia: University of Queensland Press, 1977), p. 258. Hatta also remarked that "the 1911 Revolution [in China] led by Dr. Sun influenced [*mempengaruhi*] the rise of the great Indonesian movement named Sarikat Islam". Hatta, "Pidato", p. 97.

The third image of China was characterized by a populist undertone, which had something to do with Indonesian interpretations of the Chinese revolution. Why were Mao Zedong and his Communist Party (CCP) able to defeat the seemingly mighty forces of Chiang Kai-shek, who was militarily and financially backed by powerful America? In the attempt to make sense of this intriguing question, Indonesian nationalists tended to downplay the influence of Communist ideology and persistently posited popular support for the CCP as the most important reason behind Mao's victory. As early as 1937, Sutan Sjahrir wrote about the significant differences between Chiang and Mao. According to him, Chiang's power was centred in big cities such as Nanjing and Shanghai, and he represented the interests of China's financial capital, which was in turn under the strong influence of Western power. While convinced that "a unified China, a Chinese nation, can never be expected from Shanghai",[65] Sjahrir was much more hopeful of the revolution under Mao and the CCP that had enjoyed tremendous popular support:

> To look at the other side of the picture: the lower middle class in China is now restive, and *nationalistically revolutionary*.... There are also the millions of peasants and workers and the tens of thousands of students who are stirring under the influence of idealism. They want a revolution, and they want to cleanse China of the domestic and foreign enemies of the Chinese people. They find their nuclei in the so-called communist bands, which are spread throughout China.... Actually this element amounts to a peasant revolt under Communist leadership. Its success lies neither in its military might nor in its strong and efficient organization, but rather in the response and sympathy that its aims and actions elicit from the millions of poor peasant farmers and workers in China. It has the silent support of those millions, and it finds its inexhaustible reservoir of manpower in those millions.[66]

In an essay on the Chinese revolution published in an influential magazine, the journalist Mahiddin disputed the notion that Mao was "an imitating Communist (*komunis tiruan*)"; instead, he argued that Mao's victory was fundamentally rooted in his ability to mobilize the peasantry's support.[67] The writer Armijn Pane maintained that it was not Communism

---

[65] Soetan Sjahrir, *Out of Exile*, trans. Charles Wolf, Jr. (New York: John Day, 1949 [1945]), p. 147.
[66] Ibid., pp. 148–9 (emphasis added).
[67] Mahiddin, "Tiongkok Merah", *Siasat*, 27 February 1949, pp. 4–5.

Cover of Armijn Pane, *Tiongkok Zaman Baru. Sedjarahnja: Abad ke-19 — Sekarang* (Jakarta: Arbati, 1953).

that had won the people over and that the peasants "were not aware of Communist ideology". The key reason for CCP success, according to him, was that "the majority of the people, i.e., peasants, and other social groups sided with Mao".[68] The journalist Sugardo reached a similar conclusion by asserting that "the Chinese masses, regardless of pro- or anti-communist, pledged their support for Mao".[69]

This interpretation, with its populist undertone, helped define specific images of the Chinese revolutionaries. Indonesian intellectuals tended to see Mao Zedong not principally as a Communist but as a nationalist. In this line of thinking, it was Mao, not Chiang, who was the heir to Sun Yat-sen. Asmudji emphasized that Sun Yat-sen and the communists had a great deal in common in terms of their political viewpoints and strategies.[70] Wojowasito wrote in 1947 that Chinese Communists were not composed of "a group of people who are influenced by the Soviet Union and serve as the Russians' tools; instead, they are determined to realize Sun Yat-sen's ideals".[71]

In brief, there existed three interconnected images of China in the Indonesian nationalists' eyes and minds during the first half of the 20th century: a weakening state and declining civilization, the dynamic rise of an exciting revolution, from which, with the mandate of the popular will, Mao emerged as the triumphant hero. The perceived lineage between Mao and Sun Yat-sen reinforced this line of understanding. What was consistently and conspicuously missing from this populist imagination of China, however, was the essential role of the Communist ideology and organization in leading to Mao's victory. As will be demonstrated in the next chapter, this tendency of separating Communism from China continued to be a major characteristic in Indonesian discourses of the PRC's politics throughout the 1950s.

## PERCEIVED PARALLELISMS

Having established the substance of China-images prior to 1949, let us try to unveil their characteristics, namely, a close correlation between specific

---

[68] Armijn Pane, *Tiongkok Zaman Baru. Sedjarahnja: Abad ke-19 — Sekarang* (Jakarta: Arbati, 1953), pp. 105, 118.
[69] Sugardo, "Bukan Lagi", p. 10.
[70] Asmudji, *Genderang Tiongkok Baru* (Bodjonegoro: Suara Pemuda, 1950), pp. 33–7.
[71] Wojowasito, *Tiongkok (Pembangoenan Politik)* (Yogyakarta: Badan Penerbit Nasional, [1947]), p. 44.

Chinese images and Indonesian concerns over developments at home, and a penchant for underlining parallelisms between the two countries/cultures, thus laying a foundation for translating and adapting Chinese practices into the local environments.

Indonesians' production of knowledge of China was intimately linked to their paramount interest in their own domestic issues; this contextualization helped shape the specific substance of the images *per se*. For example, the court elite's perception of a respected and powerful China was partly formulated with a conviction that this external force could be enlisted to boost political prestige at home. Likewise, with the rise of nationalism, China's revolutionary image received the most enthusiastic attention; it formed the context within which Indonesian attitudes toward the local Chinese were interconnected with the perceptions of China. Hatta wrote in 1930 that he had became aware of the changes taking place in early 20th-century China from the emerging nationalism of the local Chinese: "This great event in the Chinese mainland [the 1911 Revolution] gave rise to a spirit of nationalism in the Indonesian Chinese; their realization of their national identity and self-respect can be seen from their everyday attitudes. This situation in turn moved the hearts of the Indonesian people and helped to speed up the emergence of the first people's movement."[72] Hadji Agus Salim observed that, after the 1911 Revolution, the ethnic Chinese "no longer wanted to be treated on an equal footing with the natives and became arrogant to them".[73]

This juxtaposition of China in the Indonesian context was partly responsible for the emergence of perceived parallelisms between the two nations. Sukarno was one of the first nationalists advocating the theme of identification, as he wrote in the *Suluh Indonesia Muda* in 1928:

> People are beginning to be conscious of a sense of unity and a feeling of brotherhood between the Chinese people and the Indonesian people, that is, that both are Eastern people, both are people who are suffering, both are people who are struggling, demanding a free life.... Because the common lot of the people of Asia is certain to give birth to uniform behavior; a common fate is certain to give birth to a uniform feeling.[74]

---

[72] Hatta, "Objectives and Policy of the National Movement in Indonesia" (1930), in his *Portrait of a Patriot: Selected Writings by Mohammad Hatta* (The Hague: Mouton, 1972), p. 107.
[73] Cited in Penders, *Indonesia: Selected Documents*, p. 259.
[74] Sukarno, "Indonesianism and Pan-Asianism" (1928), in his *Under the Banner of Revolution* (Jakarta: Publication Committee, 1966), vol. 1, p. 67.

Tan Malaka saw cultural resemblances between the two countries. The values of animism and dynamism, he wrote, were "the foundations of basic Indonesian-Chinese similarities".[75] Adam Malik reminded his readers in 1950 that "Indonesians and Chinese belong to the same race, we have almost forgotten the fact that our country's oldest cultural ties with foreign nations were with China, not India."[76] Hatta commented that the two countries had similar histories, because "we were controlled by foreign countries in the past. Foreign powers colonized us and oppressed us; our independence was the product of our struggles".[77]

The perceived parallels prompted Indonesian nationalists to study closely the Chinese revolutionary experiences and their relevance. Sjahrir suggested in 1937 that the nationalists could learn some "major lessons" from recent developments in China.[78] He showed an admiration for Mao, as he wrote in 1937: "Mao Tse-tung, the genial leader of the movement is now about forty years old, and he is particularly adept at attracting the best of China's youth to his cause."[79] In October 1945, Sjahrir published a pamphlet entitled *Our Struggle*, which was considered "the most clearly articulated diagnosis of Indonesia's contemporary problems and the only coherent program for the development of the nationalist struggle".[80] It exhibited striking similarities with Mao's *On New Democracy* (1940), in terms of formulating the revolutionary goals and the means of accomplishing them. For instance, in line with Mao's analysis of China, Sjahrir defined the Indonesian Revolution as having a "dual character": simultaneously a national revolution against imperialism and a social or democratic revolution against feudalism.[81] According to a leader of the Indonesian Socialist Party, of which Sjahrir was a founding member, Sjahrir's way of thinking was so close to that of Mao's that some people were even convinced that the two had met.[82] Hazil Tanzil, one of Sjahrir's close associates, remarked in his review of *Our Struggle* in 1946,

---

[75] Quoted in Mrazek, "Tan Malaka", pp. 36–7.
[76] Adam Malik, "Tentang Persahabatan Indonesia-RRT", *Republik* 1 (1950): 12.
[77] Hatta, "Pidato", p. 97.
[78] Sjahrir, *Out of Exile*, pp. 150–1.
[79] Ibid., p. 149.
[80] Benedict Anderson, "Introduction", in Sutan Sjahrir, *Our Struggle*, trans. Anderson (Ithaca: Cornell University Modern Indonesian Project, 1968), p. 8.
[81] Sjahrir, *Our Struggle*, pp. 26–8.
[82] Quoted in Weinstein, *Indonesian Foreign Policy*, p. 60.

When *Perdjoeangan Kita* [*Our Struggle*] was seen by foreign journalists, they asked the author if he had read Mao's brochure ["On New Democracy"] before. He had analyzed the Indonesian revolution in the same way, and he came to the same conclusion about the problem of a national revolution in the formerly colonized lands, as the President of the Communist Party in Yen An did, when he wrote about the (Chinese) revolution of 1911, and about the movement as it developed afterwards.[83]

Regarding Sun Yat-sen as a symbol of Asia's progressive nationalism in the struggle for political independence and social justice, Sukarno liked to perceive himself as the Sun Yat-sen of Indonesia. "[Just as] Sun Yat-sen represented the sentiments of the Chinese people", he represented the voices of the Indonesian people and enjoyed their strong support.[84] Sukarno acknowledged a number of times that Sun Yat-sen's Three People's Principles (democracy, nationalism and socialism) was the major source of inspiration in formulating the Indonesian state ideology of Pancasila:

> Ever since then [1918], nationalism has been implanted in my heart, through the influence of the Three People's Principles. Therefore, if the whole Chinese people consider Dr. Sun Yat Sen their preceptor, be sure that Bung Karno also, an Indonesian, with the uttermost respect will feel grateful to Dr. Sun Yat Sen until he lies in the grave.[85]

---

[83] Cited in Rudolf Mrazek, *Sjahrir: Politics and Exile in Indonesia* (Ithaca: Cornell University Southeast Asian Program, 1994), pp. 275–6. It was likely that Sjahrir had read Mao's *On New Democracy*, of which there were two Indonesian versions in 1945, published by Paragon Press and Logika respectively. See Duiwai Wenhua Lianluo Weiyuanhui Ersi [Research office of the Committee of Cultural Exchanges with Foreign Countries], ed., *Yindunixiya Wenhua Gaikuang* [A survey of Indonesian culture] (Beijing, for internal circulation only, 1962), p. 186.

[84] Sukarno, "Hiruplah Pengetahuan untuk Berjuang" (1963), in his *Ilmu dan Perjuangan* (Jakarta: Inti Idayu Press-Yayasan Pendidikan Sukarno, 1984), p. 63.

[85] Sukarno, "The Birth of Pantja Sila" (1945), in *Pantja Sila: The Basis of the State of the Republic of Indonesia* (Jakarta: Department of Information, 1964), p. 27. According to Bernhard Dahm, "it was quite possible that the *Sun Min Chu I* [Three People's Principles] was a model for the idea of Pantja Sila". Dahm, *Sukarno and the Struggle for Indonesian Independence*, trans. Mary Somers-Heidhues (Ithaca: Cornell University Press, 1969), p. 339. Sukarno reiterated in 1946 that the Indonesian state's ideological foundation was similar to that of Sun Yat-sen's. See Osman Raliby, *Documenta Historica* (Jakarta: Bulan-Bintang, 1953), vol. 1, p. 213; and *Merdeka*, 10 June 1946.

China came to be deployed as a parameter in Indonesian political and cultural discourse. Political figures such as Sun Yat-sen, Mao Zedong, Chiang Kai-shek and Wang Jingwei (Wang Ching-wei), entered into Indonesian polemics with local variations. "Wang Ching-Wei-ism", for instance, was a metaphor employed by Mohamad Natsir in the 1930s to condemn some fellow nationalists' attempts to compromise with the Dutch.[86] Chinese revolutionary terms were incorporated into Indonesian military thinking. General Abdul Haris Nasution, the county's foremost military strategist, wrote in his guerrilla handbook,

> Our leaders always compared the guerrillas to fish and the people to the water, using the example from Mao Tse-tung's teaching. The Chinese leader has explained that the "water" must be nourished in its natural political and socio-economic climate to ensure the proper development of the guerrilla fighter who "swims" in it. Therefore it is very important for the guerrilla soldier to maintain that favorable "climate" with the people.[87]

Although Indonesian nationalists agreed that valuable lessons could be drawn from the Chinese experience, this did not necessarily mean that images of China were homogeneous; instead, China was presented in different lights by people with different sociopolitical orientations. Sukarno employed Sun Yat-sen's example of uniting the Nationalists and Communists to validate his own efforts to incorporate nationalism, Marxism and Islam in the 1930s.[88] To people with more radical agendas, the Chinese model represented a viable alternative for combatting imperialism and realizing "People's Democracy". Sakirman, a leading Communist theoretician, contended that Indonesia could follow the Chinese way of uniting workers, peasants and soldiers in the fight against imperialism.[89] Immediately after the founding of the PRC, a writer associated with the PKI

---

[86] Natsir, "Is There 'Wang Ching-Wei-ism' in Indonesia? No! We Respond", in *Regents, Reformers, and Revolutionaries: Indonesian Voices of Colonial Days, Selected Historical Readings, 1899–1949*, trans. and ed. Greta Wilson (Honolulu: University Press of Hawaii, 1978), pp. 123–5.
[87] Abdul Haris Nasution, *Fundamentals of Guerilla Warfare* (Singapore: Donald Moore Books, 1965), pp. 26–7.
[88] Sukarno, *Nationalism, Islam and Marxism*, pp. 40–1, 43, 58, 60.
[89] Sakirman's speech in the Indonesian parliament, *Risalah Perundingan* 2, no. 21 (September 1950): 1140–3.

commented, "As both Indonesia and China are agrarian nations, the Chinese revolution's success provides very valuable reference materials for the Indonesian revolution."[90]

Wojowasito believed that China, unlike his own country which had paid too much attention to the West, could serve as a model because it was capable of synthesizing ideas of East and West.[91] The existence of contending perceptions was manifested in the arena of Sino-Indonesian relationships. Whilst some writers saw the tributary system as a symbol of friendship between the two peoples, thus dismissing its detrimental effects,[92] others took it as a symptom of China's imperialism.[93]

## CONCLUSION

Prior to 1949, Indonesia and China had a long history of interaction of peoples and ideas dating back nearly 2,000 years. This history served as the backdrop for the Indonesian understanding of China. In the period prior to 1900, China emerged principally as a powerful state and an advanced civilization, though this image was gradually replaced, after the early 19th century, by that of a weakening nation, symbolized partially by the massive inflow of immigrants who could not survive in the mainland. At this stage, the Sino-Indonesian exchanges were primarily formed in the tangible arenas of goods and peoples. It was only at the turn of the 20th century that China (and its intellectuals in particular) began creating more

---

[90] Yusuf, "Zhongguo Renmin Geming Shengli dui Yinni Renmin Geming Douzheng de Yingxiang" [The impact of the revolutionary victory of the Chinese people upon the revolutionary struggle of the Indonesian people], *Seng Hwo Pao* (Jakarta), 4 July 1950. According to Clive Christie, the ideological leadership of Communist movements of East and Southeast Asia had been taken over in the critical decade between 1937 and 1947 by the Chinese Communist Party and its leader Mao Zedong. See Christie, *Ideology and Revolution in Southeast Asia, 1900–1980*, chapter 7.
[91] Wojowasito, *Tiongkok*, p. 3.
[92] Saleh, "Orang² Tiongkok".
[93] See some school textbooks' depiction of Chinese history, in Carl Taylor, "Indonesian Views of China", *Asian Survey* 3, 3 (1963): 165–72. This historical relationship still loomed large in the 1980s. Responding to a question on Indonesia's fear of a militarily strong China, Foreign Minister Mochtar Kusumaatmadja commented bitterly, "We used to pay tribute to China every year in the past". *Straits Times*, 25 April 1985.

equal configurations in attitudes toward the *Nanyang*. Unlike the previous era, the interaction was constructed principally in the intangible realms of ideas and cultural practices, with Indonesian nationalists held captive by China's exciting revolutionary images.

Indonesians' perceptions of China were shaped by their interests in domestic developments; hence China was often perceived in the light of its local relevance. During the first half of the 20th century, largely because the Indonesian intellectuals who were also major China observers were peripheral to political power, there was no palpable evidence of any interplay between knowledge about China and exercise of power. Nevertheless, as I have shown, China was not merely the name of a country; instead, it was constructed as an object embedded with multiple meanings that could be internalized (and politicized). These imaginations in the historical era constituted a stepping stone for creating the China metaphor in the postcolonial era. Under the new environment, when both countries faced the daunting tasks of nation-building and the forging of new cultural identities, the symbolic and metaphorical influence of China was likely to reemerge and intensify.

# CHAPTER 2

# Discourses on Chinese Politics

*In terms of everyday reality and life, China today is truly a nation by the people, from the people, of the people, and for the people.*

Barioen A.S. (1952)[1]

*I am glad and privileged to have this tour through China, because it never fails to amaze me to have observed the decidedly happy trend of development of this nation of 600 million people toward a better life.*

Roeslan Abdulgani (1956)[2]

*Confucius' thought regarding the Ta Tung (Great Harmony) has been adopted by Mao and is integrated with Chinese revolutionary ideals and Marxist-Leninist teachings. It has become the foundation of New Democracy, which is characterized by placing the common interests above individual interests.*

Armijn Pane (1953)[3]

*The Peking government has forced the whole population to become production machines and obedient aggressors. The future is very bleak, not only for the youth in China, but also for the whole world.*

Sabdo Pangon (1960)[4]

---

[1] Barioen A.S., *Melihat Tiongkok Baru: Negara Merdeka, Pandai Merdeka, Sanggup Merdeka* (Jakarta: Rada, 1952), p. 25.
[2] Roeslan Abdulgani, *Laporan Menteri Luar Negeri kepada Dewan Perwakilan Rakjat R.I. tentang Perdjalanan Presiden R.I. ke Sovjet Uni, Yugoslavia, Austria, Czecholovakia, Mongolia, dan Republik Rakjat Tiongkok (26 Agustus–16 Oktober 1956)* (Jakarta: Kementerian Luar Negeri, 1956), p. 93.
[3] Armijn Pane, *Tiongkok Zaman Baru. Sedjarahnja: Abad ke-19 — Sekarang* (Jakarta: Arbati, 1953), p. 161.
[4] Sabdo Pangon, *Angkatan Muda Tiongkok*. Seri: Kewaspadaan Nasional (Jakarta: New Nusantara Publishing Coy, 1960), p. 32.

With the founding of the People's Republic of China (PRC) in October 1949, the formal transfer of sovereignty from the Dutch to the Republic of Indonesia two months later, and the establishment of the Sino-Indonesian diplomatic relationship in mid-1950, China-images in Indonesia were to be formulated and presented in an environment substantially different from that of the pre-independence era. This chapter is concerned with Indonesians' conflicting perceptions of Chinese politics, with a focus on three defining issues: discourses on New Democracy, the cornerstone of the country's political system in the 1950s; views on the PRC's foreign policy behaviour; and images of Mao Zedong, who was regarded as the embodiment of the new China.

## "NEW DEMOCRACY": CHINESE PRACTICES AND INDONESIAN PERCEPTIONS

### Domestic and Foreign Politics of the PRC in the 1950s: A Background Note

The PRC's political system in its formative years was, at least in theory, guided by the principles of New Democracy, first elaborated by Mao in 1940. In his *On New Democracy*,[5] Mao envisioned that China was to experience a two-stage revolution: the first was "to change a colonial, semi-colonial and semi-feudal society into an independent, democratic society", and the second was "to push the revolution further and build a socialist society". China would be in the first step of the revolution during the formative years of the new nation, Mao argued. The central political institution during this transitional period was New Democracy, a "joint dictatorship of several revolutionary classes, including the proletariat, the peasantry, the intelligentsia, and other sections of the petty bourgeoisie". Together, they constituted "the basic forces which decide China's fate"; "Corresponding to this political form was the economic form of the new democracy, which involved the state ownership of all big banks, big industries, and big commercial establishments, and the state management of enterprises. However, the state should not confiscate other forms of private property or forbid capitalist production."[6]

---

[5] Mao Zedong, *On New Democracy* (Peking: Foreign Language Press, 1960).
[6] For a detailed analysis of the tenets of New Democracy, see J.H. Brimmell, *Communism in South East Asia: A Political Analysis* (London: Oxford University Press,

In practice, however, political development in the early 1950s was a departure from New Democracy theory; it was gradually replaced by the General Line for the Transitional Period that was characterized by "[class] contractions and struggles".⁷ The multiclass coalition was not based upon the principle of power-sharing, and the People's Dictatorship "was ultimately that of the Communist Party".⁸ The Communist dominance was exemplified by the Soviets' pervasive influence upon Chinese society and politics between 1949 and 1957. This model provided patterns of state organization, an urban-oriented development strategy and modern military techniques. The Stalinist economic system was established, and the Soviets were regarded as respected elder brothers. The prevailing slogans such as "The Soviet Union of today is our tomorrow" was just one example of the profound Soviet influence during the early years of the PRC.⁹ At the height of the global Cold War confrontation, "leaning toward the Soviet Union" constituted the foundation of China's foreign policy. As Mao made it clear

---

1959), pp. 139–43, and Nick Knight, "On Contradiction and On New Democracy: Contrasting Perspectives on Causation and Social Change in the Thought of Mao Zedong", *Bulletin of Concerned Asian Scholars* 22, 2 (1990): 18–35. According to Clive Christie, Mao's three essays, "On Contradiction" (1937), "On New Democracy" (1940) and "Talks at the Yenan Forum on Arts and Literature" (1942), had "a direct ideological influence on Vietnamese communism, and an indirect influence on Southeast Asian communism as a whole, during the revolutionary period of 1945 to 1947". See Christie, *Ideology and Revolution in Southeast Asia, 1900–1980*, chapter 7.

⁷ Jiang Yihua, "Guodu Shiqi Lilun yu Shijian Qudai Xinminzhuzhuyi Lishi Beijin de Yixiang Kaucha" [The historical background behind the replacement of New Democracy by the theory and practices of the transitional period], in *1950 Niandai de Zhongguo* [China in the 1950s], ed. Wu Jinping and Xu Shiyen (Shanghai: Fudan University Press, 2006), pp. 1–54; Pang Xianzhi and Jin Chongji, eds., *Mao Zedong Zhuang (1949–1976)* [A biography of Mao Zedong (1949–1976)] (Beijing: Zhongyan Wenxian Chubanshe, 2003), pp. 254–5; Liu Jianhui and Wang Hongxu, "The Origins of the General Line for the Transition Period and of the Acceleration of the Chinese Socialist Transformation in Summer 1955", *China Quarterly* 187 (2006): 724–31. Hua-yu Li's study offers convincing explanations on the policy shift from New Democracy in the early years of the People's Republic. See Hua-yu Li, *Mao and the Economic Stalinization of China, 1948–1953* (Lanham, MD: Rowman & Littlefield, 2006).

⁸ Frederick C. Teiwes, "Establishment and Consolidation of the New Empire", in *Cambridge History of China*, vol. 14, ed. Roderick MacFarquhar and John K. Fairbank (Cambridge: Cambridge University Press, 1987), p. 78.

⁹ Ibid., pp. 63, 67.

in July 1949, "We are firmly convinced that in order to win victory and consolidate it we must lean to one side."[10]

## Conflicting Intepretations from Indonesia

In their discussions of Chinese politics of the 1950s, Indonesia's China observers placed a predominant emphasis on New Democracy, manifested in the publications of a large number of writings in Indonesian and translations of Western interpretations. They appeared in the nation's influential political magazines such as *Sikap*, *Siasat* and *Liberty*.[11] Travelogues by those who had visited the PRC displayed a similar fascination with the theories and practices of New Democracy. This shared focus, however, did not lead to a consensus; instead, the narratives were diverse and sometimes conflicting. These perceptions can be divided into three: portraying New Democracy as the Chinese brand of nationalism and a manifestation of the nation's cultural tradition; a genuine democracy representing the people's mandate; and an outright Communist dictatorship.

### *New Democracy as a Symbol of Chinese Nationalism and Cultural Tradition*

According to this line of interpretation, New Democracy was a derivation of Chinese nationalism, which was in turn built upon the nation's cultural tradition. It held that indigenous nationalism, rather than imported Communism, was the key to understanding contemporary Chinese politics. In a widely read article entitled "The Problems of Communism and Nationalism

---

[10] Mineo Nakejima, "Foreign Relations: From the Korean War to the Bandung Line", in *Cambridge History of China*, vol. 14, pp. 259–92; see also Zhou Enlai, "Women de Waijiao Fangzhen he Renwu (1949)" [Our foreign policy principles and tasks], in *Zhou Enlai Xuanji* [Selected writings of Zhou Enlai] (Beijing: Renmin Chubanshe, 1984), vol. 2, p. 37. More detailed discussion on the interplay between ideology and perception in China's foreign policy can be found in Steven I. Levine, "Perception and Ideology in Chinese Foreign Policy", in *Chinese Foreign Policy: Theory and Practice*, ed. Thomas W. Robinson and David Shambaugh (Oxford: Clarendon Press, 1994), pp. 30–47.

[11] For example, "Semangat Economie Baroe", *Liberty* 15 (1946): 24; Robert North, "Politik Ekonomi Baru dan Demokrasi Baru", *Sikap* 4, 43 (1951): 18; "Komunisme dan Nasionalisme di Tiongkok", *Sikap* 4, 2 (1951): 1–10; and Soegito, "Demokrasi Baru", *Siasat* 4, 154 (1950): 10–1.

in Asia",[12] an author using the pseudonym "Realpolitiker" contended that, historically, Chinese Communism was different from Russian Communism because the former had always attached high importance to the local circumstances. In China's "search for its own road, its communism has been embedded with the spirit of nationalism". This equation of communism with nationalism had a wider resonance and acceptance. Maisir Thaib's perception of Chinese politics, for instance, was characterized by an absence of non-Chinese ideology and the presence of intimate connections between Sun Yat-sen's Three People's Principles and Mao's New Democracy. Like "Realpolitiker," Thaib stressed that China's political theory was firmly rooted in the nation's particular circumstances, such as the peasantry's vital role. After commenting that the New Democratic government was a multiclass coalition, thus ensuring representation of the people's interests, Thaib concluded, "With the implementation of these programs the CCP enters the hearts of millions of the Chinese people."[13] Mohammad Hatta, the country's vice-president between 1949 and 1956, saw Chinese communism as a variation of nationalism. In an essay entitled "The Problems of Development in the PRC", he regarded New Democracy as the foundation of the nation's political system and was convinced that Mao's thesis of the two-step revolution was appropriate because it derived from China's specific circumstances.[14]

Commentators perceived close linkages between New Democracy and China's cultural tradition. Liem Koen Hian, a leading ethnic Chinese political intellectual who had fought for an Indonesia-oriented nationalism for more than two decades, disputed the notion that China was merely a Russian follower by saying in 1949,

> I believe that the Chinese nation will not become communist like Communist Russia. Five thousand years of Chinese history have presented us with a great deal of evidence that China has never been a country that entirely swallows up imported foreign ideas. As one of the greatest countries of the world, China has been open to all foreign and new ideas, but the Chinese "cooked" [*masak*] these ideas before they were adopted in everyday life.[15]

---

[12] Realpolitiker, "Soal Komunisme dan Nasionalisme di Asia", *Sikap* 3, 10 (1950): 1–3.
[13] Maisir Thaib, *Tiongkok Merah* (Bukittinggi: Nusantara, n.d.), p. 97.
[14] Mohammad Hatta, "Masalah Pembangunan dalam RRT", *Pikiran Rakjat*, 23–24 December 1957.
[15] Quoted in Maisir Thaib, *Tiongkok Merah*, p. 84.

After reflecting upon China's experience in integrating Buddhism, Islam and Christianity into its own civilization, Liem continued,

> The communism in China is definitely different from that of the Soviet Union. It is certainly becoming a Chinese communism, the kind of communism that was practised in China a long time ago. I am thinking of the example of Wang An-shih, who lived between 1021 and 1086 and was one of the most famous statesmen in the Northern Song dynasty. He implemented certain fiscal, economic, agrarian and trade policies, which by today's standard could well be labelled as communism.[16]

After visiting China in 1951, Kwee Kek Beng reported that, contrary to the expectation that traditional values would be eliminated under the new regime, they were still very much alive.[17] Armijn Pane, a well-known writer who had personally lived in an environment of East-West cultural confrontation,[18] interpreted New Democracy as a product of acculturation between Chinese tradition and Marxism (which had been "integrated into Chinese thought"). He held that the key elements of New Democracy had been articulated in the teachings of Confucius 2,000 years earlier:

> Indeed, Confucius' thought regarding the *Ta Tung* (Great Harmony) has been adopted by Mao and is integrated with Chinese revolutionary ideas and Marxist-Leninist teachings. It has become a foundation of New Democracy, which is characterized by placing the common interests above individual interests. It is also true that from the beginning the Communist Party of China has been called the Kung-chan-tang, meaning the Party of Prosperity for All [*Berbagai Kemakuran*].[19]

## New Democracy as a Functioning Democracy

While the above perceptions of Chinese politics were mainly concerned with the theoretical dimension and historical/cultural foundation of New

---

[16] Ibid., p. 85.
[17] Kwee Kek Beng, *Ke Tiongkok Baru* (Jakarta: Kuo, 1952), pp. 30–1.
[18] On the evolution of Armijn Pane's career and cultural thought, see William H. Frederick, "Dreams of Freedom, Moments of Despair: Armijn Pane and the Imagining of Modern Indonesian Culture", in *Imagining Indonesia: Cultural Politics and Political Culture*, ed. Jim Schiller and Barbara Martin-Schiller (Athens: Ohio University Center for International Studies Southeast Asian Series, 1997), pp. 54–89.
[19] Armijn Pane, *Tiongkok Zaman Baru. Sedjarahnja: Abad ke-19 — Sekarang* (Jakarta: Arbati, 1953), p. 161. In the same spirit, Barioen said, "China's democracy was based upon a return to its own tradition". See Barioen, *Melihat Tiongkok Baru*, p. 20.

Democracy, some Indonesians were attracted to its practices. Since New Democracy duly represented the people's interests, they reckoned, a government founded upon this principle was therefore legitimately considered as being "by the people, from the people, of the people, and for the people".[20]

Barioen, an educator and writer from Sumatra, provided the most extensive and influential account on the practice of New Democracy. In late 1951, he visited China together with Armijn Pane and M. Tabrani, an ethnic policy adviser and journalist. Barioen published a book detailing his views of Chinese politics right after their return.[21] Central to his perception was that New Democracy was a genuine and functioning democracy, which "exists in the everyday reality". Because the system provided opportunities for various political parties to participate in the decision-making process, it was therefore an embodiment of the whole population's interests.[22] Chinese politics was thus characterized by all-class solidarity and harmony: "Under the People's government, the whole China is now composed of the people working only for the people's interests."[23] Barioen's views on Chinese democracy were echoed by A. Karim, a journalist associated with the *Sin Po* and president of the Indonesian Journalists' Association from 1963 to 1965:

> Some of us have a different understanding of democracy from that of the Chinese. Some people in our country think that democracy is symbolized by attacking each other. In China democracy means that every citizen must be guaranteed with appropriate material and cultural wellbeing; and it means there are no oppressions, no suffering, and no exploitations. China can proudly claim that its democracy is more valuable than democracy in the United States.[24]

In a similar vein, the journalist Arifin Bey maintained that Chinese democracy was a system founded upon the People's Representative Congress, representing people "from different generations and a variety of political

---

[20] Barioen, *Melihat Tiongkok Baru*, p. 25.
[21] His perceptions of Chinese politics had far-reaching influence, including on President Sukarno, who was attracted by Barioen's views of Chinese-style democracy, which fuelled his critique of Indonesian parliamentary democracy in the late 1950s. Interview with Mr. Soeto Mei-sen, Sukarno's personal assistant and Chinese-language interpreter.
[22] Barioen, *Melihat Tiongkok Baru*, p. 71.
[23] Ibid., pp. 25, 72.
[24] A. Karim, "Fanwen Zhongguo Guilai" [Returning from China], *Hsin Pao*, 5 June 1956.

Cover of Arifin Bey, *Dari Sun Yat Sen ke Mao Tze Tung* (Jakarta: Tintamas, 1953).

Insertion of Sugardo's *Tiongkok Sekarang* (Jakarta: Endang, 1953).

backgrounds"; this broad representation was "unprecedented in China's history".[25] Armijn Pane suggested that China's political system was exemplified by a democratic process of elections and informal meetings at the village level.[26] Speaker of Parliament Sartono commented that, unlike the Soviet Union, China's political system was not a single-party system; instead, it aimed at "encouraging all *aliran* [political, cultural and ethnic groups]

---

[25] Arifin Bey, *Dari Sun Yat Sen ke Mao Tze Tung* (Jakarta: Tintamas, 1953), p. 83.
[26] Pane, *Tiongkok*, p. 163.

to participate in politics".²⁷ Roeslan Abdulgani, minister of foreign affairs in the mid-1950s, reported to parliament about his visit to China:

> I am glad and privileged to have this tour throughout China, because it never fails to amaze me to have observed the decidedly happy trend of development in this nation of 600 million people toward a better life.²⁸

While many of the centre-oriented writers who constituted the mainstream of Indonesian intellectuals subscribed to the notion that New Democracy was an authentic democracy based on solidarity among all social groups, left-leaning intellectuals were more inclined to interpret it as a class dictatorship on behalf of the working class. Asmudji accepted the official Chinese view that New Democracy was "a democracy for the majority of the people and a dictatorship for a small minority of counter-revolutionaries".²⁹ Jusuf Adjitorop, a member of the PKI's politburo, characterized "People's Democracy" as representing genuine social justice and a "democracy against the counter-revolutionaries".³⁰

## New Democracy as Communist Dictatorship

Not every Indonesian observer shared such favourable views of New Democracy; a small number of commentators regarded it as essentially a Communist dictatorship founded entirely upon the Soviet model. They portrayed the PRC as a totalitarian regime characterized by the "suppression of the people by the people's government", and depicted its military system as the copycat of "the aggressive Soviet model" and a symbol of Communist authoritarianism.³¹ Sabdo Pangon asserted that the idea of New Democracy had first been elaborated in Lenin's New Economic Policy in the 1920s and that China was controlled by dictatorship: "While the Peking government has succeeded in eliminating individualism, it has forced the

---

²⁷ *Sin Min*, 8 August 1956; *Antara News Bulletin*, 21 August 1956.
²⁸ Roeslan Abdulgani, *Laporan Menteri Luar Negeri*, p. 93.
²⁹ Asmudji, *Genderang Tiongkok Baru* (Bodjonegoro: Suara Pemuda, 1950), p. 41.
³⁰ Jusuf Adjitorop, *Integrasi Kekuasaan Politik dan Sistim Hukum dengan Revolusi di Tiongkok Rakjat* (Jakarta: Jajasan Pendidikan dan Kebudajaan Baperki, 1964), pp. 10–1.
³¹ *Indonesia Antara Dua Blok Raksasa* (Jakarta: New Nusantara Publishing Coy, [1958]), p. 17; *Mengapa 600 djuta Rakjat RRT Bergerak Keselatan?* Seri Kewasapadaan Nasional (Jakarta: New Nusantara Publishing Coy, [1960]), pp. 6–7.

whole population to become production machines and obedient aggressors. The future is very bleak, not only for the youth in China, but also for the whole world".[32]

While this accentuation of authoritarianism stemmed largely from the relevant writers' predispositions toward anti-Communist ideology, there were associated but more nuanced criticisms by more detached observers of Chinese politics for its violations of individual human rights. They identified profound contradictions between the universal principle of human rights and Communist ideology. Their praise for the Chinese political system's broad social representation was often coupled with an aversion for the lack of protection for human rights. Asa Bafagih, a widely read author about China, represented this ambivalent mixture of admiration and revulsion. Although impressed by the significant economic progress under the Communist leadership, he was dismayed by the use of oppressive political means. He was critical of the PRC government for silencing people's voices and of its ruthless control over society (for example, Neighbourhood Committees in every city had to report to the CCP regarding every individual's activities, a gross violation of privacy).[33] In a similar vein, Sugardo found it dispiriting that basic rights such as freedom of expression and worship were extended only to "the people" and that there was no balance between Communist rule and democracy.[34] Arifin Bey reported that "although the outcomes in economic development are generally exciting, the results are tragic in the fields of developing morality and protecting basic human rights".[35]

In short, although a small minority of intellectuals found fault with New Democracy, most observers viewed it affirmatively, which led to a dominant narrative. Presented by writers from a diverse range of political and intellectual persuasions, this narrative portrayed New Democracy as a theory and practice built upon the nation's cultural tradition and indigenous nationalism. As a system representing "the people's will", it functioned well in the Chinese context. In addition to downplaying the influences of the Soviet model and communist ideology, this line of interpretation tended to

---

[32] Sabdo Pangon, *Angkatan Muda Tiongkok*, p. 32.
[33] Asa Bafagih, *RRT dari Luar dan Dalam* (Jakarta: Pengurus Besar Nahdatul Ulama, 1955), pp. 23, 27, 29.
[34] Sugardo, *Tiongkok Sekarang: Terra Incognita* (*Tanah tak dikenal*) (Jakarta: Endang, 1953), pp. 36–45.
[35] Bey, *Dari Sun Yat Sen ke Mao Tze Tung*, p. 166.

accentuate social harmony as the foundation of China's political system in the 1950s.

## CHINA IN THE INTERNATIONAL ARENA: "AN AWAKENING LION" OR "A THREATENING RED DRAGON"?

Indonesian perceptions of China's foreign policy behaviour between 1949 and 1965 were essentially an extension of their contending attitudes toward that nation's domestic politics. An approximately identical line of interpretations emerged: those writers de-emphasizing China's communist orientation regarded the nation as a power independent of Soviet influence, while those perceiving New Democracy as communist dictatorship were inclined to portray China as a tool of the Soviet empire. The former interpretation, as might be expected, did not view China as a threat to Indonesia, while the latter saw a great danger from China's presence to Southeast Asia in general and Indonesia in particular.

### China as an Independent and Peaceful Power

The debates concerning China's foreign policy started shortly before the Communist takeover in October 1949. Two influential political and literary magazines, *Sikap* and *Siasat*, both associated with the Indonesian Socialist Party (PSI), raised the question of whether the CCP was a tool of the Soviet Union. According to "Realpolitiker", Communism in China was different from that of the Soviet Union: it placed the national interest as the top priority, hence "China is not a tool of Communist Russia".[36] Liem Koen Hian wrote in 1949:

> I am also convinced that when CCP leaders come to power in the future, they will definitely not follow the Soviet Union blindly. When making policy towards a foreign country, Chinese communist leaders will be guided solely by their consideration for their country and the Chinese nation. They will not let the same, or seemingly the same, ideology guide their nation.[37]

---

[36] Realpolitiker, "Soal Komunisme". This view was echoed by another writer, who argued, "the CCP is not the tail (*buntut*) of Russia". See "Apa Artinja Kemenangan Mao Tse Tung di Tiongkok?" *Siasat* 3 (1949): 11.

[37] Quoted in Leo Suryadinata, "Liem Koen Hian: A Peranakan Who Searched for Political Identity", in his *Peranakan's Search for National Identity: Biographical Studies of Seven Indonesian Chinese* (Singapore: Times Academic Press, 1993), p. 76.

Arnold Mononutu, minister of information in the early 1950s and ambassador to Beijing from 1953 to 1955, commented in 1950, "We should not assume that all communist nations belong to the Soviet Bloc. As far as we know, the CCP is the symbol of the Chinese people's revolution."[38] Sutan Sjahrir wrote in 1951 that "China was like Yugoslavia", implying that the PRC was independent from the Soviet Union.[39] Kwee Kek Beng claimed that the Soviet Union had very little influence on China: "When travelling in the PRC, we saw very few Russians and Russian books [except in the Northeast region]".[40] Hatta reported that he did not notice any visible sign of Russian influence during his 1957 trip to China.[41] Stating that "we have seen with our own eyes that there is no sign whatsoever indicating China is being colonized by the Soviets", Barioen concluded that "China is not a satellite of the USSR".[42]

Although some writers acknowledged the existence of a special relationship between the PRC and the USSR, they did not consider it an ideological alliance. Instead, this tie was thought to stem from China's nationalistic and *realpolitik* calculations. As such, Sino-Soviet connections did not necessarily diminish China's independence. Maisir Thaib pointed out that China placed its own national interests as the top priority in its relationship with the USSR.[43] Both Sugardo and Arifin Bey felt that the deterioration of the Sino-American relationship after the Korean War left China with no other alternative but to side with the Russians. The journalist Adinegoro pointed out that the Sino-Soviet alliance was necessary because the two countries shared long and common boundaries.[44]

This conviction that China was essentially an independent polity and that the Sino-Soviet alliance was not based upon ideological affinity dissuaded many Indonesians from viewing the PRC as a threat. Following

---

[38] *Hsin Pao*, 28 July 1950.
[39] Quoted from Rudolf Mrazek, *Sjahrir: Politics and Exile in Indonesia* (Ithaca: Cornell University SEAP, 1994), p. 429.
[40] Kwee Kek Beng, *Ke Tiongkok Baru*, p. 35.
[41] Hatta, "Masalah".
[42] Barioen, *Melihat Tiongkok Baru*, pp. 31–3.
[43] Maisir Thaib, *Tiongkok Merah*, p. 93.
[44] Sugardo, *Tiongkok Sekarang*, p. 13; Bey, *Dari Sun Yat Sen ke Mao Tze Tung*, pp. 80–1; Adinegoro, *Tiongkok: Pusaran Asia* (Jakarta and Amsterdam: Djambatan, 1951), p. 84.

Napoleon, Adinegoro characterized China as an "awakening lion" in an affirmative way. China's national and social revolution, according to him, opposed Western imperialism instead of its Asian neighbours.[45] R.H. Kusnan, deputy speaker of parliament, observed that "we went everywhere in China and did not see troops or any other indications of the PRC's military preparation; neither did we spot a single Russian soldier".[46]

## China as a Stooge of the Russian Empire

In contrast to this perception of China as an independent and peaceful power in the international arena, some writers asserted that the Russian Communists dictated China's foreign policy, thus presenting a serious threat to Southeast Asia. According to such authors, the Sino-Soviet alliance would lead to the formation of "a superpower". As China did not possess adequate land for growing food to feed its 600 million people, it had to embark on a path of seeking "living space (*ruang bagi hidup*)". Since China's northern neighbour, Siberia, belonged to the Soviet Union, Southeast Asia became the only space into which the PRC could expand.[47]

Sabdo Pangon declared that China's imperialist past made it easier for the CCP to adopt the Soviet model by undertaking an aggressive foreign policy, which was reinforced by its "ambition of conquering the world". Insisting that China had been thoroughly "Russianized", Pangon foresaw "a bleak future for the whole world".[48] An essay in the *Suara Masjumi* depicted the threat to Islam by the Chinese Communists, who "are agents of the Soviet Union".[49] A number of writers shared the belief that the PRC was a threatening "Red Dragon" and claimed that the combination of China's aggressive past and Communist ideology made it "particularly dangerous".[50] After visiting China in 1954, Asa Bafagih reported, "The USSR's profound influence has been evident not only in the areas of politics, military, and economy, but also in the social and cultural fields." He did not, however, interpret the Sino-Soviet alliance as a manifestation

---

[45] Adinegoro, *Tiongkok*, p. 10.
[46] *Suluh Indonesia*, 13 October 1956; *Sin Po*, 11 October 1956.
[47] *Mengapa 600 djuta Rakjat RRT Bergerak Keselatan?* pp. 22–3, 33–4.
[48] Sabdo Pangon, *Angkatan Muda Tiongkok*, pp. 7–8, 32.
[49] "Kalau Komunis Berkuasa", *Suara Masjumi* 10 (1955): 6–7.
[50] *Mengapa 600 Djuta*, p. 4; *Indonesia antara Dua Blok*, p. 13.

of their ideological solidarity; instead, it was forged out of mutual need and was likely to break sooner or later.[51]

## "BROTHER MAO":[52] IMAGES OF MAO ZEDONG IN INDONESIA

As the paramount leader of the Chinese revolution, Mao was often regarded by Indonesians as the embodiment of the new China, just as Sun Yat-sen had been portrayed as a defining symbol of Chinese nationalism. Prior to 1949, while Indonesian nationalists were not in power and shared the ultimate goal of independence, there existed a consensus in an affirmative imagination of Sun Yat-sen. Indonesia's postcolonial development, however, was characterized by clashing and diverse agendas in nation-building and socio-economic development; the past nationalists became either power-holders or power-contenders. Discourses on Mao and his China therefore constituted a politically loaded site of contestation, which contributed to conflicting images of Mao, simultaneously portrayed as a beloved leader and a brutal dictator.

### Mao as Philosopher-King and Benevolent Ruler

To Indonesian China observers of the 1950s, Mao emerged first and foremost as the architect of the PRC's political system; they directed a significant amount of attention to understanding his political, military and cultural thought. The bulk of Armijn Pane's book on modern Chinese history, for example, was devoted to the evolution of Mao as a revolutionary thinker. His extensive references to Mao's writings demonstrated that he had studied Mao's theory in a fairly systematic and detailed manner.[53] He viewed Mao as an intellectual creatively applying Marxism to China's concrete circumstances: "From the very beginning Mao has proved himself to be different from the orthodox Marxist; he has paid special attention to the peasantry and realized that it was outside the city that the foundation of the Chinese revolution was to be located." Noting that Mao and Sun

---

[51] Bafagih, *RRT dari Luar dan Dalam*, pp. 65–6, 71.
[52] Brother Mao, or Bung Mao, was a term President Sukarno used to address Mao Zedong. Many Indonesian reporters also used this expression in reference to Mao.
[53] Pane, *Tiongkok Zaman Baru*, pp. 52–63, 159–76.

Yat-sen had a great deal in common, Pane concluded that Mao was primarily a "traditionalist and a nationalist".[54] Arifin Bey held that Mao was first and foremost a pragmatist, while Adinegoro characterized him as "a peasant, a fighter, and a scholar".[55] According to Sugardo, unlike Chiang Kai-shek, who represented the interests of "feudalism, capitalism and foreign powers", Mao was the spokesman of "the working class, peasants, and petit bourgeoisie" and was supported by over 95 per cent of the population.[56]

Indonesians seemed to be impressed by Mao's "modest life style and habit of hard work". Kwee Kek Beng observed that Mao was a person who "leads a simple life; he does not have foreign banking accounts or iron boxes full of diamonds and valuable certificates". This image of Mao offered a striking contrast to politicians of the past, who "talked like a giant and acted like a dwarf".[57] In his biographical portrayal of the PRC leadership, Kwee quoted approvingly the view of a Western journalist: "Many of the leading Chinese communists are great personalities, fanatically honest and sincere."[58] Those who had met Mao in person shared this favourable impression. Speaker of Parliament Sartono was impressed by Mao's "austere life style"; Wilopo, prime minister in 1953, was pleasantly surprised that Mao was able to receive him at 11 p.m. and hold a 45-minute talk about China's policy of reforming the national bourgeoisie.[59] Soewirjo, chairman of the Indonesian Nationalist Party (PNI), reported that Mao talked with him in "a kind and benevolent manner". "Mao is a great leader and is respected by all Chinese people," he commented approvingly, "The people respect him because all his activities are carried out in the nation's and people's interests."[60]

Mao was also portrayed as a traditional father figure. The second vice-speaker of parliament, Zainul Arifin, spoke his impression of Mao, "He is calm and possesses remarkable oriental characteristics: frank, sincere, and

---

[54] Ibid., pp. 40, 64, 157.
[55] Bey, *Dari Sun Yat Sen ke Mao Tze Tung*, p. 126; Adinegoro, *Tiongkok*, p. 90.
[56] Sugardo, *Tiongkok Sekarang*, pp. 26, 35; see also Kwee Kek Beng, *Ke Tiongkok Baru*, p. 43.
[57] Ibid., p. 124.
[58] Kwee Kek Beng, *Pendekar-pendekar R.R.T. (Who's Who in New China)* (Jakarta: Kuo, 1953), p. 7.
[59] *Antara News Bulletin*, 21 August 1956; *Seng Hwo Pao*, 15 July 1957.
[60] *Seng Hwo Pao*, 14 November 1959. The expression "kind and benevolent" was also used by Indonesia's ambassador to China, Sukardjo Wirjopranoto, in describing his impression of Mao. *Seng Hwo Pao*, 25 March 1959.

Ali Sastroamidjojo having dinner with Mao and Zhou Enlai, Beijing, 1955 (Lembaga Persahabatan Indonesia-Tiongkok, *Perkenalan Lembaga Persahabatan Indonesia-Tiongkok* [Jakarta: Rada, 1956]).

modest. He likes to exchange opinions with others and accept criticisms with an open mind. It is very difficult to find these characteristics among national leaders in the West."[61] Prime Minister Ali Sastroamidjojo recalled his 1955 meeting with Mao:

> He impressed me as being not so much the leader of a people who had succeeded in changing the course of history and the destiny of the Chinese nation, as rather a father figure, the head of a large Chinese family such as I had often met in the Chinese quarters of Indonesian towns and cities, who was respected and looked upon as an old man of great wisdom and intelligence not only by his children and his grandchildren, but also by all the local Chinese. I saw Mao then as a *pater familias* of this kind.[62]

---

[61] *Sin Po*, 24 October 1956.
[62] Ali Sastroamidjojo, *Milestones on My Journey*, ed. C.C.M. Penders (St. Lucia: University of Queensland Press, 1979), pp. 309–10. Arnold Mononutu had a similar impression of Mao as a benign ruler. He described his first meeting with Mao: "There stood Mao, large, silent, benign; he was like a god". Cited in Ross Terrill, *Mao: A Biography*, rev. ed. (New York: Simon & Schuster, 1993), pp. 256–7.

In short, Mao seems to have enjoyed a very favourable image — perhaps part of the reason that Sukarno extended eight invitations to "Brother Mao" to visit Indonesia.[63]

## Mao as Brutal Dictator

To a small number of writers, Mao personified Communism's aggressive nature. Badly in need of "food and rubber for the continuance of Chinese livelihood", Mao had to expand overseas with an intention "to conquer the whole Asia".[64] He was characterized as a ruthless dictator willing to sacrifice the masses' well-being to keep his power. It was alleged that "Mao sent children to military camps for training" and turned the whole population into "production machines" for the purpose of boosting industrial output.[65] Mao was also portrayed in a traditionalist image, but it was imbued with distinctly aggressive and sinister strategies such as those expounded by Sun Tzu in *The Art of War*.[66]

Some Indonesians thought that Mao personified a malfunctioning system. In an editorial entitled "Lessons of China", the editor of the *Indonesian Raya* "praised" Mao for admitting the existence of social and political confrontations in his country and concluded that "the people are not satisfied with merely filling their stomachs".[67] According to the *Abadi*, organ of the Masyumi Party, Mao's acknowledgement of domestic problems indicated that "freedom could not be oppressed". The newspaper ridiculed those Indonesian leaders "who, despite possessing only superficial knowledge of China, think that the PRC is like a paradise, praise its accomplishments and even want to emulate the Chinese".[68]

## CONCLUSION

The preceding discussions have highlighted a central characteristic of Indonesian perceptions of Chinese politics: the emergence of a core narrative

---

[63] Terrill, *Mao*, p. 256; and *Harian Rakjat*, 25 January 1965. Although Mao did accept one of Sukarno's invitations — making headlines in the Indonesian press in 1956 — he changed his mind and did not make the trip.
[64] *Mengapa 600 Djuta*, pp. 21–2.
[65] Ibid., p. 27.
[66] Ibid., p. 49.
[67] *Indonesia Raya*, 26 June 1957.
[68] *Abadi*, 22 June 1957.

from the competing discourses and its propensity to separate China from Communism. While most observers subscribed to the notion that New Democracy was a genuine expression of nationalism and cultural tradition and that it was a political system pursuing an independent foreign policy, a smaller number of writers characterized New Democracy as an outright Communist dictatorship under Soviet control. These clashing interpretations were extended to Mao Zedong, who was simultaneously cast as a visionary leader enjoying popular backing and a brutal dictator who pursued power relentlessly at the expense of the people. Despite the multiplicity of opinions about Chinese politics, however, it appeared that the more affirmative view of Chinese politics prevailed in intellectual imaginations and media coverage. Furthermore, the approving perceptions were formulated by leading political and cultural intellectuals of the time. Chapters 6 and 7 will provide a detailed analysis of reasons behind this phenomenon, including the important role played by the PRC government in forging such hopeful self-images.

In the core narrative about Chinese politics, there was an obvious inclination to separate China from Communism (and vice versa). By constantly accentuating the CCP's nationalistic characteristics and the historical/cultural continuity of its policies, Indonesians implicitly or explicitly delinked China from Communism. Although they did not deny the fact that China was a Communist state, their focus was on those seemingly non-Communist features, such as commonalities between Mao and Sun Yat-sen, divergences between China and the Soviet Union and the existence of a multiparty system and democratic elections. The prevailing image of Mao as a creative thinker and traditional leader reinforced this penchant for separating Communism from China. This widespread sentiment was aptly summed up by an Indonesian leader who remarked that, during the Sukarno years, "when we thought about Communism, we thought about the Soviet Union [and not about China]".[69]

In line with the separation of China from Communism, Indonesian commentators were inclined to construe Chinese politics through the lens of social harmony and political solidarity. This represented a continuation of a central theme that first emerged in the nationalists' imagining of China before the independence, which underlined popular backing as the key to the CCP's triumph over the KMT. The theory and practice of class conflict

---

[69] Quoted in Franklin Weinstein, *Indonesian Foreign Policy and the Dilemma of Dependence: From Sukarno to Soeharto* (Ithaca: Cornell University Press, 1976), p. 91.

— central to Communist ideology — received only scant attention from mainstream intellectuals. (The only exception was the views held by the PKI, which looked at China through the lens of class analysis.) The dominant image of social harmony was evident in the observation by a prominent journalist:

> It does not matter to China whether it is admired or hated. The PRC has been making steady progresses and 600 million people firmly believe the system they support is a viable one. There is a saying in the West that "the voice of the people is the voice of God". To religious people, the voice of God is the voice of truth. In the same manner, the choice for people's democracy is the voice of truth in China.[70]

This populist underpinning was so prevalent in intellectuals' judgements of Chinese politics that it was widely held that the defining nature of its political system was "the people", or the masses, not ideology. Hatta, an ardent anti-Communist at home, displayed a remarkably different attitude when speaking of China. "The measure of judging China is very simple," he wrote in 1957, "Firstly, we have to see whether or not China is making progress in comparison to its past; secondly, we have to consider whether or not this progress is beneficial to the majority of the people. After I came back from China, I found the answers to both questions are affirmative."[71]

---

[70] A. Karim D.P., "Shenke de Yinxiang" [Deep impressions], originally published in *Sin Po*, trans. Huang Aling, *Renmin Ribao*, 23 October 1956.

[71] Cited in *Jinri Xinwen*, 27 October 1957. According to an adviser of Hatta who accompanied him during the trip to China, "Hatta is anti-communist, but he is only opposed to Indonesian communists and not Chinese communists. Although Marxist ideology is worshipped by the Chinese communists, [Hatta believes] they will not be assimilated because China has a long-standing and enriching cultural tradition". "Yindunixiya Qian Fuzongtong Hada Fanhua Jiedai Jianbao" [Newsletter on the reception of former vice president Hatta of Indonesia during his visit to China, issues no. 1–2] (25 September 1957), file no. 204-00046-03 (1), Archives of the Ministry of Foreign Affairs, PRC.

# CHAPTER 3

# Social Dynamism and Economic Progress

*China used to be "everybody's colony, nobody's responsibility". Today the situation is totally different; the New China is "nobody's colony, everybody's responsibility".*

Kwee Kek Beng (1952)[1]

*Peking, Shanghai, Wuhan/Wearing Blue Clothes, People Are Working indefatigably/From Dawn to Afternoon, till Night/Under the Sky/Smokes Emitting from Thousands of Socialist Chimneys/Symbols of the Twentieth Century are Emerging from Here/... Today We Will be Departing/The Future of My Motherland/Is Surfacing from the Imagination.*

Sitor Situmorang (1961)[2]

*During three weeks of my stay in China, I was constantly reminded of a saying, "Keep your clothing clean and shun away from any forms of impurity." How could I not? Everything was immaculate, orderly, and pristine.*

Danubroto (1956)[3]

---

[1] Kwee Kek Beng, *Ke Tiongkok Baru* (Jakarta: Kuo, 1952), p. 151.
[2] Sitor Situmorang, "Lagu² Tiongkok Baru", in his *Zaman Baru: Sadjak-Sadjak* (Jakarta: Madjalah *Zaman Baru*, 1961), p. 15. See also "Xin Zhongguo Zige" [Song of the new China], in Xitoer Xidumolang (Sitor Situmorang), *Shiji* [Selected poems], trans. Chen Xiaru (Beijing: Zuojia Chubanshe, 1963), p. 10.
[3] Danubroto [vice mayor of Greater Jakarta], "Tiongkok Laksana Sarang Labah: Setiap Orang Bergerak dan Bekerdja", *Sin Po*, 11 July 1956. This essay also appeared in *Seng Hwo Pao*, 12 July 1956.

> [*Watching the National Day Parade in Peking in 1956*] *The whole panorama before us inspired awe and fear. There were people everywhere, regimented people who marched in endless procession with disciplined body movements, yet gay, forceful, and excitedly flawless, and seemingly coordinated by remote control. It was an impressive sight to behold but nonetheless a most frightening one.*
>
> Ganis Harsono (1956)[4]

As people living in a newly independent country facing the exciting yet daunting task of nation-building, Indonesian intellectuals were naturally attracted by experiences of other new nations. It was within this context that China entered Indonesian discourses on society and economy. This chapter examines Indonesians' perceptions of social and economic developments in China and their attempts to make sense of these changes. Unlike the contentious nature of narratives about politics, there existed a significant degree of consensus, regardless of the writers' political persuasions, in descriptions of China's impressive progress in the socio-economic arena. Interpretations of the causes of this progress, however, were varied and came to be intimately associated with politics. It was at this later phase that this social imagining was defined and shaped by Indonesian intellectuals' own agendas at home. This chapter focuses on three interrelated narratives on society and economy in the PRC: social harmony and solidarity, the "amazing" economic growth and the people's commune as the epitome of socio-economic progress.

## THE PURPOSEFULNESS AND ORDERLINESS OF AN EGALITARIAN SOCIETY

A number of keywords emerged, quite consistently, in Indonesian writings about Chinese society: purposefulness, harmony and the unity of the people. They collectively constituted the core of the main narrative on social change, which can be further divided into two sub-narratives, highlighting the favourable first impressions of the mainland as well as of the Chinese people.

---

[4] Ganis Harsono, *Recollections of an Indonesian Diplomat in the Sukarno Era* (St. Lucia: University of Queensland Press, 1977), p. 162.

## "The Border-Crossing Syndrome": Setting Foot in an Exciting New World

Indonesians' knowledge of Chinese society was often derived from their personal visits; like most visitors to a foreign country, the first impression tended to be powerful and sometimes lasting. As the majority of Indonesians entered the PRC en route from Hong Kong, the physical crossing of borders from the British colony to Shenzhen (or in some cases, to Guangzhou (Canton)) was frequently accompanied by what I call the "border-crossing syndrome". This was a combination of excitement, exhilaration and admiration; many regarded the border-crossing as a symbolic and metaphorical step in approaching something fundamentally different from Hong Kong.

The account by Sumanang, a member of parliament and head of the 1955 Sumatra People's Delegation, was typical of reactions to entering China: "My first impression of China is that all the people have a sense of orderliness and discipline, and that they are working happily."[5] Barioen, an educator and writer from Sumatra, reported that "the first impression of arriving in China is the energetic and bustling scene of construction".[6] The journalist Sugardo was equally amazed by what he saw as soon as he entered China:

> Crossing the border, everything appeared to be different. Here, every Chinese works under their own government, for their own well-being, and collectivism becomes the driving force behind their work. All the posters, magazines, newspapers and books are about economic construction.[7]

Zainul Arifin, second vice-speaker of parliament and vice-chairman of the Nahdatul Ulama (NU), commented that "the Chinese characteristics are discipline, orderliness and hard work".[8] The editor-in-chief of the newspaper *Berita Indonesia* reported, "as soon as I crossed the Chinese border

---

[5] Sumanang, "Perdamaian dan Persahabatan", in *Tiongkok Baru jang Kami Lihat* (Peking: Pustaka Bahasa Asing, 1955), p. 19.
[6] Barioen, *Melihat Tiongkok Baru: Negara Merdeka, Pandai Merdeka, Sanggup Merdeka* (Jakarta: Rada, 1952), p. 69.
[7] Sugardo, *Tiongkok Sekarang: Terra Incognita (Tanah tak dikenal)* (Jakarta: Endang, 1953), p. 69.
[8] *Hsin Pao* (Jakarta), 24 October 1956.

I saw signs of harvesting in the vast land. Both city and countryside are orderly, clean, and peaceful".[9] Gatot Mankupradja, a veteran revolutionary, enthusiastically told an Indonesian audience in a four-hour speech pertaining to his China trip in 1956:

> Arriving at Canton, I found streets were clean and orderly; I did not see a single piece of waste paper. Janitors hired by the government needed only to sweep fallen leaves from the trees alongside the streets. This is not only the case in Canton, but also in Peking; it is same all over China.[10]

Sitor Situmorang recorded his memory of China trip in 1962 in a poem:[11]

> In the Canton-Peking express train, I memorize
> Thirty years earlier, gazing at the scenery of China
> I recall my father saying —
> staring from the hillsides —
> "Son, look at the mist over the valley!
> Life is there! Peace is there!"

Praise for discipline and orderliness was often made in the context of comparing the PRC with Hong Kong, which was taken as a symbol of decadent Western capitalism. Sugardo had this to say about Hong Kong: "It is under the British rule, and all the newspapers there are about 'fighting for food'. Advertisements portray sexually appealing women (some are teenagers) in order to attract men's attention. We also saw children of six or seven years of age begging for money."[12] The journalist Hadi Usmany sensed the differences between the mainland and Hong Kong "immediately after crossing the Chinese border". Hong Kong's extravagant scene was merely "superficial"; people in China "lead simple lives, they dress simply, eat simply; and this simplicity constitutes a driving force for building their nation with a high spirit".[13] Hong Kong in Kwee Kek Beng's description was a place "full of taxi girls and superficial prosperity". This degenerate situation was a direct contrast to the PRC, where "not a single British

---

[9] Cited in *Jinri Xinwen*, 16 December 1963.
[10] *Seng Hwo Pao* (Jakarta), 3 November 1956.
[11] "Surat dari Tiongkok untuk Retni" (1962), cited from "The Passion of the Sound and the Wanderer [interview with Situmorang]", *Tempo* 46 (18–24 July 2006).
[12] Sugardo, *Tiongkok Sekarang*, p. 70.
[13] Hadi Usmany, "Surat dari Perdjalanan: Hari Pertama didaratan Tiongkok", *Minggu Merdeka*, 1 September 1957.

# Udara Pagi di Peking

### Sitor Situmorang

Dari djendela hotel kami lihat,
Tembok besar kota dalam.
Dikedjauhan menara Tjandi Kajangan,
Tjerobong² pabrik kota luar.

Diatas tembok besar dan tua,
kami lihat anak² mentjari sesuatu
Mestinja jang berguna-kukira,
sekadar alasan menghirup warna hidup muda,
kitjau burung angkasa musim bunga
paginja pembangunan sosialisme.

Inilah pagi Ibu Kota Revolusi,
sibuk membangun sistem hidup!
Diatas kebesaran imperial, kini
tersusun konsep kedjajaan rakjat!

Paris: Pangkal Idee! Peking: Kota Komune!
Tertjakup bulat pengalaman rakjat
sebagai penjair pembangunan dan
tentera pertempuran
Revolusi Rakjat jang berkelandjutan!

Kuo Mo-djuo, Wk. Ketua Komite Tetap KRN dan Ketua Perserikatan Sasterawan dan Seniman Tiongkok, menerima Ketua Delegasi Nasional Pengarang Indonesia Sitor Situmorang pada tg. 29 April

Poem of Situmorang and photo of him with Guo Monuo, Beijing, 1961 (*Tiongkok Rajat*, no. 7, 1961).

soldier is spotted and where women do not have to dance in night clubs in order to make a living".[14] Sudarman, head of a 1956 women's delegation, remarked that, before 1949, prostitutes had been abundant in the streets of Shanghai. This phenomenon was eliminated in the new China, "where women enjoy an equal social and political status with men". Hong Kong, however, seems to have reminded her of pre-1949 Shanghai: "In our trip to China via Hong Kong, we saw with our eyes that prostitutes were openly soliciting clients in the streets." She concluded pointedly, "Hong Kong and the liberated China are two different worlds."[15]

## Social Harmony and Solidarity

As noted in the previous chapters, Indonesians' interpretations of the CCP victory and Chinese political system were characterized by a strong populist undertone and the notion that political and social confrontation had been minimized, if not eradicated entirely. This populist interpretation also figured prominently in Indonesian discourses on Chinese society. Social harmony, collectivism and class solidarity became celebrated symbols of the society, while signs of tangible and potential social and class conflicts were conspicuously ignored or downplayed.

According to Sugardo, China in the 1950s was "a collectivist world, with the government in the people's hands. The development is carried out by the people and for their benefit". Unlike individualism in the West, "this collectivist ideology provides a great deal of opportunities for the social well-being". Furthermore, this collectivism valued collective contribution, which was a stark contrast to "capitalist society where money is worshipped and feudal society where power was respected; the symbols of China's collectivism are working heroes, mothers of the people, and so on".[16] Barioen reported that everyone in China wanted to become a "patriot and working hero". Egalitarianism was another characteristic of the new society: "Someone is valued because of his own work, not because of sharing others' fame."[17] Suwardi observed that he could not distinguish high-ranking officials from low-level civil servants, because "everyone dressed simply and moderately".[18]

---

[14] Kwee Kek Beng, *Ke Tiongkok Baru* (Jakarta: Kuo, 1952), p. 174.
[15] *Seng Hwo Pao*, 20 October 1956.
[16] Sugardo, *Tiongkok Sekarang*, pp. 66–7.
[17] Barioen, *Melihat Tiongkok Baru*, pp. 22, 57.
[18] *Mingguan Seng Hwo Pao*, 14 November 1963.

Ramadhan K.H., a noted writer, recorded an "unforgettable" experience while visiting Sichuan province in 1957, where he was "very surprised to learn" that a young peasant he met was a professor's son. This was taken to be an illuminating symbol of an egalitarian society. "A professor's son in Indonesia would undoubtedly stay in the city or college and become a member of high society", he marvelled, "But in China, he came to the countryside to work for the nation."[19] After recounting that generals and ordinary people queued together in front of the stores, he pointedly reminded his readers, "Remember what the case in our own country is."[20] The prevailing impression of a united and vibrant China was aptly summarized in the report by Foreign Minister Roeslan Abduglani to parliament in 1956:

> In the People's Republic of China we witnessed the existence of the complete consistency and unity of 600 million people who are activated by their consciousness and conviction that lasting change to their state is dependent upon the product of their work and their own attitudes as members of the community of nations. In Peking there is to be found the heart of a living society, full of vitality and power, and with faith in itself and maturity. It is widespread and has its roots in the villages throughout the country.[21]

The attraction to and fascination with China's social harmony was a theme expounded by intellectuals and politicians of different persuasions. Discussion on the absence of strikes in China is an illuminating case in point. A number of writers noted that there were no strikes in China which was taken as a sign of social harmony. Refuting the notion that the government banned strikes, Barioen suggested, "It is not true that strikes are not permitted; the truth is that no one wants to strike."[22] According

---

[19] Ramadhan K.H., "Kesan² Perdjalanan Ke RRT (V): Si Nenek Boleh Piara Babi dan Anak Profesor Djadi Petani", *Siasat* 11, 549 (1957): 12–3, 21.

[20] Ramadhan K.H., "Kesan² Perdjalanan Ke RRT (II): Amatlah Bedanja, Amatlah Bedanja", *Siasat* 11, 546 (1957): 15.

[21] Roeslan Abdulganl, *Laporan Menteri Luar Negeri kepada Dewan Perwakilan Rakjat R.I. tentang Perdjalanan Presiden R.I. ke Sovjet Uni, Yugoslavia, Austria, Czecholovakia, Mongolia, dan Republik Rakjat Tiongkok (26 Agustus–16 Oktober 1956)* (Jakarta: Kementerian Luar Negeri, 1956), pp. 47, 55 (the English translation is original and taken directly from this text).

[22] Barioen, *Melihat Tiongkok Baru*, p. 57.

to Kwee Kek Beng, "China does not ban strikes, an activity intended to improve workers' conditions, which are already very good."[23] Journalist A. Karim D.P. claimed, "China does not have to face the problem of strikes. It is not because strikes are forbidden, but because there is no need to stage strikes."[24] Sukiman, vice-chairman of the anti-Communist Masyumi Party, displayed a similarly approving attitude. His remarks, though apparently meant for the militant workers at home, underscored a familiar theme of social harmony: "I sincerely hope that trade unions in our country should not stage strikes so frequently at will. You see, are there any strikes in the new China? All the people there are busy building their nation; we should learn from the new China's example."[25]

## A New Society and New Human Beings

The most frequently used word in Indonesians' descriptions of Chinese society was "baru" (new). Many saw the emergence of a new society in which everyone was working for the collective social good. "In China everyone talks about production results," according to Barioen. "Regardless of whether he is a peasant, worker, merchant, minister, high-ranking civil servant, professor, artist, writer, technician, street sweeper, or doctor, teacher, etc., they all talk about work and work results, which are important for societal and national well-being."[26] The vice-mayor of Greater Jakarta, Danubroto, regarded the new Chinese society as a stark contrast to the "old China", characterized by disunity, corruption and poverty:

> We have witnessed the great movement of a nation that knows self-respect and self-confidence. This nation is now concentrating all its strength in building a modernized and free society. The whole of China is just like a spider web — everyone talks about actions, everyone is working — men, women, the young, the elderly — day and night — they are racing with time — everyone is united.[27]

Indonesians believed that the new social engineering had created a new human being. "Within just 15 years", Amarzan Hamid marvelled in

---

[23] Kwee Kek Beng, *Ke Tiongkok Baru*, p. 124.
[24] *Hsin Pao*, 8 June 1956.
[25] *Hsin Pao*, 18 October 1956.
[26] Barioen, *Melihat Tiongkok Baru*, p. 21.
[27] Danubroto, "Tiongkok Laksana Sarang Labah: Setiap Orang Bergerak dan Bekerdja", *Sin Po*, 11 July 1956; *Seng Hwo Pao*, 12 July 1956.

1964, "new human beings have been born in China, new human beings with new creativity, new initiatives, new thinking and new feelings".[28] According to Aslan, a PKI member, these new human beings "are patriotic, purposeful, and unified like one".[29] Kwee Kek Beng reckoned in 1952 that the revolution had transformed the society: "The Chinese have placed the interests of the nation and people above those of individual and family."[30] A writer commented approvingly that individualism was regarded by the new human beings as an obstacle to social integration.[31]

This enthusiastic endorsement on the new social engineering and its powerful impact was also evident in descriptions of the improvement of women's social status in China. According to Tjiptodarsono, the establishment of the PRC had brought about significant progress with respect to women's position: "In the past, men were considered to be superior to women, who had to obey orders of their parents and husbands. In the new China, women are free and have freedom in deciding their own careers and marriages."[32] Kartowijono observed, "In the new China, women are full citizens, participating in all sorts of activities. They are now enjoying an equal legal and social status as men."[33] Sudarman commented, "The progress [in China] is particularly apparent with respect to women, who have obtained equal rights as men and have made full use of this improved status to serve the new nation."[34]

In brief, Indonesians regarded the creation of a new society and new human being as a key feature of China's post-revolutionary transformation. Central to this new society was new social engineering, with initiatives emerging from among the people who had only one unified and noble goal — building a "prosperous and just society". Indonesians shared views

---

[28] Amarzan Ismail Hamid, "Melihat RRT sesudah 15 tahun: Revolusi Menempa Manusia Baru", *Harian Rakjat*, 12 November 1964.

[29] Aslan, "Dari Dunia Baru: Tiongkok Hari Ini", *Bendera Buruh* 3 (1954): 15–6.

[30] Kwee Kek Beng, *Ke Tiongkok Baru*, p. 43.

[31] Ibnu Parna, "Angin dari Utara: Laporan Ke RRT dan Korea-Utara, XV", *Mingguan Pekerdja* 34 (1964): 7.

[32] Tjiptodarsono, "Kawin dan Tjerai di Negara RRT", *Mimbar Indonesia* 6, 42 (1952).

[33] Nj.S. Kartowijono, "Keadaan Wanita di RRT", *Suara Guru* 14 (1959).

[34] *Seng Hwo Pao*, 20 October 1956. Similar comments on Chinese women's improved social status can be found in Adinegoro, *Tiongkok: Pusaran Asia* (Jakarta and Amsterdam: Djambatan, 1951), pp. 40–2.

An Indonesian woman's writing about China: "We Come, We See, We Learn…" [*Panjawarna* 2, 104 (October 1964)].

held by some Western observers of China in this respect. The words of British sinologist Joseph Needham were approvingly quoted by Setianegara to support his depiction of new Chinese society: "The West cherishes the idea that the population is dragooned to perform tasks. On the contrary, everywhere one sees spontaneity, often outrunning government planning, a new type of social engineering, the product of leadership from within, not from above."[35]

---

[35] Setianegara, *Sedikit tentang Komune-Komune Rakjat di RRT* (Jakarta: Bintang Terang, 1960), p. 13.

## NEW CHINA'S "AMAZING" ECONOMIC GROWTH

China experienced rapid economic growth from 1950 to 1957; its national income grew at an average annual rate of 8.9 per cent (measured in constant prices), with agriculture and industrial output expanding annually between 1953 and 1957 by about 3.8 and 18.7 per cent, respectively. During the same period, per capita income increased at 6.5 per cent (compared with 2.5 per cent per capita growth in India during the same period).[36] It is generally agreed that two of the most important factors responsible for this success were the effective implementation of the First Five-Year Plan (1953–57) and indispensable Soviet assistance — both were closely related to political policies and the nature of the regime. According to Nicholas Lardy, "measured in terms of economic growth, the 1st FYP was a stunning success"; the plan was prepared under classic Marxist theory.[37] The rapid development of the production sector "depended critically on capital goods acquired from the Soviet Union", Lardy argues, "The importance of Soviet technical assistance and capital goods would be difficult to overestimate."[38] Rapid economic growth was severely interrupted by the Great Leap Forward Movement, launched in 1958, which aimed at mobilizing the whole population to create a massive economic miracle. The gross failure of this utopian project contributed directly to an unprecedented famine in the early 1960s, resulting in the deaths of 16 to 27 million people.[39]

Throughout most of the 1950s, fascination with "the remarkable speed of economic growth and significant improvement of people's living

---

[36] Nicholas R. Lardy, "Economic Recovery and the 1st Five-Year Plan", in *Cambridge History of China*, ed. Roderick MacFarquhar and John K. Fairbank (Cambridge: Cambridge University Press, 1987), vol. 14, pp. 155–6.

[37] Ibid. Alexander Eckstein remarks that "Maoism [was] a defining aspect of China's economic strategy". See his *China's Economic Revolution* (Cambridge: Cambridge University Press, 1977), pp. 32–7.

[38] Lardy, "Economic Recovery", pp. 177–8. For a fuller discussion of the Soviets' role in the making of Mao's economic policies and China's economic development in the early years of the People's Republic, see Li, *Mao and the Economic Stalinization of China, 1948–1953*.

[39] Nicholas Lardy, "The Chinese Economy under Stress, 1958–1965", *Cambridge History of China*, vol. 14, p. 370. See also Chen Xuewei, *Lishi de Qishi: Shinian Jiansheshi Yanjiu, 1957–1966* [Lessons from history: A study of socialist construction from 1957 to 1966] (Beijing: Qiushi Chubanshe, 1989).

standard" was a recurring theme in Indonesian descriptions of the Chinese economy. Barioen was impressed that the PRC had made significant progress within just a short span of time: "In 1948 the country was experiencing rampant inflation and was almost broken, and people were miserable. In the new China, prices have been stabilized and people have enjoyed substantial improvements in their living standard."[40] Adinegoro, head of the Indonesian New Agency (PIA), who had visited China in the 1930s, proclaimed that China had entered "the age of modern industrialization".[41] After visiting the country's industrial base in the northeast, Kwee Kek Beng reported that Shenyang was "equal to any other Western industrial cities in terms of industrial capacities". He shared the view of an Indian visitor who said that "the people of China are clearly on the road to industrialization and soon they will be able to surpass Japan and the USA in the industrial field".[42] Dr Soeharto, Sukarno's personal physician, displayed a similar feeling: "Like many advanced industrial nations, there are countless new factories emerging in China."[43] The chairman of the Indonesian Nationalist Party (PNI), Soewirjo, was surprised to learn that "in just ten years after the Liberation [in 1949], China's industrial growth has increased by eleven times".[44] The president of Hassanudin University, Tirtodiningrat, was immensely impressed by the fact that one truck was manufactured every three minutes, while a member of parliament marvelled, "cars are priced at only 1,000 *yuan* each; in just a few more years every Chinese family can afford to own a car".[45]

Agricultural growth in China commanded much attention in Indonesia, also an agrarian nation. The focus was on how peasants had improved their lot as a result of the agrarian reform. "By liberating peasants and giving them land", Barioen remarked, "agricultural growth becomes possible in China". Sugardo praised China for having realized Sun Yat-sen's noble goal, that "tillers have their own land".[46] Subandrio regarded China's land reform

---

[40] Barioen, *Melihat Tiongkok Baru*, pp. 36, 54–5.
[41] Adinegoro, *Tiongkok*, p. 33.
[42] Kwee, *Ke Tiongkok Baru*, p. 122.
[43] *Seng Hwo Pao*, 20 July 1956.
[44] *Seng Hwo Pao*, 14 November 1959.
[45] *Seng Hwo Pao*, 8 July 1959; 29 November 1959.
[46] Barioen, *Melihat Tiongkok Baru*, p. 46; Sugardo, "Petani Tiongkok", *Mimbar Indonesia* 7, 7 (1953): 10–1.

as "a tale of a whole people in the grip of a mighty passion, and [as] an important guide to the future of prosperity, liberty, [and] democracy".[47]

Mohammad Hatta was a leading political intellectual who had a profound interest in and professional knowledge about China's economic growth. An economist by training, he played a key role in designing and implementing Indonesia's economic strategy during his tenure as the country's vice-president between 1950 and 1956. When meeting with Huang Zhen, the PRC ambassador to Jakarta, Hatta raised a number of well-informed questions regarding China's economic development, such as how to carry out industrial and commercial transformation, the percentage of the budget set aside for education and social welfare programmes, and so on.[48] This enthusiastic interest in the Chinese experience was further amplified during Hatta's three-week long visit to China in 1957. He went to open markets in Beijing to find out the price of eggs and buttons, and posed questions to officials regarding macroeconomic policy-making, including the First Five-Year Plan and strategies of economic transformation in the 1950s.[49] During his lengthy meeting with Mao and Zhou Enlai, Hatta's questions — which were all framed with a view to addressing similar problems at home — included how China had developed cooperatives in the countryside and how to persuade peasants to join them (because "Indonesia too is an agrarian country where the arable lands are scarce while the peasantry are populous", said Hatta); how to nurture good discipline among the Chinese people who had been undisciplined in the past ("some people in Indonesia are crazy for independence just for the sake of being independent, thus having poor efficiency", remarked Hatta); what were the focuses of China's economic constructions and whether it had undertaken national campaigns to encourage savings.[50]

---

[47] Subandrio, "State and Peasantry in Indonesia" (1950), in his *Indonesia on the March* (Jakarta: Djambatan, 1959), p. 56.
[48] Interview with Chen Lishui, Huang Zhen's interpreter; see also Yi Jiamin, *Huang Zhen Jiangjun de Dashi Shenya* [The Ambassador Career of General Huang Zhen] (Nanjing: Jiangsu Renmin Chubanshe, 1998), p. 126.
[49] Interview with Huang Aling, who accompanied the Hatta delegation in China.
[50] "Mao Zedong Zhuxi he Zhou Enlai Zongli Jiejian Yindunixiya Qian Fuzongtong Hada de Tanhua Jilu" [Records of talks between Chairman Mao Zedong and Premier Zhou Enlai during their meeting with former vice-president of Indonesia Hatta] (3 October 1957), file no. 105-00345-01, Archives of the Ministry of Foreign Affairs, PRC.

During and after his trip, Hatta wrote and spoke extensively about economic development in the PRC, and these writings and speeches were marked by an overwhelming sense of amazement and admiration:

> What we have seen in the past ten days is very amazing and exciting. Amazing, because everywhere we saw people were energetically working for development. New factories, which did not exist before and had not even been thought about by the old government, are emerging all over the place.[51]

In his serialized essay entitled "The Problems of Development in the PRC",[52] Hatta commented, "Any sane and objective person must admit that China has carried out massive nation-building." The speed of China's "amazing economic growth was beyond my expectation", he told Indonesian reporters, saying that he admired the nation for having achieved "unthinkable progress in such a short time".[53] The building of the Yangtze River Bridge was used to illustrate his favourable view: This two-storey bridge — 1,800 metres long and 18 metres wide — was completed in "just two years and three months". Workers finished this project not only "ahead of the original schedule", but spent just "80 percent of the initial budget". This was an extraordinary achievement:

> To the USA, such a bridge would perhaps be commonplace, but to the backward country China is, this project has a very great value as a feat. Considerable also in the effect it has on the imagination and fantasy of the Chinese people and on its esteem for the Chinese people's government and the communist regime.[54]

The same bridge was similarly employed by the writer Ramadhan as an embodiment of economic dynamism: "For Americans and Europeans, building such a bridge is not a big deal. But for a country like China, it is

---

[51] Mohammad Hatta, "Selamat Tinggal (Pidato pada Jamuan Makan yang Diadakan Duta Besar Indonesia di Peking, pada Tanggal 2 Oktober 1957)", in his *Kumpulan Pidato*, p. 99.

[52] Mohammad Hatta, "Masalah Pembangunan dalam RRT", *Pikiran Rakjat*, 23–24 December 1957.

[53] *Sin Min*, 14 October 1957; *Cankao Xiaoxi*, 24 October 1957.

[54] Mohammad Hatta, "Not Communism but Chinese Qualities Made People's China Rise", *Indonesian Spectator*, 1 December 1957, pp. 10–1.

definitely a great achievement and an indication that the people trust their government; it is also a proof of their improved fate."[55]

## THE PEOPLE'S COMMUNE AS AN EPITOME OF SOCIAL AND ECONOMIC PROGRESS

As an important component of the Great Leap Forward movement, the people's commune system was officially introduced in 1958. According to the "Resolution on Some Questions Concerning the People's Commune", issued by the CCP in August 1958, "the people's commune is the basic unit of the socialist social structure of our country, combining industry, agriculture, trade, education, and military affairs; at the same time it is the basic organization of the socialist state power."[56] The people's communes quickly spread all over China; by the end of 1958, over 120 million households, or more than 99 per cent of the nation's peasant households, had joined the communes. Although the opening phase of the commune movement was marked by prevailing optimism and confidence, many problems emerged, causing overwork, discontent and the agricultural crisis of 1959–61. The commune system was dramatically modified after 1960 and finally abandoned in the late 1970s. In short, "this commune experiment was largely a failure".[57]

Despite its ups and downs in China, the practice of the people's commune was enthusiastically watched by a wide circle of Indonesian intellectuals and politicians. For example, the commune's inauguration was ranked by a magazine as the most important event in 1958.[58] The people's commune soon became a central topic in writings and speeches concerning China; as a well-known journalist pointed out, "When we talk about China, we have to talk about the people's commune. It is a topic attracting

---

[55] Ramadhan K.H., "Kesan² Perdjalanan ke RRT (VI): Itu Kebiasaan jang Djelek", *Siasat* 11, 550 (1957): 5.
[56] Cited from George P. Jan, "The People's Communes in Communist China", in *Government of Communist China*, ed. Jan (San Francisco: Chandler Publishing Company, 1966), p. 424.
[57] Ibid., p. 421. See also George P. Jan, *The Chinese Commune: A Communist Experiment that Failed* (Lewiston: Edwin Mellen Press, 2004). A Chinese critical reevaluation of the people's commune experiment can be found in Chen Xuewei, *Lishide Qishi: Shinian Jainsheshi Yanjiu, 1957–1966*, pp. 27–104.
[58] "Memasuki Tahun Baru 1959", *Pesat* 15, 1 (1959): 3.

attentions from friends and foes alike."⁵⁹ An analysis of Indonesian perceptions of the commune, therefore, helps decipher the images of Chinese society and economy.

The views of Satya Graha were representative of Indonesians' largely enthusiastic receptions of the people's commune. As vice-editor-in-chief of the PNI-associated and Jakarta-based daily *Suluh Indonesia*, he was also the secretary-general of the Indonesian Journalists' Association (PWI) between 1959 and 1965. During this period, he paid three extended visits to China and wrote lengthy commentaries. Stating that the commune was created in order to "expand production and organize the people effectively", Graha regarded it as the best social and economic organization for the Chinese.⁶⁰ His enthusiasm for the commune experiment did not diminish with the passing of time and the emergence of apparent difficulties. In 1963, he revisited some communes and reported that he had seen abundant and inexpensive farm products. Refuting the view that peasants were forced to work, Graha wrote, "peasants can be forced to work for one day, but it is impossible to force them to work for five years — from 1958 till today".⁶¹ "The people's commune will be a subject of my study of a lifetime", he concluded, "It is the first of its kind ever to emerge on the earth; it is not only a great agrarian revolution of China, but a great revolution in the peasant life of the world."⁶²

Sukardjo Wirjopranoto, ambassador to Beijing from 1956 to 1960, also played a part in shaping his nation's (mis)perceptions of the people's commune. He told a Jakarta audience in 1959, "The people's commune has brought many benefits to the Chinese people". As peasants shared their production yields, the commune "should not be seen as a slave system". Responding to a question on what would happen to those who did not want to join the commune, he answered, "The people's commune was initiated from below instead of from the top. The communes have hospitals and schools, which had not existed before. If someone does not like the commune, it is because he is lazy."⁶³

---

⁵⁹ Satya Graha, "Tantan Renmin Gongshe" [On the people's commune], *Zhong Cheng Bao* (Jakarta), 10 November 1963.

⁶⁰ All these quotations are from Satya Graha, "Melihat Komune Rakjat dari dekat", parts 1–2, *Pesat* 14 and 15 (1959): 5–8; these serialized reports also appeared in the *Suluh Indonesia*, 16–19 March 1959.

⁶¹ Satya Graha, "Tantan Renmin Gongshe".

⁶² *Shanxi Ribao*, 30 April 1964.

⁶³ *Hsin Pao*, 25 March 1959.

As might be expected, the commune was fully endorsed by left-leaning intellectuals and politicians. In his Jakarta speech about a recent China trip in early 1959, Aidit praised the people's commune as "the most suitable form of Chinese socialism and its transition to communism". In 1963, he believed that difficulties facing the commune were only temporary: "As a powerful social organization, the people's commune has steadily increased its influence; it has demonstrated its advantages in organizing the peasantry and coping with natural disasters."[64] An editorial in the *Bendera Buruh* (Worker's Flag) stated in 1959 that the commune had laid the "foundation for China's transition to communism".[65] Even some right-wing politicians were impressed by progress made under the commune, Zainal Ahmad, third deputy speaker of parliament and a Masyumi Party leader, admitted that peasants were guaranteed to have adequate food to eat and clothes to wear.[66] Mohamad Isa, president of the University of Sriwidjaja, was convinced that the commune was "the right way for the Chinese people".[67] In a report by the Indonesian Department of National Research, Koentjaraningrat and Selo Soemardjan provided thorough observations on the commune system, agreeing that China's agrarian reform aimed at "eliminating feudalism, developing production and mobilizing the peasant class".[68] A journalist shared this cherished impression: "Everyone in the people's commune looked very happy, they could eat all they wanted in the community kitchens, which have plenty of food. From children's healthy faces we know that the Chinese people are very content and fortunate."[69] Setianegara observed, "The people's communes have their own performing teams, film projectors, radios, and televisions.... The commune is not just about rice, wheat, and cotton; it is also about poetry and painting."[70]

Indonesians seemed to believe the grotesquely dubious statistics manufactured by the Chinese authorities in order to shore up the commune's

---

[64] *Renmin Ribao*, 13 April 1959; *Nanfang Ribao*, 26 September 1963; *Harian Rakjat*, 1 October 1963.
[65] *Cankao Xiaoxi*, 10 November 1959.
[66] *Seng Hwo Pao*, 31 October 1958.
[67] *Harian Rakjat*, 23 July 1963.
[68] *Laporan Kundjungan Delegasi Ilmiah Departemen Urusan Research Nasional ke Republik Rakjat Tiongkok, tanggal 25 April–17 Mei 1965* (Jakarta: n.p., 1965), pp. 23–6, 32–8.
[69] *Seng Hwo Pao*, 13 April 1959.
[70] Setianegara, *Sedikit*, p. 31.

"huge success". Kusnan, head of a workers' delegation in 1959, told the Indonesian press,

> I was much interested in the fact that during China's Great Leap Forward in agriculture, a yield equivalent to 900 tons of rice per hectare had been achieved. It was amazing because it was the first time such high yields had appeared in human history. Nearly all agricultural plants had yielded extraordinary results. I was surprised that every rubber tree could yield 5,000 cc of rubber juice per day. China has surpassed the United States in production of wheat and cotton.[71]

A member of parliament was "amazed" to learn — and to believe — that in China 22,000 kilos of grain per *mu* (1/15 hectare) were yielded.[72] The favourable view of the commune was well caught in a phrase used by a Western observer and borrowed approvingly by Setianegara: "The records of yesterday are shattered this morning, and what was planned for tomorrow was done three days ago."[73]

In short, a large segment of Indonesian commentators displayed genuinely high regards for the perceived achievements under the people's commune. This unsuspecting acceptance betokened their profound interest in a new type of social engineering, namely, initiatives from below and from among the people. Furthermore, affirmative depictions of the commune as an ideal socio-economic institution seemed to validate an Indonesian ideal. Some observers were convinced that under Indonesia's *gotong royong* (mutual assistance) system, which was the basis for political discourse concerning the nature of authority and the characteristics of village society, they too could realize such a prosperous society in the countryside.[74]

## MAKING SENSE OF CHINA'S SOCIO-ECONOMIC PROGRESS: POLITICS OR CHINESENESS?

As noted, Indonesians displayed almost reverential interest in China's socio-economic transformation; they were attracted not only by the appearance

---

[71] Quoted in *Sino-Indonesian Relations, 1950–1959* (*Research Backgrounder*) (Hong Kong: Union Research Institute, 1960), p. 97.
[72] *Seng Hwo Pao*, 29 August 1959.
[73] Setianegara, *Sedikit*, p. 32.
[74] Satya Graha, "Melihat Komune Rakjat dari dekat". For a detailed discussion of the multiple meanings of *gotong royong* and its social and political roles, see John Bowen, "On the Political Construction of Tradition: Gotong Royong in Indonesia", *Journal of Asian Studies* 45, 3 (1986): 545–61.

of social harmony, egalitarianism, purposefulness and orderliness, but also by the country's "amazing" economic growth. The genuine admiration was shared even by prominent anti-Communist politicians and intellectuals such as Hatta and Sukiman. How did Indonesians account for the remarkable achievements in a new nation that was founded at the same time as their own? Here, the consensus on the phenomenon of socio-economic growth were replaced by competing discourses and huge variation in the reasons put forward for China's socio-economic development. Although some emphasized the significance of a "top-down" approach in the organizational strengths of a centralized Communist leadership, most observers underscored a "bottom-up" method in the new social engineering. They regarded spontaneity and the cultural characteristics of the Chinese people as essential factors behind the nation's extraordinary socio-economic development. This populist/culturalist reckoning therefore explicitly downplayed the roles of Communist ideology and CCP mobilization capacities.

## Organizational Capacities of the Chinese Communist Party (CCP)

Writers associated with the Communist Party of Indonesia (PKI) attributed China's success to the CCP's powerful organizational capacities. Sakirman, a member of the PKI leadership who spent six months in China in the late 1950s studying its economic transformation, argued that it was government policies such as the First Five-Year Plan and the "General Guidelines for Socialist Construction" that made rapid economic development a reality: "The socialist revolution's victory in the economic sphere goes hand in hand with victory in the realms of politics and ideology." The Chinese example was a testimony that "only under the CCP leadership can peasants get rid of poverty" and that "politics must be the commander".[75] Njoto, a major theoretician of the PKI, praised the CCP's superb organizational capacity, thought to be responsible for "fundamental changes in people's thinking, spirituality, and morality".[76] Jusuf Adjitorop held that the government played a key role in engineering social change: "It is only under the people's democratic government that China can make such great successes in socialist construction."[77] A member of the Indonesian women's

---

[75] Sakirman, *Pembangunan Ekonomi Raksasa Tiongkok Rakjat*, Seri Perdjalanan (Jakarta: Pembaruan, 1960), pp. 14, 52, 57.
[76] *Guangming Ribao*, 26 November 1959.
[77] Jusuf Adjitorop, *Integrasi Kekuasaan Politik dan Sistim Hukum dengan Revolusi di Tiongkok Rakjat* (Jakarta: Jajasan Pendidikan dan Kebudajaan Baperki, 1964), p. 14.

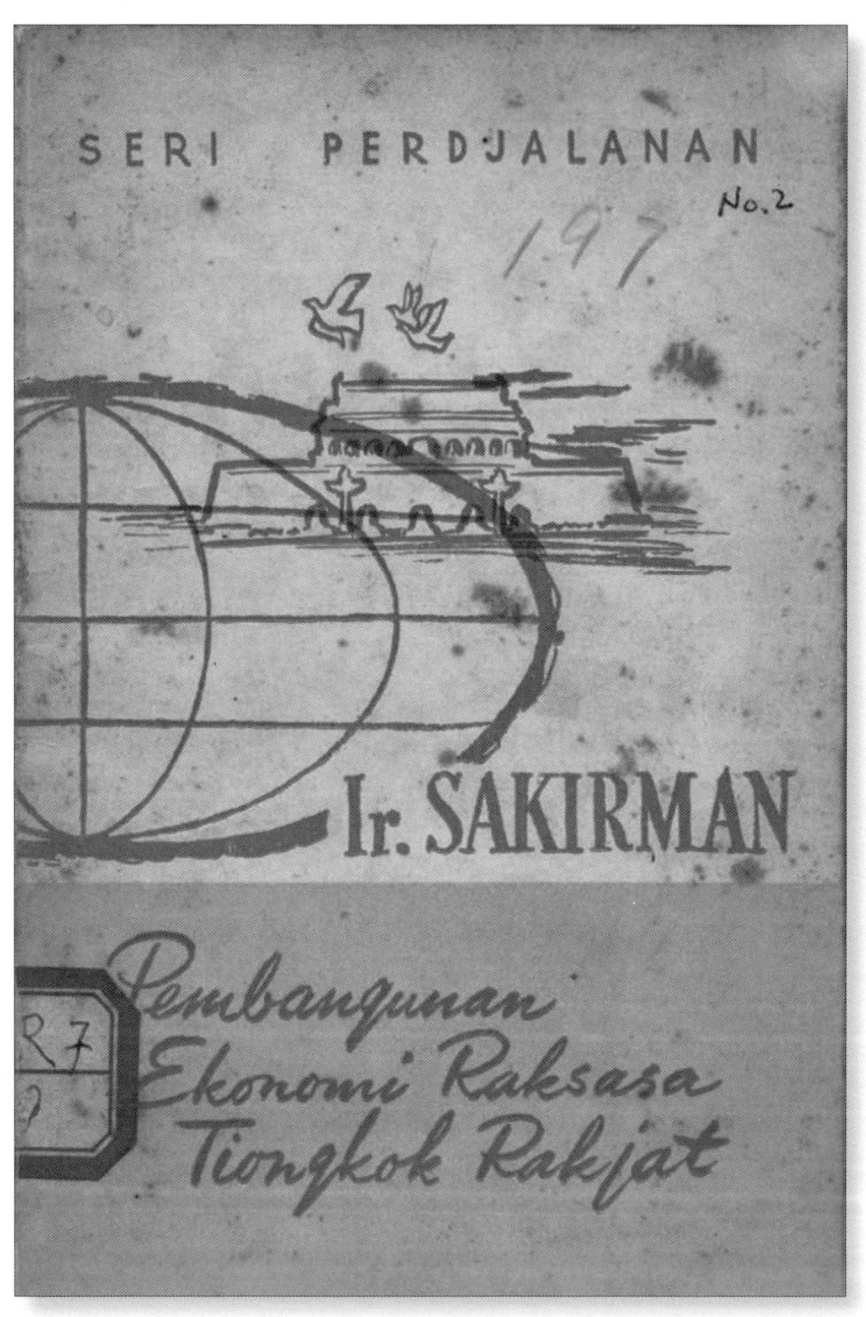

Cover of Sakirman's *Pembangunan Ekonomi Raksasa Tiongkok Rakjat* (Jakarta: Pembaruan, 1960).

delegation stated in 1959 that the CCP leadership should be given sole credit for liberating women from the household work that had burdened them for centuries, while the chairman of the Indonesian Catholic Party believed that China's economic success resulted from combining "sound management, effective governance, and an authority broadly accepted by the disciplined people".[78]

Indonesians regarded the First Five-Year Plan as a key factor in accelerating economic development. In a series of parliamentary debates, Thaher Thajeb reported that China's overall economic growth rate was 77.5 per cent from 1950 to 1958 and that the country was "in the process of surpassing Japan and Britain in the industrial field". He maintained that differences between China and Indonesia, two countries with similar natural resource endowments, lay largely in the policy arena. "While China has a well-founded Five-Year Plan, Indonesia has experienced protracted debates over the feasibility of such planning", he commented ruefully.[79] Echoing this view, a fellow member of parliament, Runturambi, pointed out that the Five-Year Plan had contributed considerably to China's extraordinary economic development and that the Indonesian government should learn from this successful example.[80]

## "Chineseness" as the Source of New Social Engineering

Most observers in Indonesia, however, had formulated different explanations for China's impressive record of socio-economic change; they attributed it to a most important factor: the character of the Chinese people. According to this view, political change had only provided a necessary environment for social and economic development; it was the character of the Chinese (hardworking, discipline, thrifty, pragmatic, etc.) that was ultimately responsible for that country's achievements. The view of Hatta was representative in this regard. In a serialized essay, "The Problem of Development in the PRC", he posed the question of why China was able to accomplish so much in such a short time. "What do we have to credit most for all this?" he asked, "The communist system with its well-knit organization and tight discipline, or the Chinese people's inclination toward thrift, diligence, punctuality in work and sense of realism?" His answer:

---

[78] *Harian Rakjat*, 13 May 1959; *Hsin Pao*, 19 October 1956.
[79] Konstituante Indonesia, *Risalah Perundingan*, session 143 (19 September 1958): 3478–83.
[80] Ibid., session 139 (16 September 1958): 3323–4.

"It has mainly been the Chinese people's own characteristic talent that made those achievements possible." Although he did not completely ignore the role of the political system, it was considered secondary in creating socio-economic transformation:

> However powerful the communist regime with its organization and discipline may be, all that has been achieved in China could not have been, were it not that construction efforts there have been carried out industriously, thriftily, and with punctuality, and with a sense for realism in a typically Chinese way. One should not forget that out of the 600 million Chinese people only about 10 million are communists.

"Many aspects of development efforts in People's China are not specifically communist in nature", he concluded. "A people under a democratic system which possesses leadership and moral discipline can achieve the same results. Indonesia, too, can practice this device without having to adhere to the communist ideology and system."[81] Ramadhan K.H. concurred with Hatta's assessment: "Development in China is being carried out with firm programs, orderly organizations, strong discipline, and genuine leadership, with a view to benefit the Chinese people who are industrious, prudent, and meticulous. But all these are not necessarily based upon that country's system."[82]

There were numerous references to the character of the Chinese people and its tremendous role in economic growth. Kwee Kek Beng remarked in 1952, "The new China is a country with a disciplined people."[83] According to A. Aziz, president of the Indonesian Journalists' Association (PWI) between 1953 and 1955 and editor-in-chief of the *Surabaya Post*, "The Chinese people are generous, kind, and hard-working, and they are full of confidence, and imbued with a new national spirit."[84] Rasuna Said, a member of parliament from Sumatra, observed that "the Chinese are a strong-willed and meticulous people; it is because of this quality that their country is

---

[81] Mohammad Hatta, "Not Communism but Chinese Qualities Made People's China Rise", *Indonesian Spectator*, 1 December 1957, pp. 10–1 (all citations originally in English). Ambassador Huang Zhen commented in 1957 that "Although Hatta is anti-communist at home, he is not against the People's Republic of China." See Yi Jiamin, *Huang Zhen*, p. 127.
[82] Ramadhan K.H., "Kesan² Perdjalanan ke RRT (VI)".
[83] Kwee Kek Beng, *Ke Tiongkok Baru*, p. 73.
[84] *Renmin Zhongguo Tongxun* 12 (1956): 63–4.

becoming a prosperous and happy nation".[85] Hidajat, vice-chairman of the Constitutional Assembly, was convinced that "discipline is the key to national development and women's emancipation in China".[86] Sitor Situmorang remarked that "What has been attained in China and Cuba can also be realized in Indonesia, *as long as there is sufficient discipline.*"[87] Ambassador Sukardjo Wirjopranoto commented that the Chinese way of thinking was the most important element leading to their awakening and great accomplishments.[88]

In short, most Indonesian observers attributed China's economic success to the cultural and moral character of the Chinese people. The notion of "Chineseness" was employed as a key explanatory variable, and it was placed above Communist ideology and organizational capacities. Implicit in this line of reasoning is that any people with similar cultural attributes would be able to achieve comparable accomplishments. As will be discussed in subsequent chapters, this belief not only facilitated the transfer of perceptions about China to the China metaphor, but also prompted the translation from ideas about a foreign country into domestic policies.

## Social Regimentation and Human Sacrifice

Throughout the Sukarno era, Indonesia was a plural society, with competing social and political agendas. As a reflection of this plurality, assessments of China's socio-economic transformation were not always uniformly affirmative; praise for its remarkable economic growth was sometimes mixed with criticism over social regimentation. The 1954 report by a college-student delegation exemplifies this sense of ambivalence. Although its members were genuinely impressed by the dynamism, simplicity, high working spirit and patriotism evident among fellow Chinese students, they faulted the country's rigid social control and resultant human sacrifice: "It is perhaps excessive that in China everything is being controlled and pre-arranged."[89] Rivai Atmadja, a member of the PSI-led labour union delegation in 1955, conceded that "China's industry has been in a better shape than that

---

[85] *Tay Kong Sian Po* (Surabaya), 4 November 1959.
[86] *Sin Po*, 7 October 1957; *Sin Min*, 15 October 1957.
[87] Cited from Harry Aveling, *A Thematic History of Indonesian Poetry: 1920 to 1974* (Center for Southeast Asian Studies, Northern Illinois University, 1974), p. 50 (emphasis added).
[88] *Seng Hwo Pao*, 25 March 1959.
[89] Suprapti Samil and Sabam Siagian, "Mahasiswa Indonesia ke RRT", *Kompas untuk Generasi Baru* 4, 10 (1954): 17, 24.

Cover of the *Kompas untuk Generasi Baru* magazine (1954), on Indonesian college students visiting China.

under Chiang Kai-Shek, but this accomplishment comes with a price." For instance, political leaders were "blindly worshipped and praised" by the masses.[90] In an interview conducted in the late 1960s, a policy-maker recalled that although he "admired the success [of China in the 1950s] in providing the basic necessities of life for all the people and in virtually eliminating starvation, unemployment, corruption, and stealing", he was critical of the social regimentation and lack of freedom.[91]

These negative commentaries focused on the human costs resultant from the employment of authoritarian mechanisms. "What has been achieved in Russia and in People's China", commented a Jakarta-based magazine, "was attained through extraordinary sacrifices, through laying emphasis on the problem of forced labor".[92] According to a series of commentaries entitled "People's China's Economic Machine", appearing in the right-wing newspaper *Nusantara*,

> The difference [between the PRC and Indonesia] in methods and means is a consequence of the difference in the political system of the State. People's China is a totalitarian state ... [and] the economic system of People's China is a mammoth machine run by the communist party, controlling and intervening in all aspects of economic life so that there is not much left of individual freedom.[93]

These critical observers identified different meanings in the same objects that had been glorified by mainstream intellectuals. They too had a "border-crossing syndrome", but it was the British colony Hong Kong, rather than the Chinese city Shenzhen, that was taken as a symbol of freedom and prosperity. Cheng Lim Fei's account of his 28-month ordeal as a college student in China started with this remark: "After leaving communist China I felt that I had left a mountain of tigers and returned to heaven." Having been detained for no reason, he claimed to have bribed with $500 the Chinese police before getting an exit permit to "enter Hong Kong — and freedom".[94] Instead of being amazed by egalitarianism,

---

[90] *Pedoman*, 9 June 1955.
[91] Weinstein, *Indonesian Foreign Policy*, p. 92.
[92] "Editorial", *Indonesian Spectator*, 15 August 1958.
[93] The major points of these essays are summarized in "Economy: Toward a Synthesis", *Indonesian Spectator*, 15 June 1958, pp. 17–8 (originally in English).
[94] Cheng Lim Fei, "Saja Pernah Sekolah di Tiongkok", *Gadjah Mada* 9, 2 (1959): 92, 96.

the writer Trisno Sumardjo asserted that the Chinese leadership was not democratically elected and that they enjoyed special privileges. Hadji Saleh Suaidy, head of the Press and Radio Section of the Ministry of Religious Affairs, claimed that in contrast to the propaganda on egalitarian ideals, a new ruling elite had actually emerged in China.[95]

According to this line of interpretation, the fact that most Chinese wore dark blue clothes was not praised as a sign of egalitarianism, but taken to symbolize social monotony and regimentation. Similarly, the fact that women engaged in menial work was not celebrated as a symbol of their emancipation; instead, it was lamented as the loss of womanhood and the end of homemaking.[96] The family system under Communism was portrayed as a broken institution: "Children no longer belong to their parents; just like anything else, they become the state's property."[97] The picture painted by Kristiatma was more terrifying and bleak: "Children in China have been put in reform camps to be forcefully educated in Marxist ideology. Many tried to escape or commit suicide." For him, "the new human beings that the Communist Party intends to create constitute merely an impossible dream, no matter what kinds of techniques are being employed".[98]

## CONCLUSION

Most Indonesian observers, regardless of their political persuasion, agreed that China had experienced remarkable social development and economic growth in the 1950s. They were especially impressed by the purposefulness, orderliness and the seemingly egalitarian nature of its society. This master narrative depicted China as a harmonious society in which everyone was working for collective social good; the people's commune, alongside the emerging "new human beings", commanded a great deal of genuine admiration.

---

[95] Trisno Sumardjo, "Sebulan di Tiongkok", *Budaja* 7, 1 (1958): 19; Hadji Saleh Suaidy, "Kesan² Saja selama di RRT", part 4, *Abadi*, 20 June 1956.
[96] See, for example, Rivai Atmadja's comments in *Pedoman*, 6 June 1955; Trisno Sumardjo, "Sebulan"; Asa Bafagih, *RRT*, p. 42; Kristiatma, "Brainwashing di Tiongkok (II)", *Basis* 7, 3 (1957): 85.
[97] Editorial comments on Feng Ting's essay, "Bagaimana Bentuk 'Keluarga Baru' Model RRT?" *Siasat Baru* 13, 623 (1959): 9–11.
[98] Kristiatma, "Brainwashing", pp. 85, 91.

The consensus on the phenomenon of economic growth, nevertheless, was not extended to explanations put forward for this phenomenon. While a small number of intellectuals underscored, either favourably or disapprovingly, the essential roles of the political system and Communist ideology, most China observers articulated and propagated the view that "the Chinese character" (hardworking, thrifty and discipline) was the key factor leading to the nation's progress. Their praise for the spontaneity of a high-spirited people was often accompanied by a conspicuous neglect of the importance of Communist ideology and organizational capacities as well as Soviet aid. The familiar propensity to decouple China and Communism, therefore, resurfaced systemically and forcefully in the discourses about the country's society and economy.

CHAPTER 4

# Of Culture, Religion and Intellectuals

*We have observed in China that great attention has been paid to culture. There is a clear-cut mission for art and literature, namely, to serve the society as a whole, especially workers and peasants. Art and literary workers stand in the ranks of national struggle and national progress.*

Armijn Pane, M. Tabrani and Barioen A.S. (1951)[1]

*Literature [in China] has become a real revolutionary weapon for the purposes of unifying the people, educating the people, and defeating the enemy.*

Njoto (1950)[2]

*Art in China is "art engagé", art for the enhancement of the people, whether they are manual workers or intellectuals.*

Prijono (1954)[3]

*Art has degenerated to become informational instructions and pure propaganda. We watched the play "The Long March", a story about the Red Army's struggle. Its prose and style reminded us of what was written during the Japanese occupation [of Indonesia].*

Trisno Sumardjo (1958)[4]

---

[1] "Statment [sic] of the Indonesian People's Delegation", Hangchow [Hangzhou], 27 October 1951, in Barioen A.S., *Melihat Tiongkok Baru* (Jakarta: Rada, 1952), Appendix 16.
[2] Njoto, "Literatur Baru: Bagaimanakah Pendapat Mao Tze-Tung tentang Literatur?" *Republik* 1, 4 (1950): 36.
[3] Quoted from "Kesan² Prof. Dr. Prijono tentang Kundjungannja ke RRT", *Merdeka*, 21 October 1954.
[4] Trisno Sumardjo, "Sebulan di RRT", *Budaja* 7, 1 (1958): 24.

This chapter is concerned with Indonesian perceptions of culture, religion and intellectual freedom (or the lack of it) in China. It addresses three closely related questions: What were Indonesians' views of the relationship between culture and politics in the PRC? How did they perceive Chinese intellectuals' role in the nation-building process? What were their observations on the place of religion in society? These questions must be understood in the context of Indonesia's cultural polemics after the 1930s. With the founding of the *Pudjangga Baru* (New Writer) in 1933, the quest for an Indonesian national culture and identity had figured prominently in the country's intellectual discourse.[5] As creators of cultural norms, intellectuals were particularly interested in their Chinese counterparts' role in shaping national culture and socio-economic development. The question of religious freedom was intimately linked with the subject of cultural development, thanks in part to the fact that 90 per cent of Indonesians were Muslims; the status of Islam in China therefore commanded much attention, even though Muslims accounted for less than 2 per cent of the whole population.

## "NEW CULTURE" AND NATION-BUILDING

### New Culture as the People's Culture and Agent of Socio-economic Change

In their writings about culture in the PRC, most Indonesian observers emphasized its close linkages with the people and the Chinese tradition. Barioen provided the most extensive and influential treatment of the new culture. Central to his idea was that the new culture was first and foremost characterized by its populist appeal and by its responsibility to the society at large. As a product of the Chinese revolution, the new culture transformed national culture from a feudal culture to "a people's culture". For instance, "the most important element in Chinese films is expression of general public's interests, rather than interests of individuals or political parties".[6] Barioen's view was shared by a large number of writers. Armijn

---

[5] Heather Sutherland, "*Pudjangga Baru*: Aspects of Indonesian Intellectual Life in the 1930s", *Indonesia* 6 (1968): 106–27; Jim Schiller and Barbara Martin-Schiller, eds., *Imagining Indonesia: Cultural Politics and Political Culture* (Athens: Ohio University Center for International Studies Southeast Asian Series, 1997).

[6] Barioen, *Melihat Tiongkok Baru*, pp. 98, 109.

Pane believed that Chinese *Yangko* dance was "closer to the people" in comparison with similar artistic forms in Indonesia.[7] According to a report of an Indonesian university student delegation: "Art for the people means not only to provide the masses with vast opportunities to creatively engage in the arts, but also to imbue them with new themes such as development and awakening of the *semangat* [spirit]".[8]

"In today's China," noted the painter and dancer Bagong Kussudiardjo, "the arts are really from the people and for the people". The artist Wisnoe Wardhana stated that since the arts in China were created from within the masses' real and colourful life, they were "both dynamic and down to earth".[9] In his elaboration of Mao Zedong's cultural theory, Njoto stressed that the arts were responsible for "workers, peasants, soldiers and petit bourgeoisie" and that literary creativity in China derived "not from abstract concepts but from realities".[10] The sense of a dynamic new culture was well captured by Anantaguna, a poet associated with Lekra (People's Institute of Culture), who claimed that in the exciting process of forming a new national culture, boundaries between poets and farmers had vanished: "Peasants could produce poems immediately after they were able to read and write, which is truly a miracle in cultural history; they will be able to compose great symphonies in future".[11] The revitalization of Chinese indigenous arts and classical literature also captured Indonesian attention and veneration. According to Wisnoe Wardhana, China's national arts were developed "from within a wide variety of local cultures, which have been assimilated into the new culture", thus avoiding the danger of "provincialism".[12]

The new culture in China was not only people-oriented but, more importantly, responsible for nation-building. After a visit to China in the early 1950s, an Indonesian culture delegation declared approvingly, "There is a clear-cut mission for art and literature, namely, to serve the society as a whole, especially workers and peasants. Art and literary workers stand in

---

[7] Cited in Kwee Kek Beng, *Ke Tiongkok Baru* (Jakarta: Kuo Ming, 1952), p. 39.

[8] Suprapti Samil, *Laporan Kundjungan dua Utusan "Perserikatan Perhimpunan² Mahasiswa Indonesia"* (Jakarta: n.p., May/June 1954), p. 25.

[9] B. Kussudiardjo, "Kesan-kesan Perlawatan ke RRT", *Budaya* 4, 1 (1955): 6; Wisnoe Wardhana, "Tari dan Opera di RRT", *Budaya* 4, 4/5 (1955): 187.

[10] Njoto, "Literatur Baru: Bagaimanakah Pendapat Mao Tze-Tung tentang Literatur?" *Republik* 1, 4 (1950): 36.

[11] S. Anantaguna, "Tiongkok Baru selalu Baru", *Harian Rakjat*, 15 November 1958.

[12] Wisnoe Wardhana, "Tari dan Opera", p. 188.

the ranks of national struggle and national progress".[13] Barioen reiterated this point by suggesting that "art and culture have certainly played a very important role in the development of society and the human beings in today's China".[14] To Prijono, a professor and later minister of culture and education, "Art in China is *art engagé*, which is for the enhancement of the people".[15] Njoto emphasized that literature in China "is a real revolutionary weapon for the purposes of unifying the people, educating the people and defeating the enemy".[16]

In short, Indonesian intellectuals defined China's new culture as people-oriented and socially responsible, presenting a stark contrast to elite-oriented culture of the past. This new culture was different from the culture based upon abstract concepts, and it reflected not only people's aspirations, but the social environment. The new culture's popular representation, vitality and realism led one observer to characterize the cultural development of 1950s China as a "national renaissance".[17]

## Nurturing a New Culture: Roles of the State and Education

After establishing the contents and functions of China's new culture, Indonesian observers went on to ponder upon the reasons behind the national renaissance and identified a crucial role by the state and education in nurturing this new culture. This was by no means a coincidence. The relationship between the state and cultural development in the efforts to forge a "new Indonesian culture" was an issue close to the hearts and minds of many intellectuals. In the First Cultural Congress held in Yogyakarta in 1948, the participants agreed generally that the state should have an important place in the development of culture, though some (for example, Sastroamidjojo) cautioned against returning to the practices of the Japanese occupation when "culture was directed, led by the centre with a particular purpose".[18]

---

[13] "Statment [sic] of the Indonesian People's Delegation", 27 October 1951, in Barioen, *Melihat Tiongkok Baru*, Appendix 16.
[14] Barioen, *Melihat Tiongkok Baru*, p. 111.
[15] "Kesan² Prof. Dr. Prijono tentang Kundjungannja ke RRT", *Merdeka*, 22 October 1954.
[16] Njoto, "Literatur Baru", p. 36.
[17] Suprapti Samil, *Laporan Kundjungan*, p. 25.
[18] Tod Jones, "Indonesian Cultural Policy, 1950–2003: Culture, Institutions, Government" (Ph.D. dissertation, Curtin University of Technology, 2005), pp. 98–102.

Barioen, Pane and Tabrani in Hangzhou, 1951 [Barioen, *Melihat Tiongkok Baru* (Jakarta: Rada, 1952)].

In 1951, Barioen, Armijn Pane and M. Tabrani jointly stated, "In China, great attention has been paid to culture [by the Chinese government]."[19] Pramoedya stated that the new government in Beijing had attached "a great deal of importance to culture and classic literature".[20] Wisnoe Wardhana commented approvingly that the state was like a great patron of the arts and promoter of new culture and that traditional arts such as Peking Opera were revitalized as a result of the government's progressive policy. By establishing new institutions such as the Academy of Arts, local and classical cultures were intensively studied and incorporated into national culture.[21] According to Kussudiardjo, preserving the Forbidden City was a clear indication that the government "has been paying attention to culture". The comparison with his homeland reinforced this view: "As I conclude my essay, my only hope is that culture in general and

---

[19] Cited in Barioen, *Melihat Tiongkok Baru*, Appendix 16.
[20] Pramoedya Ananta Toer, "Manakah Pengarang dari Golongan Keturunan Tionghoa?" *Pendorong*, 13 July 1956.
[21] Wisnoe Wardhana, "Tari dan Opera", pp. 188–9.

art in particular would receive comparable careful attentions from our own government, like what we have witnessed in the PRC".²²

Apart from the government's essential role, Indonesians believed that China's new culture was fostered by an educational system that prioritized social responsibilities. Barioen wrote that education in the PRC aimed to "raise people's cultural standard and to train them for nation-building", while Pramoedya was amazed that the Chinese were indoctrinated from a very young age with principles of social responsibility and loyalty to the nation.²³ The educator Zachri noted that education in China was accorded the same degree of importance as economic development, leading to a consensus that "education is development and development is education". Sudjono found that the educational system in China provided a wide variety of opportunities for people with different needs.²⁴

Between 1955 and 1965, there were some Indonesian students studying at Chinese universities; their firsthand reports highlighted the emphasis placed in education on social responsibility and practicality. M.U. Sardjono, a student at Peking University and chairman of the Indonesian Student Union in China, recounted favourably his experience in participating in industrial production and working in the countryside.²⁵ Moedjijoewono Partokoesoemo, studying at the China Foreign Trade Institute, reported that Chinese students were integrated into society by way of participating in politics and other activities.²⁶ Professor Sudjono Pusponegoro, minister for national research, was impressed by the "close connections between scientific research and production, especially agriculture". Members of an Indonesian research delegation approvingly reported that students at Tsinghua University spent ten to fifteen weeks a year in "productive work as a means of participating in national construction".²⁷

---

²² Kussudiardjo, "Kesan-kesan", pp. 5, 11.
²³ Barioen, *Melihat Tiongkok Baru*, pp. 120–2; *Sin Po*, 5 January 1957.
²⁴ A. Zachri, "Menindjau Republik Rakjat Tiongkok: Kesan Selajang Terbang pada bidang Pendidikan", *Suara Guru* 7, 11 (1957): 4–5; Sudjono, "Tiongkok Baru Selajang Pandang", *Suara Guru* 3, 11/12 (1953): 5.
²⁵ M.U. Sardjono, "Kami Diuniversitas Tiongkok", *Tiongkok Rakjat* 12 (1958): 49–52.
²⁶ Partokoesoemo, "Beladjar, Persahabatan dan Setiakawan", *Tiongkok Rakjat* 4 (1962): 50. See also Gede Nassa, "Pengalaman Beladjar di RRT", *Tiongkok Rakjat* 12 (1962): 17.
²⁷ *Zhong Cheng Bao*, 24 August 1964; *Laporan Kundjungan Delegasi Ilmiah Departemen Urusan Research Nasional Ke Republik Rakjat Tiongkok, Tanggal 25 April–17 Mei 1965* (Jakarta: NP, 1965), pp. 27–8.

Indonesian visitors in Tiananmen Square, July 1965 (Courtesy of Irawati Durban).

In short, Indonesian observers focused on the social relevance and people-oriented nature of the new culture that was being supported by the state. In addition to celebrating the role of culture in nation-building, they accentuated its contribution to forging solidarity and new identity. Communist ideology figured marginally in this description of Chinese culture, and few commentators looked at how this new culture was deployed by the CCP as a tool for transforming the society from above. The depoliticization of culture, in fact, was an extension of the tendency to portray China in a non-Communist and nationalistic perspective, as discussed in previous chapters.

## INTELLECTUALS IN THE PRC: "ENGINEERS OF HUMAN SOULS" OR "TOOLS OF PROPAGANDA"?

Indonesia's intellectuals were naturally interested in their Chinese counterparts' role in society, politics and cultural development. Unlike their generally favourable attitudes toward the new culture, there existed no consensus in their observations of relationships between intellectuals and power. Although many writers admired Chinese intellectuals for being closely integrated into society, their assessments of these intellectuals' relationship with the state were deeply divided. While some were attracted by Chinese intellectuals' direct participation in political change and their role as "the engineers of the human souls",[28] others were critical of them for serving as "tools of propaganda". In other words, China constituted a politically loaded zone of contestation.

Indonesians' complex perceptions of intellectuals in China were partly a reflection of cultural transformation at home during the 1950s, when both countries faced profound challenges in the quest for a balance between artistic creativity and social commitment. Therefore, a brief overview of intellectual history of the PRC between 1949 and 1965 will be helpful in placing Indonesian perceptions in context.

## Dilemmas of Intellectuals in the PRC

With the founding of the PRC in 1949, the relationship between intellectuals and power was to undergo fundamental changes. As Merle Goldman points out, the CCP's policy after 1949 was characterized by an oscillation "between periods of repression in which intellectuals were subjected to thought reform campaigns and periods of relative relaxation in which they were granted some responsibilities and privileges in order to win their cooperation in carrying out modernization".[29] Intellectuals viewed the state with considerable ambivalence. As heirs of the long-established Confucian tradition, they considered criticizing official misdeeds to be their natural obligation. They sought to connect themselves to the society and people,

---

[28] This expression was first made famous by Joseph Stalin, who said in 1932: "The production of souls is more important than the production of tanks.... And therefore I raise my glass to you, writers, the engineers of the human soul" (Joseph Stalin, *Speech at Home of Maxim Gorky*, 26 October 1932). The reference was widely used in China during the 1950s <http://en.allexperts.com/e/e/en/engineers_of_the_human_soul.htm> [accessed 29 September 2009].

[29] Merle Goldman, "The Party and the Intellectuals", in *Cambridge History of China*, ed. Roderick MacFarquhar and John K. Fairbank (Cambridge: Cambridge University Press, 1987), vol. 14, p. 218. For more details on the relationship between intellectuals and politics in contemporary China, see Merle Goldman and Leo Ou-fan Lee, eds., *An Intellectual History of Modern China* (Cambridge: Cambridge University Press, 2002), and Eddy U, "The Making of Chinese Intellectuals: Representations and Organization in the Thought Reform Campaign", *China Quarterly* 192 (2007): 971–89.

and most intellectuals were ready to make an effort to help the new regime, because they had become "sick of the inefficiencies of the old China and had lost any faith that the Guomindang [KMT] could bring an enduring and constructive change".[30]

The Communist Party's conciliatory policy toward intellectuals reached its height in 1957. Between May to June, following Mao's call made one year earlier (letting "a hundred flowers bloom" in the field of culture and "a hundred of schools of thought contend" in the field of science), intellectuals responded by protesting CCP control over culture and the slavish imitation of Soviet models. This intellectual vehemence, however, was ended abruptly with the launch of the "Anti-rightist Campaign" in late July. It is estimated that around 400,000 to 700,000 intellectuals lost their jobs and were sent to labour camps or the countryside into what was essentially a punitive exile.[31] In the Great Leap Forward Movement of the late 1950s, a new slogan was advanced, calling on people in all walks of life, intellectuals in particular, to be simultaneously "red and expert", with the emphasis being geared toward "red" (politically siding with the Party). Intellectuals were generally denigrated because they were "imbued with the bourgeois concepts of individualism, liberalism, and anarchism".[32]

The years between 1949 and 1965, in short, mixed both intellectual suppression and limited intellectual freedom, with the former being a defining feature of the intellectual history of the time. Within this changing and often hostile environment, however, Chinese intellectuals were not alienated from society, and remained convinced that they could contribute to the nation-building project. What was the role of Chinese intellectuals in the process of nation-building and socio-economic transformation? Seen in the Chinese (or Asian) context, how to forge an ideal balance between artistic creativity and social commitment? These were questions that Indonesian observers sought to answer — against the backdrop of changing cultural politics at home.

---

[30] Jonathan D. Spence, *The Search for Modern China* (New York: W.W. Norton, 1990), p. 564.
[31] Ibid., p. 572; Goldman, "The Party and the Intellectuals", p. 257.
[32] Merle Goldman, "The Party and the Intellectuals: Phase Two", in *Cambridge History of China*, ed. Roderick MacFarquhar and John K. Fairbank (Cambridge: Cambridge University Press, 1991), vol. 15, p. 433.

## Intellectuals as a Respected Class

That intellectuals were accorded a respected place in society and were monetarily well treated by the government was a recurring theme in Indonesian writings about China. As one of the most prominent writers of his time, Pramoedya Ananta Toer's views captured sentiments of many fellow intellectuals. In 1956 and 1958, he undertook two extended visits to China and met a number of renowned writers and ranking cultural officials (among them Zhou Yang, Ba Ren and Liu Baiyu).[33] His writings displayed a genuine admiration for the writers' social and political contributions: "Chinese writers are the spiritual engineers of the nation. They occupy a high place and their voices are listened to by the society at large, their role is very important in China's nation-building process. This helps explain why writers are very well treated by the society."[34] According to Pramoedya, an indication of writers' high social status was lucrative monetary rewards for their creative work. "One thing that attracts much of my attention as a writer is the life security enjoyed by writers in the new China", he commented, "Over there, a writer can lead a decent life by virtue of his pen."[35] The novelist Liu Tje Sie (Liu Zixia), according to Pramoedya, was paid 400,000 *yuan* in royalties for his novel *Railway Guerrilla*, which was "approximately 240 times a Chinese cabinet minister's monthly salary". Ramadhan K.H. marvelled that a poet could earn 1,500 *yuan* per month by publishing just a few poems, while Mao Zedong's monthly salary was merely 600 *yuan*.[36]

The generous reward for writers, Pramoedya was convinced, not only exemplified the fact that "culture is supported by the highest authorities in China", but also provided a stark contrast to Indonesia. He noted that, while Chinese writers were paid Rp. 1,000–3,000 for every three pages of

---

[33] Interview with Chen Xiaru, Pramoedya's interpreter in China. Zhou Yang (Chou Yang) (1908–89) was a literary theorist and one of the most important policy-makers on culture in the 1950s in his capacity as Vice-Minister of Propaganda and Vice-Minister of Culture. Ba Ren (pen name of Wang Ren Shu, 1901–72) was China's first ambassador to Indonesia (1950–52) and director-general of the People's Literature Publishing House in the 1950s. Liu Baiyu (1916–2005) was a famous writer.
[34] Pramoedya Ananta Toer, "Sedikit tentang Pengarang Tiongkok", *Mimbar Indonesia*, 19 January 1957, p. 21.
[35] "Pramudya Ananta Tur di RRT", *Sin Tjun* 2 (1957): 107.
[36] Ramadhan K.H., "Serakan Bintang Sekitar Yang-Tse", *Konfrontasi* 4, 12 (1957): 62; see also Sumardjo, "Sebulan di RRT", p. 21.

published work, Indonesians got only Rp. 30 per short story. In order to barely survive, the latter had to publish at least ten stories every month, in addition to seeking part-time employment.[37] Equally amazed by Chinese intellectuals' social position, Prijono pointed out: "Artists and writers occupy a high place in China. Their lives are secure and remuneration is very good. Ting Ling [Ding Ling] got 300,000 *yuan* for her novel, *The Sun Shines over the Sanggang River*; this remuneration is approximately 150 times of a physician's monthly salary".[38] Kussudiardjo observed that dancers in China were provided with milk, eggs and regular food supplies every morning by the government, while Indonesian artists had to strive for recognition. A journalist was impressed that in China "everything, from housing to education, is provided for intellectuals by the government, and they do not have to worry about their livelihoods".[39]

## Intellectuals as "the Engineers of Human Souls"

To Indonesians, there was a direct correlation between Chinese intellectuals' respected status and their contributions to nation-building. Adinegoro contended that intellectuals' participation in the revolution was a key factor in overthrowing the Chiang Kai-shek regime.[40] Asmudji believed that intellectuals were a crucial factor leading to the establishment of the PRC. Barioen felt that "the Artist Front played no small role in the Chinese revolution's victory".[41] In his book on the modern history of China, Armijn Pane consistently emphasized the functions of ideas in political transformation: "Since the May 4th Movement in 1919, new intellectuals have become pioneers again."[42] Chinese intellectuals' integration with people and into society was considered to be a source of artistic creativity. The observation by Barioen, Armijn Pane and M. Tabrani in 1951 set the tone for this line of interpretation:

---

[37] Pramoedya Ananta Toer, "Keadaan Sosial Para Pengarang: Perbandingan Antarnegara", *Siasat* 11, 506 (1957): 28.
[38] "Kesan² Prof. Dr. Prijono".
[39] Kussudiardjo, "Kesan-kesan", p. 8; "Kehidupan Seniman RRT Terdjamin", *Suluh Indonesia*, 14 November 1963.
[40] Adinegoro, *Tiongkok: Pusaran Asia* (Jakarta: Djambatan, 1951), pp. 42–9.
[41] Asmudji, *Genderang Tiongkok Baru* (Bodjonegoro: Suara Pemuda, 1950), p. 23; Barioen, *Melihat Tiongkok Baru*, p. 111.
[42] Armijn Pane, *Tiongkok Zaman Baru* (Jakarta: Arbati, 1953), p. 20.

In China, we have observed that great attention is paid to culture. There is a clear-cut mission for art and literature; namely, to serve society as a whole, especially workers and peasants. Art and literary workers stand in the ranks of national struggle and national progress.[43]

More specifically, Barioen stated, "While artists have contributed their artistic products, writers and poets have produced creative works that could be understood by the people, needed by the people, and become wholly people's arts."[44] Sardjono was impressed that "China's young intellectuals regard manual work as a respected job and value the chance of working and living together with workers and peasants". Two professors from the Bandung Technological Institute thought that Chinese college students had made "greater social contributions" than their counterparts at home, because they took part in activities such as "installing railway tracks, constructing roads together with workers, and helping peasants".[45]

## Intellectuals as Tools of Propaganda

There were dissenting voices among Indonesia's China observers with respect to intellectuals' role in society, with an important segment of intellectuals holding critical views on the relationship between art and politics in the PRC. Their criticisms were focused on two interrelated areas: the arts in China had become "pure propaganda", and by placing political loyalty and social commitment above aesthetic and artistic standards, intellectuals had degenerated into "tools of propaganda".

Trisno Sumardjo was one of the most outspoken critics of cultural and intellectual development in the PRC. Hoping for an answer to the vexing question of "moral code" — how to forge a balance between "artistic creativity" and "social responsibility" — he led a cultural delegation to China in 1957.[46] Sumardjo failed, however, to find any viable solutions. Although he was impressed by the people's orderliness, discipline and high spirit, he was appalled by an apparent lack of intellectual vitality and freedom. According to him, writers he met were only interested in "talking

---

[43] Barioen, *Melihat Tiongkok Baru*, Appendix 16 (originally in English).
[44] Ibid., p. 111.
[45] M.U. Sardjono, "Kami Diuniversitas"; *Cankao Ziliao*, 10 June 1964.
[46] Trisno Sumardjo, "Sebulan di RRT", p. 15. Sumardjo was one of the key writers actively involved in the debates about culture and its relationship to the state in Indonesia. See Jones, *Indonesian Cultural Policy, 1950–2003*, chapter 2.

about ideology and procedural techniques (such as practices of publication and honoraria). They tended to evade questions of individual freedom and free expression in art in particular and in the society in general." He viewed the One Hundred Flowers movement with considerable apathy: "My impression is that only a few flowers are allowed to blossom within the limits of the Constitution; anything beyond is considered reactionary and to be wiped out." The lack of intellectual freedom was evidenced by the fact that there existed only one literary theory: socialist realism. Defined as "something that is understood by the people", it was "promoted by the authorities and has replaced classic Chinese literary principles". In his view, this literary doctrine could only produce "work of poor value". Sumardjo faulted intellectuals for using literature to serve the agendas of "rekindling spiritual sentiments of workers, peasants, and soldiers" and concluded that the arts had degenerated into informational instruction and pure propaganda.[47]

The writer Balfas shared Sumardjo's criticisms. While acknowledging that China's economic construction was "amazing", he criticized its practices of using the arts as a "tool for development". Balfas found it discouraging that there was only one topic in contemporary Chinese novels, namely, "development".[48] Ramadhan K.H. was similarly suspicious of the cultural practice that subjected writers to the government's political agendas and subordinated the arts to power: "By equating art with life, work, and development, Socialist Realism grossly simplifies the complexities and beauties of the arts." To him, the One Hundred Flowers movement had only "symbolic meaning", as restrictions were placed upon the freedom of expression.[49] He was apprehensive of the celebrated literary doctrine that held "a work is valuable as long as it reflects development and the people's life". Underlying his observation was a strong revulsion for the principle of "politics as commander" in the arena of the arts, which led to writers' self-censorship.[50]

---

[47] Sumardjo, "Sebulan di RRT", pp. 18–20, 25.
[48] "Kesan² Sastrawan Indonesia tentang Tiongkok", *Sin Min*, 3 December 1957.
[49] Ramadhan K.H., "Serkan Bintang Sekita Yang-Tse", *Konfrontasi* 4, 12 (1957): 60–72. A shorter version of this essay was published in Ramadhan, "Kesan² Perdjalanan ke RRT (VIII)", *Siasat* 11, 552 (1958): 13, 21.
[50] Ramadhan, "Serakan Bintang", pp. 66–7; Ramadhan, "Kesan² Perdjalanan ke RRT (I–IX)".

In brief, Indonesians presented clashing and ambivalent narrations on the role of culture and intellectuals in national development. While a majority of them concluded that intellectuals constituted a respected class well taken care of by the government, there was no consensus on their social and political functions. Writers such as Pramoedya were enthusiastic about the practices that empowered intellectuals in nation-building; they were less concerned about the potential pitfalls of intellectuals' close association with the establishment. The agenda of serving the people and nation seemed to justify the means of using the arts as an instrument of changing society. On the other end of the spectrum, writers like Sumardjo were critical of the lack of freedom of expression resultant from subjecting art to politics. To them, the artistic and aesthetic value of literary work figured much more prominently than the doctrine that "art must reflect the people's life". It was perhaps this explicit disagreement between the two groups that led editors of the literary journal *Siasat*, whose views were largely in tandem with those of Sumardjo and Ramadhan, to insert an unusual editorial statement when publishing Pramoedya's essay, which spoke highly of the respected social status of Chinese writers, cautioning readers that this essay "overlooks the issue of intellectual freedom in the concerned country".[51]

## A QUESTION OF RELIGIOUS FREEDOM

Just like the conflicting interpretations of cultural and intellectual development in the PRC, Indonesians' perceptions on religion, especially Islam, were mixed with admiration and aversion. Partly because Islam was a subject under heated and politically charged debate at home, Indonesian views of Muslim life in China exhibited a greater degree of diversification and contestation than discourses on culture in general. Although some writers insisted that religious freedom was largely protected by the Chinese authorities and that Islam enjoyed healthy growth, others maintained that Muslims were oppressed and that Islam had experienced a serious setback under the Communist regime. Between these two poles, some portrayed Islam in China as being full of contrasting characteristics: a limited degree of religious freedom was overshadowed by a powerful regime that was essentially atheist.

---

[51] See *Siasat* 11, 506 (1957): 25. Pramoedya's essay was entitled "Keadaan Sosial Para Pengarang Perbandingan Antarnegara".

Mohammad Hatta's largely favourable view was representative of the first kind of perception. During his 1957 visit to Xinjiang, a region with a high concentration of Muslims, he claimed that remarkable progress had been made: "While studying economics in Rotterdam [before World War II], I learned that Singkiang [Xinjiang] was a region populated mostly by Muslims who were oppressed by the government of the time. Now I have seen with my own eyes all kinds of progress in such a short time."[52] Hatta attributed this progress to the government's judicious policies. "Having talked to Muslims in China, I found no evidence of religious suppression there", he remarked, "Unlike the Soviets, the Chinese government has taken a sensible policy. Maybe in the beginning, there were incidents of religious suppression, but now they have recognized that it was wrong."[53] Kwee Kek Beng commented that China's religious policy was "wise and respectful" to Islam, while Barioen similarly pointed out that "religious freedom does exist in China".[54]

Professor H.A. Soenarjo, president of the National Islamic Institute in Yogyakarta (IAIN), remarked that Muslims in China used to be economically backward and discriminated against under the old regime. The PRC government, by contrast, provided them with various kinds of assistance, such as building new mosques and finding them employment.[55] Hadji Zainul Arifin, member of the conservative Nahdatul Ulama (NU) and second deputy speaker of parliament, contended that there were constraints on freedom of worship in China.[56] A leader of the Masyumi Party left China with a cherished impression that all religious rituals there were "the same as in Indonesia", signalling that "there is freedom of religious worship in the PRC".[57] Dr Djalaludin, member of a parliamentary delegation to China in 1956, succinctly summed up the prevalent sentiment of the above perceptions on Islam: "It is totally groundless to say that there

---

[52] Mohammad Hatta, "Pidato Pada Jamuan Makan oleh Wakil Ketua Daerah Otonom Uighur Singkiang (4 Oktober 1957)", in *Kumpulan Pidato* (Jakarta: Inti Idaya Press, 1983), vol. 2, p. 104.

[53] *Nanyang Siang Pao* (Singapore), 31 October 1957.

[54] Kwee Kek Beng, *Ke Tiongkok Baru*, p. 59; Barioen, *Melihat Tiongkok Baru*, p. 28.

[55] H.A. Soenarjo, "Sepintas tentang Agama Islam di Tiongkok", *Tiongkok Rakjat* 3 (1965): 50.

[56] *Sin Po*, 24 October 1956; *Suluh Indonesia*, 25 October 1956.

[57] *Seng Hwo Pao*, 16 July 1957.

Hatta in Xinjiang, 1957 (*Indonesian Spectator*, 1 October 1957).

is no religious freedom in China; on the contrary, religious freedom is a reality."[58]

The second category of narrative held that religious freedom was severely restricted in China. Arnold Mononutu, ambassador to Beijing between 1953 and 1955, claimed that "conditions imposed on the exercise of religious freedom are that religious leaders must be Chinese, that religion must not oppose to the present regime and must not be active in politics".[59] Although acknowledging that the government had provided "adequate assistance" for building facilities such as mosques, Ramadhan was sceptical that Marxist ideology would permit religious education.[60] According to the *Mudjahid Islam Indonesia* (Defender of Indonesian Islam), restricted religious freedom in China was further blemished by a declining and ageing Muslim population and by the penetration of Marxism into religious

---

[58] *Sin Po*, 8 October 1956.
[59] *Antara News Bulletin*, 26 May 1955.
[60] Ramadhan K.H., "Kesan² Perdjalanan ke RRT (IX): Assalamualaikum…'dia Islam'", *Siasat* 11, 553 (1958).

worship. The report thus identified an irony in the troubling coexistence of Communism ideology and Islam: "The library of the mosque is full of portraits of Stalin, Lenin, Marx, Engels, Mao Tse-tung, and a few other Communist Party leaders who are anti-religious, and books by and about Marx, Lenin and Stalin are abundant."[61]

Asa Bafagih offered the third type of interpretation on the condition of Islam in China. As the founder and editor of the Jakarta daily *Duta Masjarakat* (Envoy of Society), organ of the Nahdatul Ulama, he was an influential political commentator. After a month-long tour of China in 1954, he published a widely read book entitled *RRT dari Luar dan Dalam* (The PRC from Without and Within). Although Bafagih was impressed by the country's social and economic development, his observations on Islam were both pessimistic and critical. His inquiry started from a curious statistical gap: before the Communist takeover in 1949, there had been about 50 million Muslims, a number reduced to only 10 million five years later. The fate of these "forty million missing Muslims" became a haunting question that loomed large in Bafagih's mind. After a painstaking investigation, he concluded, "these tens of millions of Chinese Muslims, who no longer appear in the census reports as Muslims, must still exist…. In their daily life and quite possibly in their family life, they are forced to make a secret of their religion".[62] This view was echoed by Hadji Saleh Suaidy, director of the Press and Radio Section of the Ministry of Religious Affairs. Seeing only signs of "regimentation and retrogression" among the Chinese Muslims, he was convinced that Islam there was "at best fifty years behind the times". Chinese Muslims, for example, generally did not know Arabic and thus could not perform or understand religious services properly. His conclusion was indeed grim: "For the Chinese Muslims, there is no freedom or progress, only suppression and eventual elimination, if not of them personally, then of their religion."[63]

This view of the lack of religious freedom was often associated with criticisms of Islamic leaders and scholars, who "help the degeneration of Islam in China". Suaidy, for instance, ridiculed the leaders of the All-China

---

[61] Mudjahid Islam Indonesia, *Supplement bagi Perdamaian Dunia: Pudji dan Kritik bagi Bangsa Tionghoa dan Republik Rakjat Tiongkok* (Jakarta, 1953), pp. 5–6.
[62] Asa Bafagih, *RRT dari Luar dan Dalam* (Jakarta: Pengurus Besar NU, 1955), p. 80; see also Willard Hanna, "The Case of the Forty Million Missing Muslims", *American Universities Field Staff*, Southeast Asia Series, no. 15 (20 September 1956), p. 9.
[63] H. Saleh Suaidy, "Kesan² Saja selama di RRT", part 4, *Abadi*, 20 June 1956.

Muslim League "for merely acting as the government's propaganda tool". Their activities reminded him of the Jawa Hokokai, the puppet organization set up by the Japanese in Java during World War II.⁶⁴ Bafagih felt that this organization resembled "the organization set up during the Japanese occupation in our country, for whom the important and ultimate objective has been to assist, assist, and always to assist the authorities in power". The degeneration of Islamic scholarship was seen as another indication that intellectuals had become a propaganda tool. Bafagih was dismayed that a Muslim scholar wrote a verse in praise of Mao, converting the godless Mao into a figure deserving Muslim reverence.⁶⁵ He used the example of Muhammad Makien (Ma Zhen), widely regarded by Indonesians prior to 1949 as the leading Islamic scholar in China, to illustrate the loss of intellectual independence. Bafagih recorded that he seemed to encounter in 1954 a totally different Makien, who claimed that Chinese Muslims "have enjoyed equal rights and could look forward to a brilliant future".⁶⁶

Indonesian views of Islam in China, in short, were not only at variance, but also politically charged. The simultaneous coexistence of these contradictory and ambivalent perceptions pertaining to religious freedom (or the lack of it) was well captured by the fact that members of the same Indonesian parliamentary delegation returned from China in 1956 with vastly differing assessments. While Suaidy's critical view was shared by two fellow members who concluded that Muslims were oppressed and that "Islam would be eliminated in China",⁶⁷ two other members, H. Siradjuddin Abbas (Independent) and Dr H. Ali Akbar (Masyumi Party), proclaimed that they had observed the "unimpeded practice of religious freedom in China", and that "every Muslim was able to perform religious rituals freely in mosques, a reality we observed with our own eyes".⁶⁸

---

⁶⁴ Ibid., part 1, *Abadi*, 16 June 1956.
⁶⁵ The verse: "The waters of Mount Tiensang are without end and the virtues of leader Mao will never be forgotten". Bafagih, *RRT dari Luar dan Dalam*, pp. 85, 87.
⁶⁶ Cited from Hanna, "The Case of the Forty Million Missing Muslims", pp. 9–10.
⁶⁷ *Keng Po*, 25 October 1956.
⁶⁸ Hanna, "The Case the Forty Million Missing Muslims", p. 16; *Seng Hwo Pao*, 23 October 1956. The internal document by the Chinese Ministry of Foreign Affairs confirmed the existence of diverse views within this delegation after its return to Indonesia. See "Guanyu Yindunixiya Guohui Daibiaotuan Fanghuahou de Fangyin" [Reactions of the Indonesian parliamentary delegates after visiting China], file no. 105-00451-04 (6–14 December 1956), Archives of the Ministry of Foreign Affairs, PRC.

## CONCLUSION

Indonesians' discourses about cultural and intellectual life in the PRC bore a number of similarities to their perceptions of Chinese politics and society. First, images of China's new culture were ambiguous and sometimes conflicting. Representations of intellectuals' respected status coexisted with harsh criticisms over the dearth of freedom of expression; admiration for their social commitment was mixed with disdain for the evaporation of aesthetic taste in their literary work. The status of Islam was simultaneously and contradictorily described as "in a stage of healthy growth" and "in the process of extinction". Second, despite these incongruous presentations, mainstream writers repeatedly praised the full integration with society of intellectuals in the PRC, whose enviable treatment (financially and politically) by the government was seen as a natural outcome of their vital social contribution. This line of representation implicitly or explicitly overlooked the other side of the picture such as the sacrifice of freedom of expression resulting from intellectuals' close ties with the establishment. As a consequence, the ordeal of intellectuals under the Communist regime received only scant attention. This neglect further reinforced the familiar pattern of envisioning China principally as a nationalistic state, with Communist characteristics fading into a remote background. Finally, China's new culture was presented as people-oriented, with its creativity and aspirations originating from the masses. This effort to "popularize" Chinese culture was essentially in tandem with the prevailing portrayal of a populist China, in which social harmony and all-class solidarity reigned supreme.

# PART II

## Constructing the China Metaphor

## CHAPTER 5

# Indonesian Dreams and the "Chinese Realities": The Sociopolitical and Intellectual Dimensions

*The image not only makes society, society continually remakes the image.*

Kenneth E. Boulding (1966)[1]

*As soon as I arrived at Peking, I was immediately reminded of Yogyakarta in the early days of our revolution where everybody was heroic.*

M. Tabrani (1951)[2]

*Whilst I admire the superb organization and marvellous capacity for action of the Chinese people under Mao Tse-tung's leadership, I also see our own conditions in the mirror.*

Satya Graha (1963)[3]

*"It is necessary to establish a conception of national culture at the top and then to spread it downwards," [said Achmad], "this is why I agreed with brother Yasrin's plan to study the development of the people's culture in RRT [the PRC]. He will probably learn a lot and be inspired by their example."…*
*"Look at RRT," [said Suryono], "how tremendous the progress which has*

---

[1] Kenneth E. Boulding, *The Image: Knowledge in Life and Society* (Ann Arbor: University of Michigan Press, 1966), p. 64.
[2] *Hsin Pao* (Jakarta), 6 November 1951.
[3] Quoted in *Warta Bhakti* [*Zhong Cheng Bao*] (Jakarta), 5 November 1963.

> been initiated by Mao Tse-tung in all fields — the liberation of the people from the oppression and corruption of Chiang Kai-shek's clique. If it can be done there, why not here?"
>
> Mochtar Lubis (1957)[4]

We have demonstrated that there was a large quantity of writings and speeches about China aimed at the general and educated public in Indonesia between 1949 and 1965. Collectively, these led to the formation of a diverse range of perceptions and images of the PRC. While most observers regarded China as a newly emerging *nationalist* state making impressive progress in the social, economic and cultural arenas, a considerably smaller number of commentators perceived the PRC as a Soviet satellite pursuing a policy of aggressive expansion abroad and oppression at home. These varied reactions aside, a certain degree of consensus did exist among mainstream intellectuals, who depicted China as an independent, populist and nationalistic state. Politically, its New Democracy was hailed as a democracy "for the people, by the people, and of the people", while its foreign policy was interpreted as peaceful and friendly, with Mao Zedong being portrayed as a scholar and soldier who worked diligently for the nation's interests. Socially, China was regarded as an orderly, harmonious, dynamic and egalitarian society, with its disciplined people striving to work for the collective good. Whereas China's "new culture" was thought to represent the masses' genuine sentiments, intellectuals were admired for being spiritual leaders of nation-building and for enjoying enviable social respect. Underlying these master narratives was an implicit inclination to separate Communism from China, whose nationalistic and populist dimensions were constantly accentuated at the expense of Marxist ideology. This largely favourable interpretation of China was upheld and shared by prominent political and cultural intellectuals, including those with strong anti-Communist persuasions such as Hatta and leaders of the Masyumi Party. We have also demonstrated that there were perceptional gaps between Indonesian narratives about China and Chinese realities. Not only was China in fact a Communist state closely following the Soviet model (particularly during the PRC's formative years), but class struggle was also a pronounced theme in both theory and practice, which led to the purging of intellectuals for being outspoken critics of the Communist Party.

---

[4] Mochtar Lubis, *Twilight in Djakarta*, trans. Clair Holt (New York: Vanguard Press, 1964 [1957]), pp. 51, 57.

How do we account for the coexistence of differing and often conflicting China in the public and intellectual discourses? Why did political and cultural intellectuals, including those taking a staunch anti-Communist stance at home, portray Communist China in a fundamentally affirmative and sometimes idealized light? Why was China persistently disassociated from Communism and intimately linked with nationalism? Why did themes of social harmony and popular democracy figure so prominently while class conflicts and Communist ideology were conspicuously ignored or downplayed? These are fundamental questions concerning not only the perceptions of China but, more importantly, the nature and characteristics of China observers themselves and the changing sociopolitical environment in Sukarno's Indonesia.

Through extensive reading and analysis of Indonesians' writings and speeches about China, the preceding chapters have been devoted to establishing the phenomenon of this study, namely, the contents, substance and variations of narratives about China *per se*. The following two chapters move beyond textual analysis and seek to unveil the complex context within which specific knowledge formation and discursive practices took place. I argue that the texts about China should be read as strategic and ingenious reactions to postcolonial transformations in Indonesia. These narratives served as political points of reference and cultural devices to reflect upon, and more importantly cope with, fluid and intricate situations at home. In so doing, knowledge, discourse, power and the concrete process of sociopolitical transition were intimately intertwined; this interplay provided fertile ground for further political action. This and the next chapters will also examine the multilayered linkages between the (perceived) undesirable results of domestic sociopolitical transformation and a tendency to idealize foreign examples thought to be successful. As should be evidenced in the following pages, the inclination to treat China as an antithesis to Indonesia significantly affected public intellectuals' perceptions of China and facilitated the transformation of views of China into the China metaphor.

## POLITICAL INSTABILITY AND CULTURAL ANTAGONISMS AT HOME

Indonesians' knowledge about China was formulated and constructed amidst turbulent domestic changes between 1949 and 1965, inevitably playing an important part in shaping China-imagining — in both setting/timing and substance. The fact that these image-makers were active public intellectuals and politicians, rather than detached academicians or indifferent observers, reinforced the linkages between Indonesia's changing sociopolitical landscape and the construction of perceptions of China. It is therefore necessary briefly to examine Indonesia's postcolonial transformation and the diverse reactions by the educated public to the process of this transformation.

## Quest for an Indonesian Political Format

Political change in Indonesia from 1949 to 1965 was first and foremost characterized by an unrelenting search for a political format that would fit the new nation's culture and environment. Robert Elson points out that the real political problem of how to build a consensus in the 1950s was "not just on the composition of the state but, more important, on what the state should be and do".[5] The deep-seated social, political, ideological and cultural cleavages, together with the "conceit and complacency of the new state's leaders", however, made consensus-building arduous and challenging. The clashing agendas held by competing groups constituted a major cause of political instability during the Sukarno era. As M.C. Ricklefs puts it, "Given the circumstances facing Indonesian governments in the years 1950–7, it is not surprising that the democratic experiment foundered, for there were few foundations upon which representative democracy could be built."[6]

One of the most haunting quests facing Indonesia was the trial and ultimate failure of Western-style parliamentary democracy. In December 1949, after the transfer of sovereignty to the Republic, a constitutional democracy modelled after the Dutch and British systems was established. The president under the new political system was merely a figurehead, while parliament and the prime minister appointed by parliament held ultimate political power. During the country's first free election in 1955, 28 parties claimed at least one seat in parliament, with only four parties gaining more than eight seats: the Indonesian Nationalist Party (PNI), the Masyumi Party, the conservative Islamic party Nahdatul Ulama (NU) and the Communist Party of Indonesia (PKI). Cabinets had to be formed by multiparty agreements and coalitions. The different and often conflicting

---

[5] Robert Elson, *The Idea of Indonesia: A History* (Cambridge: Cambridge University Press, 2008), p. 153.
[6] M.C. Ricklefs, *A History of Modern Indonesia*, 3rd ed. (Basingstoke: Palgrave, 2001), p. 289.

interests represented by the major parties, however, made this power-sharing practice extremely difficult, if not impossible, resulting in a high frequency of power turnover. There were six prime ministers between 1950 and 1957; a new cabinet was formed every 12.4 months.[7] These cabinets' short lives were "dependent in large part on the competing interests of the changing coalition of party partners", commented Audrey and George Kahin, veteran observers of Indonesian affairs. "Their weakness stemmed not only from the interparty rivalries but also from the increasing friction between political leaders and President Sukarno over control of the armed forces".[8]

In the meantime, social conflict and economic stagnation became serious problems eroding the foundation of the Indonesian state. Although the nation's GNP grew at 5.6 per cent per annum between 1950 and 1955 (which was about average by the Asian standard of the time though slower than China and Japan), the average annual growth was 1.7 per cent per annum from 1958 to 1965, implying falling per capita income, as the population was growing by around 2 per cent per annum in the decades from 1950 to 1970.[9] The escalating rate of inflation, running at about 100 per cent annually between 1950 and 1957, was accompanied by rampant corruption, especially among civil servants who could barely live off their meagre incomes.[10] The problems of inefficiency and maladministration were aggravated by a stagnated economy, and there is "strong evidence of a general deterioration in living standards" from 1955 to 1965.[11]

---

[7] The most comprehensive political history of Indonesia between 1950 and 1957 is Herbert Feith, *The Decline of Constitutional Democracy in Indonesia* (Ithaca: Cornell University Press, 1962).

[8] Audrey R. Kahin and George McT. Kahin, *Subversion as Foreign Policy: The Secret Eisenhower and Dulles Debacle in Indonesia* (New York: The New Press, 1995), p. 48.

[9] Ann Booth, *The Indonesian Economy in the Nineteenth and Twentieth Centuries: A History of Missed Opportunities* (London: Macmillan, 1998), pp. 55, 65.

[10] In 1930, the colonial civil service totalled about 145,000, representing approximately one official for every 418 inhabitants. In 1960, the number increased to 807,000, representing about one for every 118 inhabitants. Ricklefs, *A History of Modern Indonesia*, p. 291. See also Adrian Vickers, *A History of Modern Indonesia* (Cambridge: Cambridge University Press, 2005), p. 135.

[11] Booth, *The Indonesian Economy*, p. 118; see also Douglas S. Paauw, "From Colonial to Guided Economy", in *Indonesia*, ed. Ruth McVey (New Haven, CT: HRAF Press, 1963), pp. 155–247; and Thomas Lindblad, "The Political Economy of Realignment in Indonesia during the Sukarno Period", in *Europe-Southeast Asia in the Contemporary*

The combination of political instability and economic difficulties accelerated confrontations between Java and the outer islands, whose residents and politicians had long thought they were unfairly exploited by the central government. This conflict was exacerbated by the armed forces' intervention in politics. The army stationed in the outer islands established close connections with various regional and ethnic groups, a situation that was partially responsible for a series of regional military revolts that broke out between 1956 and 1960, some of which were backed by the United States and the Nationalist authorities in Taiwan.[12] The intertwining of racial, religious, economic and foreign interests in these rebellions pushed Indonesia to the brink of dissolution. With the support of the army under General Abdul Haris Nasution's leadership, President Sukarno declared martial law in March 1957. Two years later, the system of Guided Democracy was formally established, signifying the final demise of parliamentary democracy.

Guided Democracy was founded on Indonesia's 1945 Constitution, giving ultimate authority to a powerful presidency. Like constitutional democracy, however, the new system was plagued by insurmountable conflicts of interests. Lacking strong institutional backing, Sukarno had to play a balancing game between the army and the PKI, the two best organized institutions in the nation. Nevertheless, the deep-rooted ideological and political enmities between a conservative, pro-American army leadership and a radical, (largely) pro-China PKI proved to be unbridgeable, and reinforced by the international Cold War. Meanwhile, Sukarno's rhetorical call for continuing the "Unfinished Revolution" and returning to radical nationalism could not halt the worsening of the economy. In 1965, inflation ran as high as 500 per cent; by the end of 1965, the price of rice was rising at an annual rate of 900 per cent.[13] The final showdown came on 30 September 1965. A coup staged by a battalion of the palace guard commanded by Lieutenant-Colonel Untung triggered a counter-coup led

---

*World: Mutual Images and Reflections 1940s–1960s*, ed. Piyanart Bunnag, Franz Knipping and Sud Chonchirdsin (Baden-Baden: Normos Verlagsgesellschaft, 2000), pp. 149–72. According to Lindbald, "There was probably a slight absolute income decline of about 0.3% on average during these years [1958–65]."

[12] Jacques Bertrand, *Nationalism and Ethnic Conflict in Indonesia* (Cambridge: Cambridge University Press, 2004), pp. 34–40; Audrey and George Kahin, *Subversion as Foreign Policy*.

[13] Ricklefs, *A History of Modern Indonesia*, p. 338.

by General Suharto. In the subsequent months, amidst the massacre of PKI members and followers, Sukarno was ousted and the New Order regime headed by Suharto was formally installed in March 1967.[14]

It should be emphasized that the Sukarno era, especially the years between 1950 and 1957, was marked by some significant achievements in the social and political spheres, including the existence and functioning of a free press, popular participation in politics on the ground, an increasing pace of education and maintenance of a unified state, despite powerful centrifugal forces from within and without. Ann Laura Stoler points to the existence of "another civil society in Indonesia" during the Sukarno era and considers the 1950s "to be more cosmopolitan, 'modern' and politically progressive" than it has usually been portrayed. She contends that "it was a time that held promise … [and] former members of progressive labor and literary organizations retain vivid memories of a vibrant intellectual and political environment."[15] It is precisely these lively intellectual and sociopolitical landscapes that made the emergence of competing images of China possible and sustainable for much of the Sukarno era.

To summarize, the above simplified overview of Indonesia's post-colonial transformation underscores the fact that the years 1949–65 were primarily characterized by political instability, social cleavages, cultural antagonisms, economic stagnation and ethnic/regional confrontations. Although one should not overstate this gloomy facet, it was evident that "more and more Indonesians became impatient with the unfulfilled promise

---

[14] There is still no consensus on the origins of the 30 September 1965 movement. For some earlier studies, see Benedict Anderson and Ruth McVey, *A Preliminary Analysis of the October 1, 1965, Coup in Indonesia* (Ithaca: Cornell Modern Indonesia Project, 1971); and Harold Crouch, *The Army and Politics in Indonesia* (Ithaca: Cornell University Press, 1978). Victor Fic, *Anatomy of the Jakarta Coup, October 1, 1965: The Collusion with China Destroyed the Army Command, President Sukarno and the Communist Party of Indonesia* (New Delhi: Abhinav Publications, 2004) claims that both the Chinese government and Sukarno were involved in the Movement. This thesis is dismissed by John Roosa as "sheer speculation". See his much more solid work, *Pretext for Mass Murder: The September 30th Movement and Suharto's Coup d'état in Indonesia* (Madison: University of Wisconsin Press, 2006).

[15] Stoler, "Untold Stories: On the Other Side of 1965 Lay a Vibrant Indonesia Worth Remembering", *Inside Indonesia*, October–December 2001, p. 7. For a reassessment of the "forgotten 1950s", see useful discussions in David Bouchier and John Legge, eds., *Democracy in Indonesia: 1950s and 1990s* (Clayton: Centre of Southeast Asian Studies, Monash University, 1994), especially pp. 3–49.

of progress",[16] which constituted the defining environment shaping Indonesians' views of domestic and external developments. As will be detailed in the following pages, general sentiments of disappointment among the "political public" as well as alienation of intellectuals were direct responses to the (perceived) failure of the post-revolutionary transformation.

## "My Sun No Longer Shines": Indonesian Dreams and Despairs

According to Herbert Feith, the winning of independence was accompanied by the emergence of at least three expectations among the Indonesian people.[17] The first was material aspiration. The economic system was expected to produce a rapidly expanding volume of goods and services to "the mobilized people". The second expectation was that of increased social status. The society was expected to create a great number of white-collar positions and many "leadership roles" in politics and administration, or in social life generally. The third expectation was psychological. With society changing so rapidly, values were thrown into confusion. As old status barriers were destroyed or in the process of crumbling, many Indonesians became uncertain of their place in society and sought for stability.

These expectations and a general belief that independence would automatically lead to "a golden bridge to a just and prosperous society",[18] however, were not fulfilled in the tumultuous postcolonial transformation. The feelings of discontent were gradually manifested in intellectual and political discourses. Mohammad Natsir, at one time the prime minister in the early 1950s and a leader of the Masyumi Party, captured the public sentiments in his Independence Day speech in 1951:

> When we look around, we see very few joyful expressions. It is as if the independence we have obtained had brought but few benefits. It would seem that expectations have not been fulfilled. The gain is like a loss.... There is a disappointment, ideals have been lost sight of. Everywhere there prevails a feeling of dissatisfaction, a feeling of frustration, a feeling of hopelessness.[19]

---

[16] Vickers, *A History of Modern Indonesia*, p. 135.
[17] Feith, *The Decline*, p. 598.
[18] Sukarno was the most eloquent spokesman of this theme of a post-independence "promising future". See, for example, Sukarno, *Indonesia Accuses*, ed. and trans. Roger K. Paget (Kuala Lumpur: Oxford University Press, 1975), esp. pp. 49–52.
[19] Mohammad Natsir, "Lassitude and the Display of False Glitter", in *Indonesian Political Thinking, 1945–1965*, ed. Herbert Feith and Lance Castles (Ithaca: Cornell University Press, 1970), p. 72.

In 1955, a group of university students looked back to the country's early years of independence and similarly found no signs of joyfulness:

> Up to now, we have been administering our free country for nearly ten years. Meanwhile we could ask ourselves what results have been obtained and what we have given to be the essence of our freedom. If the answer is based on the daily facts, then we are to confess, that we have not attained much; on the contrary the retrogression and splitting up of our community indicate dangerous symptoms.[20]

This sense of frustration was intensified two years later, as vividly illustrated in the responses to an essay contest on the question of "What are we as a nation and as a country?", organized in 1957 by Soedjatmoko, one of the most distinguished intellectuals of the time. The 355 essays were submitted by people from all walks of life, including students, teachers, journalists, writers, civil servants and white-collar workers.[21] They could be seen as representatives of what Herbert Feith calls "the political public", who were "outside the political elite … [but] nevertheless saw themselves as capable of taking action which could affect national government or politics".[22] These entries reflected profound disappointment with not being able to witness "Indonesia playing the role of examplar, teacher, or arbiter of the world." One of the recurrent statements was "We do not yet enjoy the fruits of our independence." There were persistent complaints about corruption, internal division, social inequality and economic stagnation. Although "too many people are poor, lack housing and clothing", a few "dance inside magnificent mansions forgetting the beggars outside who ask for alms".[23] Metaphors were used to express feelings of despair; examples like the following were abundant: "We are like mushrooms which grow

---

[20] "Desintergration [sic] in all Fields", *Gadjah Mada* 6, 2 (1955): 72 (originally in English).
[21] These entries are extensively analysed by Guy Pauker in his "Indonesian Images of Their National Self", *Public Opinion Quarterly* 22, 2 (1958): 305–24. An Indonesian specialist, Pauker was a consultant for the then CIA-sponsored RAND Corporation and was directly involved in decision-making for the CIA, the Pentagon and the State Department regarding Indonesia. See Budiawan, "Seeing the Communist Past through the Lens of a CIA Consultant: Guy J. Pauker on the Indonesian Communist Party before and after the '1965 Affair'", *Inter-Asia Cultural Studies* 7, 4 (2006): 650–62.
[22] Feith, *The Decline*, p. 109.
[23] Cited in Pauker, "Indonesian Images", p. 316.

and die in the same spot, leaving no trace of what they accomplished while alive", and "Now the road is winding, the goal is unknown, I lost my way and drift." The sense of optimism evident in the first years of independence was replaced by prevailing pessimism. "My sun no longer shines," one essay contestant lamented, "My feet are wounded, and so is my soul." "We are a fruit beautiful to look at but empty", wrote another.[24]

Many blamed political leaders for the problems Indonesia was facing. An editorial appearing in a university student journal commented bitterly:

> Up till now the term "politics" is not popular.... This term has meanings, such as "opportunity to enrich oneself", sharing subsistence with relatives and friends, "display and power".... It only concentrates on a minority of people living in the countries. The slogan used are [sic] indeed "for the people", but the ways of acting are in accordance with personal desires. The "sterility" of such leaders has become more and more obvious [sic], and finally, the day will come that they will be exposed.[25]

In sum, political instability and economic stagnation became conspicuous features of the country's postcolonial transformation, which led to growing discontent among the "political public" during the 1950s. The failure of parliamentary democracy propelled the educated not only to look for other alternatives, but also to compare their own country with other new nations with similar natural endowments and sociocultural environments. It was within this domestic context that Indonesia's China observers understood and interpreted China, and presented their narratives to the public.

## DISILLUSIONMENT AND ALIENATION OF INTELLECTUALS

Indonesians' images of China were shaped not only by their nation's changing conditions, but also by the China-image-makers — political and cultural intellectuals of the time. As Indonesian intellectual history between

---

[24] Ibid. This pessimism was in stark contrast to the optimism that had prevailed just two years earlier. In 1955, an Indonesian cabinet minister boasted, "no one starves in this country. No one freezes. There are always bananas on the trees and there is always a sun in the sky". *New York Times*, 8 June 1955.
[25] "What Changes Are to be Expected in Political Life?" *Gadjah Mada* 6, 6 (1955): 440 (originally in English).

1949 and 1965 has been largely a neglected area of research, it is necessary to provide some contextualization and examine major themes that emerged in the cultural and intellectual scene of the 1950s.

## "Crisis in Literature" and Debates about Cultural Identity

Indonesia's intellectual journey, just like its political trajectory, was marked by turbulence and diversity. After 1949, the search for an Indonesian cultural identity was increasingly shaped by the clashing agendas of various political forces, including nationalism.[26] Within this changing sociopolitical milieu, intellectuals were persistently formulating and reformulating their visions for the new nation-state. As analogues to public discontents, many intellectuals were frustrated by the disappointing results of nation-building, amply evidenced by the recurrent theme of "crisis" in political and cultural discourses.

Shortly after the transfer of sovereignty in 1949, some intellectuals began to argue that the 1945–49 Revolution had failed to tackle the country's fundamental social, religious, cultural and economic problems. The notion of "crisis" gradually came to dominate much social, political and literary writing. In late 1950, the poet Rivai Apin proclaimed, "We are now in a crisis, which is a reality."[27] Takdir Alisjahbana, a prominent intellectual and social activist, declared the next year that a static way of thinking had caused an impasse and that only a new dynamic in thought could get society and culture going again.[28] Suparna Sastradiredja claimed in 1951 that Indonesia was facing "one thousand and one crises", including "political crisis, economic crisis, cultural crisis, and military crisis; or, using vocabularies easier to be comprehended by workers and peasants, crisis of democracy, crisis of rice price, crisis of low wage, crisis of corruption, crisis of strikes, and so on".[29] It was by no means a coincidence that Usmar Ismail (1921–71), considered to be the father of modern Indonesia

---

[26] On the role of nationalism in postwar Indonesia, see Coen Holtzappel, "Nationalism and Cultural Identity", in *Images of Malay-Indonesian Identity*, ed. Michael Hitchcock and Victor T. King (Kuala Lumpur: Oxford University Press, 1997), pp. 63–107, which argues that "Indonesian nationalism also became the source of Indonesia culture" during the Sukarno era.

[27] Rivai Apin, "Berdasar Pada Krisis", *Siasat* 4, 192 (1950): 9.

[28] Cited in A. Teeuw, *Modern Indonesian Literature* (The Hague: Martinus Nijhoff, 1979), vol. 1, p. 40.

[29] Sastradiredja, "Mengatasi Krisis", *Pikiran Rakjat*, 5 March 1951.

cinema, whose films "have artistic integrity and reflect a national identity",[30] entitled two of his films as "Crisis" (Krisis,1953) and "Crisis Again" (Lagi-Lagi Krisis, 1955).

Throughout the first half of the 1950s, "crisis in literature" (hereafter without quotation marks) became a dominant theme in much of the nation's cultural discourse. Although focused on literature, these public discussions had broader implications. As Teeuw has pointed out, the debate over crisis in literature was an attempt "to discover the Indonesian identity, to give shape to the ideals of the revolution, and to determine the Indonesian place in the modern world".[31] Three major themes emerged in this polemic, and they constituted some of the defining issues in the intellectual history of the 1950s.

The first theme pertained to the origin of the crisis-in-literature debate, which was widely held to have come about because of a "failed revolution". This notion was first elaborated by W.F. Wertheim, an influential Dutch scholar, who argued that "modern Indonesian literature and the national revolution are inseparable". He pointed out in 1953 that, as a social revolution, the Indonesian revolution had "failed and stopped halfway", which led to many social problems (such as corruption) and pervasive pessimism in literature.[32] The theme of a failed revolution was quickly taken up and expounded upon by intellectuals back home who were dismayed to see that idealism and national unity were being displaced by cynicism and social cleavages. As G. Siagian put it, "the élan of the 1945 revolution had dwindled before a national spirit took shape and direction".[33] Another writer, Buyung Saleh, contended that the so-called crisis in literature was merely a sign of widespread structural crisis, symbolizing the failure of the Revolution, while Soedjatmoko characterized it as a "psychological crisis".[34]

---

[30] H. Misbach Yusa Biran, "Brief History of the Indonesian Film", *Journal of Film Preservation*, no. 69 (2005): 2–6; Krishna Sen, "Politics of Melodrama in Indonesian Cinema", in *Melodrama and Asian Cinema*, ed. Wimal Dissanayake (Cambridge: Cambridge University Press, 1993), pp. 205–17.

[31] Teeuw, *Modern Indonesian Literature*, vol. 1, p. 139.

[32] Pramoedya Ananta Toer, "Prof. Dr. Wertheim tentang Kesasteraan Indonesia Modern", *Medan Bahasa* 3, 11 (1953): 39–43; this essay also appears in *Siasat* 7, 336 (1953): 14–5.

[33] Cited in Teeuw, *Modern Indonesian Literature*, vol. 1, p. 141.

[34] Saleh, "Latarbelakang Kesedjarahan Krisis Indonesia", *Siasat* 8, 387 (1954): 24–5; and Ajip Rosidi, *Ichtisar Sedjarah Sastra Indonesia* (Bandung: Bintjipta, 1969), p. 138.

The second and related theme was the conviction that the crisis was in part precipitated by the West's "negative influence". This view was in tandem with the escalating attack at the time on Western-style democracy. According to H.S. Gazalba, "this crisis is generated by Western culture, which has brought new ways of thinking and feelings that are in total contrast to ways of thinking and feelings in our society". Consequently, "new arts, which stem from Western influence, have not been in harmony with the spirit of the majority of the people; modern art has become alien to the majority of people".[35] Politicians and intellectuals held that the continuing presence of "decadent" Western influence hindered the creation of national culture and national education.[36]

The third theme was that intellectuals had been isolated from the people, and that this disassociation between men of thinking and men of action reinforced the estrangement of intellectuals. "The more advanced our writers' thinking becomes, the greater the distance between them and the people", wrote Gazalba, "Therefore, society at large finds it more and more difficult to understand them. Our writers have not fulfilled their responsibilities to the society."[37] In a similar vein, Pramoedya complained of "the Salon-intelligentsia, who have been detached from the truly revolutionary problem of the Indonesian people".[38] The uneasy views concerning the relationship between the arts and the masses reflected the ongoing controversies about the direction of Indonesian culture in general. Should art be pursued purely for its own sake, or should it reflect the sentiments of the people? This uncertainty was clearly illustrated in the resolutions of the Second Cultural Congress held in Bandung in October 1951. The Congress acknowledged "a difference of opinion as to the basis of art: (a) art based on the existing law; (b) art for society, and (c) free art".[39]

---

[35] Gazalba, "Ada Krisis".
[36] Lee Kam Hing, *Education and Politics in Indonesia, 1945–1965* (Kuala Lumpur: University of Malaya Press, 1995), pp. 165–8.
[37] Gazalba, "Krisis Indonesia Dewasa ini", *Indonesia* 5, 12 (1954): 696.
[38] Cited in Teeuw, *Modern Indonesian Literature*, p. 140.
[39] "Decisions of the Second Cultural Congress at Bandung", *Indonesia* 3, 1/3 (1952): 481–2. For more details about issues under debate at this congress, see Tod Jones, "Indonesian Cultural Policy, 1950–2003: Culture, Institutions, Government" (Ph.D. dissertation, Curtin University of Technology, 2005), pp. 103–5.

In short, although some writers (notably H.B. Jassin, a renowned literary critic of the time) denied the existence of a crisis in literature,[40] the very fact that this debate featured so prominently in the mass media was itself illuminating. It demonstrated not only prevailing sentiments of confusion and discontent among intellectuals, but also wider problems on the national scale. As a manifestation of cultural crisis, Gazalba observed, the crisis in literature "reflected real crises in economics, politics, society, science, the arts, philosophy, and religion".[41] Even General Nasution spoke of a "moral crisis" in 1953: "The happy and hopeful atmosphere, prevailing at the transfer of sovereignty, has turned into one of demoralization with crises developing in all fields because the responsible leaders have dialed in their duty."[42]

## Search for Political and Cultural Solutions

Despite the disillusionment, public intellectuals continued to search for ways of overcoming mounting difficulties with two major alternatives: the first was culturalist, calling for a return to the "Eastern spirit" in general and an Indonesian identity in particular; the second was nationalistic, advocating unity among all social groups, particularly between intellectuals and the people.

The call for a return to an Indonesian identity was a by-product of the growing criticisms over the West's negative influences. Politically, with the failure of parliamentary democracy and seemingly unmanageable social disarray, calls for state authority to be strengthened were widely voiced. Sukarno had complained as early as in 1952, "for decades we have longed for an authority of our own. And now that we have our own authority, we do not respect it".[43] Minister of Information Roeslan Abdulgani declared that the country's existing democracy was a system that "often develops excesses and becomes a caricature of itself", and he stated that "we have too much democracy, what we need is discipline and leadership".[44] By

---

[40] H.B. Jassin, "Kesasteraan Indonesia Modern Tak Ada Krisis", *Mimbar Indonesia* 49–52 (1954).
[41] Gazalba, "'Ada Krisis' dalam Kesasteraan Indonesia Modern: Pembakangan terhadap Jassin", *Siasat* 9, 398 (1955): 22–3.
[42] Cited in Elson, *The Idea of Indonesia*, p. 163.
[43] Sukarno, "The Crisis of Authority", in Feith and Castles, *Indonesian Political Thinking*, p. 74.
[44] Cited in Feith, *The Decline*, pp. 326–7.

1957, unfavourable feelings toward parliamentary democracy had become more intense and widespread. Many believed that the ideal type of democracy should be "an Indonesian democracy, and not an American democracy — one based on justice, prosperity, solidarity, cooperation, which are the characteristics of our spirits". More specifically, it was held that "the present Western-style democracy must be transformed into a democracy Oriental in spirit, based on solidarity, honesty, and stability".[45]

Culturally, criticisms over Western influence were accompanied by a yearning for an Indonesian identity, situated within a broadly defined Eastern tradition. According to Gazalba, "the starting point to overcome our cultural crisis is a recognition that in terms of spirit, logic, rationale, and objective, Western culture is different from ours". Therefore, Indonesian culture needed to be brought back to its own tradition.[46] Convinced that "Indonesia's traditional oriental characteristics have been polluted by the materialist spirit of the West", some writers proposed that "Western culture must be discarded in favor of traditional culture in order to avoid divisive and debilitating cultural clashes."[47] Others believed that some foreign cultural elements should be selected, reinterpreted and integrated into Indonesian culture.[48]

The second alternative for coping with social and political problems was the forging of national unity. Suparna Sastradiredja was convinced that "strengthening our union is the most important remedy [in order to overcome the crisis]".[49] By 1957, many insisted that national unity, along with social egalitarianism and economic progress, should be made the nation's objective. Unity between intellectuals and the people was an important aspect of national solidarity. Gazalba contended that in order to get out of the crisis, intellectuals should "fulfill their social responsibilities and identify themselves with the people".[50]

---

[45] Cited in Pauker, "Indonesian Images", p. 319.
[46] Gazalba, "Krisis Indonesia".
[47] Cited in Pauker, "Indonesian Images", p. 310.
[48] Selosoemardjan, "Some Social and Cultural Implications of Indonesia's Unplanned and Planned Development", *Review of Politics* 25, 1 (1963): 64–90.
[49] *Pikiran Rakjat*, 5 March 1951.
[50] Gazalba, "Ada Krisis". This theme of the unity between intellectuals and the people was advocated in particular by left-leaning intellectuals associated with Lekra. See Keith Foulcher, *Social Commitment in Literature and the Arts: The Indonesian "Institute of People's Culture" 1950–1965* (Clayton: Center of Southeast Asian Studies, Monash University, 1986).

The quest for an Indonesian identity in the framework of a perceived Oriental tradition was the context within which knowledge about China was formulated and contested. Two major factors further explain Indonesians' attraction to the Chinese experience. First, prior to 1949, Indonesian nationalists had been inclined to believe that the two nations shared some fundamental similarities in terms of historical development and natural resources endowment. This theme of identification continued in the postcolonial era. "As soon as I arrived at Peking," wrote the veteran journalist Tabrani in 1951, "I was immediately reminded of Yogyakarta in the early days of our revolution where everybody was heroic."[51] It was widely held that the two countries were facing the same problems of nation-building. As Prime Minister Wilopo put it in 1953, "There are profound commonalities between our two nations, which are both at the time of transformation. This is the reason why I am coming to China to study at a close distance how the Chinese people have solved the problems arising from the transition."[52] After recounting past friendship and common struggles against colonialism and imperialism, Prime Minister Ali Sastroamidjojo proclaimed in 1955 that Indonesia and China shared similar aims in nation-building that "have brought us nearer together".[53] China represented an exciting, ongoing experiment of nation-building that was different from the West and the Soviet Union. Zainul Arifin, second deputy speaker, explained why China was more attractive and relevant to his country: "It is very important for us to know the process of change, yet the Soviet Union has already completed this process." After visiting both China and the Soviet Union, an Indonesian reported that, while accomplishments in the latter were obtained by the use of machinery, China's achievements were "reached through manpower, which is the most interesting experience to us".[54]

Second, despite the fact that the PRC was a Communist state, many Indonesians continued to regard China primarily as an Asian nation belonging to the Oriental tradition. Shortly after independence, a number of intellectuals lamented that Indonesia had paid too much attention to the West and that it was necessary to redress the balance by looking to its Eastern neighbours; China was singled out as an example of this Oriental

---

[51] *Hsin Pao* (Jakarta), 6 November 1951.
[52] *Renmin Ribao*, 30 June 1957.
[53] *Indonesia: A Feature Bulletin* (Beijing: Embassy of the Republic of Indonesia, 1955), p. 31.
[54] "Melawat ke Sovjet Uni dan RRT", *Suara Guru* 12, 12 (1958): 19–22.

tradition.⁵⁵ At the Indonesian Cultural Conference held in August 1950, which focused on the theme of "National Culture and Its Relationship with Cultures of Other Nations", Ki Hadjar Dewantara, one of the three main speakers, charged that all cultural exchanges in the past were via the Netherlands, and that Indonesia had neglected cultural relations with her immediate neighbours in Asia. His view was echoed by other participants.⁵⁶ In 1955, Professor Prijono spoke of the need to seek inspiration from the East, instead of continuing to look to the West.⁵⁷ Advocating close cultural ties with the PRC, Adam Malik pointedly reminded his readers at home in 1950, "Indonesians and Chinese belong to the same race."⁵⁸ A number of political and cultural intellectuals pointed out during their visits to China in the 1950s that, because both Indonesians and Chinese were Oriental, it was quite easy for them to establish mutual understanding and to learn from one another.⁵⁹ The mayor of Greater Jakarta, Sudiro, remarked in 1956 that China's progress made him "proud" to be an Asian.⁶⁰

These perceived parallels, which had their historical precedents (as we established in Chapter 1) reinforced the feelings of affinity and led to an (over)emphasis on the cultural elements of China's sociopolitical transition (such as character of the people) that might be transferrable within an imagined Oriental tradition. As a consequence, Indonesians were drawn to nationalism while downplaying Communist ideology, thus decoupling China from Communism. In other words, the formation of Indonesian knowledge about China became intimately intertwined with changing priorities and agendas at home.

---

⁵⁵ "Pengantar", in *Tjerita-Tjerita Tiongkok*, trans. and ed. Beb Vuyk, Mochtar Lubis and S. Mundingsari (Jakarta: Pembanguanan, 1953), pp. 7–19; Adinegoro, *Tiongkok: Pusaran Asia* (Jakarta: Djambatan, 1951), pp. 7–10; Wojowasito, *Tiongkok (Pembangoenan Politik)* (Yogyakarta: Badan Penerbit Nasional, n.d.), "Kata Pengantar".
⁵⁶ Jones, *Indonesian Cultural Policy, 1950–2003*, p. 102.
⁵⁷ *Pikiran Rakjat*, 15 April 1955.
⁵⁸ "Tentang Persahabatan Indonesia-RRT", *Republik* 1 (1950).
⁵⁹ Yao Zhongming et al., *Jiangjun, Waijiaojia, Yishujia — Huang Zhen Jilian Wenji* [General, diplomat and artist — A collection of essays in commemorating Huang Zhen] (Beijing: Jiefangjun Chubanshe, 1992), p. 367; interview with Chen Lishui, who was personal assistant and chief interpreter to Chinese ambassadors between 1950 and 1960.
⁶⁰ Cited in R. Howie, "Sino-Indonesian Relations, 1950–1959: A Study of the Chinese People's Republic's Policy towards a Non-Communist State in South East Asia" (M.A. thesis, University of Western Australia, 1966), p. 104.

Sudiro with students at Tsinghua University, Beijing, 1956 [Lembaga Persahabatan Indonesia-Tiongkok, *Perkenalan Lembaga Persahabatan Indonesia-Tiongkok* (Jakarta: Rada, 1956)].

## PRECONCEPTIONS ABOUT INDONESIA AND THE CONSTRUCTION OF CHINA-IMAGES

How were Indonesians' perceptions of China related to their country's political and intellectual transitions? What was the linkage between intellectuals' visions for their nation and specific China-images? I argue that Indonesians deployed their China perceptions as political and cultural devices for reflecting upon and confronting situations at home. The largely affirmative attitudes toward China were mainly a product of Indonesians' dissatisfaction with their own process of nation-building. This is a major reason why admiration for China's "amazing" development was, as a rule, repeatedly accompanied by criticism of the lack of progress at home. In other words, China observers tended to transpose their ideals and preconceptions about their nation into the constructions and presentation of specific China-images. China thus became not only a metaphor, but a site of political and cultural contestation.

## China as a Point of Reference and a Political/Cultural Device

As demonstrated earlier, there existed significant gaps between expectation and reality in Indonesia's postcolonial transition; the dream of a just and prosperous society was shattered by political instability and economic stagnation. It was against this backdrop that specific dimensions of China's development and the characteristics of its people — such as idealism, egalitarianism, discipline, hard work, collectivism, strong leadership, unity between intellectuals and the people, high *semangat* [spirit], social harmony, orderliness and economic progress — were given special attention in the dominant narratives, as these were exactly Indonesians' ideals for their country. The following points highlight the main social and political themes of comparison when China was referred to in Indonesian writings.

(1) *Democracy*. In striking contrast to Indonesia's "chaotic and imported democracy", New Democracy in China was portrayed as a system based upon the people's interests and traditional culture. Barioen's approving narrative was apparently framed within his negative view of democracy at home:

> Which country — Indonesia or China — has true democracy? In Indonesia people say that they have democracy, but it exists only as an illusion and in theory, and it is merely a democracy in name. Democracy in China, on the other hand, does not exist as a theory debated on podiums and ranted about in newspapers, it is an everyday reality and practice.[61]

With the intensification of criticism over constitutional democracy after the mid-1950s, democracy in China was constructed by some commentators not only as a negation of politics at home, but as a realization of Indonesians' ideals. In the words of A. Karim, a journalist affiliated with the *Sin Po*, democracy evoked different meanings in the two countries. It was symbolized by "political parties attacking one other" at home, while democracy in China meant that "all citizens must be guaranteed with appropriate material and cultural well-being". Karim further utilized the China example to shore up the call for a new political format in Indonesia:

> I am reminded of what President Sukarno said right after the [1955] election: "If all political parties can unify and be guided under agreed

---

[61] Barioen A.S., *Melihat Tiongkok Baru* (Jakarta: Rada, 1952), p. 70.

principles, what is the use of the opposition?" He also advocated establishing the Guided Democracy, namely, a democracy under strong leadership. Judged from my conversations with representatives of nine democratic parties in China, I am convinced that China's democracy is actually based upon such a guiding principle supported by all the parties and that it is a system under a democratic leadership.[62]

(2) *National unity.* Throughout the Sukarno years, national unity was a paramount concern for a great majority of politicians and intellectuals. This ideal of unity, however, was overshadowed by political turmoil, social divisiveness and regional rebellions. Formulated against this backdrop, image of a unified China was both powerful and appealing. Indonesians' admiration for its national unity was frequently blended with hope for a similar situation at home. Satya Graha, vice-editor-in-chief of the PNI-affiliated daily *Suluh Indonesia*, spoke of the prevailing sentiment when reporting his impressions of the PRC:

> Just imagine: 650 million people have been meticulously organized and robustly unified, and undertaking revolutionary activities. What a powerful force it is! Are there any precedents in human history? The unity of 650 million people means the unity of one-fourth of the whole world's population. In an exciting way, the dream of unity aspired by Bung Karno has been realized in China.[63]

Not surprisingly, this China was taken as a stark contrast to sad realities at home: "While I admire the superb organization and marvellous capability of the Chinese people under Mao Tse-tung's leadership", he remarked sarcastically, "I also see our own conditions in the mirror."[64] The promising image of a unified China was often followed by the proposition that Indonesia should learn from its example. Henk Ngantung, a prominent painter and mayor of Greater Jakarta between 1960 and 1965, suggested that China had in effect realized some of the ideals espoused in his nation: "The PRC has made remarkable progress. In fact we can use China's methods of development in our nation."[65] Soewirjo, chairman of the PNI, was impressed by the mechanisms for unifying all social groups in China and contended that these "should be taken as models for Indonesia,

---

[62] *Hsin Pao* (Jakarta), 8 June 1956.
[63] *Warta Bhakti* (*Zhong Cheng Bao*), 2 November 1963.
[64] *Warta Bhakti* (*Zhong Cheng Bao*), 5 November 1963.
[65] *Tay Kong Sian Po* (Surabaya), 4 November 1959.

because we are also striving to form a national front".⁶⁶ In his acclaimed novel about cultural politics in the mid-1950s, *Twilight in Djakarta*, Mochtae Lubis vividly depicts widely held views among intellectuals:

> "It is necessary to establish a conception of national culture at the top and then to spread it downwards," [said Achmad], "this is why I agreed with brother Yasrin's plan to study the development of the people's culture in RRT [the PRC]. He will probably learn a lot and be inspired by their example…"
>
> "Look at RRT," [said Suryono], "how tremendous the progress which has been initiated by Mao Tse-tung in all fields — the liberation of the people from the oppression and corruption of Chiang Kai-shek's clique. If it can be done there, why not here?"⁶⁷

(3) *Social engineering and economic growth*. As noted in Chapter 3, social engineering was perceived to be responsible for the making of the "new human beings" who were in turn a driving force behind economic progress in China. This favourable portrayal was frequently accompanied by propositions for Indonesia to adopt some methods of China's socio-economic development for its own use. After learning from Hatta that China had eliminated prostitution, Minister of Social Affairs Muljadi announced that he wanted to study its methods of dealing with this social problem plaguing his country. Similarly, a Masyumi Party member in the Jakarta city council urged the government to learn from China on how to eradicate the problem of prostitution and beggars.⁶⁸ Sukardjo Wirjopranoto, ambassador to Beijing between 1956 and 1960, suggested that more delegations be sent to China in order to observe and closely study its development: "Because China is full of manpower and possesses little advanced equipment, its methods of development can be implemented in Indonesia."⁶⁹

(4) *Collectivism and egalitarianism*. Indonesian intellectuals regarded collectivism and egalitarianism as an integral component of a just and prosperous society. Some used China as an antithesis for registering their frustrations with rampant individualism at home and as a strategic device for promulgating their views on what ought to be done. Prior to visiting

---

⁶⁶ Cited from *Cankao Xiaoxi* (Beijing), 17 October 1959.
⁶⁷ Mochtar Lubis, *Twilight in Djakarta*, pp. 51, 57.
⁶⁸ *Sin Po*, 18 November 1957; *Hsin Pao*, 27 July 1956.
⁶⁹ *Seng Hwo Pao* (Jakarta), 25 March 1959.

China, Sugardo reported that he had attempted to sort out some perplexing questions facing his country: "Indonesia is now experiencing a revolution, what ought to be its goals? After gaining political independence, how can we achieve social justice?"[70] The Indonesian experience of the early 1950s apparently dashed his hope that independence meant "the building of a golden bridge to justice and prosperity". Instead, he found that the country was facing a series of crises.[71] Sugardo's China trip appeared to promise solutions to his problems. Unlike individualism in the West, collectivism in China provided vast opportunities for the people, so he advocated imitating some of its methods.[72] To Pramoedya, the prevalence of collectivism and social harmony in China demonstrated, ironically, what had gone wrong at home: "In Indonesia, people only think of themselves; over there, everyone thinks of others. Here, people have to be greedy in order to survive; over there, the avaricious instinct has been totally eliminated."[73]

(5) *Political discipline.* The China example was deployed not only as a reflective mirror to underscore what went wrong in Indonesia but, more importantly, as a political device for substantiating certain agendas and priorities for transforming things domestically. Deeply disturbed by the internal power struggle and the army's intervention in politics, Sukarno was evidently hoping for an unchallenged civilian leadership when he repeatedly spoke about unity and strong leadership in China. "In the PRC", Sukarno claimed after his 1956 trip to that country, "leaders do not play political games, which is exactly the opposite to here in Indonesia, and we are now on the verge of falling apart".[74] Apparently referring to rampant regional military rebellions at home, Sukarno in late 1956 spoke approvingly about China, where "soldiers are obedient to political leadership and do not form any military cliques".[75] Sukiman, a leader of the anti-Communist Masyumi Party, reported favourably that there were no strikes in China, before urging his fellow countrymen to learn from this example.[76] It was not because he had changed his political attitude; instead, China was deployed as a political strategy for justifying his anti-labour stance at home.

---

[70] Sugardo, *Si Djembel Mentjari Keadilan Sosial* (Jakarta: Dharma, 1952), p. 7.
[71] Sugardo, "Krisis = Kita Sekarang", *Mimbar Indonesia* 5, 49 (1951): 3.
[72] Sugardo, *Tiongkok Sekarang* (Jakarta: Endang, 1953), pp. 66–77.
[73] *Sin Po*, 5 January 1957.
[74] *Hsin Pao*, 1 November 1956.
[75] *Hsin Pao*, 12 November 1956.
[76] *Hsin Pao*, 18 October 1956.

As a result of the attempt to project Indonesian expectations and ideals onto perceptions of China, the latter became politically loaded narratives subject to animated contestation. For one thing, Indonesians tended to focus selectively on specific aspects of China that offered contrasting characterizations to developments at home. This is why China's dominant image was imbued with recurring catchwords such as discipline, orderliness, people-orientation, leadership and dynamism, which were, after all, yet-to-be realized ideals at home. The intention and lens through which Indonesians appropriated China as a mirror and/or a political device further complicated the process. "The Chinese subjects" as seen through the rose-tinted spectacles could easily be misrepresented, intentionally or inadvertently. Disdain for "chaotic" democracy at home, for instance, was partly responsible for Indonesians' uncritical acceptance of China's New Democracy, whose representativeness was overstated in order to fit with the Indonesian ideal.

With respect to the interplay between culture and politics, Indonesians, especially those with anti-Communist persuasions, faced a central dilemma in presenting an idealized and promising picture of the PRC: how could they reconcile seemingly irreconcilable ideological differences and come to terms with favourable attitudes toward Communist China while upholding anti-Communist stances at home? How could they justify the call to adopt some of China's methods in a nationalist Indonesia? As I have demonstrated, one of the most effective and frequently used ways of circumventing this dilemma was systematically accentuating China's nationalistic and populist characteristics while downplaying its Communist features. Herein lies the central reason why people like Mohammad Hatta and Ramadhan K.H. repeatedly stressed that it was the hard work and discipline of the Chinese people — not the communist system — that were responsible for the country's rapid economic growth. In a similar vein, after visiting China in 1962, Sitor Situmorang came to conclude that what had been attained in China could also be realized in Indonesia, as long as there was sufficient discipline.[77]

Indonesians' ambivalent perceptions and conflicting presentations of China can be understood within the broad context of intellectuals' ambiguous responses to domestic sociopolitical transitions. Their discontentments and agonies were a key factor responsible in reinforcing the admiration for

---

[77] Cited in Harry Aveling, *A Thematic History of Indonesian Poetry: 1920 to 1974* (DeKalb, Illinois: Center for Southeast Asian Studies, Northern Illinois University, 1974), p. 50.

China's perceived success. On the other hand, many Indonesian intellectuals were educated and socialized in a predominantly Western cultural world prior to independence. The ideas of freedom and human rights constituted an integral component of their way of thinking. Although some Indonesian intellectuals might attribute their country's problems to a chaotic democracy, they were not prepared to give up freedom of expression, which was fundamental to a vibrant cultural life and their very survival as a social class. This attitude helped explain why some intellectuals were critical of China's restrictions on individual freedom and social regimentation while simultaneously hailing that country's economic progress as a potential model for Indonesia to emulate.

Many China observers were prominent political and cultural intellectuals whose overriding and ultimate concerns were geared toward understanding and solving problems at home. Differing domestic priorities and predispositions therefore shaped the different constructions of China. The contradictory reactions to the presence (or absence) of freedom in China is a case in point. For liberal intellectuals such as Trisno Sumardjo and Ramadhan K.H., freedom of expression was deemed to be of foremost importance. Their criticisms of China derived in no small part from contempt for its denial of the freedom of expression. In an editorial entitled "The Lessons of China", appearing in the *Indonesia Raya*, a newspaper associated with the PSI and under Mochtar Lubis's editorship, China represented something that Indonesia should not emulate: "To Indonesians the lesson from China is that people are not satisfied with just filling their stomachs; instead, they long for a free spirit. The authoritarian regime will fail eventually."[78] On the other hand, for some political intellectuals such as Sukarno, freedom of expression was secondary to political stability and control. Their perceptions of China would remain favourable despite an awareness that freedom of expression was severely restricted there. In the words of Sukarno, the rationale for placing "freedom from want" as the top priority in China was both convincing and acceptable: "Because the stomach does not wait."[79]

## Indonesian Lens and Chinese Mirror

Apart from the larger sociopolitical setting that shaped Indonesians' perceptions of China, their views were also moulded by the conceptual devices

---

[78] *Indonesia Raya*, 26 June 1957.
[79] Sukarno, *Marhaen and Proletarian* (Ithaca: Cornell University Indonesian Project, 1960 [1957]), pp. 19–20.

through which they saw that nation. When representing China, Indonesian commentators tended to employ specific concepts that were indigenous to their culture and easily understood by the public. I have already pointed out that a dominant image of China in the Sukarno era was that of harmony and solidarity, whereby people's interests were duly represented by the government and its leaders. This depiction of peaceful and orderly China contrasted with both theory and practice, which were based on the guiding principle of class confrontation and proletarian dictatorship. Part of the answer to the discrepancies between image and reality, I believe, lies in the utilization of an "Indonesian looking glass" in examining Chinese society and politics. Indonesians were inclined to employ concepts developed in their own historical and cultural settings to comprehend and judge the PRC, thus leading to potential misappropriations. Two cultural concepts were particularly pertinent: views of "the people" and "social harmony".

Herbert Feith has demonstrated that one of the main features of Indonesian thought was the tendency "to see society as undifferentiated", which led to inattention to "conflict between ethnic groups and virtually none to class conflict, except among the communists". With this propensity, "the people were commonly thought of as a whole, with leaders being duty bound to represent the interests of this whole".[80] This perspective of an undifferentiated society and people was prevalent. As William Frederick has pointed out, Indonesian writers held that "modern culture must represent society as a whole". Furthermore,

> They ardently sought a formula for assuring that their creation would mirror society as a whole. In particular, many insisted, the culture which they fashioned should mirror the *rakyat*, the common folk, for it was they who were intrinsically happy and good, and it was ultimately on them, therefore, that the nation and national culture must rely for its purest values.[81]

Intellectuals' inclination to see society as an undifferentiated entity and to identify themselves with "the people" constituted a central thrust of the "holistic perspective". This view displayed little concern for the

---

[80] Feith, "Introduction", in *Indonesian Political Thinking*, ed. Feith and Castles, pp. 18–9. See also Elson, *The Idea of Indonesia*, p. 155.

[81] William Frederick, "Dreams of Freedom, Moments of Despair: Armijn Pane and the Imagining of Modern Indonesian Culture", in *Imagining Indonesia: Cultural Politics and Political Culture*, ed. Jim Schiller and Barbara Martin-Schiller (Athens: Ohio University Research in International Studies Southeast Asia Series, 1997), pp. 56–7.

individual and showed "a marked preference for collective forms of social organization, a dislike of the profit motive and *enrichissez-vous*, and a notion of the ideal state as one which was organic and a source of personal meaning to its members".[82] This holistic perception was in turn a product of the country's historical and cultural tradition, which valued highly social harmony and solidarity. As Supomo, a prominent theoretician of the Indonesian state ideology, wrote succinctly in 1952,

> The traditional objective of the Indonesian community is to achieve harmony: harmony between individuals and groups, harmony between man and nature, and harmony in all fields of life. This traditional aim is the search for spiritual happiness, and the continuance of social happiness can be assured only within the harmony mentioned above.[83]

In his criticism of parliamentary democracy in 1955, Natsir opined: "In this Indonesia of ours there is no chance that any system based on the conflict of group with group or class with class will emerge. The system which meshes with *the Indonesian national mentality is harmony of life as a fixture*, but there is *gotong royong* [mutual assistance] as well."[84]

This perspective of an undifferentiated people and a harmonious society, therefore, served as a vital looking-glass through which Indonesians perceived China. This mindset was further reinforced by the elite's self-imposed task of morally and materially uplifting "the people" through the institutions of the government, which was central to social power.[85] It was this cherished view of social harmony that led many writers to identify with and romanticize the people's commune. This social institution seemed to have reflected at least partially some Indonesian dreams and ideals such as collectivism, harmony and the people's well-being. More specifically, this conceptual predisposition prompted many commentators to utilize their own culturally specific concepts to characterize China, such as the extensive use of *gotong royong* in reconstructing Chinese society in general and the village in particular,[86] in an attempt to accentuate social harmony and

---

[82] Feith, "Introduction", p. 19.
[83] Supomo, "The Question of Our Cultural Policy", *Indonesian Affairs* (Jakarta) 2, 1 (1952): 38.
[84] Cited in Elson, *The Idea of Indonesia*, p. 162. Emphasis is mine.
[85] Ibid., p. 155.
[86] See, for example, Arifin Bey, *Dari Sun Yat Sen ke Mao Tse Tung* (Jakarta: Tintamas, 1953), p. 172; Sugardo, *Tiongkok Sekarang*, pp. 11–4; Adinegoro, *Tiongkok: Pusaran Asia*, p. 102; and Asmudji, *Genderang Tiongkok Baru* (Bodjonegoro: Suara Pemuda, 1950), p. 4.

mutual cooperation. By characterizing and constructing China with such culturally bounded conceptions, Indonesians ignored or downplayed the potential for social conflict and class struggle that were both pronounced and fundamental to the PRC's ideology and policy.

## CONCLUSION

Indonesians' perceptions of China were formulated and constructed within the changing sociopolitical and intellectual environments at home. Public discontent and intellectual disillusionment played a significant part in shaping the largely affirmative images of China. The sense of frustration resulting from political instability, social confrontation and economic stagnation was a vital factor in explaining Indonesians' admiration for China, which was further taken to represent an antithesis. The discourses about China were, therefore, inseparable from the ongoing nation-building projects and their outcomes. Many commentators evoked an imagined China as a mirror for illustrating what had gone wrong at home. Furthermore, China entered the Indonesian scene at the time of an intensified search for a new political and cultural identity. The failure of Western-style democracy paved the way for seeking alternative, perhaps more authoritarian, means of governance. This timing and setting for China-imagining explained why there was a marked increase of writings and commentaries about the PRC in the mid-1950s when Indonesia was moving toward the end of constitutional democracy and crying out for a new socio-political system. The call to return to an (imagined) Oriental tradition, within which the new Indonesian identity was to be situated, further facilitated identification with China. Indonesians employed the PRC as a political device and a potential model for rejecting or validating domestic agendas. The political use of knowledge about China resulted in the transposition of Indonesian ideals into specifically reconstructed PRC images; it also led to the downplaying of China's Communist ideology and to the overstatement of its nationalistic and populist underpinnings. The incorporation of Indonesia's own cultural conceptions, such as "the undifferentiated people", reinforced the propensity to separating Communism from China. By creating China in their own image, in short, Indonesians transformed their perceptions of China into the China metaphor.

CHAPTER 6

# An "Inner China" and External PRC: The Ethnic and Diplomatic Dimensions

*Until my visit to China I have known China and the Chinese only from political, economic and social literature and from my own personal experience in Indonesia. The picture I have thus gained about the Chinese in general is that they are dirty, rude and a people fond of gambling and smuggling. The impression I gained from my visit to China on the other hand is that of a tidy, friendly and kind people.*

Mohammad Hatta (1957)[1]

*Maybe the Chinese in the PRC are not as rich as their compatriots living in Indonesia, but they dress neatly, whiten their teeth, and respect their hosts.*

Satya Graha (1960)[2]

---

[1] Mohammad Hatta, "Not Communism but Chinese Qualities Made People's China Rise", *Indonesian Spectator* (Jakarta), 1 December 1957, p. 10. In his conversation with the Chinese ambassador, Huang Zhen, on 6 August 1957, Foreign Minister Subandrio said that Hatta's understanding of China was "based upon writings by Russian exiles", which were biased. "Zhu Yindunixiya Shiguang Baohui Yinni Waizhang Subandeliyue tan Qian Fuzongtong Hada Fanghua Shi" [Report by the embassy in Indonesia concerning the talk with Indonesian foreign minister Subandrio on the visit to China by former vice president Hatta] (6 August 1957), file no. 105-00344-02, Archives of the Ministry of Foreign Affairs, PRC.
[2] *Suluh Indonesia*, 18 January 1960.

> *Southeast Asian countries have different views from the imperialists with respect to the questions of war and peace. We must strive to ensure their neutrality at the time of war and to prevent them from siding with the imperialists at the time of peace.*
>
> Zhou Enlai (1949)[3]

> *The Indonesian people can draw necessary lessons not only from their own experiences, but also from the experience of China.*
>
> Sha Ping (Hu Yuzhi) (1949)[4]

The preceding chapter has examined the close correlation between knowledge about China and specific problems facing Indonesia's postcolonial transition. Indonesians' perceptions of the PRC were shaped not only by the sociopolitical environment at home, but by a complex set of ethnic and diplomatic factors both internal and external to the country. The existence of more than two million ethnic Chinese residing locally presented an intricate circumstance in the making of China-images. Thanks in no small part to the intermediaries of local Chinese, Indonesians "experienced" China's presence at first hand, and they tended to compare, often unfavourably and harshly, Indonesian Chinese with their compatriots in the mainland. Meanwhile, ethnic Chinese were actively involved in formulating images of their ancestral homeland, which partly influenced indigenous Indonesians' attitudes toward that country.

As I have demonstrated, the making of the China metaphor was undertaken within a shifting milieu of Sino-Indonesian diplomatic relations between 1949 and 1965, which was characterized by both amity and confrontation against the backdrop of the Cold War and Sino-American confrontation. Throughout these years, China worked enthusiastically in trying to win Indonesians' hearts and minds. This effort was carried out simultaneously on two fronts. In Indonesia, Beijing attempted to create a favourable climate of opinion and presented its self-image directly or indirectly to the public. In China, the moulding of affirmative self-perceptions was implemented by impressing visiting Indonesians, who as a

---

[3] Zhou Enlai, "Women de Waijiao Fangzhen he Renwu" [Our foreign policy principles and tasks], in *Zhou Enlai Xuanji* [Selected writings of Zhou Enlai] (Beijing: Renmin Chubanshe, 1984), vol. 2, p. 90.

[4] Sha Ping (Hu Yuzhi), "Lessons from Indonesia", *China Digest* 5, 12 (1949): 5.

rule reported their observations of China through mass media such as newspapers and magazines to a broad audience at home. Formal and informal diplomacy, therefore, constituted a major context in shaping knowledge about China and its subsequent transition to the policy arena.

Not intending to undertake a thorough analysis of the Sino-Indonesian community in Indonesia or of Sino-Indonesian diplomacy during the Sukarno era, this chapter examines three interconnected issues: perceptions of China formulated by three different local Chinese sociocultural and political groups; indigenous Indonesians' views of the local Chinese and how the latter were projected onto China-images; and mechanisms and strategies of China's cultural and informal diplomacy and its implementation in Indonesia. This chapter concludes with observations on the multifarious interplay between ethnicity and the state in the making of the China metaphor.

## INDONESIAN CHINESE SOCIETY AND THE CONSTRUCTION OF IMAGES OF THE ANCESTRAL HOMELAND

The Chinese started migrating to the Indonesian archipelago as early as the first years of the Christian era. By the early 15th century, sizeable Chinese communities had emerged in different parts of the archipelago. With the coming of the Dutch after the end of the 16th century and the advent of colonialism, demand for Chinese labourers and middlemen increased dramatically. The inflow of immigrants continued until the end of the 1930s and led to the formation of two heterogeneous communities: "the *totoks* (literally, 'of pure blood') being those who had recently immigrated, spoke Chinese and were culturally oriented towards China, and the much older *peranakan* communities being characterized by the use of vernacular language for everyday purposes and by a distinctive set of cultural traits which were neither wholly Chinese nor wholly Indonesian".[5] It was estimated that in the mid-1950s there were around 2.45 million ethnic Chinese in the country (accounting for less than three per cent of the

---

[5] J.A.C. Mackie and Charles A. Coppel, "A Preliminary Survey", in *The Chinese in Indonesia: Five Essays*, ed. J.A.C. Mackie (Honolulu: University Press of Hawaii, 1976), p. 5.

nation's population, which numbered 97 million in 1961); among them were approximately 1.4 million *totoks*.⁶

Three major factors shaped Indonesian Chinese perceptions of their ancestral homeland: distinctions between the *totok* and the *peranakan*, ideological divergences, and differing views of Indonesian Chinese identity. In the first place, as can be expected, the *totok* tended to be China-oriented. According to G. William Skinner's survey of Chinese youth in urban Java conducted in the late 1950s, more than 80 per cent of the *totok* Chinese were either "strongly or moderately China-oriented". By contrast, over four-fifths of *peranakan* Chinese had weak or no China-orientation.⁷ Second, divided political loyalties between the Nationalist regime in Taiwan and Communist China played a part in shaping local Chinese perceptions of the PRC. After 1949, the KMT government devoted a great deal of energy to organizing and mobilizing its supporters abroad; much of this endeavour was concentrated in Indonesia. During the 1950s, KMT membership in that nation was the largest outside Taiwan, with 41,584 KMT members in 1950 and more than one-fifth being new recruits.⁸ It is not surprising, therefore, that approximately 30 per cent of Chinese residents were reportedly pro-KMT.⁹ The two governments' attempts at winning the hearts

---

⁶ G. William Skinner, "The Chinese Minority", in *Indonesia*, ed. Ruth McVey (New Haven, CT: HARF Press, 1963), pp. 97–117; and Twang Peck-yang, "Political Attitudes and Allegiances in the Totok Business Community, 1950–1954", *Indonesia* 29 (1979): 65–83. According to an internal report prepared by the Chinese embassy in Jakarta, there were 2.51 million Chinese living in the country in the early 1950s. See file no. 117-00265-01 (18–31 March 1953), Archives of the Ministry of Foreign Affairs, PRC. Another report prepared by the Chinese embassy in 1957, however, revealed that the number of the ethnic Chinese living in Indonesia was 2.15 million. See file no. 105-00704-03 (11–12 August 1960), Archives of the Ministry of Foreign Affairs, PRC.
⁷ G. William Skinner, *Communism and Chinese Culture in Indonesia: The Political Dynamics of Overseas Chinese Youth* (unpublished manuscript written in 1962, deposited at the Kroch Library, Cornell University), pp. 19–20.
⁸ James Chien-Chen Yang, "A Statistical Appraisal of Kuomintang's Overseas Movements in 1950–1963", paper presented at the International Conference "The Last Half Century of the Chinese Overseas (1945–1994): Comparative Perspectives", Hong Kong University, 19–21 December 1994.
⁹ Van Hassens, "The Campaign against Nationalist Chinese in Indonesia", in *Indonesia's Struggle, 1957–1958*, ed. B.H.M. Vlekke (The Hague: Netherlands Institute of International Affairs, 1959), p. 68.

and minds of local Chinese led to the so-called "dual structure in Indonesian Chinese society", whereby two sets of contending sociopolitical organizations, newspapers and other publications coexisted uneasily.[10] While pro-PRC organizations saw China in a profoundly affirmative light, the PRC's image presented by those pro-KMT Chinese was overwhelmingly negative. For example, an editorial in a major KMT-affiliated newspaper published in Jakarta asserted, "The PRC has become the Soviet Russia's satellite and been degenerated into slavery to the Slavic nation."[11]

The third and most important factor in shaping Indonesian Chinese views of China was their self-perceptions and changing identity, which in itself was a heatedly debated issue besetting many local Chinese. In an essay entitled "Our Dilemma", its author asked pointedly, "Do you feel Chinese first or Indonesian first? Do the Chinese government and the so-called pure Indonesians consider you as a Chinese first or as an Indonesian first?"[12] This identity dilemma was not only concerned with local Chinese self-perceptions, but also closely linked to their ambiguous attitudes toward the ancestral homeland and their land of domicile. Three strands of thought emerged in the polemics about Chinese identity during the 1950s and early 1960s: the overseas Chinese identity, the pluralist identity, and the assimilationist identity.[13] Each group formulated its own images of China

---

[10] "Perpetjahan dalam Masjarakat Tionghoa", *Star Weekly*, no. 378 (28 March 1953). On the CCP-KMT conflicts in Indonesia, from the perspectives of Beijing and Taipei respectively, see Zhu Lin, *Dashi Furen Huiyilu: Xiongyali, Yinni, Faguo, Meiguo* [Memoir of an ambassador's wife: Hungary, Indonesia, France and the USA] (Beijing: Shijie Zhishi Chubanshe, 1991); and Cai Weiping, "Zhu Yinni Gongzuo Huiyi" [Reflections of my work assignments in Indonesia], *Zhongguo yu Yinni* [China and Indonesia] (Taipei), no. 12 (1986): 49–58.

[11] *Tiangsheng Ribao Xuanji* [Selected editorials from the *Harian Thien Sung Yit Po*] (Jakarta: Harian Thien Sung Yit Po, 1951), pp. 75–6.

[12] Liem Wie Tiong, "Dilemma Kita", *Ta Hsueh Tsa Chih* [College Student Magazine] (Jakarta) 21, 4 (1953): 11–2.

[13] This classification is based upon Leo Suryadinata, ed., *Political Thinking of the Indonesian Chinese, 1900–1995: A Sourcebook* (Singapore: Singapore University Press, 1997). On the evolution of Indonesian Chinese society and debates on Indonesian Chinese identity in the postwar era, see Leo Suryadinata, *Pribumi Indonesians, the Chinese Minority and China*, 3rd ed. (Singapore: Heinemann Asia, 1992) and Mary Somers, "Peranakan Chinese Politics in Indonesia" (Ph.D. dissertation, Cornell University, 1965).

"Our Dilemma" — cover of *Ta Hsueh Tsa Chih* [College Student Magazine], 1951.

and projected them onto a wider audience, thus further complicating China-images in Indonesia.

**Overseas Chinese and the PRC Image**

To those who kept their PRC citizenship, China remained the motherland and ultimate subject of political loyalty and cultural identification. Considering themselves as sojourners and guests in Indonesia, they kept a distance from local politics. Nevertheless, they tried to attain the rights of a minority group and saw themselves as representatives of China, serving as "a bridge between Indonesia and the PRC".[14] This self-identity had a significant impact upon overseas Chinese perceptions of the homeland; they were proud of being PRC citizens and actively promulgated information concerning China's progress among the indigenous people. As Sung Chung-Ch'uang, president of the Ch'iao Tsung (The General Organization of Overseas Chinese) put it, "Their [overseas Chinese] hearts are with Peking." They were immensely impressed by "the significant achievements in the political, economic, and cultural fronts" of the new China, and "understand their motherland better and hence love their motherland more".[15] During the early 1950s, Chinese-language newspapers associated with Beijing frequently used catchwords such as "democracy, strength in unity, cooperation, united front" to describe that country.[16] An essay entitled "Cheers for the Motherland's Great Accomplishments" proudly proclaimed, "Since October 1, 1949, when Chairman Mao declared the PRC's founding, our great motherland has been like a rising sun, emitting indefinite light and heat".[17]

According to Soeto Tjan, a *totok* community leader, "Our great motherland has made glorious and amazing progress since the Liberation [in 1949]".[18] Some writers conceived that the founding of the PRC had transformed local Chinese from "overseas orphans" to "respected citizens

---

[14] "Overseas Chinese and the Round Table Conference" (1949), in Suryadinata, *Political Thinking*, p. 84.
[15] "Ten Years of the Ch'iao Tsung" (1962), in Suryadinata, *Political Thinking*, pp. 87–90.
[16] M.J. Meijer, "The Chinese in Indonesia" (unpublished working paper, 1953, deposited at the Kroch Library, Cornell University), pp. 33–8.
[17] *Seng Hwo Pao Xinnian Tekan* (Jakarta, 1953), p. 52.
[18] *Seng Hwo Pao Xinnian Tekan* (Jakarta, 1954), p. 30.

of a strong and rapidly growing new democratic nation".[19] They were now "the motherland's messengers", whose first and foremost responsibility was "to report all kinds of new developments in their motherland to the local populace". This "new task of transmitting up-to-date information regarding the PRC", a writer remarked, "can be carried out in the forms of reportage, translations, exhibitions, movies, theatre performance, even conversations with the indigenous".[20] This newfound sense of mission led to the portraying of China in a positive manner.

The example of Weng Fulin is a case in point.[21] Born in 1906 in Longyan, Fujian Province, Weng went to Indonesia at age 20 and developed personal and business connections with nationalists like Achmad Subardjo and Adam Malik, the future minister of foreign affairs and vice-president, respectively. After 1945, Weng was actively involved in overseas Chinese activities and became a leader of the pro-PRC organization, the Ch'iao Tsung. In early 1948 he founded Nanxin (Southern Star) Bookstore and Nanxin Motion Picture Company, importing books and movies from the mainland. In March 1951, as a result of the government's restrictive policy aimed at Chinese importers, Weng restructured his companies and renamed his bookstore as Rada Book Import and Export Corporation, which remained in the same location (Pintu Besar, Selatan 3A, Jakarta). Rasuna Said, a member of parliament from Sumatra, became the chairperson of its board while her husband, Barioen A.S., was appointed manager. Weng's motion picture company was renamed as the Mubarti Movie Importation Company during the 1950s, with Adam Malik taking charge of its daily operations. Through importation of books and films from

---

[19] *Yinhua Jinji* (Jakarta), no. 4 (1956), p. 61.

[20] Oey Tong Ping, "Cong Haiwai Guer dao Zhuguo Xinshi" [From overseas orphanages to messengers of the motherland] (1951), in his *Duangao Erji* [Short essays: Two collections] (Singapore: Island Cultural Publisher, 1993), pp. 466–7. I am grateful for Mr Oey (1923–), one of the most prolific writers in Indonesia, for providing me with his writings about the Chinese and China published between 1950 and 1965 and for granting me an interview in Singapore pertaining to the attitudes of the Indonesian Chinese toward China in the 1950s and 1960s.

[21] The information about Weng Fulin is based upon an interview with Weng Xihui in Guangzhou. As Weng Fulin's nephew, he is an Indonesian specialist who translated S. Rukiah's *Tandus* into Chinese during the 1960s. He is the author of an unpublished manuscript, "Yinni Aiguo Huaqiao Weng Fulin" [Weng Fulin, a patriotic overseas Chinese from Indonesia]; the abbreviated version of this manuscript appears in *Huaqiao Huaren Lishi Yanjiu*, 4 (1993).

the PRC, as well as publication of Indonesian writings about China (such as Barioen's influential *Melihat Tiongkok Baru*), Weng and his associates helped create a promising image of China. For example, Sukarno's personal assistant, Soeto Mei-sen, frequently visited Weng's bookstore in the mid-1950s to acquire books and magazines about China, to satisfy the president's wide-ranging interests in China's social, economic and political developments.[22]

## The Pluralists and the PRC Image

Represented predominantly by the *peranakan* who were closely associated with the BAPERKI (*Badan Permusjawaratan Kewarganegaraan Indonesia*, Consultative Council on Indonesian Citizenship), the pluralists held quite different views of Chinese identity and the PRC. Founded by Siauw Giok Tjhan in 1954, BAPERKI was modelled after the National Association for the Advancement of Colored People (NAACP) in the United States. Siauw maintained that Indonesian citizens of Chinese descent were already Indonesians and that the *peranakan* should be recognized as a *suku* (ethnic minority) of the nation. He was opposed to forced assimilation and favoured gradual integration of the Chinese into Indonesia.[23] The pluralists' attitudes toward China were less clearcut, however. On the one hand, their foremost task was to integrate ethnic Chinese into local society, a strategy that was essential for their survival in an independent and increasingly nationalistic Indonesia. For this reason, BAPERKI promoted local Chinese identification with the hostland while discouraging institutional associations and emotional affinities with the ancestral homeland. On the other hand, the PRC was an important external factor affecting the pluralists' destiny, partly because the issue of Indonesian Chinese nationality was dependent upon Beijing's readiness to negotiate with Jakarta.[24] Some

---

[22] Yuan Houchun, *Yige Canyu Chuangzao Lishi de Huaren — Situ Meisheng Chuanqi* [A Chinese who participated in the making of history: A biography of Soeto Mei-sen] (Beijing: Renmin Wenxue Chubanshe, 2006), p. 82.
[23] Suryadinata, *Political Thinking*, p. 91; Jacques Bertrand, *Nationalism and Ethnic Conflict in Indonesia* (Cambridge: Cambridge University Press, 2004), pp. 62–3.
[24] On the Indonesian Chinese citizenship issue and the Sino-Indonesian Dual Nationality Treaty of the 1950s, see Donald Willmott, *The National Status of the Chinese in Indonesia, 1900–1958* (Ithaca: Cornell Modern Indonesia Project, 1961), and Mochtar Kusuma Atmadia, "The Indonesian-Chinese Dual Nationality Treaty", *Indonesian Review of International Affairs* 1, 3/4 (1972–4): 36–53.

Over 20,000 Chinese in Jakarta celebrating the establishment of Sino-Indonesian diplomatic relationship, May 1950 [*Seng Hwo Pao Chuangkan Shizhounian Jiniankan, 1945–1955* (Jakarta, 1955)].

*peranakan* were absentee landlords who had properties and relatives in the mainland, causing them to be deeply concerned about developments in the PRC.

In an essay published in the *Star Weekly*, Khoe Woen Sioe described China as "Indonesia's largest neighboring country and a potentially large market." He commented, "We hope China will be strong. If it is strong it will be of some benefit to us. But let us not hinge our fate on China's strength or weakness."[25] A number of pro-Beijing *peranakan* were supportive of Mao's domestic policies in the early 1950s, pointing out that there was a star in the PRC flag for national capitalists and that New Democracy was not Communist.[26] The biweekly *Republik*, published by Siauw Giok Tjhan in Surabaya, covered extensively the PRC's domestic evolution, and produced large numbers of commentaries including reports by its own correspondents and translations from the mainland and foreign presses.[27] Many were favourable descriptions of, for example, New Democracy and socio-economic progress under Mao's leadership. Siauw came to know a great deal about China from Tan Kah Kee, a prominent overseas Chinese leader who was pro-Communist and was exiled in East Java during the Japanese occupation.[28] After visiting the United States and China in 1957, Siauw praised the former's "positive democracy" for having "encouraged people's contributions to society".[29] Like many indigenous intellectuals of the time, the pluralist *peranakan* Chinese were impressed by China's socio-economic progress. Tan Eng Tie, a Leiden-educated physician and a founding member of the BAPERKI, marvelled that within just three years China had been transformed from "a land of famine" to "a land of

---

[25] "The Persatuan Tionghua and Politics" (1949), in Suryadinata, *Political Thinking*, p. 98.

[26] William Skinner, *Report on the Chinese in Southeast Asia* (Ithaca: Cornell University Southeast Asia Program, 1951), pp. 70–1.

[27] For example, "Rakjat Tiongkok Membangun", *Republik* 1, 2 (1950); "Politik Ekonomi Tiongkok", *Republik* 1, 5 (1950); and "Perkembangan Demokrasi di Tiongkok Baru", *Republik* 1, 23 (1951).

[28] Siauw Tiong Djin, "Siauw Giok Tjhan: Perjuangan Seorang Patriot Membangun Nasion Indonesia dan Masyarakat Bhineka Tunggal Ika" (Ph.D. dissertation, Monash University, 1998). The Chinese translation of this dissertation appears as *Xiao Yucan Zhuan* [A biography of Siauw Giok Tjhan], trans. Lin Liushun and Zhou Nanjing (Hong Kong: Nandao Chubanshe, 2001), p. 49.

[29] *Sin Po*, 23 August 1957; *Sin Min*, 26 August 1957.

abundance". Sie Boen Lian, Sukarno's personal physician, shared the sense of optimism prevailing during the Great Leap Forward era: he was led to believe in 1958 that China would soon overtake Britain in industrial capacity and become the third-strongest economy in the world.[30]

In comparison with those overseas Chinese who remained PRC citizens, the pluralists viewed China with a greater sense of detachment. Unlike the *totok* Chinese who published mostly through Chinese-language venues with a predominantly ethnic readership, the *peranankan* wrote and debated about China in vernacular mass media such as *Sin Po* and *Star Weekly*, which were widely read and commented on by indigenous readers. The pluralists' views of China were therefore closely integrated into the knowledge production process relating to China in Indonesia.

## The Assimilationists' Image of the PRC

Mostly Western-educated, the assimilationists were mainly those *peranakan* associated with the LPKB (*Lembaga Pembinaan Kesatuan Bangsa*, the Institute for the Promotion of National Unity) founded in 1963. Central to their beliefs was the notion that the existence of racial discrimination in Indonesia could primarily be attributed to the local Chinese themselves, who tended to retain their group identity and segregate themselves from indigenous society, thus constituting a principal barrier to national unity. The only solution was total assimilation. As an assimilationist put it, "It is known that our 'Chineseness' is still strong while our 'Indonesianness' is still very weak."[31] Asserting that "Indonesia is free of racial prejudice, and it is free of religious prejudice",[32] Ong Hok Ham, a prominent *peranakan* writer and historian educated at Yale University, insisted that the only

---

[30] Tan Eng Tie, "Keadaan Makanan dan Agraris di Tiongkok", *Star Weekly*, no. 372 (14 February 1953), pp. 9–11; Sie Boen Lian, "Tiongkok Susul … Diri Sendiri", *Sin Tjun* 4 (1959): 127–9.

[31] Lauw Chuan Tho, "Why Should the Chung Hwa Hui and Similar Organizations be Dissolved" (1952), in Suryadinata, *Political Thinking*, p. 140. Major arguments of the assimilationist school can be found in *Lahirnya Konsepsi Asimilasi* (Jakarta: Yayasan Tunas Bangsa, 1977 [1962]).

[32] "The Case for Assimilation" (1960), in *Indonesian Political Thinking 1945–1965*, ed. Herbert Feith and Lance Castles (Ithaca: Cornell University Press, 1970), p. 349. See also Benny G. Setiono, *Tionghoa dalam Pusaran Politik* (Jakarta: Elkasa, 2003), pp. 727–30.

way out of racial discrimination was "assimilation or one hundred percent fusion. Thus the *peranakan* become 'indigenous' Indonesians".[33] This approach of total assimilation required not only changing Chinese names to Indonesian-sounding ones, but also dissolution of all ethnic Chinese organizations. "The Assimilation Charter" (1961) stated unambiguously, "assimilation means the entry and acceptance of individuals of Chinese descent into the single body of the Indonesian nation in such a way that the special group they have originally belonged to will eventually cease to exist".[34]

The assimilationists' self-perception and proposed remedy for eliminating racial discrimination was partially responsible for their negative views of China, which symbolized the "shadow of a foreign power" and constituted a major obstacle to total assimilation. Their criticisms of China were often accompanied by identification with and idealization of Indonesia. Thung Liang Lee presents a case in point. Born in Bogor and educated in London and Vienna, Thung had been deeply involved in both Chinese and Indonesian politics prior to 1945, including serving as the private secretary of Wang Jingwei (1883–1944), head of the puppet government set up by the Japanese in Nanjing in 1940. He was convinced in the 1950s that ethnic Chinese were fortunate to have found "a heaven of relative security and prosperity", after escaping from "the land of oppression and corruption". He was dismayed that many of his compatriots still remained "obsessed" with Chinese nationalism, an attitude that "hampered their outlook and hindered their political advancement". They failed to recognize that China "never wanted them; their aspirations were directed toward a China which, in actual fact, only exists as an idealization of a dream-world". He urged local Chinese to come to terms with reality — "China is a country ruled over by individuals who, having no heart for their own people and regarding them [overseas Chinese] only fit as objects of exploitation, can certainly have no sympathy and understanding for expatriates thousands of miles away."[35] Advocating "total assimilation" into

---

[33] "The Assimilation of the Peranakans" (1960), in Suryadinata, *Political Thinking*, p. 147.

[34] "The Assimilation Charter" (1961), in ibid., p. 152.

[35] Thung, "The Unreality of Chinese Nationalism in Indonesia: An Apologia and a Reorientation", *Indonesia Review* (Jakarta) 2, 1 (1954): 69–75. On Thung's political involvement in Indonesia and China, see Setiono, *Tionghoa Dalam Pusaran Politik*, p. 675.

local society, Thung declared unapologetically: "Our true fatherland is this country of Indonesia…. Our loyalty belongs to the Republic of Indonesia and it must be one and undivided."[36] Tan Eng-Kie, editor of the *Keng Po*, an influential Indonesian-language newspaper, shared much of Thung's critical views of China. Despite the fact that local Chinese had vested their hopes in the ancestral homeland and sent back millions of dollars, he opined, "China had disappointed us" and had done "nothing in return for us". Tan's condemnation of China was reinforced by his identification with Indonesia, where "no political discrimination" existed and "members of any minority group are welcomed by the major parties". Local Chinese, in short, should realize that "their living depends upon Indonesia and not upon China, a foreign country in every sense of the word".[37]

In brief, like the knowledge about China produced by indigenous Indonesians, the perceptions of the PRC formulated by local Chinese were intertwined with differing political, cultural and communal allegiances. China was, again, a site of contestation, simultaneously portrayed as the glorious motherland, a potential market and a land of oppression.

The discourses on Indonesian Chinese identity and the corresponding formation of conflicting images of the PRC contributed to the making of a China metaphor. The aforementioned debates were carried out in the vernacular mass media, through which Indonesians partially acquired their (mis)understandings of China. Moreover, knowledge about China was intimately intertwined with the changing political configuration, with the pluralists and assimilationists siding with different political forces. While those politically active overseas Chinese might support the PKI, the BAPERKI was increasingly backed by Sukarno, with the LPKB being linked closely with the army and right-wing intellectuals.[38] As will be detailed in the next two chapters, the blending of perceptions of China with changing cultural and racial politics during the closing years of the Sukarno regime had a profound impact on the country's future trajectory.

---

[36] Thung, "The Unreality of Chinese Nationalism in Indonesia", p. 74.
[37] Tan Eng Kie, "The Question of Minorities: A Hopeful View of a Present Problem", *The Atlantic Monthly* (Supplement, 1956): 61–4.
[38] On the complex relationship between Indonesian Chinese and political changes in the early 1960s, see Charles Coppel, *Indonesian Chinese in Crisis* (Kuala Lumpur: Oxford University Press, 1983); Setiono, *Tionghoa*, chapters 41–6; and Mary Somers, *Peranakan Chinese Politics*, pp. 224–81.

## BROTHERS OF DIFFERENT KINDS: INDONESIANS' PARADOXICAL VIEWS OF THE CHINESE

Indonesians' perceptions of China were inseparable from their views of local Chinese. As Armijin Pane put it, "In the past we tended to look at China through the medium of the Chinese living in our country".[39] According to Franklin Weinstein, who conducted extensive interviews with Indonesian foreign policy-makers during the late 1960s, "when asked what they thought about China, the foreign policy elite members frequently responded with comments on the Indonesian Chinese".[40] How, then, did Indonesians perceive ethnic Chinese at home and in the mainland? What was the relationship between these two sets of different but connected perceptions? I argue that Indonesians created contrasting types of Chineseness, praising the Chinese in the PRC while portraying their local compatriots in an unfavourable light. The construction of "brothers of different kinds" thus complicated the intriguing linkages between ethnicity and the state; the denigration of local Chinese reinforced, paradoxically, Indonesians' admiration for China and its people.

### Indonesian Views of Local Chinese

Throughout the Sukarno years, the indigenous (*pribumi*) views of the local Chinese, or non-*pribumi* (non-indigenous) as they were called during this period, were diverse, politically loaded and changing, partly reflecting the nature and characteristics of the country's post-independence transition.[41]

Indonesians were inclined to see the Chinese as an undifferentiated entity, despite the fact that there existed profound social and cultural

---

[39] *Hsin Pao*, 31 October 1951.
[40] Franklin Weinstein, *Indonesian Foreign Policy and the Dilemma of Dependence: From Sukarno to Soeharto* (Ithaca: Cornell University Press, 1976), p. 120.
[41] Rizal Sukma suggests that there at least five major stereotypes of the Chinese widely held by the majority of Indonesians: (1) that the ethnic Chinese are a separate *bangsa* (race, nation); (2) the privileged position of the Chinese enabled this group to establish its position as a powerful economic force in the country; (3) the discriminatory social structure during the colonial era created a deep social gap between the Chinese community and the *pribumi* Indonesians; (4) that the Chinese are changeless; and (5) the Chinese minority is an ethnic group whose concerns rest only with their own safety and economic well-being. Sukma, *Indonesia and China: The Politics of a Troubled Relationship* (London: Routledge, 1999), pp. 56–7.

differences within this ethnic group. As Mohammad Hatta admitted, a majority of Indonesians found it difficult to distinguish the *totoks* from the *peranakans*.[42] Feelings of distrust and animosity toward the Chinese, though not always justifiable, prevailed through much of the 20th century. Historically, the Chinese were seen as a tool of Dutch colonialism. In the words of Hatta, they represented "a continuation of foreign capitalism in Indonesian society". The indigenous people were particularly resentful of the perceived fact that "under different colonial regimes the Chinese were always on the top, enjoying superior economic status".[43] Economically, the Chinese were accused of controlling and manipulating the local economy. In 1956, a prominent member of the PNI declared in parliament, "My party does not want the economy of this country to be controlled by an exclusive group which only looks after its own interests in an egoistic and materialistic manner."[44]

Politically, local Chinese were depicted as opportunists lacking loyalty to their host nation. Abu Hanifah, minister of education and culture in 1950, stated bitterly, "These Chinese were always loyal either to the Dutch or to their homeland, China. They had no sense of loyalty toward the country which fed them or to its inhabitants."[45] Some foreign policy elite even went so far as to allege that the local Chinese had reversible portraits hung in their walls at home, with Mao Zedong on one side and Chiang Kai-shek on the other.[46] Responding to the complaints (on the recurring robberies and killings of local Chinese) made by the PRC consul in an official meeting in 1951, a director of the Asian Bureau of the Indonesian

---

[42] Hatta, "Warganegara Indonesia Turunan Tionghoa", *Star Weekly*, no. 578 (26 January 1957), pp. 2–4; and Z.M. Hidajat, *Masyarakat dan Kebudayaan Cina di Indonesia* (Bandung: Tarsito, 1977), p. 101.

[43] Hatta, "Message to the Chinese Group Conference", in his *Portrait of a Patriot: Selected Writings* (The Hague: Mouton, 1972), p. 472; Hatta, "Warganegara Indonesia Turunan Tionghoa".

[44] Cited in Hassens, "Campaigns against the Nationalist Chinese in Indonesia", p. 69.

[45] Hanifah, *Tales of a Revolution* (Sydney: Angus and Robertson, 1972), p. 253. It should be pointed out that Indonesian Chinese contributed to the Indonesian revolution and nation-building. See, for example, Twang Peck Yang, *The Chinese Business Elite in Indonesia and the Transition to Independence, 1940–1950* (Kuala Lumpur: Oxford University Press, 1998); and Hong Liu, "Social Capital and Business Networking: A Case Study of Modern Chinese Transnationalism", *Southeast Asian Studies* (Kyoto University) 39, 3 (2001): 357–81.

[46] Weinstein, *Indonesian Foreign Policy and the Dilemma of Dependence*, p. 121.

Ministry of Foreign Affairs bluntly attributed these incidents to the victims: "When the Japanese came, the Chinese became close to them; when the Dutch returned, the Chinese befriended them. Moreover, the Chinese tended to overcharge their customers, further leading to Indonesians' discontent."[47] Some Indonesians regarded ethnic Chinese as a threat to national security, and military leaders believed that they could become intermediaries through which China and the PKI influenced domestic politics. A high-ranking army officer told foreign correspondents in 1957: "We must force the Chinese to take Indonesian names and citizenship. If we are going to fight anyone, it will not be the Americans. It will be the Chinese."[48]

Although these anti-Chinese statements were made primarily for political scapegoating and enhancing certain indigenous groups' own agendas in the name of nationalism, the existence of enduring and widespread stereotypes did reveal profound distrust toward the local Chinese among the indigenous elite and public; it also reflected the precarious and marginal position of the Chinese in the country's political system. They were often considered as "the other" in much social and cultural discourse, thus becoming easy targets of violence.[49] The prevailing negative attitudes facilitated the frequent outbreak of anti-Chinese activities during the Sukarno years, including the 1956 Assaat Movement, aiming at eliminating Chinese economic influence, as well as the 1959–60 and 1963 anti-Chinese riots in Java.[50]

Despite the prevailing anti-Chinese sentiment, a small number of indigenous Indonesians were critical of their fellow countrymen's anti-Sinicism and came to the defence of ethnic Chinese. Iwan Simatupang, a

---

[47] "Zhu Yindunixiya Shiguan Yijiuwuyi Nian Waijiao Huitan Jiyao Huibian" [Records of diplomatic meetings of the PRC embassy in Indonesia in 1951], file no. 118-00399-01, Archives of the Ministry of Foreign Affairs, PRC.

[48] Cited in Hassens, "Campaigns", p. 70; a similar view was expressed in Adiputra, "Overseas Chinese dan Indonesia", *Mimbar Indonesia* 6, 30 (1952): 8, 27.

[49] Jacques Bertrand, *Nationalism and Ethnic Conflicts in Indonesia* (Cambridge: Cambridge University Press, 2004), pp. 62–5; Asvi Warman Adam, "The Chinese in the Collective Memory of the Indonesian Nation", *Kyoto Review of Southeast Asia* (March 2004) <http://kyotoreview.cseas.kyoto-u.ac.jp/issue/issue2/index.html> [accessed 12 May 2009].

[50] For details about these anti-Chinese activities, see J.A.C. Mackie, "Anti-Chinese Outbreaks in Indonesia, 1959–1968", in *The Chinese in Indonesia*, ed. Mackie, pp. 77–138.

prominent liberal intellectual, faulted the anti-Chinese pamphlet *The Chinese Problem in Indonesia* as being oversimplified and biased. He criticized its author, A.J. Muaja, for exaggerating Chinese influence over the economy and for failing to view their place in a historical context.[51] Buyung Saleh, a writer associated with Lekra, contended that the so-called Chinese problem was a historical legacy. By documenting their cultural and economic contributions to the country, he advocated the unification of indigenous Indonesian and ethnic Chinese.[52] At the height of anti-Chinese sentiments in 1960, Pramoedya wrote and published a 200-page book entitled *The Chinese in Indonesia*, providing a thorough and passionate account of their significant contributions to the nation's social, cultural and economic developments, concluding that the ethnic Chinese should be treated as Indonesians' "comrades-in-arms".[53] This book, however, was banned shortly after its publication and Pramoedya was jailed for nine months because of his sympathetic attitudes toward the Chinese.

## Intriguing "Chineseness"

The preceding pages have shown that indigenous Indonesians' attitudes toward local Chinese were largely disparaging and unfavourable. We may recall that many Indonesians attributed the PRC's socio-economic progress to Chinese characteristics such as loyalty, discipline, collectivism and work ethic. How do we account for the considerable discrepancy between Indonesians' admiration for the Chinese in the mainland and their vilification of local Chinese? What was the implication of these seemingly

---

[51] See Simatupang's review of A.J. Muaja's *The Chinese Problem in Indonesia*, in *Indonesia* 10, 10 (1959): 469–73.

[52] Buyung Saleh, "Yindunixiya de Shaoshu Mingzu Wenti" [Minority problems in Indonesia], *Nanyang Wenti Ziliao Yicong* 3 (1957): 35–7; and "Yindunixiya Huayi Gongmin Dui Yindunixiya Xiandai Wenhua de Gongxian" [Contributions of the ethnic Chinese to the development of modern Indonesian culture], *Nanyang Wenti Ziliao Yicong* 4 (1957): 94–8. The original Indonesian version of this essay appeared in a Jakarta magazine in 1957.

[53] Pramoedya Ananta Toer, *Hoakiau di Indonesia* (Jakarta, 1960), Setiono, *Tionghoa*, pp. 793–4. Pramoedya's book was republished in 1998 in Jakarta after the fall of Suharto. See more details in Hong Liu, Goenawan Mohamad and Sumit Kumar Mandal, *Pram dan Cina* (Jakarta: Komunitas Bambu, 2008). The English translation of Pramoedya's book (by Max Lane) is published as *The Chinese in Indonesia* (Singapore: Select Books, 2008).

contradictory interpretations of "Chineseness" upon Indonesian perceptions of China?

It has been suggested that Indonesians projected negative views of ethnic Chinese onto their perception of China, leading to unfavourable images of the PRC.[54] This line of analysis, however, misses the multifaceted and intriguing connections between the two sets of images and their divergent sociopolitical contextualization. The nation's prevailing anti-Chinese sentiment was in no small part generated by economic competition, cultural distrust and religious confrontations. It was also a symbol of political instability; as J.A.C. Mackie points out perceptively, "the fact that outbreaks of violence have occurred more frequently in Indonesia than in other plural societies of Southeast Asia may tell us more about the limitations of the government authority in Indonesia in the turbulent aftermath of the revolution than it does about the intensity of anti-Chinese feeling there".[55]

Indonesian perceptions of China, on the other hand, were constructed and presented as a kind of political discourse for confronting a series of profound sociopolitical and cultural problems emerging in the nation-building process. In other words, attitudes toward local Chinese as an ethnic group and China as a nation-state were formulated with different sets of reference points — while the former was shaped by long-standing stereotypes and internal racial politics, the latter was conditioned by Indonesians' preconceptions about the country's tumultuous postcolonial transformation. Indigenous writers' criticisms of local Chinese did not automatically lead to the formation of anti-China sentiments; on the contrary, the unfavourable portrayal of local Chinese buttressed hopeful images of China. In other words, Indonesians' anti-Chinese feelings were partially responsible for the idealization of China and its people; their praise for the mainland Chinese was generated in part by disdain for local Chinese. Herein lies the central reason why Indonesians' admiration for

---

[54] See, for example, Carl Taylor, "Indonesian Views of China", *Asian Survey* 3, 3 (1963): 165–72; Peter Hauswedell, "The Anti-Imperialist International United Front in Chinese and Indonesian Foreign Policy 1963–1965: A Study of Anti-Status Quo Politics" (Ph.D. dissertation, Cornell University, 1976), pp. 176–83; Lie Tek Tjeng, "The Sinic East Asia Image in Southeast Asia as Seen from Jakarta", *Korean Journal of International Studies* 14, 4 (1983): 381–90; and Sukma, *Indonesia and China*, pp. 56–8.
[55] Mackie, "Anti-Chinese Outbreaks", p. 77.

the Chinese in the PRC was often accompanied by condescending remarks about local Chinese; it also helps explain the simultaneous existence of anti-Chinese riots amidst largely amiable perceptions of China.

After returning from China in the early 1950s, Sugardo was overwhelmed by the Chinese people's way of "placing social well-being above individual interests", but he emphatically pointed out that they were very much different from local Chinese, who "came here only for the purpose of making money and damage their motherland's reputation".[56] H.A. Aziz, editor-in-chief of the *Surabaya Post*, observed, "I had been abroad for eight times and this trip to China was the most fulfilling one. The Chinese have shown, in every small detail of their daily life, politeness, modesty, and sincerity, which is a striking contrast to the Chinese I know in Southeast Asia."[57] Reflecting upon his China trip in 1957, Hatta commented: "The picture I have thus gained about the Chinese in general [before visiting China] is that they are dirty, rude and a people fond of gambling and smuggling. The impression I gained from my visit to China on the other hand is that of a tidy, friendly and kind people."[58] One of his associates told his Chinese host, "a big headache for the Indonesian government is how to deal with Dutch and Chinese capitalists, and we hope the PRC government could regularly advise Indonesian Chinese that they should learn from the example of their compatriots in the mainland".[59] Satya Graha, who had proposed enthusiastically learning from the people's commune, noted pointedly in 1960, "Maybe the Chinese in the PRC are not as rich as their compatriots in Indonesia, but they dress neatly, whiten their teeth, and respect their hosts."[60] During a trip to China in the late 1950s, Rasuna Said, president of the Indonesian-China Friendship Association, commended Chinese people for their high spirit in serving the nation. This affirmative comment, however, was followed by a blunt remark: "It would be ideal if the Chinese in Indonesia could be replaced by the

---

[56] Sugardo, *Tiongkok Sekarang* (Jakarta: Endang, 1953), p. 5.
[57] *Hsin Pao*, 22 May 1956.
[58] Mohammad Hatta, "Not Communism but Chinese Qualities Made People's China Rise", *Indonesian Spectator* (Jakarta), 1 December 1957, p. 10.
[59] "Yindunixiya Qian Fuzongtong Hada Fanghua Jiedai Jianbao" [Briefing about former vice president of Indonesia Hatta's visit to China, no. 5] (13 October 1957), file no. 204-00046-04, Archives of the Ministry of Foreign Affairs, PRC.
[60] *Suluh Indonesia*, 18 January 1960.

PRC Chinese". A local Chinese community leader admitted that thousands of indigenous people would echo her view.[61]

The previous chapters have documented admiring attitudes toward the PRC held by Ruslan Abdulgani, foreign minister in the mid-1950s. His view of the local Chinese, however, was surprisingly negative, as he opined in an interview in June 1957: "The overseas Chinese are concerned only with profits ... It is only material considerations that count with them; they are without any spiritual or political convictions".[62] In late 1959, his successor, Subandrio, rejected Beijing's statement that overseas Chinese had made significant contributions to Indonesia, and asserted that they were essentially "capitalists and monopolists" who did not deserve Beijing's protection. He proclaimed in his letter to Chinese Foreign Minister Chen Yi, "I should like to emphasize that the Chinese community in Indonesia does not have the same character and behavior as the socialist community in China, while its activities do not conform with the socialist policy of the government of the People's Republic of China."[63]

In sum, there existed two radically different kinds of Chinese in the Indonesian public perception and imagination; while the mainland Chinese were lavishly praised for their discipline, hard work, loyalty and altruism, local Chinese were viewed harshly and unfavourably for lacking any of these characteristics. As I have suggested in previous chapters, the intention to employ knowledge about China as a reflective devise and a viable model became a major rationale for Indonesians' tendency to disassociate Communism from China. By presenting the PRC Chinese as a favourable antithesis to their "distrusted" local compatriots, Indonesian writers reinforced the assumption that it was the "good" Chinese character instead of Communism that made China's socio-economic success possible. This is the key reason why an "Inner China" — symbolized by the existence of nearly 2.5 million ethnic Chinese — was an indispensable component in Indonesian discourses about China and, furthermore, the making of the China metaphor.

---

[61] Hong Yuanyuan [Ang Goan Jan], *Hong Yuanyuan Zizhuan* [An autobiography of Ang Goan Jan], trans. Liang Yingming (Beijing: Zhongguo Huaqiao Chuban Gongsi, 1989), pp. 231–3.
[62] Cited in Robert Elson, *The Idea of Indonesia: A History* (Cambridge: Cambridge University Press, 2008), p. 176.
[63] *Antara News Bulletin*, 14 December 1959.

## SINO-INDONESIAN DIPLOMATIC RELATIONS AND THE MAKING OF THE CHINA METAPHOR

Indonesians' perceptions of China were formulated and presented against the backdrop of a changing diplomatic relationship between the two nations. As a vital context for the construction of knowledge about the People's Republic and for relevant discourses in Indonesia, this relationship helped define and shape the characteristics of China as a site of political contestation and cultural imagination. While this study is not primarily concerned with Sino-Indonesian diplomatic history *per se*, it is necessary briefly to examine how diplomacy, both formal and informal, had an impact upon the making of China perceptions in Sukarno's Indonesia.

Sino-Indonesian diplomatic relations between 1949 and 1965 were characterized by recurring cycles of amity and enmity. In January 1950, Mohammad Hatta, then prime minister and minister of foreign affairs, expressed his government's intention to establish diplomatic ties with China. He suggested that, because the PRC was founded prior to the Republic of Indonesia, Beijing should recognize Jakarta first.[64] On January 26, Mao Zedong cabled Liu Shaoqi (acting chairman of the People's Government) from Moscow during his state visit to the Soviet Union, requesting him to undertake some preparatory work on establishing a diplomatic relationship.[65] Zhou Enlai, premier and minister of foreign affairs, agreed in May 1950 to send Wang Renshu (alias Ba Ren) as the first ambassador to Jakarta. Born in Zhejiang province in 1900 and having joined the Communist Party before the Pacific War, Wang was known as a writer who was in exile in Sumatra and expelled by the Dutch because of his participation in the anti-Dutch movement during the 1945–49 Revolution. Prior to this appointment, he served as deputy director of the Second Bureau of the Ministry of United Fronts. Upon arriving in Jakarta,

---

[64] *Merdeka*, 29 March 1950. On the evolution of Sino-Indonesian relationship, see David Mozigo, *Chinese Policy toward Indonesia, 1949–1967* (Ithaca: Cornell University Press, 1976); Ide Anak Agung Gde Agung, *Twenty Years Indonesian Foreign Policy 1945–1965* (Yogyakarta: Duta Wacana University Press, 1990), pp. 408–43; and Sukma, *Indonesia and China*, pp. 16–43.
[65] "Jiu Zhongguo Yindunixiya Jianjiao Shi Mao Zedong Zidian Liu Shaoqi" [Mao Zedong cabled Liu Shaoqi pertaining to the establishment of Sino-Indonesian diplomatic relations] (26 January 1951), file no. 105-00003-07, Archives of the Ministry of Foreign Affairs, PRC.

Wang actively sought local Chinese support and called for establishing a United Front among overseas Chinese.[66] He wrote and published an essay criticizing Sukarno and the Indonesian government, which was later found out despite his use of a pseudonym.[67] This action partially led to Jakarta's suspicion of the PRC's intentions and to a strained diplomatic relationship. In the early years of the global Cold War confrontation, especially during the Sukiman cabinet period (May 1951–March 1952), America forged close ties with Indonesia. As Secretary of State Dean Acheson put it, "the importance of keeping Indonesia in the anti-Communist camp is of greater and greater importance. The loss of Indonesia to the Communists would deprive the United States of an area of the highest political, economic and strategic importance".[68] The anti-Communist cabinet under Mohammad Natsir even refused to turn over the embassy building of nationalist China to Wang Renshu, who was only permitted to set up his office in the Hotel des Indes.[69] The Sino-Indonesian relationship reached its nadir when Wang was declared *persona non grata* because of his public anti-American statements; he was subsequently recalled back to Beijing in late 1951.

---

[66] "Wozhu Yinni Shiguan Dashi Wang Renshu zai Huaqiao Huanyinghui shang de Yenjianggao' [Text of speech by Ambassador Wang Renshu in the welcome party hosted by overseas Chinese] (1 August 1950), file no. 105-00070-05, Archives of the Ministry of Foreign Affairs, PRC.

[67] In his letter to Hatta dated on 31 May 1951, Zhou Enlai introduced Wang Renshu as "a man of letters" and noted that he had "resided in Sumatra from 1945 till 1947 and worked in the overseas Chinese community of East Sumatra". See "Guanyu Renmin Wang Renshu Wei Zhu Yinni Dashi de Liangguo Zongli Hanjian ji Youguan Wenjian" [Communications between the two premiers on the appointment of Wang Renshu as China's ambassador to Indonesia] (26 May–9 June 1950), file no. 105-00003-05, Archives of the Ministry of Foreign Affairs, PRC. On the life and career of Wang Renshu, see Zhou Nanjing, ed., *Baren yu Yindunixiya* [Ba Ren and Indonesia] (Hong Kong: Nandao Chubanshe, 2001), especially the section on "Chronicle of Ban Ren (1948–52)", pp. 374ff. According to Wang's personal and confidential files (*dangan*), "From August 1950 to January 1952, I was ambassador to Indonesia … However, because I lacked discipline and was not following closely the established protocols, I made some mistakes. As I did not master policies well, I was often criticized by the Ministry of Foreign Affairs … I subsequently asked to be reassigned and sent back home". Ibid., p. 400.

[68] Quoted from Robert J. McMahon, *The Limits of Empire: The United States and Southeast Asia since World War II* (New York: Columbia University Press, 1999), p. 49.

[69] Cheng Hsueh-chia, *Whither Indonesia? PKI and CCP* (Taipei: Asian People's Anti-Communist League, 1960), p. 15.

Indonesian policy toward China underwent significant changes after 1953. The PNI-dominated cabinet under Ali Sastroamidjojo implemented a "neutral and active" foreign policy, which distanced itself from the Western bloc. In August 1953, Arnold Mononutu, a veteran revolutionary and former minister of information, was dispatched as the first ambassador to Beijing.[70] Huang Zhen, a high-ranking general, was appointed the new ambassador to Jakarta in 1954, when China began actively building friendly relations with its Asian neighbours, symbolized by the introduction of the Five Principles of Peaceful Coexistence.[71] The 1955 Bandung Asian-African Conference represented a turning point in Sino-Indonesian diplomacy. Prime Minister Zhou Enlai's extraordinary performance and amiable personality won him (and China) widespread respect in Indonesia and other Asian-African nations.[72] Zhou refuted the claim that China might make use of the overseas Chinese as a means of intervening in their host nations' domestic affairs; instead, "China is trying to resolve the dual

---

[70] Arnold Mononutu, *Seorang Pejuang yang Berkarakter* (Jakarta: Gunung Agung, 1980), and R. Nalenan, *Arnold Mononutu: Potret seorang Patriot* (Jakarta: Gunung Agung, 1981), pp. 217–25. According to the letter of credential provided by the Indonesian Ministry of Foreign Affairs, Mononutu was born in 1898 in Manado, North Celebes. After receiving preliminary education in Indonesia, he studied at the College of Commerce in Holland and Leiden University, in addition to reading political science in Paris. He was a French-language lecturer in a Jakarta college and became in 1946 the chief editor of the daily newspaper, *Menara Merdeka* [Tower of Independence] in Jakarta. He was vice-chairman of the Parliament of the East Indonesian State in 1949 and subsequently appointed Minister of Information of the Republic of Indonesia. "Yindunixiya Zhuhua Dashi Chengti Guoshu Cailiao ji Yinni Jiankuan" [Indonesian ambassador submitting credential and brief notes about Indonesia] (18–21 March 1953), file no. 117-00265-01, Archives of the Ministry of Foreign Affairs, PRC.
[71] The five principles include (1) mutual respect for sovereignty and territorial integrity, (2) non-aggression, (3) non-interference in other countries' internal affairs, (4) equal and mutual benefit, and (5) peaceful coexistence. For background on China's changing policies, see Chen Jian, "China and the Bandung Conference: Changing Perceptions and Representations", in *Bandung Revisited: The Legacy of the 1955 Asian-African Conference for International Order*, ed. See Seng Tan and Amitav Acharya (Singapore: NUS Press, 2008), pp. 132–59.
[72] On Zhou Enlai's performance in Bandung, see Ruslan Abdulgani, *The Bandung Connection: The Asian-African Conference in Bandung in 1955* (Singapore: Gunung Agung, 1981); George Kahin, *The Asian-African Conference, Bandung, Indonesia, April 1955* (Ithaca: Cornell University Press, 1956); and G.V. Ambekar and V.D. Divekar, eds., *Documents on China's Relations with South and South-East Asia (1949–1962)* (Bombay: Allied Publishers, 1964).

Zhou Enlai in Bandung, 1955 [Lembaga Persahabatan Indonesia-Tiongkok, *Perkenalan Lembaga Persahabatan Indonesia-Tiongkok* (Jakarta: Rada, 1956)].

nationality problem."[73] As Zhou conceded to his colleagues in Beijing in 1957, "The new China has not just stood up, but also become increasingly stronger as a major power in Asia. People [in other Asian countries] are afraid of dual nationality, and we have come to realize this after visiting countries such as India and Burma."[74]

To win Indonesians' hearts and minds and to dilute their suspicions of the ethnic Chinese, Beijing had to act swiftly and firmly in establishing

---

[73] "Zhou Enlai Zongli zai Yafei Huiyi Quanti Huiyi shang de Buchong Fayan" (1955) [Supplementary speech by Premier Zhou Enlai in the Asian-African Conference (1955)], in *Zhonghuarenmin Guoheguo Wenjianji, 1954–1955* [Documents of the People's Republic of China, 1954–1955] (Beijing: Shijie Zishi Chubanshe, 1958), p. 251.

[74] Cited in Xia Liping, "Zhou Enlai de 'Danyi Guoji' Shixiang Yanjiu" [A study of Zhou Enlai's thought on single nationality], *Waijiao Pinglun* [Review of Foreign Affairs] 102 (2008): 11–7.

the state's supremacy in defining the national interest, leading to "essentially China-centred" overseas and foreign policies, with the latter taking the unchallenged priority.[75] The fundamental shift in the PRC's policy toward overseas Chinese was manifested in the Sino-Indonesian Treaty on Dual Nationality, signed during the Bandung Conference in April 1955. The treaty made it clear that dual nationals should have the right to choose freely between two nationalities, thus signalling the end of the PRC's claim to all overseas Chinese nationals (if they opted for local citizenship). In the second half of the 1950s, further policies to remove the overseas Chinese problem from the PRC's relations with Southeast Asia were implemented; these included strong official advocacy that overseas Chinese should choose local nationality and that Chinese nationals should not interfere in local politics.

The signing of the Dual Nationality Treaty paved the way for the improvement of diplomatic relations. President Sukarno's state visit to the PRC in October 1956 symbolized Indonesia's increasingly friendly policy toward the People's Republic. By 1957, trade between the two countries had increased by a dramatic 2,500 per cent, and Jakarta and Beijing began to forge mutual support and collaboration on a wide range of international matters.[76]

The Sino-Indonesian conflict in 1959–60 concerning the overseas Chinese issue cast a dark shadow over this cordial diplomatic relationship. In May 1959, Minister of Trade Djuanda announced the presidential decree, or PP10, stipulating that, from the following January, alien retail traders would be banned in the countryside; this affected at least 300,000 Chinese. This policy was accompanied by a series of regulations issued by military commanders in Java, forcing the Chinese to move into cities and towns. Beijing intervened on behalf of its citizens by protesting against the new regulations and repatriating 119,000 Chinese back to China.[77]

However, China dealt with this confrontation by downplaying its importance and by highlighting the common causes bonding the two

---

[75] Stephen Fitzgerald, *China and the Overseas Chinese: A Study of Peking's Changing Policy, 1949–1970* (Cambridge: Cambridge University Press, 1972), pp. 74–91.
[76] Sukma, *Indonesia and China*, p. 26.
[77] The anti-Chinese move was mainly instigated by the army leadership; the PP10 was announced when Sukarno was abroad. Sukarno actually attempted to defend the Chinese against heavy pressure from the army and Muslim parties. See Fitzgerald, *China and the Overseas Chinese*, pp. 145–7, Siauw Tiong Djin, *Siauw Giok Tjhan*, p. 212; Setiono, *Tionghoa*, pp. 792–3; and M.C. Ricklefs, *A History of Modern Indonesia since c. 1200*, 3rd ed. (Basingstoke: Palgrave, 2001), p. 324.

countries together, an indication that China placed its national interests well above the diaspora's interests.⁷⁸ Foreign Minister Chen Yi told Indonesian journalists in August 1960: "We are willing to maintain friendship with Indonesia, *the overseas Chinese problem is just a minor issue* and we hope it will not become bigger ... Our common cause of anti-imperialism and anti-colonialism is a main concern for us".⁷⁹ The two countries resumed close ties immediately after Beijing made some concessions on the issue of overseas Chinese citizenship in 1961. "The overseas Chinese problem is *a small matter in the relationship between our two countries*", Chen Yi told Sukarno, who was visiting Beijing in March 1961, "And it has been resolved now." Sukarno responded that he was in full agreement with this view.⁸⁰

In the final years of the Sukarno regime (1963–65), China and Indonesia forged a symbolic alliance in "the struggle against imperialism and neo-colonialism", known as the Jakarta-Peking Axis, officially declared in Sukarno's Independence Day speech in August 1965. This radical international anti-status-quo united front, however, was unstable and short-lived; it was completely broken up after the 30 September 1965 movement. Alleging that Beijing was behind the plot to overthrow the government, the new Suharto military regime froze the diplomatic relationship with China in 1967; it was not restored until 1990.⁸¹

---

⁷⁸ For a more detailed analysis of the complex interplay between diplomacy and the diaspora in the context of Sino-Indonesian relationship, see Hong Liu, "An Emerging China and Diasporic Chinese: Historicity, State and International Relations", *Journal of Contemporary China* 20, 71 (2011).

⁷⁹ "Yindunixiya Shibao Jizhe he Renmin Ribao Jizhe Fanhua Jianbao" [Briefing on the China visit by journalists from *The Indonesian Times* and *Harian Rakjat*] (1–23 August 1960), file no. 105-00985-03, Archives of the Ministry of Foreign Affairs, PRC (emphasis added).

⁸⁰ "Chen Yi Fuzongli tong Yindunixiya Zhongtong Su Jianuo Huitan Jiyao" [Minutes of meeting between Vice Premier Chen Yi and President Sukarno of Indonesia] (31 March 1961), file no. 111-00339-13, Archives of the Ministry of Foreign Affairs, PRC (emphasis added).

⁸¹ Hauswedell, "The Anti-Imperialist International United Front". See also R. Howie, "Sino-Indonesian Relations, October 1965–April 1967" (Ph.D. dissertation, University of London, 1968). For background on changing Chinese diplomatic policy in the early 1960s, see Niu Jun, "Yijiuliuer: Zhongguo Duiwai Zhengce 'Zuo' Zhuang de Qianye" [1962: Eve of a "left" turn in China's foreign policy], *Lishiyan Yanjiu* [Historical Research] 3 (2003).

Sukarno dancing with Marshal Chen Yi, Jakarta, 1961 (Photograph by Liu Qingrui, by permission of the Xinhua News Agency, ID: 12475489).

The changing Sino-Indonesian diplomatic relationship affected the production and dissemination of knowledge about China in the public sphere. Four different facets of interactions between diplomacy and perception-formation can be identified. In the first place, there were discrepancies between foreign policy-makers and public intellectuals in their attitudes toward the PRC in the early 1950s. Despite Jakarta's anti-China foreign policy, a number of leading intellectuals displayed genuine admiration for that country. Their favourable views of China were formulated primarily through visits to the People's Republic as private citizens. More than 300 Indonesians visited China in the early 1950s, while hundreds of prominent Indonesians attended China's National Day reception in the Jakarta embassy every year.[82] After returning home, many wrote and published positive accounts about China, which were read by a significant segment of the country's "political public". Armijn Pane, Barioen A.S., M. Tabrani and Kwee Kek Beng, for example, published their travelogues first in serialized form in the newspapers and then as books. The discrepancies between policy-makers and intellectuals in their attitudes toward the PRC demonstrated that, in an environment of free press and expression, perceptions of China could be conceived and presented independent of official diplomatic policy. The gradual emergence of pro-China views among the educated public might have been one of the main reasons leading to a more friendly government policy toward the PRC after the mid-1950s. Sukarno, for example, was very interested in the characteristics of the Chinese political system, described in detail in Barioen's *Melihat Tiongkok Baru* (Looking at the New China).[83]

Second, the improvement of Sino-Indonesian diplomatic relations between 1955 and 1959 created a conducive environment for the making and circulation of positive images of the PRC. The imagining of a nationalistic China converged nicely with Jakarta's nationalist turn in foreign policy. Domestically in Indonesia, it was a time of rapid transition when many established political practices were being challenged or phased out, prompting vigorous quests for alternative models of political and social development, especially from those nations facing similar problems of

---

[82] Zhu Qi, *Zhongguo he Yindunixiya Renmin de Youyi Guangxi he Wenhua Jiaoliu* [Friendship and cultural exchanges between the Chinese people and Indonesian people] (Beijing: Zhongguo Qingnian Chubanshe, 1956), p. 22. "Zhu Yindunixiya Shiguan Guanyi Qingzhu 1952 Nian Guoqing Kongzuo Zongjie" [Report of the embassy in Indonesia concerning the work of celebrating the National Day in 1952] (15 October 1952–26 January 1953), file no. 117-00214-03, Archives of the Ministry of Foreign Affairs, PRC.

[83] Interview with Soeto Mei-sen, Sukarno's personal interpreter and assistant in the 1950s and early 1960s.

nation-building and identity-formation. This confluence in turn generated an atmosphere within which the populist imagining of China could be easily comprehended and accepted. These years also saw a growing number of visitors to China, especially technical, professional and parliamentary delegations sponsored by the Indonesian government.[84] The noticeable increase reflected political and cultural intellectuals' intention to observe and learn from some of China's practices in the nation-building process. As will be demonstrated in the following two chapters, respectively, it was principally during this period that Indonesians started mingling perceptions of China with visions for their own nation, thus initiating the process of internalizing an external development model.

Third, the anti-Chinese movement in 1959–60 fostered the (re)emergence of negative and critical portrayals of China, especially by right-wing newspapers and magazines associated with orthodox Muslims and the army leadership. The anti-Chinese and anti-China rhetoric was often imbued with hidden domestic anti-Communist agendas. For example, the organ of the Masyumi Party, *Abadi*, implicated the PKI as a part of China's "expansionism".[85] The setback for China in 1959–60, nevertheless, was only temporary, and a positive China-image quickly reemerged. Shortly after settling the dispute on the overseas Chinese issue, an editorial in the centrist and nationalist newspaper, *Suluh Indonesia*, likened the two countries to "husband and wife":

> It seems to be the law-of-life that conflicts sometime happen between two close friends, like between husband and wife. This will come more to the fore should the husband and wife each have a strong personality. Such conflicts, however, will not bring about a break between two close friends or between husband and wife. On the contrary, their love for each other could grow stronger.[86]

Finally, from 1961 to 1965, China-images were predominantly conceived and presented within the framework of Indonesia's increasingly radical turn in both domestic and foreign policies. China's anti-imperialist image and the Sino-Indonesian alliance received overriding attention in

---

[84] *Sino-Indonesian Relations, 1950–1959 (Research Backgrounder)* (Hong Kong: Union Research Institute, 1960), pp. 75–8.
[85] Mackie, "Anti-Chinese Outbreaks".
[86] *Antara News Bulletin*, 29 March 1961 (originally in English).

the mass media. The convergence of China's public image with Indonesia's foreign policy took place against a backdrop of growing authoritarianism in domestic politics. The partial suppression of press freedom during the Guided Democracy era helped silence dissenting voices, including anti-China ones, and knowledge about that country became increasingly monopolized by those associated with power. The editorials below, from the centrist and nationalist newspapers, were typical examples of the views prevailing about China and Sino-Indonesian ties during the closing years of the Sukarno regime:

> Chinese solidarity with Indonesia has a strong foundation. It is based on a fact, a must that both countries need each other ... Both countries have the same aims and purposes. Both are the worst enemies of capitalism and imperialism. Both are interested in destroying them.[87]

> The Peking-Djakarta Axis is a genuine axis forged into being by two people with revolutionary spirit and with heroic tradition in the struggle for freedom and peace.[88]

In sum, the changing Sino-Indonesian diplomatic relationship constituted a significant variable in shaping perceptions of China and their internalization. Indonesians' ambivalent images of the PRC were devised partly to accommodate the shifting ties between the two nations. The need to rationalize a nationalist foreign policy or a Peking-Jakarta alliance reinforced the tendency to portray China not only in a favourable light, but specifically with a populist and nationalistic colouring. However, diplomacy and imaginings of China were undertaken in separate arenas, with differing sets of parameters and agendas. For the former, the predominant frame of reference was national interest and national security; its operation was confined to the official sphere in the transnational setting. The construction of images of China, on the other hand, was mainly shaped by political and intellectual evolution in the domestic arena, whereby China was taken as a yardstick of reference and comparison, with contestations about China as a state (of mind) occurring mainly in the public domain. It was only after 1957 that the two arenas (official and public) began to converge, partly facilitated by Sukarno's ascendance to power and by the country's increasing drift toward radicalization.

---

[87] *Berita Indonesia*, cited in *Editorials from Djakarta Press*, 2 October 1963.
[88] *Suluh Indonesia*, cited in *Editorials from Djakarta Press*, 21 January 1965.

## CHINA CREATES ITS OWN IMAGES

### China's Foreign Policy Goals in Indonesia

Historically, China's self-images had had some influence on outsiders' perceptions.[89] Beijing's strategies of creating an affirmative self-image in Indonesia were subordinate to its overall foreign policy, which was in turn shaped by Chinese leaders' views of the world. After the PRC's founding, with a conviction that the postwar world had been divided into socialist and capitalist camps, CCP leaders pursued a policy of "leaning toward one side". As Zhou Enlai stated in 1949, "our current task in foreign policy is twofold: establishing brotherly friendship with the Soviet Union and other people's democracies [in East Europe], and opposing imperialism".[90] This was the general framework in which China developed its relationships with newly independent nations in Southeast Asia, considered "one of the most important areas in the colonial world".[91] There was widespread conviction that the region's anti-colonial nationalist movements were "influenced and inspired by the Chinese revolution", which, according to an editorial of the *People's Daily*, "provides the people in the East with extremely valuable lessons".[92] According to Lu Tingyi (Lu Dingyi), director of the CCP's Propaganda Department,

> The victory in China of Marxism-Leninism and Comrade Mao Tse-tung's theory of the Chinese revolution will help the people of Asian countries free themselves from the influence of bourgeois democracy of the old style, resolutely take the path of the new democratic revolution of the people, and after the victory of the people's democratic revolution, continue their march forward towards a better social system — the system of socialism and communism.[93]

---

[89] Rupert Hodder, "China and the World: Perception and Analysis", *Pacific Review* 12, 1 (1999): 61–77.
[90] Zhou Enlai, "Xin Zhongguo de Waijiao" [New China's diplomacy], in *Zhou Enlai Waijiao Wenxuan* [Selected writings of Zhou Enlai on foreign affairs] (Beijing: Zhonggong Zhongyang Wenxian Chubanshe, 1990), pp. 1–2.
[91] Shi Zhen, "Dongnanya Guojia de Minzu Jiefang Yundong" [National liberation movements in Southeast Asia], *Shijie Zhishi* 2 (1955): 14.
[92] *Renmin Ribao* [People's Daily], 17 February 1948; "Dongnanya Geguo de Minzu Jiefang Yundong" [National liberation movements in Southeast Asian countries], in *Changjiang Ribao*, 3 May 1952.
[93] Cited in Alan Lawrence, ed., *China's Foreign Relations since 1945* (London: Routledge and Kegan Paul, 1975), p. 159.

During the 1950s, Chinese policy-makers and practitioners believed that Southeast Asian countries would likely follow China's road of New Democracy; this conviction strongly influenced Beijing's diplomacy in the region.[94] The belief in the reproducibility of China's experiences in Southeast Asia was so prevalent that some leaders were convinced that "China's today is Southeast Asia's tomorrow." As Chen Yi, minister of foreign affairs, stated in 1960,

> Chinese success in revolution and construction was … tremendous encouragement to all the oppressed nations and peoples of the world fighting for their liberation. In the Chinese people they see their own tomorrow. They feel that everything the Chinese people accomplished they too should be able to accomplish. They draw unlimited confidence and courage from the victory of the Chinese people…. The Chinese people see their yesterday in all oppressed nations.[95]

Being the largest nation in Southeast Asia, Indonesia was accorded the highest priority in the PRC's foreign policies toward the region. Shortly before the PRC's founding, Sha Ping (Hu Yuzhi),[96] one of the CCP's leading specialists on Southeast Asia, remarked, "The Indonesian people can draw necessary lessons not only from their own experiences, but also from the experience of China", including the essential roles played by the

---

[94] Interview in Xiamen with Huang You, Vice Chairman of the Fujian Overseas Chinese Affairs Commission.

[95] Quoted in A.M. Halpern, "The Foreign Policy Use of the Chinese Revolutionary Model", *China Quarterly* 7 (1961): 10.

[96] Hu Yuzhi (1896–1986) was once a deputy chairman of China's National People's Congress. He joined the CCP in 1933 and was dispatched by Zhou Enlai to Singapore in 1940 to undertake anti-Japanese propaganda. He was the editor-in-chief of the *Nanyang Siang Pau*, a newspaper owned by the patriotic entrepreneur Tan Kah Kee. Hu was in exile in Indonesia during the Japanese occupation and started learning the Indonesian language. He wrote widely about the issue of overseas Chinese and Southeast Asia, in addition to participating in China-oriented political activities such as organizing the branches of Chinese Democratic Union (Ming-Men). He returned to China in 1948 and served as the director of CCP Publication Bureau and Deputy Minister of Culture after the founding of the PRC. See Liu Bing, "Hu Yu Zhi and the Nanyang Overseas Chinese", in *Tonan Ajia Kakyo to Chugoku: Chugoko-kizoku-ishiki kara Kajin-Ishikie* [Overseas Chinese in Southeast Asia and China: Conversion of the object of their identity from China to the host countries], ed. Fujio Hara (Tokyo: Institute of Developing Economies, 1993), pp. 133–54.

united front, correct leadership, armed struggle and the Communist Party with a broad mass base.⁹⁷ By the mid-1950s, China's Indonesian policy goal was explicitly spelled out by the new ambassador, General Huang Zhen, under the guideline of "striving to obtain Indonesia's cooperation in the cause of anti-imperialism and anti-colonialism, pushing forward economic collaborations and cultural exchanges, and promoting the development of Sino-Indonesian relationships in an all-round way".⁹⁸

To win Indonesians' hearts and minds, Beijing adopted a pragmatic overseas Chinese policy, encouraging their conversion to local citizenship and non-interference in local politics.⁹⁹ It emphasized national and cultural commonalities between China and Indonesia in addition to promulgating its own experiences, as Zhou Enlai informed the visiting Prime Minister Ali Sastroamidjojo in 1955,

> There exists between the Chinese and the Indonesian peoples a traditional friendship of long standing. In recent generations, we have had common experiences and lived through similar conditions. And at present, our countries not only have the same aspiration and need to defend peace in Asia and the world and safeguard our respective sovereignty and territorial integrity, but are both engaged in a struggle to further oppose foreign intervention to shake off economic backwardness and to achieve complete national independence. All this constitutes a deep and broad basis for the development of friendship and co-operation between our two countries.¹⁰⁰

This strategy of promoting China's successful experiences was carried out primarily within the framework of cultural exchange, defined by the Chinese authorities as "one of the important channels for establishing and promoting relationships between countries and *as an essential component of diplomatic activities*".¹⁰¹ Undertaken simultaneously in both countries, this

---

⁹⁷ Sha Ping [Hu Yuzhi], "Lessons from Indonesia", *China Digest* 5, 12 (1949): 5.
⁹⁸ Yao Zhongming *et al.*, *Jiangjun, Waijiaojia, Yishujia — Huang Zhen Jilian Wenji* [General, diplomat and artist — Essays commemorating Huang Zhen] (Beijing: Jiefangjun Chubanshe, 1992), p. 334. Yao was Huang's successor from 1961 to 1966.
⁹⁹ On the policies concerning Chinese nationality, non-interference and resettlement, see Fitzgerald, *China and the Overseas Chinese*, pp. 141–4.
¹⁰⁰ Cited in *Sino-Indonesian Relations*, pp. 51–2.
¹⁰¹ Teng Yun, ed., *Dangdai Zhongwai Wenhua Jiaoliu Shiliao* [Primary materials on cultural exchanges between China and foreign countries in the contemporary era] (Beijing: Wenhua Yishu Chubanshe, 1990), p. 1 (emphasis added).

cultural diplomacy was implemented by a number of coordinated agencies charged with disseminating a wide range of information concerning China. At the time of the Cold War confrontation, this information war was also engaged against the United States and Nationalist government in Taiwan, which was eager to gain the support of the Chinese diaspora in Southeast Asia and elsewhere.[102]

**The Indonesian Front**

The most effective way of influencing Indonesians' views was directly presenting them with affirmative information about China. Three main types of agencies were tasked with this agenda: the Chinese embassy in Jakarta, the Foreign Language Press and Radio Peking, and various official and semi-official delegations to Indonesia.

Headed by General Huang Zhen throughout most of the 1950s, the PRC embassy in Jakarta was "one of the very few key Chinese embassies" in the world.[103] A veteran revolutionary and articulate diplomat, Huang befriended many Indonesians, including Sukarno. This personal diplomacy significantly facilitated one of his major agendas — "explaining China's foreign policy and making the circumstances of the new China known to Indonesians, including the leftists, centralists and rightists".[104] Through

---

[102] Meredith Oyen, "Communism, Containment and the Chinese Overseas", in *The Cold War in Asia: The Battle for Hearts and Minds*, ed. Yangwen Zheng, Hong Liu and Michael Szonyi (Leiden and Boston: Brill, 2010), pp. 59–94. For discussions on the general mechanisms and effects of China's cultural exchanges with foreign countries, see Nicolai Volland, "Translating the Socialist State: Cultural Exchange, National Identity, and the Socialist World in the Early PRC", *Twentieth-Century China* 33, 2 (2008): 51–72.

[103] Yao Zhongming, *Jiangjun*, p. 385. Huang Zhen (1908–90) was appointed major-general in 1946. After serving as ambassador to Indonesia for more than six years (1954–61), Huang was promoted to Vice-Minister of Foreign Affairs (1961–64). In his capacity as the first ambassador to France (1964–72), Huang conducted a series of secret negotiations with American diplomats on the establishment of diplomatic relations. Between 1973 and 1977, Huang was appointed head of the PRC Liaison Office in Washington (equivalent to an ambassadorship) and became Minister of Culture from 1977 to 1981. See Zhu Hong, *Huang Zhen Zhuang* [A biography of Huang Zhen] (Beijing: Renmin Ribao Chubanshe, 2000). The memoir of Huang's wife, who served as the first secretary of Chinese embassy in Jakarta, provided detailed accounts of his diplomatic career. See Zhu Lin, *Dashi Furen Huiyi Lu*.

[104] Yao Zhongming, *Jiangjun*, p. 371.

Huang's arrangement, Sukiman, a staunch anti-Communist politician, was invited to visit China and to meet Mao Zedong and Zhou Enlai,[105] which might have partly contributed to Sukiman's subsequent favourable report on China. Yao Zhongming, Huang's successor from 1961 to 1966, followed his example in reaching out to a wide circle of Indonesians. He seemed to be pleased with the results of the work. During his tenure in Jakarta, he wrote a play depicting how a Chinese ambassador in an unnamed country had tried resolutely and succeeded in transforming the nation's president from a "reactionary" to a devout anti-American and pro-China nationalist.[106]

The Chinese embassy in Jakarta and various consulates served as an important information hub frequented by political and cultural intellectuals, who came to obtain the latest news about China, watch Chinese movies or just have a chat.[107] In 1954 alone, the embassy hosted 48 receptions for local guests.[108] In 1955, three movies (two of which were documentaries about China's economic and social progress) were shown 97 times in ten districts of Indonesia, with a total audience of 79,000.[109] The Medan consulate showed seven feature and documentary films a total of 20 times, attracting an audience of 5,401.[110] During the mid-1950s, Sukarno regularly dispatched his personal assistants to the embassy to acquire Mao's writings and other publications about China.[111] When

---

[105] Ibid., p. 344; interview with Chen Lishui, Huang's personal assistant and interpreter.
[106] Interview with Chen Wenxian, who worked in the Jakarta embassy as an interpreter.
[107] Yao Zhongming, *Jiangjun*, pp. 333–405; and Zhu Lin, *Dashi Furen*, pp. 44–89.
[108] "Zhu Yindunixiya Shiguan Yijiuwushinian Jiaoji Gongzuo Zongjie Baogao" [Report of the embassy in Indonesia on public relations work in 1954] (10 February 1955–10 February 1956), file no. 117-00371-12, Archives of the Ministry of Foreign Affairs, PRC.
[109] "Zhu Yajiada Zong Linguan Yijiuwuwunian Huaqiao Wenhua Jiaoyu Kongzuo Zongjie" [Report of the consulate general in Jakarta on overseas Chinese cultural and educational work in 1955] (1 February–13 March 1956), file no. 118-00560-04, Archives of the Ministry of Foreign Affairs, PRC.
[110] "Zhu Mianlan Linshiguan Guanyi Shukan Fenfa, Dianying Fangyi Ji Huaqiao Baozhi Kongzuo de Baogao" [Report by Medan consulate on the distribution of books and magazines, showing of movies, and works relating to overseas Chinese newspapers] (24 January 1956), file no. 118-00560-05, Archives of the Ministry of Foreign Affairs, PRC.
[111] Interview in Hong Kong with Soeto Meisen, Sukarno's personal assistant and interpreter. See also "Sujianuo Zongtong Fanhua Yaoqing Jingguo" [Chronicles regarding the process of inviting President Sukarno to visit China] (18 January 1956), file no. 204-00030-01, Archives of the Ministry of Foreign Affairs, PRC.

Sima Wensen in Surabaya, 1956 [Lembaga Persahabatan Indonesia-Tiongkok, *Perkenalan Lembaga Persahabatan Indonesia-Tiongkok* (Jakarta: Rada, 1956)].

meeting with the Chinese consul in 1954, the secretary-general of the Ministry of Foreign Affairs, Roeslan Abdulgani, requested publications from the PRC and showed a strong interest in literary works published recently in China. He even borrowed some Chinese music albums with the intention of copying and playing them for the youth, who, according to him, were used to listening to "decadent" Western music.[112] The embassy's cultural section was very active in reaching out to various circles of intellectuals. Sima Wenshen, the cultural attaché, went to the countryside for meetings with local artists.[113] The embassy was charged with the task of recommending Indonesians to visit China. It was reported that intellectuals

---

[112] "Wo Zhu Yinni Shiguan Chanzhan yu Yinni Waijiaobu Mishuzhan Lushilan Aduganni jiu Yinni Wengongtuan Fanhuashi Huitan Jiyao" [Minutes of meeting between the Chinese consul and Roeslan Abdulgani, secretary-general of the Indonesian Ministry of Foreign Affairs, pertaining to the upcoming visit of Indonesian cultural delegation to China] (3 June 1954), file no. 105-00260-12, Archives of the Ministry of Foreign Affairs, PRC.

[113] Interview in Beijing with Chen Wenxian, who worked in the Cultural Section of the Chinese embassy.

with rightist or centrist orientations were particularly encouraged to go, with the hope that their views of China would be changed for the better, which would in turn "greatly expand our influence in Indonesia".[114]

To project a positive self-image, the PRC embassy maintained regular contacts with a variety of local organizations. For example, overseas Chinese organizations usually followed its instructions with respect to disseminating information about China. During a two-month period in early 1954, the PRC's Overseas Chinese Broadcasting and Editorial Department (*Huaqiao guangbo bianji bu*) put out a total of 648 articles; 623 or 95.6 per cent of them were used by Chinese newspapers in countries like Indonesia.[115] The Indonesian-Chinese Friendship Association was one of the major non-government organizations that the embassy worked closely with. Established in 1955 for the purpose of "studying and understanding China's experiences, especially in the sphere of cultural and socio-economic development", its membership included both leftist and centrist intellectuals and politicians, such as Prijono (a professor at the University of Indonesia and later minister of culture and education), Djawoto, head of the Indonesian News Agency *Antara* and later ambassador to Beijing, and Henk Ngantung, a prominent painter who later became governor of Jakarta. In addition to regularly supplying the organization with films and books, Chinese officials, including Ambassador Huang and his wife Zhu Lin, met regularly with its members.[116]

Printed materials were another effective venue for generating self-publicity. A large number of Indonesian-language books were published between 1950 and 1965, primarily by the Foreign Language Press in

---

[114] "Yaoqing Yindunixiya Shehui Minliu Fanhua Shi" [Matters pertaining to the invitation for prominent Indonesians to visit China] (8 August–27 September 1958), file no. 105-00862-02, Archives of the Ministry of Foreign Affairs, PRC; and interviews in Washington DC and Beijing with Huang Shuhai, who worked as an interpreter in the Jakarta embassy and the Ministry of Foreign Affairs.

[115] Zhang Yunfei, "Dui Dagemin ji Qiaoju Yinni de Huiyi" [Recollections on the great revolution and sojourning in Indonesia], in *Wenshi Ziliao Xuanji* [Selected materials on culture and history] 16 (1988): 51–75; Oyen, "Communism, Containment and the Chinese Overseas".

[116] "Konsepi: Lembaga Persahabatan Tiongkok-Indonesia", *Zaman Baru* 4, 22/23 (1953): 13–6; *Perkenalan Lembaga Persahabatan Indonesia-Tiongkok* (Jakarta: Rada, 1956), p. 99; see also Hong Yuanyuan, *Hong Yuanyuan*, pp. 224–33; Zhu Lin, *Dashi Furen*, pp. 61–89.

Beijing. This organization was officially responsible for translating and publishing books and magazines pertaining to "China's successful revolution and construction". From 1950 to 1965, the number of Indonesian-language books ranked second in the press's overall publications. (The first, predictably, was English-language books.[117]) These books were composed mainly of translations of cultural and political writings by CCP leaders and favourable depictions of the new China. They also included literary works such as *The White-haired Girl*, a novel about rural class war, which was translated by Pramoedya from English into Indonesian. The Foreign Language Press edited and published a number of Indonesian-language magazines, including *Tiongkok Rakjat* (People's China). At the request of D.N. Aidit, the PKI chairman, an Indonesian version of *Peking Review* was published in 1963.[118]

These publications were distributed through China's International Book Company, the embassy and consulates in Indonesia, bookstores owned by sympathetic overseas Chinese (such as Weng Fulin as described in Chapter 6) and PKI affiliates; many were given as gifts to individuals or organizations such as university libraries.[119] For instance, in 1955 alone, the PRC consulate in Medan distributed a total of 6,426 copies of the following regularly published magazines in the region: (1) *People's Pictorials* (Chinese version): 336 copies; (2) *China Pictorials* (Indonesian version): 3,578 copies; (3) *People's China* (English version): 607 copies; (4) *China Construction* (English version): 782 copies; and (5) *People's Literature* (English version): 114 copies. In addition, the consulate distributed 16 irregularly published magazines (a total of 1,846) and donated 1,623 books. The recipients included: (1) major military, political and police officials in Northern and Central Sumatra: 127; (2) Indonesian news agencies: 16; (3) mass organizations and schools in Northern and Central Sumatra: 145; (4) Indonesian writers, physicians and other prominent persons: 48; (5) foreign consulates in Medan: 6; (6) other foreign organizations: 9; and (7) Peranakan physicians and prominent figures, overseas Chinese associations and schools: 107.

---

[117] Interview with Jiang Bolin, head of the Indonesian Section, Foreign Language Press, Beijing.

[118] Interview in Beijing with Jiang Bolin. Aidit sent a few Indonesians to Beijing to help with the translation and editorial work, among them his younger brother Sobron Aidit, a noted poet himself.

[119] Interview in Beijing with Chen Youli, head of the Indonesian Section of Foreign Language Press in the 1950s.

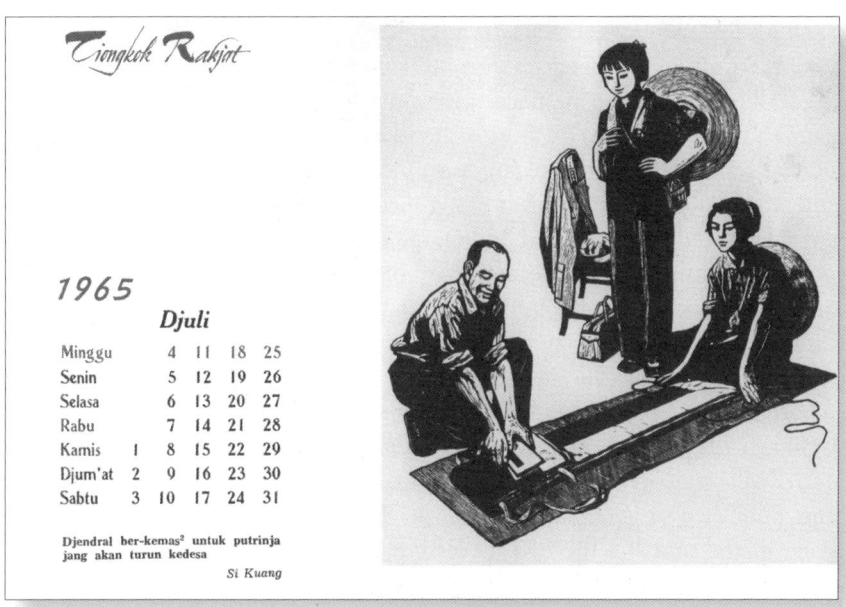

Calendar poster attached to and distributed with *Tiongkok Rakjat*, 1965: "A General sends his daughters to the countryside".

Calendar poster attached to and distributed with *Tiongkok Rakjat*, 1965: "Preparing for the tilling of the land in winter".

In the same year, the consulate received 311 requests from various Indonesian governmental agencies and individuals for magazines and books.[120]

China seemed to be making significant inroads in terms of its propaganda programme. After a tour of Southeast Asian nations in 1956, a U.S. official reported that the region was "flooded with Red Chinese literature and consumer goods".[121] More significantly, these magazines and books were read and well received by an important segment of educated Indonesians. Armijn Pane, for example, quoted extensively Indonesian versions of Mao's works in his book about China. After reading the Chinese publications, a bureau director in the Medan municipal government reportedly said that "everyone should be aware of China's progress". Another reader reported that China's rapid progress and patterns of development should be taken "as a model".[122] *Song of Youth*, a novel about anti-Japanese and anti-KMT student movements in 1930s China, was translated by Shannu and published as *Njanjian Remadja* in 1961 and became an instant bestseller of the time.[123] The PKI leadership designated this novel as a compulsory reading for its members, and the movie adapted from it was watched by large numbers of Indonesian youths.[124]

Radio Peking was another agency to transmit information about China. Its agenda fell within the official guideline, which was to "comprehensively and promptly present China's planned development and report new progress of the Chinese people in the process of building socialism".[125]

---

[120] "Zhu Mianlan Lingshiguan Guanyi Shukan Fenfa, Dianying Fangyi Ji Huaqiao Baozhi Kongzuo de Baogao" [Report by Medan consulate on the distribution of books and magazines, showing of movies, and works relating to overseas Chinese newspapers] (24 January 1956), file no. 118-00560-05, Archives of the Ministry of Foreign Affairs, PRC.

[121] Cited in Oyen, "Communism, Containment and the Chinese Overseas".

[122] "Zhu Mianlan Lingshiguan Guanyi Shukan Fenfa…".

[123] It has been pointed out that novels like this were sold well in the early 1960s, and that they dealt with regional heroes who were against corrupt government officials, feudal warlords or brutal dictators. Although they were aimed at the situation in China, they could be "read as having relevance to the situation in Indonesia, the book seller said cautiously". Cited in Maslyn Williams, *Five Journeys from Jakarta: Inside Sukarno's Indonesia* (Westport, CT: Greenwood Press, 1965), pp. 187–8.

[124] Interviews with Shannu and Huang Shuhai in Beijing and Washington, DC; and personal correspondence from Chen Wenxian.

[125] Internal speech in 1953 of Wu Linxi, director of the Xinhua News Agency, in *Xinhuashe Wenjiang Ziliao Xuanbian* [Selected documents of the New China News Agency] (Beijing, n.d.), vol. 3, p. 7.

The early 1950s saw a "spectacular increase" in its output, from 16 hours per week in 1948 to 116 hours in 1954.[126] A major division within Radio Peking, the Indonesian Section was founded in October 1950, charged with the task of "promulgating the new China's accomplishments and explaining its foreign policy" to Indonesians; both Zhou Enlai and Chen Yi were closely involved in the setting of its strategic direction.[127] The section was equipped with advanced facilities and had two frequency channels. According to Indonesian reports, Radio Peking was the most frequently listened to foreign radio in the country.[128] Informal surveys showed that the audience was composed mostly of civil servants, teachers, students and workers — the core of the political public. Some officials were even able to recognize the voices of Chinese broadcasters when the latter visited Indonesia. It was reported that the Indonesian Section of Radio Peking received more than 10,000 letters each year from its audience in the early 1960s; many expressed a strong interest in China's domestic socio-economic transformation, such as the people's communes.[129]

Official and semi-official delegations to Indonesia were another effective channel through which information about China was conveyed. One of the most successful events was the 1955 cultural delegation led by Zheng Zhenduo, vice-minister of culture. The delegation toured the country for 54 days and was received enthusiastically, with each performance reportedly being watched by at least 50,000 people. Sukarno said that he had received numerous letters from various parts of the country pleading him to send this delegation to their districts. The performance programmes were filled with themes of glorifying the new China's progress and celebrating the integration of arts, life and the people.[130] According to a (somewhat exaggerated) internal report prepared by the embassy's

---

[126] John C. Clews, *Communist Propaganda Techniques* (London: Methuen & Co., 1964), p. 123.

[127] Interviews in Beijing with Huang Aling and Lin Liushun, both heads of the Indonesian Section of Radio Peking between the early 1950s and the end of 1980s.

[128] J.J.K., "Siaran Gelombang Pendek: Radio Republik Rakjat Tiongkok", *Siasat* 9, 440 (1955); "Siaran Gelombang Pendek: Presiden Sukarno di Peking", *Siasat* 10, 488 (1956).

[129] All this information is drawn from interviews with Huang Aling and Lin Liushun.

[130] *Guangming Ribao*, 12 August 1955; see also Zhou Erfu, *Dongnanya Sanji* [Random notes on Southeast Asia] (Beijing: Zhongguo Qingnian Chubanshe, 1956), pp. 84–145. For the programme guides, see *Pertundjukan Delegasi Kebudajaan Republik Rakjat Tiongkok* (Jakarta: PRC Embassy, 1955).

Cultural Division, "this cultural delegation has left significant impact upon the Indonesians in their endeavours to revitalize and improve their national arts. After this visit, Indonesian dancing arts, especially those reflecting the people's life, have further flourished".[131]

Throughout their meetings with their local hosts, visiting Chinese delegates highlighted common interests between the two countries. A religious delegation called on the minister of religions in 1951, emphasizing specifically "all Muslims under the sky are one family".[132] In 1956, Soong Ching Ling (Sun Yat-sen's widow) told a Jakarta mass rally, "As newly independent nations, our fundamental interests are similar; we have identical views on many issues facing us today."[133] A visiting delegation to North Sumatra declared in 1965 that both Indonesia and China had "identical destinies and objectives", and the head of a journalist delegation proclaimed, "The Asian-African people's primary and most important task at present is to oppose imperialism and colonialism, old and new."[134]

Although it is difficult to establish direct empirical links between China's deliberate efforts in transmitting positive information and Indonesians' perceptions of that country, there is no doubt that these endeavours laid a fertile ground for interpreting and imagining China in a largely positive light. Indonesians' knowledge about China, therefore, was acquired with some explicit foreign manipulation. This could backfire, however, as resentment of the infiltration of China's cultural and political influence caused uneasiness and criticism, especially by the anti-Communist intellectuals. H.B. Jassin reported that the importation of books from China had caused "an ideological war" in the early 1950s.[135] The wide-

---

[131] Duiwai Wenhua Lianluo Weiyuanhui Ersi [Research office of the Committee of Cultural Exchanges with Foreign Countries], ed., *Yindunixiya Wenhua Gaikuang* [A survey of Indonesian culture] (Beijing, internal circulation, 1962), p. 54.

[132] "Zhu Yindunixiya Shiguan Yijiuwuyinian Waijiao Huitan Jiyao Huibian" [Compiled records of diplomatic meetings of the embassy in Indonesia in 1951], file no. 118-00399-01, Archives of the Ministry of Foreign Affairs, PRC.

[133] *Xinhua Yuebao* 8 (1956): 13.

[134] *Medan Press Summary*, 11 May 1965; *Afro-Asian Journalists* (Jakarta), no. 1 (March 1964), p. 8.

[135] H.B. Jassin, *Surat-Surat, 1943–1983* (Jakarta: Gramedia, 1984), p. 91. The Indonesian government kept a close eye on books about and imported from China. An official at the Ministry of Interior inquired with the Chinese consul in 1951 about the status of Chinese books being translated into Indonesian and requested that relevant information be sent to him. See "Zhu Yindunixiya Shiguan Yijiuwuyinian Waijiao Huitan Jiyao Huibian" [Compiled records of diplomatic meetings of the embassy in Indonesia in 1951], file no. 118-00399-01, Archives of the Ministry of Foreign Affairs, PRC.

spread distribution of Chinese publications also alarmed Indonesian intelligence agencies at the time of the Sino-Indonesian conflicts in 1960; an official was dispatched to the PRC embassy to investigate the distribution channels of these publications, while some local military authorities banned their distribution.[136]

## The China Front

The PRC's efforts in fashioning and presenting its self-image were simultaneously carried out in China proper. Unlike the strategies in Indonesia, which were targeted at influencing "the political public" in general, the endeavours on the China front were more sharply focused, aiming specifically at selected members of the political elite and opinion-makers. For example, 105 Indonesians were invited to visit China in 1954; they represented a wide range of professions such as arts and culture, agriculture, education, trade unions, youth and journalism. The embassy recorded 1,835 cases of formal and informal interactions with local Indonesians.[137] Through their enthusiastic travelogues and speeches about China after returning home, Indonesian observations contributed to the collective imagining of China.

It has been argued that visits to the PRC by foreign guests were essentially a kind of "guided tourism" manipulated by the hosts, who selectively displayed the country's accomplishments to foster its image in foreign public opinion.[138] There is a certain truth to this argument, but it should not be overstated. To be sure, Indonesians' judgements of China were inevitably clouded by the ways they were treated and by what they were able to see. Like other foreign visitors of the time, Indonesians were well received and amiably treated as soon as they landed in the PRC. Trisno Sumardjo remarked that, unlike in the United States where he was

---

[136] "Yindunixiya Jinzhi Wo zai Yinni Chuban Fanxin Xuanchuanpin Qingkuan" [Report on the Indonesian ban on the publication and distribution of our publicity materials] (12 July–8 September 1960), file no. 105-00986-02 (1), Archives of the Ministry of Foreign Affairs, PRC.

[137] "Zhu Yinni Shiguan 1954 Nian Jiaoji Gongzuo Zongjie Baogao" [Report on the work of publicity of the Indonesian embassy in 1954] (10 February 1955–10 February 1956), file no. 117-00371-12, Archives of the Ministry of Foreign Affairs, PRC.

[138] Herbert Passin, *China's Cultural Diplomacy* (New York: Praeger, 1963); Paul Hollander, *Political Pilgrims: Travels of Western Intellectuals to the Soviet Union, China, and Cuba* (Lanham, MD: University Press of America, 1990), pp. 347–99.

treated like a "college student", he was an honoured state guest in China. Members of a college-student delegation reported that they were received as if they were "princes".[139] Bagong Kussudiardjo was very pleased that his 60-person cultural delegation was able to take a specially chartered train from the south China border to Beijing and was personally received by Zhou Enlai. "In China, we are not ordinary persons, but respected guests", he commented appreciatively.[140]

In most cases, Indonesian visitors were able to see only a small portion of China (usually industrial centres such as Shanghai, Shenyang and Guangzhou), which could lead to the mistaken impression that these cities were representative of the whole country. The Chinese were willing to go a step further to impress selected guests. Mohammad Hatta's 1957 visit is a case in point. Despite having stepped down as vice-president in 1956 (mainly because of his disagreements with President Sukarno), Hatta remained an influential political intellectual. After he expressed the intention to visit the PRC, Ambassador Huang Zhen extended an invitation without delay. (The Chinese, however, proceeded to obtain the prior consent of Sukarno, who was of the view that Hatta should take the trip in order to "expand his narrow vision and correct his unrealistic views [about Indonesia] and biases [toward China]".[141]) Upon arriving in Beijing as a private citizen, Hatta was pleasantly surprised to be received as if he were still the incumbent vice-president. He and his entourage were even provided with two private jets for a trip to Xinjiang, where most Chinese Muslims resided and which was rarely accessible to foreigners. Hatta was allowed to tour an airplane-manufacturing factory in the industrial city of Shenyang, a secret military facility that had never been open to any other foreign visitors before. (His host, however, did not show him the engine production section.[142])

---

[139] Trisno Sumardjo, "Sebulan di Tiongkok", *Budaja* 7, 1 (1958): 15–25; Suprati Samil and Sabam Siagian, "Mahasiswa Indonesia ke RRT", *Kompas untuk Generasi Baru* 4, 10 (1954): 22.
[140] Kussudiardjo, "Kesan-kesan", p. 12.
[141] "Zhu Yindunixiya Shiguang Baohui Yinni Waizhang Subandeliyue tan Qian Fuzongtong Hada Fanghua Shi" [Report by the embassy in Indonesia concerning the talk with Indonesian foreign minister Subandrio on the visit to China by former vice-president Hatta] (6 August 1957), file no. 105-00344-02, Archives of the Ministry of Foreign Affairs, PRC; Yao Zhongming, *Jiangjun*, pp. 343–4; interview with Chen Lishui.
[142] Interviews in Beijing with Zhang Ailing and Huang Aling, both of whom were with the Hatta delegation in 1957.

One should not, however, exaggerate the significance of "guided tourism" and dismiss it purely as propaganda; otherwise, we cannot explain why members of the same delegations returned home with different, and at times conflicting, impressions of China (see Chapter 4). Hatta himself was clearly aware of the limitations of what he could see in merely three weeks.[143] In their respective commentaries on trips to the PRC in 1954 and 1957, Asa Bafagih, Trisno Sumardjo and Ramadhan K.H. admitted that, even though they were well received by their hosts, it did not prevent them from being very critical (Bafagih and Sumardjo) or mildly critical (Ramadhan) of China's political and cultural policies.[144] Some visitors reported that they had enjoyed a certain degree of freedom in deciding what they wanted to see during the trip. In a letter to his family, Tabrani wrote that he went to China with suspicion and uneasiness, but these feelings were soon replaced by admiration and amazement. His delegation, which included Armijn Pane and Barioen A.S., paid an unscheduled visit to a village without prior approval of the host, which led to his belief that "prosperity in the countryside is indeed a reality, not propaganda".[145] Yuti (Melik Sayuti), a noted columnist who accompanied the Sukarno delegation to China in 1956, observed that because the delegation frequently changed its itineraries, the warm receptions were spontaneous and genuine; he liked to quote what Sukarno said there, "Smiles cannot be prearranged."[146]

In any event, most Indonesian visitors returned home with improved impressions regarding China.[147] Roeslan Abdulgani, for example, reported to parliament that his tour of China had "corrected some erroneous impressions which I was bound to make because I only got them from text books".[148] Like Sukarno, he too reckoned that Hatta's trip to the PRC

---

[143] Hatta, "Masalah Pembangunan dalam RRT", *Pikiran Rakjat*, 23–24 December 1957.

[144] Asa Bafagih, *RRT dari Luar dan Dalam* (Jakarta: Pengurus Besar Nahdlatul Ulama, 1955); Sumardjo, "Sebulan di RRT"; and Ramadhan, "Serakan Bintang Sekitar Yang-Tse", *Konfrontasi* 4, 12 (1957): 60–72.

[145] *Hsin Pao*, 6 November 1951; Barioen, *Melihat Tiongkok Baru* (Jakarta: Rada, 1952), p. 9.

[146] "Limabelas Hari di Tiongkok", *Suluh Indonesia*, 26–30 October 1956.

[147] This information is drawn from Franklin Weinstein's interviews with the Indonesian foreign policy elite who visited China prior to 1965. See his *Indonesian Foreign Policy*, p. 92.

[148] Abdulgani, *The Foreign Minister's Report to Parliament on President Sukarno's Second Tour, August 26–October 16, 1956* (Jakarta: Department of Foreign Affairs, 1956), p. 93.

would prompt a change of mind for many intellectuals who were biased against China.[149] Beijing seemed genuinely pleased that its efforts had paid off. Officials were convinced (sometimes wishfully) that Indonesians' visits led not only to changes of their attitudes toward the PRC, but also their views of development at home. An internal report of the Chinese embassy in Jakarta boasted, "Having visited China in 1959, the president of Hassanuddin University, Tirtodiningrat, was impressed by the country's rapid progress, which in turn reinforced his conviction in the need to strengthen Indonesia's national education".[150]

## CONCLUSION

In conclusion, both the ethnic Chinese in Indonesia and China's wide-ranging formal and informal diplomacy helped shape the production and dissemination of perceptions of the PRC. Three brief observations could be drawn from the preceding discussion. In the first place, ethnic Chinese were partially responsible for the formulation of conflicting perceptions of their ancestral homeland. Their views of China, ranging from exceptionally affirmative to very negative, contributed to the emergence of differing Chinas in the public discourse. Some indigenous Indonesians' disdain for the local Chinese, in the meantime, partially fuelled an admiration for a different kind of Chinese and Chineseness; ironically, Indonesians' praise for the latter served as a powerful pretext for chastising the local Chinese.

Second, a variety of institutions and agencies were established to transmit information about China and project it onto the Indonesian scene. They constituted the core of cultural diplomatic efforts not only in moulding China's affirmative self-image but also in engaging in an information war with the Americans and Taiwanese for the purpose of winning Indonesians' hearts and minds. The medium of this warfare included magazines, pamphlets, newspapers, books and even calendars circulated widely in Indonesian, films and documentaries about China, and messages broadcast from thousands of miles away. The recurring messages by visiting Chinese delegates on Sino-Indonesian mutual interests and cultural

---

[149] "Zhu Yindunixiya Shiguan Baohui youguan qian fuzongtong Hada fanghua shiyi" [Report by the embassy concerning matters relating to former vice-president Hatta's forthcoming visit to China] (13 June 1957), file no. 105-00344-02, Archives of the Ministry of Foreign Affairs, PRC.
[150] Duiwai Wenhua, *Yindunixiya*, p. 124.

commonalities coincided nicely with the selective showcasing in China for Indonesian guests, thus reinforcing a perception that China could become a viable model. Looking back, the episode of Beijing's exhaustive cultural diplomacy in Sukarno's Indonesia may well be taken as a successful precedent of China's increasing soft power in Southeast Asia, which has attracted much media and academic attention since the turn of the 21st century.[151]

Finally, images of China were cast against the shifting backdrop of the Sino-Indonesian relationship, characterized by both amity and enmity. While national interests and security were supreme factors in shaping official diplomacy, intermittent conflicts were thus inevitable, the formation of public views about China was more often linked with Indonesian opinion-makers' overriding interests in domestic issues, which tended to be long-standing and recurring. The intertwining of these two sets of frameworks and points of reference facilitated the gradual transition of China from being on the margin of Indonesian discourse to a central position in the closing years of the Sukarno era. In the early 1950s, China was remote — geographically, cognitively and metaphorically — and its attraction was limited to a small number of intellectuals who had personally visited the country or read widely about it. The apathy toward China was reinforced by the lukewarm diplomatic relationship and Indonesians' confidence in their own experimentation with constitutional democracy. By the mid-1950s, however, the attention to and attraction by the Chinese experience had increased dramatically, reflecting not only growing Sino-Indonesian diplomatic ties, but more importantly the (perceived and actual) failures of sociopolitical experiments at home. China became a site of political contestation and cultural imagination on the very idea of Indonesia, including the format of the political system, the pattern of social engineering, models of economic development and the role of intellectuals. From the end of the 1950s to 1965, the Guided Democracy regime's search for workable models for managing domestic sociopolitical transition further brought China into the Indonesian imagination and policy reformulations. In other words, despite the fact that the PRC encountered mixed receptions (ranging from admiration to hostility) in the official and diplomatic arena, China as an idea and potential model in the

---

[151] Joshua Kurlantzick, *Charm Offensive: How China's Soft Power Is Transforming the World* (New Haven: Yale University Press, 2007); Hong Liu, "The Historicity of China's Soft Power: The PRC and the Cultural Politics of Indonesia, 1945–1965", in Zheng, Liu and Szonyi, eds., *The Cold War in Asia*, pp. 147–83.

public sphere was attractive to many Indonesians. In the intriguing process of mingling knowledge and power, and as a result of the ascendance of political and cultural intellectuals like Sukarno and Pramoedya during the first half of the 1960s, discourses about China were translated into policy and practice. China no longer stayed merely as a site of contestation in the intellectual arena; instead it ventured into, intentionally or unintentionally, an uncharted and precarious terrain of political and cultural transformation.

# PART III
## Shaping a New Trajectory

# CHAPTER 7

# Sukarno, the China Metaphor and Political Populism

*If men define situations as real, they are real in their consequences.*

W.I. Thomas (1928)[1]

*During my visits to the newly emerged people's democratic countries I witnessed the realization of my ideals formulated since 1929.... In the PRC I saw the practice of a guided democracy (*demokrasi terpimpin*); only this democracy with guidance can bring people into a new world, a truly just and prosperous new world.*

Sukarno (1956)[2]

*I came back from my visit to ... the People's Republic of China with a tremendous sense of amazement.... I no longer dream.... I propose that the leaders of the people confer and decide to bury all parties.*

Sukarno (1956)[3]

Sukarno was arguably the single most important politician in determining the trajectory of postcolonial Indonesian history up to 1965. His multifaceted and far-reaching influences upon Indonesia's domestic and foreign

---

[1] W.I. Thomas, *The Child in America* (New York: Knopf, 1928), p. 527, quoted in David Shambaugh, *Beautiful Imperialist: China Perceives America, 1972–1990* (Princeton: Princeton University Press, 1991), p. 17.
[2] *Harian Rakjat*, 17 October 1956, and *Tay Kong Sian Po* (Surabaya), 18 October 1956.
[3] Quoted in Arnold C. Brackman, *Indonesian Communism: A History* (New York: Frederick A. Praeger, 1963), p. 227.

205

politics have been meticulously documented and extensively analysed.[4] Although there is a consensus regarding Sukarno's significant contributions to Indonesian political development, scholars disagree about the sources of his thought. While some perceive him to be essentially a statesman whose views were shaped by his Western education and by his experiences in the nationalist movement, others see him as a modern version of a Hindu-Javanese ruler, whose actions were guided by traditional Javanism. The relevance of Sukarno's perceptions of the experiences of other Asian nations (such as China) to the evolution of his thinking has escaped scholarly scrutiny.

This chapter examines the construction of Sukarno's perception of the PRC and suggests how it is centrally relevant to the evolution of his thought. It argues that his largely favourable views of China were fashioned predominantly by his predispositions about Indonesia. The hopeful China-images created and presented by Sukarno, therefore, reflected more his own political discontent and intellectual ambiguity than they did Chinese realities. In reformulating his agendas for Indonesia, Sukarno consistently and deliberately drew upon different dimensions of the Chinese model of social and political development. His notion of what went wrong with Indonesia was constantly set against his perception of what went right in the PRC. By using China as a political point of reference and a social strategy, Sukarno incorporated some of the PRC's conceptual inspiration and practical alternatives in his determined drive to replace Western-style parliamentary democracy with Guided Democracy. In so doing, Sukarno converted his own image of China into a China metaphor, a mirror that contained transformable ramifications of far-reaching significance beyond its original connotations.

It should be noted that this chapter is not a study of Sukarno's political thinking *per se*; its focus is on how Sukarno's China perception was contrived and, more importantly, on its significance to Indonesia's critical political transformation between 1956 and 1959, a turning point in Sukarno's

---

[4] See, for example, John D. Legge, *Sukarno: A Political Biography* (Sydney: Allen and Unwin, 1990 [1972]); Bernhard Dahm, *Sukarno and the Struggle for Indonesian Independence*, trans. Mary Somers-Heidhues (Ithaca: Cornell University Press, 1969); C.L. Penders, *The Life and Times of Sukarno* (Kuala Lumpur: Oxford University Press, 1974); Benedict Anderson, "Bung Karno and the Fossilization of Soekarno's Thought", *Indonesia* 74 (2002): 1–19; and Bob Hering, *Soekarno: Founding Father of Indonesia, 1901–1945* (Leiden: KITLV Press, 2002).

career as a politician and a thinker. In many respects, what happened during the period between 1960 and 1965 was a continuation of major themes expounded by Sukarno himself during these previous and crucial four years.

## SUKARNO AND CHINA BEFORE 1956

When Sukarno first visited China in October 1956, he was already familiar with its political and social development. He had long recognized the importance of China, as he remarked in 1930, "Whoever holds the environs of China will control the affairs of the entire Eastern world."[5] Like many of his fellow nationalists (as described in Chapter 1), Sukarno's knowledge of China during the Dutch East Indies era was derived from two major sources: publications about China and personal contacts with the Indonesian Chinese. The former included works by and about Dr. Sun Yat-sen, Mao Zedong and Chiang Kai-shek, and reports about China by sympathetic Western journalists such as Günther Stein, whose *The Challenge of Red China* was translated by Liem Koen Hian and published as *Chungking dan Yenan* in 1949.[6] Edgar Snow's *Red Star Over China* was perhaps the single most important written account influencing Indonesian nationalists' understanding of China. It was translated in 1938 by Siauw Giok Tjhan and published in a serial form in the *Sin Tit Po*.[7] Sukarno developed close personal ties with those Indonesian Chinese who were supportive of his cause and held regular discussions with them regarding strategies for nationalist activity. The ethnic Chinese community in the East Indies played an important part in the sociopolitical awakening of the country; their aspiration to modernity, political emancipation and advocacy for a Pan-Asian imaginary had a positive impact on the nationalist cause in Indonesia. Kwee Keng Beng, editor-in-chief of *Sin Po* between 1925 and

---

[5] Sukarno, *Indonesia Accuses*, ed. and trans. Roger K. Paget (Kuala Lumpur: Oxford University Press, 1975), p. 17.
[6] On writings about China published in Indonesia prior to 1950, see Claudine Salmon, *Literature in Malay by the Chinese of Indonesia: A Provisional Annotated Bibliography* (Paris: Éditions de la Maison des Sciences de l'Homme, 1981), pp. 66–7, 75–6; Kwee Kek Beng, *Doea Poeloe Lima Tahoen Sebagai Wartawan, 1922–1947* (Batavia: Kuo, 1948), pp. 32–43.
[7] Mary Somers, "Peranakan Chinese Politics in Indonesia" (Ph.D. dissertation, Cornell University, 1965), p. 100.

1947, was a contributing editor to Sukarno's *Soeloeh Indonesia Moeda* during the late 1920s and early 1930s. He was one of the foremost supporters of Sukarno's PNI, often printing the PNI periodicals free of charge and distributing them.[8] China's revolutionary image, presented to him partly through the ethnic Chinese, might have accounted for Sukarno's strong interest in establishing contacts with the revolutionaries in China.[9]

The perceptions of China that Sukarno developed prior to 1956 had three major characteristics. First, his China images were imbued with a strong nationalistic colouring, becoming a source of inspiration. As a devoted nationalist, Sukarno's overriding concern during the pre-World War II era was winning independence, and it was within this context that China entered his reconstruction of the outside world. Sukarno considered Indonesia's nationalist movement to be an integral part of "Eastern nationalism"; as he put it in 1928, "the [nationalist] movement in Indonesia was born, among other things, because of inspiration from the movements in other Asian countries".[10] China served as one of the major models of Asian nationalism, with Sun Yat-sen at the centre of this nationalist imagining. Sukarno regarded himself to be "a pupil of Dr. Sun Yat-sen", whom he described as "a very great nationalist leader" and "the father of the Chinese masses".[11] He acknowledged that Sun Yat-sen had been a source of intellectual stimulus in developing his nationalism and the Indonesian state ideology, the Pancasila. In a 1945 speech to the committee drafting Indonesia's constitution, Sukarno declared that "ever since then [1918], nationalism has been implanted in my heart, through the influence of [Sun Yat-sen's] Three People's Principles [democracy, nationalism and socialism]".[12] He remarked that "Sun Yat-sen through his *San Min Chu I*

---

[8] Hering, *Soekarno*, pp. 62–7.

[9] Kwee Kek Beng, *Doea Poeloe Lima*, p. 35; Hong Yuanyuan [Ang Goan Jan], *Hong Yuanyuan Zizhuan* [An autobiography of Hong Yuanyuan], translated from the unpublished English manuscript by Liang Yingming (Beijing: Zhongguo Huaqiao Chuban Gongsi, 1989), p. 79.

[10] Sukarno, "Indonesianism and Pan-Asianism" (1928), in his *Under the Banner of Revolution*, vol. 1 (Jakarta: Publication Committee, 1966), pp. 67–71.

[11] Sukarno, *Nationalism, Islam and Marxism* (Ithaca: Cornell University Modern Indonesian Project, 1984 [1926]), p. 43; Sukarno, *Indonesia Accuses*, p. 55; and *Sin Min* (Semarang), 14 November 1956.

[12] Sukarno, "The Birth of Pantja Sila" (1945), in *Pantja Sila: The Basis of the State of the Republic of Indonesia* (Jakarta: Department of Information, 1964), p. 27.

[Three People's Principles] has been instrumental in getting [Sukarno] back to nationalism from erstwhile cosmopolitan ideas he had cherished as a 16-year-old youngster for a while." So the three principles "flourished in his heart and he "feels forever grateful to Dr. Sun Yat-sen".[13]

Second, Sukarno believed that Indonesia and China had identical goals and common aspirations in their struggles for national independence. This conviction was an extension of his pan-Asianism, as he wrote in the newspaper *Suluh Indonesia Muda* in 1928:

> People are beginning to be conscious of a sense of unity and a feeling of brotherhood between the Chinese people and the Indonesian people, that is, both are Eastern people, both are people who are suffering, both are people who are struggling, demanding a free life.... Because the common lot of the people of Asia is certain to give birth to uniform behavior; a common fate is certain to give birth to a uniform feeling.... In opposing British imperialism and others of the kind, the Egyptian people, the Indian people, the Chinese people, the Indonesian people face a single enemy ... therefore we should all forge on Asian community and oppose the foreign strongholds of imperialism.... That is the reason why we must adhere to the principle of Pan-Asianism.[14]

He concluded by saying that Indonesian and the Chinese peoples were "comrades-of-one-fate, comrades-of-one-endeavor, comrades-of-one-front". Sukarno told a visiting KMT official in 1946 that Indonesia's state theory was not much different from that of Sun Yat-sen's.[15] As a result of this perceived parallel, Sukarno liked to point to Sun Yat-sen's strategy of uniting nationalists and Communists as a vindication for his own efforts to unite nationalism, Marxism and Islam.[16]

---

[13] Hering, *Soekarno*, p. 353.

[14] Sukarno, "Indonesianism and Pan-Asianism", p. 67; Hering, *Soekarno*, p. 153.

[15] Raliby Osman, *Documenta Historica*, vol. 1 (Jakarta: Bulan-Bintang, 1953), p. 213; *Merdeka*, 10 June 1946. In his meeting with the first Chinese ambassador to Jakarta in 1950, Sukarno remarked that he had studied Sun's Three People's Principles closely and was in complete agreement with his proposal of Asian cooperation. See "Wo Zhu Yinni Dashi yu Sujianuo Zongtong Tanhua Jiyao" [Records of Chinese ambassador's meeting with President Sukarno] (27 August 1950), file no. 105-00070-02, Archives of the Ministry of Foreign Affairs, PRC. Bernhard Dahm suggests that Sukarno's call for unlimited cooperation among all Asian peoples was "no doubt under the influence of Sun Yat-sen". Dahm, *Sukarno*, pp. 115–6.

[16] Sukarno, *Nationalism, Islam and Marxism*, pp. 40–1, 43, 58, 60.

Third, the post-1949 China remained a nationalistic and populist state in Sukarno's perception. Like many Indonesian intellectuals of his time, he viewed Mao's theory of New Democracy as a genuine expression of Chinese nationalism and an extension of the Three People's Principles.[17] As Sukarno had acknowledged earlier that these principles constituted one of the major intellectual foundations of Indonesia's state ideology, he developed a sense of affinity with the PRC and with Mao Zedong, whom he perceived as a successor of Sun Yat-sen and heir to the Chinese tradition.[18] He followed China's political development closely throughout the first half of the 1950s and was deeply impressed by its "democratic centralism". He suggested in 1954 that Indonesia should establish a People's Congress similar to the one in China.[19] Sukarno was fairly familiar with the political and cultural writings of Mao and Lu Xun, a renowned left-leaning Chinese writer.[20]

Sukarno's China, in brief, was characterized by its nationalistic underpinnings. The separation of China from Communism was a central feature in Sukarno's construction of pre-1956 China. A major reason for downplaying the role of Communism was that Sukarno's images of China were fashioned primarily by his domestic concerns. When national independence was his overriding consideration, he saw China mainly through the lens of nationalist inspirations. By the same token, his increasing frustrations with and criticisms of Western-style democracy sparked an interest in

---

[17] This information on Sukarno's view of New Democracy is provided by Mr Soeto Meisen, Sukarno's personal assistant on China affairs and his Chinese interpreter (personal interview in Hong Kong). According to him, Sukarno's understanding of the Chinese political system was very much influenced by Barioen's *Melihat Tiongkok Baru* (Jakarta: Rada, 1952), which paints China in a favourable populist light.

[18] When Sukarno met Mao in 1956, he told Mao three times that he regarded him as "a good disciple of Confucius". Wu Jiangxiong, ed., *Mao Zedong Pingdian Guoji Renwu* [Mao Zedong comments upon international figures] (Hefei: Anhui Renmin Chubanshe, 1998), vol. 2, p. 1155.

[19] Cited in R. Howie, "Sino-Indonesian Relations, 1950–1959: A Study of the Chinese People's Republic's Policy towards a Non-Communist State in South East Asia" (M.A. thesis, University of Western Australia, 1966), pp. 109–10.

[20] Interview in Beijing with Chen Lishui, the Indonesian-language interpreter for Chinese ambassadors throughout the 1950s, who met with Sukarno on a number of formal and informal occasions.

the PRC experience; a non-Communist China appeared to have provided a plausible alternative.

Despite the fact that Sukarno was largely a figurehead president with only symbolic power in the first half of the 1950s, the Chinese authorities considered him to be the paramount leader holding ultimate authority over Indonesia's domestic and external policies. Sukarno was at the centre of Beijing's endeavours to win Indonesia's hearts and minds. The Chinese apparently hoped that a pro-China president would have a positive influence on the attitudes of the general public and policy-makers toward the PRC. Before taking up his post as ambassador to Jakarta in 1954, Huang Zhen had decided to focus his diplomatic efforts on Sukarno. Convinced that "President Sukarno is a patriot and a nationalist leader of Indonesia", Prime Minister Zhou Enlai instructed Huang to cultivate close ties with Sukarno.[21] China's strong interest in Sukarno was manifested not only in the policy dimension, but at the personal level. The Chinese, for example, regularly provided Sukarno with *dim sum* (one of his favourite foods) made by the ambassadors' chefs.[22] A mutual interest in painting also contributed to close personal ties between Sukarno and Huang. In the summer of 1956, at the request of Sukarno, Huang Zhen arranged the publication of a six-volume set *Paintings from the Collection of Dr. Sukarno* (in Chinese) in Beijing, which had not appeared in any other language, including Indonesian.[23] A volume of Sukarno's selected speeches, emphasizing the themes of anti-imperialism and Afro-Asian solidarity, was published in Chinese at

---

[21] Zhu Lin, *Dashi Furen Huiyilu: Xunyali, Yinni, Faguo, Meiguo* [Memoirs of an ambassador's wife: Hungary, Indonesia, France and the USA] (Beijing: Shijie Zhishi Chubanshe, 1991), p. 44; and Yao Zhongming *et al.*, *Jiangjun, Waijiaojia, Yishujia — Huang Zhen Jilian Wenji* [General, diplomat and artist — A collection of articles in commemorating Huang Zhen] (Beijing: Jiefangjun Chubanshe, 1992), pp. 342–3.
[22] Zhu Lin, *Dashi*, pp. 63–4.
[23] Huang graduated from the prestigious Shanghai Art Academy before joining the CCP. At the request of Sukarno in 1958, China extended Huang's tenure as the ambassador for three additional years. This was unprecedented in the diplomatic practice of both China and Indonesia. See Yao Zhongming, *Jiangjun*, pp. 341–3, 361. On Sukarno's artistic sensibility and its political implications, see Angus McIntyre, "Sukarno as Artist-Politician", in *Indonesian Political Biography: In Search of Cross-Cultural Understanding*, ed. Angus McIntyre (Clayton: Centre of Southeast Asian Studies, Monash University, 1993), pp. 161–210.

the same time. It was an indication that China apparently saw Sukarno as a major anti-Western leader in the newly independent nations. No other Indonesian leader of that time, not even the Communist Party chairman, D.N. Aidit, had been accorded similar recognition.[24] Sukarno was apparently quite pleased with the publication of his writings and painting collections in China, which, he said, "has made Indonesian arts known throughout the world".[25] In the meantime, the significant improvement of the Sino-Indonesia relationship after the 1955 Bandung Conference undoubtedly contributed to Sukarno's positive opinion about China. The signing of the Sino-Indonesian Dual Nationality Treaty in the same year further paved the way for his upcoming visit to the PRC.[26]

Sukarno's attraction to the PRC thus converged nicely with the latter's attempt to cultivate his support. One of his advisers visited the Chinese embassy in Jakarta on 18 January 1956, conveying the view that Sukarno "was extremely interested in visiting China" and requesting materials about its socio-economic developments so that he would have a better understanding of the country. A week later, the Chinese Ministry of Foreign Affairs responded to the embassy report by saying that the central government "attached very high importance" to Sukarno's proposed visit and an invitation was subsequently forwarded, thus initiating the historic 1956 visit.[27]

---

[24] Yao Zhongming, *Jiangjun*, pp. 633–4; Zhu Lin, *Dashi*, p. 64; and David Mozingo, *Chinese Policy toward Indonesia, 1949–1967* (Ithaca: Cornell University Press, 1976), p. 150.

[25] Interview with Chen Lishui in Beijing. This view was confirmed in a confidential briefing by the Chinese ministry of foreign affairs about Sukarno's visit to China in 1956. File no. 2004-00030-04, Archives of the Ministry of Foreign Affairs, PRC.

[26] See, for details, Ronald C. Keith, *The Diplomacy of Zhou Enlai* (London: Macmillan, 1989), pp. 80–7; and Mozingo, *Chinese Policy toward Indonesia*, Chapter 4. See Seng Tan and Amitav Acharya, eds., *Bandung Revisited: The Legacy of the 1955 Asian-African Conference for International Order* (Singapore: NUS Press, 2008).

[27] "Sujianuo Zongtong Fanhua Yaoqing Jingguo" [The process of inviting President Sukarno to visit China], file no. 204-00030-01 (18–25 January 1956), Archives of the Ministry of Foreign Affairs, PRC. Willard A. Hanna's contention that China extended an invitation to Sukarno *after* he had been invited by the United States and the Soviet Union is mistaken. See Hanna, "Sukarno: The Devolution of a Revolutionary", in his *Eight Nation Makers* (New York: St. Martin's Press, 1964), p. 71.

# MR SUKARNO GOES TO BEIJING

## The Context

Sukarno travelled to China in autumn 1956. It was a critical time both in Indonesia's postcolonial history and in his personal odyssey.[28] It had become apparent at the end of 1955 that the high expectations born with the winning of independence were largely unfulfilled; the dream of establishing a just and prosperous society had been shattered by the realities of political instability, economic stagnation and social disarray. The first national election in 1955 further exacerbated the country's problems by deepening existing cleavages. Within this turbulent environment, Indonesia's political and intellectual leaders were confronted with daunting questions: What had gone wrong with their nation? Was Western-style democracy the most viable political system for the country? If not, what was a suitable alternative? Sukarno was a leading politician in articulating the nation's profound sense of estrangement and frustration while painfully searching for a way forward. Even before 1956, Sukarno had been an outspoken critic of parliamentary democracy, but he was not sure exactly what political and social institutions might best replace the existing system; nor was he certain as to what theoretical foundation should underlie the new system. Although he did mention the concept of Guided Democracy in the early 1950s, many questions remained unanswered. For example, how to balance leadership with democracy? How to mobilize the people for socio-economic construction, yet at the same time maintain political stability? What was the most effective ideological guidance for the proposed new structure? Sukarno did not have any clear-cut answers to these pressing questions. It was at this critical juncture that the China model emerged as a significant factor influencing his plan to reform Indonesia.

Sukarno's 1956 overseas trips were crucial in providing him with conceptual and practical examples of nation-building, and would in turn

---

[28] John Legge points out that "the end of 1956 marks a turning point in Sukarno's political career". See his *Sukarno*, p. 271. Willard A. Hanna concurs, "For both Sukarno and for Indonesia, the year 1956 was by far the most critical since 1945. It was a year of chaos, when every individual national leader was privately and publicly seeking for the 'way out', but everybody blocked everybody else's exit. In the past Bung Karno had always provided the nation with the formulas which inspired action, but in 1956 Bung Karno, like everyone else, seemed to be baffled". See his "Sukarno: The Devolution of a Revolutionary", p. 70.

play a key role in (re)formulating his own vision for Indonesia. These trips were also significant because they afforded him opportunities to observe and compare the world's two major social systems.[29] After his visit to the United States and Western Europe between May and June 1956, Sukarno travelled to Yugoslavia, Czechoslovakia, the USSR, Mongolia and the PRC. Prior to starting these state visits, Sukarno declared that he had a far-reaching agenda in mind: "After my return from these foreign visits, I will be able to say for certain what would be the best course for us to follow in our task of nation building."[30] In a similar vein, Foreign Minister Roeslan Abdulgani subsequently reported to parliament regarding the president's foreign trips: "What we have seen can at least be used as matter for comparison and study in our own task of upbuilding and in our endeavors to achieve greater production than we have done up to now.... In various ways we are able to draw upon their experience."[31]

By his own account, Sukarno's trip to the United States was more or less a disappointment. Although he was impressed by its material progress, Sukarno realized that the two nations were at different stages of development and that it would be difficult for his nation to catch up with America. While Indonesia was a newly independent nation, the United States had long since established itself as the most industrialized country in the

---

[29] Sukarno travelled extensively and was widely exposed to both the West and East: between 1959 and 1963, he spent almost one year outside Indonesia, visiting 41 countries in 319 days abroad. Although some of these trips were private affairs, many travels were on state business. These trips included: Japan (60 days, including 33 on mostly private trips), Austria (44 days, mostly on private holidays) and Italy (20 days). The United States ranked high with 15 days (1959, 1960 and 1961); 14 days in the Soviet Union, 5 in Cuba, 17 days in Yugoslavia and 26 days in other countries of the Eastern Bloc. Thus he spent approximately 50 per cent of his time in Asia, Africa and Latin America, 30 per cent visiting North America and Western Europe, and 20 per cent in Communist countries. See Jeroen Touwen, "Indonesia's Foreign Policy and Trade, 1957–1965: Economic Reorientation versus Political Realignment", in *Europe-Southeast Asia in the Contemporary World: Mutual Images and Reflections 1940s–1960s*, ed. Piyanart Bunnag, Franz Knipping and Sud Chonchirdsin (Baden-Baden: Normos Verlagsgesellschaft, 2000), p. 176.
[30] Quoted in Ganis Harsono, *Recollections of an Indonesian Diplomat in the Sukarno Era* (St. Lucia: University of Queensland Press, 1977), p. 145.
[31] Roeslan Abdulgani, *The Foreign Minister's Report to Parliament on President Soekarno's Second Tour, August 26–October 16, 1956* (Jakarta: Department of Foreign Affairs, 1956), p. 47.

world. Meanwhile, as a politician who despised capitalism and the social inequality it produced, Sukarno was unlikely to be attracted by the modern American experience. This was perhaps a major reason why Sukarno liked to inform his Indonesian audiences that he did not consider the American trip politically significant.[32]

Although Sukarno and his party were well received by the Russians, they were not very pleased with the trip to the Soviet Union, which was described as "something considerably less than an unqualified success".[33] Sukarno and his entourage were surprised to discover the existence of serious social problems in the USSR. For example, despite the Soviet Union's tremendous material progress, the Indonesians encountered filth, poverty, squalor, and 19th-century rather than 20th-century conditions of life and work. They were also dismayed by the Russians' ill treatment of Muslims. In the words of Zainul Arifin, second deputy speaker of parliament, "Here the Moslem religion resembles a lamp in which the light has almost died out and the oil has not been renewed."[34] According to one of Sukarno's aides, in spite of the Russians' well-orchestrated effort to win Sukarno's sympathy, "I did not see any indication on the part of Bung Karno to change his outlook, and I guess *Time* magazine of 17 September [1956] was right in saying that 'though Sukarno was a brother he was by no means a comrade'".[35]

There was perhaps a cultural element in Sukarno's unenthusiastic attitude toward the USA and the USSR. As noted earlier, Sukarno had long embraced the idea of pan-Asianism and tended to see the world as divided

---

[32] See, for example, "Mengapa Presiden Ambil Tjontoh Pembangunan dari RRT?" *Sin Min*, 31 August 1957. The United States ambassador to Indonesia, Hugh S. Cumming, seemed to have the same impression. "There isn't a great deal to say [about Sukarno's trip to the U.S. in 1956]", Cumming recalled later. "Sukarno's own book shows his disappointment at not having been treated with greater intimacy.... He was disillusioned a little bit — disillusioned in that respect; overwhelmed in another — with the hopelessness of ever bringing his people up to us". See "A Transcript of a Recorded Interview with Ambassador Hugh S. Cumming, Jr." (1 December 1966), *The John Foster Dulles Oral History Project* (Princeton University Library), pp. 23–4.

[33] Willard A. Hanna, "Moscow Comes to Bung Karno — And So Does Peking", *American Universities Field Staff* (Southeast Asia Series), no. 20 (30 November 1956), p. 4.

[34] Ibid., p. 6.

[35] Harsono, *Recollections*, p. 160.

between East and West, and he had come to believe that the East could serve as the moral leader of the world. This conviction was clearly manifested in one of his 1956 speeches, entitled "The Spiritual Movement in Asia as a World Moral Force", delivered at Heidelberg, West Germany. Asserting that the economic and military power and efficiency on which Western nations set such great store were far less important than the moral principles of the East, Sukarno proclaimed,

> The strongest power in this world is the idea. Our philosophy rests on ethical principles and our state is founded on this ethical basis. And ethical principles determine the whole of our life.... The power of the idea is superior to all other forces and all nations have at all times recognized this and have established a spiritual and moral order. But you have often misused this order and have given it a materialistic imprint with the result that there is a conflict between principles and practice.[36]

In short, Indonesia's undesirable domestic situation propelled Sukarno to compare his own country with the outside world in an effort to search for an alternative, while the disappointing impressions of his American and Soviet trips compelled him to look to China as a source of inspiration. Sukarno's intention to establish the nation's future political system within a broadly defined Eastern tradition reinforced the potential attraction of the PRC model.

## Sukarno in China: Metamorphosis through Personal Experiences

Sukarno arrived in Beijing on 30 September 1956. Immediately upon landing, he sensed that the receptions for all his other state visits were dwarfed by the magnificent scale of the PRC reception. Praising Sukarno as "the most distinguished visitor and a staunch champion of anti-colonialism", the Chinese hailed his visit as the most significant event in Sino-Indonesian relations.[37] A Chinese reporter vividly described the colourful welcoming scene:

> The importance of President Sukarno's visit to China was amply reflected in the fervour of the welcome accorded to him by the Chinese people. Everywhere he went he was greeted by huge crowds, acclaiming him

---

[36] Cited in Penders, *The Life and Times of Sukarno*, pp. 154–5.
[37] *Presiden Sukarno Mengunjungi Tiongkok* (issued by the Chinese Embassy in Jakarta, 1956), p. 1.

Sukarno was welcomed by Mao and the Chinese in Beijing, 1956 (Photograph by Yuan Ling, by permission of the Xinhua News Agency, ID: 13187795).

with deafening cheers.... Practically the whole Chinese government went to the airport to meet him. The car in which he and Chairman Mao rode was followed by an endless line of others. When the first car entered the walled city many others had not yet left the airport, so long was the file.[38]

More than 300,000 Chinese lined up along the streets from the airport to downtown to welcome Sukarno. In the words of his personal aide, "It was a throbbing red human carpet that engulfed Sukarno upon arrival, led personally by Chairman Mao Tse-tung. This human carpet shouted and cheered 'Hidup Bung Karno' (Long Live Bung Karno)".[39] Roeslan Abdulgani was equally overwhelmed by the reception, "which was so colorful it was as though it reflected the glory and the thousands of years old history and culture of China".[40]

---

[38] Wang En-yuan, "President Sukarno in Peking", *People's China*, no. 21 (1 November 1956), p. 8.
[39] Harsono, *Recollections*, p. 162.
[40] Roeslan Abdulgani, *Foreign Minister's Report*, p. 54.

Sukarno was moved to tears by the magnificent scale of welcome accorded to him.[41] As his aide put it, "the line of communication between the two leaders [Sukarno and Mao] seemed to be immediately established and they hugged each other as if they had known each other for a long time".[42] This sensation of personal affinity was reinforced by the Chinese leaders' constant emphasis on the themes of mutual interests and Asian solidarity. In his welcoming speech, Mao complimented Sukarno for his "outstanding leadership" in the struggle against colonialism and reminded his guests that both countries shared the same aspirations. "What are the ideals of the Indonesian people?" Mao posed the question pointedly, "They are ideals of independence, peace, and a new world. These are precisely the same ideals of the Chinese people".[43] Echoing Mao, Sukarno declared, "The Chinese and Indonesian peoples have many things in common.... Your ideal is to build a new world free from exploitation, misery, and oppression — a world in which people can live freely and happily. Such are also our ideals".[44] Sukarno regarded the Chinese not only as "brothers" but as "comrades-in-arms". "The victory of China is the victory of Indonesia," he proclaimed, "And the victory of Indonesia is the victory of China".[45]

---

[41] "Sujianuo Zongtong Fanhua Jiedai Jianbao" [Briefing on the reception of President Sukarno's visit to China, No. 1] (1–7 October 1956), file no. 2004-00030-03, Archives of the Ministry of Foreign Affairs, PRC.

[42] Harsono, *Recollections*, p. 162.

[43] Michael Y.M. Kau and John K. Leung, eds., *The Writings of Mao Zedong, 1949–1976*, vol. 2 (Armonk, NY: M.E. Sharpe, 1992), pp. 143, 145. Mao told Sukarno that he had read his "remarkable" address to the US Congress and complimented him for being "the representative of the whole Asia", with which Sukarno happily concurred, and informed Mao that American political leaders were not very pleased with what he had said. He Ming, ed., *Weiren Mao Zedong* [Mao Zedong, the great man] (Beijing: Zhongyan Wenxian Chubanshe, 2003), vol. 2, p. 851.

[44] Cited in Zou Sheng, ed., *Su Jia Nuo Zongtong zai Zhongguo* [President Sukarno in China] (Hong Kong: Zhonghua Shuju, 1957), pp. 167–8. This is a collection of Sukarno's speeches in China; the Indonesian version, entitled *Presiden Sukarno di Tiongkok*, was published by the Foreign Language Press in Beijing in 1956. After comparing the Chinese version with the Indonesian one as well as with those speeches appearing in the Indonesian newspapers, I found the Chinese translation to be an accurate reflection of the original texts.

[45] *Sin Min*, 5–6 Oct. 1956. Unlike the previous tours to the USA and the USSR, Sukarno's China trip was widely and positively covered by the Indonesian press.

Within this amiable atmosphere, Sukarno toured China for 17 days and visited the cities of Beijing, Shenyang, Anshan, Changchun, Luda, Nanjing, Shanghai, Hangzhou, Wuhan, Guangzhou (Canton) and Kunming. Like many other Indonesians who visited China in the mid-1950s, Sukarno's impressions were profoundly favourable. He was particularly amazed by China's seemingly remarkable economic progress, strong leadership and political stability, and the mobilization of a people with high spirit.

Sukarno displayed a genuine admiration for China's massive economic development. An engineer by training, he was especially interested in China's ongoing big projects, such as the construction of the Yangtze River Bridge.[46] Hailing the PRC for entering an era "with a bright future", Sukarno said that further achievements in the economic sphere would surely follow the "existing marvellous accomplishments".[47] The report to parliament by Foreign Minister Roeslan Abdulgani, which may be taken as a reflection of Sukarno's fascination with China's progress, stated that the delegation returned with concrete impressions that "the People's Republic of China is now catching up with the level of the West in the field of production and industry".[48] To Sukarno, the key to China's success lay not in its Communist ideology, but in its political stability, which was symbolized by the unification of the Chinese people who constituted "a single entity". "Because of this solidarity", he announced, "the PRC will never be eliminated".[49] This political stability was further facilitated by the existence of a strong and unified leadership. Sukarno told Indonesian journalists that "Chinese leaders are model working human beings; they talk little and work a lot".[50]

---

See, for example, A. Karim D.P., "Dengan Bung Karno Melihat Dunia Baru: Perobahan Tjara Berpikir di RRT", *Sin Po* (Jakarta), 13–16 November 1956; Juti (Melik Sayuti), "Limabelas Hari di Tiongkok", *Suluh Indonesia* (Jakarta), 26–30 October 1956; and Adinegoro, "Xin Shijie: Suitong Zhongtong Chuguo Fanwenji" [A new world: Visiting foreign countries with the president] *Hsin Pao* (Jakarta), 23 October–1 November 1956.

[46] Interview with Soeto Mei-sen (Hong Kong).
[47] Zou Sheng, *Su Jia Luo*, pp. 162–3.
[48] Roeslan Abdulgani, *Foreign Minister's Report*, p. 47.
[49] Zou Sheng, *Su Jia Luo*, p. 154.
[50] A. Karim D.P., "Dengan Bung Karno Melihat Dunia Baru", *Sin Po*, 16 November 1956.

Sukarno's most profound impression was the high *semangat* (spirit) of the Chinese people, thus sharing a populist interpretation with the majority of Indonesia's China observers. This populist undertone was characterized by the assumption that responsibility for the PRC's remarkable achievements lay primarily with the people rather than the Communist Party. Implicit in this explanation was a tendency to minimize the influence of Communist ideology and the theory of class struggle. Sukarno attributed China's rapid progress to two major factors: China was endowed with all the essential natural resources for economic development; and more importantly, the Chinese people — "the PRC's most valuable asset" — who worked industriously and were willing to sacrifice individual interests for the nation's well-being. This emphasis on the *semangat*, hard work and discipline of the people ran through all of Sukarno's observations regarding China. "When Chairman Mao Zedong lived in the mountains [during the anti-Japanese and anti-KMT wars], what did he possess? What did his followers possess?" Sukarno posed these questions to his Chinese audiences and gave his answer: "All they possessed was high morale and burning *semangat*, which explains why Chairman Mao was eventually able to establish the PRC".[51] This spirit could generate tangible consequences. "Because of the fervent hearts and burning *semangat*," he said to workers in an industrial city, "you are able to build up this gigantic industrial enterprise here". Sukarno concluded that the mighty *semangat* was the single most effective weapon both Indonesia and China possessed.[52]

To be sure, the emphasis on spiritual power, strong leadership and unity were all essential ingredients in Sukarno's thinking long before his visit to China. What he saw in the PRC, however, proved for the first time that these elements were not only fundamental for a successful nationalist movement, but critical for the very process of nation-building. The Chinese example thus reaffirmed for Sukarno the validity of his long-held ideas. This newfound inspiration was to become a vital driving force in Sukarno's subsequent efforts to transform the Indonesian society and political system. With such an understanding of China's progress and its dynamics, Sukarno became very interested in its methods of forging unity and igniting the people's spiritual power, and raised a number of pointed questions with Chinese leaders regarding their approaches to national development. His inquiries were framed with the hope of finding solutions for his own

---

[51] Zou Sheng, *Su Jia Nuo*, p. 117.
[52] Ibid., pp. 117, 132.

nation's domestic problems. One of his central concerns was the relationship between democracy, dictatorship, political stability and leadership. Mao Zedong, who had long held that democracy was merely "a means to an end", suggested to him that "it is necessary to have democracy; but it is also imperative to have solidarity and to avoid chaos". Both Mao and Zhou Enlai reportedly said that Sukarno should not be a Communist but a Sun Yet-sen who could unify all political factions.[53] Marshal Chen Yi, the vice-premier (and after 1958 the foreign minister), played an important part in conveying positive information regarding China to Sukarno. Chen had met Sukarno at the 1955 Bandung Conference and accompanied the Indonesian delegation throughout its China journey. At the request of Sukarno, Chen gave him detailed explanations of China's experiences in economic development.[54] At one point Sukarno asked him about the techniques used to control the military (apparently reflecting Sukarno's attempt to cope with the increasingly strained civilian-military relationship in Indonesia at the time). Chen Yi remarked that one of the most effective methods was the regular rotation of regional military commanders.[55] He further explained to Sukarno the fundamentals of China's "democracy with leadership" and how it differed from the "sham" democracy of the West. During his China trip, Sukarno remarked a number of times that the main problem with Indonesia was the lack of strong leadership, which had led the country to "anarchic democracy".[56] He asked Chen about methods of governing such a huge country like the PRC. "Chairman Mao Tse-tung has formulated the best leadership methods", answered Chen Yi, "he used to say that the most important ones are to offer inspiring ideas and to make

---

[53] Interview with Chen Lishui, who was present at the Mao-Sukarno meeting. When visiting Indonesia in April 1961, Marshal Chen Yi, Chinese vice-premier and minister of foreign affairs, said to Sukarno that "we treat you like our friend. I think there is no harm in being a bourgeoisie revolutionary; Mr. Sun Yat-sen was one of our great historical figures". See Hu Shiyang, *Chen Yi Zhuang* [A biography of Chen Yi] (Beijing: Dantai Zhongguo Chubanshe, 1991), p. 574.

[54] He Xiaolu, *Yuanshuai Waijiaojia* [The marshal diplomat] (Beijing: Jiefangjun Wenyi Chubanshe, 1985), p. 187; Jiang Hongwu, *Chen Yi Zhuang* [A biography of Chen Yi] (Shanghai: Shanghai Renmin Chubanshe, 1992), pp. 702–3.

[55] Interview with Chen Lishui (Beijing).

[56] "Sujianuo Zongtong Fanghua Jiedai Jianbao" [Briefing on the reception of President Sukarno's visit to China, Nos. 9 and 15] (9–15 October 1956), file no. 2004-00030-06, Archives of the Ministry of Foreign Affairs, PRC.

Sukarno and Mao Zedong, Beijing, 1956 [*Presiden Sukarno Mengundjungi Tiongkok* (Jakarta: Kedutaan Besar Republik Rakjat Tiongkok di Indonesia, 1956)].

good use of cadres." Chen then proceeded to describe in detail the application of these methods, which greatly impressed Sukarno.[57]

Sukarno's 1956 trip to China was a key factor in shaping his perception of the PRC. Considering the PRC to be a successful example of socio-economic development in newly independent nations, he liked to employ China as a foil for revealing the deficiencies of Indonesia's postcolonial transformation. He was convinced that the PRC had in effect realized some of his own ideals for Indonesia. On his way back home, Sukarno told reporters that "during my visits to the newly emerged people's democratic countries I witnessed the realization of my ideals formulated since 1929…. In the PRC I saw the practice of a guided democracy (*demokrasi terpimpin*), and only this democracy with guidance can bring people into a new world, a truly just and prosperous new world".[58]

---

[57] Ibid. He Xiaolu, *Yuanshuai*, p. 188; Hu Shiyang, *Chen Yi Zhuang*, pp. 573–4. In his frequent meetings with Ambassador Huang Zhen, Sukarno was similarly interested in the issues regarding China's socio-economic development and its mechanisms. See Yao Zhongming, *Jiangjun*, pp. 376–8.

[58] *Harian Rakjat*, 17 October 1956; *Hsin Pao*, 18 October 1956.

# SUKARNO'S PERCEPTION OF CHINA AND VISION FOR INDONESIA

## The Transition to Guided Democracy and the China Inspiration

The years between 1956 and 1958 were crucial for Sukarno in reformulating his blueprint for Indonesia. In this process, he consistently utilized the example of China as a point of reference to validate his call for fundamental change. This was illustrated by the numerous references to China in almost all of his major speeches after his return. More specifically, his presentation of China-images was unambiguously linked to his views for transforming Indonesian society, which can be seen from three interlinked dimensions: the necessity of change, the direction of change and the methods of change.

In the first place, the China example reinforced Sukarno's belief that Indonesia should fundamentally restructure its existing political system. The chaotic domestic situation presented a stark contrast to what he had witnessed in China. As soon as he landed in Jakarta on 17 October 1956, Sukarno remarked that he "felt revolted (*muak*) at seeing our conditions here" and that he was appalled by the "degeneration" of Indonesia's political parties.[59] On 28 October, in his first public speech after coming back from his recent overseas trip, Sukarno stated that he had been immensely impressed by the Chinese people's efforts at building a new society. This favourable comment served as a pretext for criticizing the disturbing situation at home: "we made a very great mistake in 1945 when we urged the establishment of parties, parties, and parties".[60] Two days later, Sukarno revealed that he had a "conception" (*konsepsi*) for coping with the country's problems. He had long been dissatisfied with the way in which parties had become vehicles for serving the personal interests of their leaders, said Sukarno, but he had never publicly expressed his dissatisfaction before. The China trip seemed to have led to a partial change of mind. "I came back from my visit to the Soviet Union and the PRC with a tremendous sense of amazement", declared Sukarno, "I no longer dream and I propose

---

[59] *Sin Min*, 1 November 1956.
[60] Sukarno, *Indonesia, Pilihlah Demokrasimu Jang Sedjati* (*Pidato Presiden Sukarno pada Hari Sumpah Pemuda tgl. 28 Oktober 1956 dan Pidato Presiden Sukarno pada Resepsi Kongres P.G.R.I. ke-8 tgl. 30 Okt. 1956*), 2nd printing (Jakarta: Jajasan Prapantja, 1961), p. 11.

that the leaders of the people confer and decide to bury all parties".[61] In a speech delivered at Banjarmasin on 22 July 1957, Sukarno resumed his attack on parliamentary democracy as unsuitable for the country and urged Indonesians to take China's approach in order to get out of the current predicament.[62]

Second, the perceived China example provided Sukarno with a feasible model for the direction of change. If change was deemed necessary, as most Indonesians agreed, what direction should this change take? Sukarno had made it clear that Western-style democracy did not work in Indonesia and concluded that both the United States and the Soviet Union were too advanced for his country to learn any practical lessons from. His observations of China's practices, on the other hand, reinforced his opinion that Asia was different and that problems in the region should be dealt with by using "Asian formulas". As a newly independent Asian country that had made remarkable accomplishments, the PRC clearly had great appeal to him. Following Mao, he came to believe that democracy was merely "a means to an end", and came to be convinced that the two essential ingredients of the proposed new system would be "leadership" and "socio-democracy". This emerging conviction was partly inspired by what he had personally witnessed in China, namely, the vital role of the leadership, and stability in nation-building. In his "Conception Speech" on 30 October 1956, Sukarno announced,

> The democracy I would like to have for Indonesia is not the liberal democracy of the West.... What I like to have for Indonesia is a guided democracy, a democracy with leadership. A guided democracy, something which is guided but still democratic ... especially if we want to build as people have in other countries I have seen, for example, in the PRC.[63]

The Chinese practice of socio-democracy, as understood by Sukarno, left an imprint on the specific content of his remedies for Indonesia. On 3 July 1957, Sukarno delivered what he considered as "one of the most important speeches of his entire life" before the Indonesian Nationalist

---

[61] Quoted in Arnold C. Brackman, *Indonesian Communism: A History* (New York: Frederick A. Praeger, 1963), p. 227.

[62] Associated Press dispatch (Jakarta), 20 July 1957, quoted in *Cankao Xiaoxi* (Beijing), 22 July 1957.

[63] Sukarno, *Indonesia, Pilihlah*, p. 24.

Party Conference at Bandung.[64] Distinguishing socio-democracy from parliamentary democracy (the "philosophy of a rising bourgeoisie" in the West), Sukarno argued that Indonesia should adopt a socio-democracy that would lead to economic prosperity and social equality. For this purpose it was necessary to place the concept of "freedom" in an appropriate context. "In the United States of America priority is given to *freedom of speech* and *freedom from want* comes later", but this practice, Sukarno insisted, created social inequality. On the other hand, in the Soviet Union and the PRC, "what is given priority, what is sought first is *freedom from want*; *freedom of speech*, if need be, comes late".[65] He then spoke in detail of his conversation with Madame Soong Ching Ling (Sun Yat-sen's widow) in Beijing a few months earlier, and cited approvingly Soong's answer to his question of why China placed freedom from want before freedom of speech: "because the stomach does not want to wait".[66] He concluded that Indonesia should have a system of socio-democracy, "within which Parliament has the authority to determine the nation's political and economic policies, as in the PRC and the Soviet Union".[67]

Third, the PRC served as a viable model for how to generate constructive political change. With the question of the need for change and the direction of change answered, the question of how to implement the necessary transformation came to the fore. Once again, Sukarno employed China to validate his own approach. Two methods particularly caught his attention: the mobilization of the people and the establishment of a cadre system. Mass mobilization had long been Sukarno's favourite approach to social change; the PRC experiences strengthened his confidence in its effectiveness. For instance, he pointed out that China had made remarkable progress in industrial production, and Indonesia could imitate some of its methods.[68] After coming back from the PRC, Sukarno further elaborated his opinion that China's success mainly lay not in its political system, but in a mobilized and highly spirited people.[69] The question, then, was how

---

[64] See George Kahin's preface to Sukarno, *Marhaen and Proletarian* (Ithaca: Cornell Modern Indonesian Project, 1960), p. iii.
[65] Ibid., p. 19 (emphasis is original).
[66] Ibid., pp. 19–20.
[67] *New China News Agency*, 14 November 1956. See also, "Mengapa Presiden Ambil Tjontoh Pembangunan dari RRT?" *Sin Min*, 31 August 1957.
[68] *Tay Kong Sian Po* (Surabaya), 11 June 1957.
[69] *Seng Hwo Pao* (Jakarta), 20 April 1957; and Brackman, *The Communist Party of Indonesia*, p. 227.

to mobilize the people. Sukarno was perhaps reminded of his extended discussions with Chen Yi, who had suggested that the essential elements of China's leadership methods were "offering inspiring ideas and making good use of cadres". On his way back home, Sukarno approvingly referred to the China example: "Because the Chinese people have clear goals and high *semangat*, they are able to carry out massive construction successfully. Indonesian leaders should inspire the people with ideals so that economic growth can be achieved."[70] In his 30 October 1956 "Conception Speech", he affirmed the view that China's massive mobilization was the product of a well-organized cadre system, which could effectively unify the nation; he called for the establishment of a similar system to enkindle the people's spirit and facilitate national unity.[71] Sukarno felt strongly that Indonesia should adopt China's approach of "achieving solidarity through constructive criticisms" in an attempt to get out of the existing political and economic difficulties.[72] In a speech before a group of military officers in Bandung, Sukarno referred to the example of the Chinese military, which "is subordinated to the revolution and does not form a military clique", in justifying his plea for maintaining civilian supremacy over the military. He urged the government to send delegations to China to study the issue of how to balance the civilian-military relationship.[73]

Sukarno's interpretations of the PRC experience and the resultant changes to his ideas constituted one of the key rationales for the establishment of Guided Democracy in 1959. The new political system was characterized by three major institutional arrangements. First, under the 1945 Constitution the president had ultimate authority over domestic and foreign policies. Second, the cabinet operated on the principle of *gotong-royong* (mutual assistance), and all main parties (including the Communist Party) participated in the decision-making process. Third, the National Council (*Dewan Nasional*) replaced the parliament. The Council was a high advisory body in which various functional groups — workers, peasants, national businessmen, youth, women and so on — were represented; it

---

[70] *Hsin Pao*, 18 October 1956.
[71] Sukarno, *Indonesia, Pilihlah*, pp. 21–2.
[72] Associated Press dispatch (Jakarta), 20 July 1957, quoted in *Cankao Xiaoxi*, 22 July 1957.
[73] *Hsin Pao*, 12 November 1956; *Sin Min*, 13 November 1956.

operated through consultation (*musyawarah*) and consensus (*mufakat*) rather than by voting.[74]

Sukarno continued to be captivated by China throughout the Guided Democracy era. In September 1965 alone, he sent more than six government delegations to China, with the primary mission — according to Sukarno's instructions — of learning "what happened in China which could be of use to Indonesia at a later date".[75] The China factor came to be increasingly manifested in Indonesian domestic politics. During the closing years of the Guided Democracy regime, Sukarno became increasingly concerned about his inability to control the military, which had developed into a relatively independent political force. Apart from setting up a "fifth force" of armed workers and peasants to counterbalance the growing power of the army,[76] a more effective method appeared to be to directly influence military officers' way of thinking. Impressed by China's techniques of political indoctrination, Sukarno asked Marshal Chen Yi, on short notice, to come to Jakarta to lecture his generals in August 1965. One of the sessions lasted five hours, during which Chen Yi spoke in great detail about China's outlook on the world and his own analysis of the international situation.[77]

---

[74] The best studies of Indonesian politics during the Guided Democracy era remain Daniel Lev's *Transition to Guided Democracy: Indonesian Politics, 1957–1959* (Ithaca: Cornell University Modern Indonesian Project, 1966); and Herbert Feith, "Dynamics of Guided Democracy", in *Indonesia*, ed. Ruth McVey (New Haven: HRAF Press, 1963), pp. 309–409. See also David Bouchier and John Legge, eds., *Democracy in Indonesia: 1950s and 1990s* (Clayton: Centre of Southeast Asian Studies, Monash University, 1994).

[75] Quoted from Radhi S. Karni, ed., *The Devious Dalang: Sukarno and the So-called Untung Putsch, Eye-Witness Report by Bambang S. Widjanarko* (The Hague: Interdoc, 1975), p. 100.

[76] This scheme was first suggested by PKI leaders and it was reported that the PRC enthusiastically supported the plan. See Ide Anak Agung Gde Agung, *Twenty Years Indonesian Foreign Policy*, pp. 441–2; and Mozingo, *Chinese Policy toward Indonesia*, p. 227.

[77] Interviews (Washington, DC) with Huang Shuhai, who was Chen Yi's interpreter and with Soeto Mei-sen (Hong Kong). Some details of this talk were later repeated in an important press conference by Chen himself in Beijing on 29 September 1965. In this press conference, he dealt with a variety of international issues, including the Sino-Indian Boundary question, the Second African-Asian Conference, China's development of nuclear weapons, and the Sino-U.S. relationship. Chen Yi concluded

## The Experiment in New Social Engineering

It should be evident by now that Sukarno's perception of the PRC was contrived primarily to deal with domestic issues, and that China as seen through the eyes of Sukarno became a yardstick for intellectual judgement and a point of reference for political thinking. In other words, China was constructed as a mirror for demonstrating his own discontent — and aspirations — with respect to Indonesia's postcolonial transformation. This China metaphor not only constituted a significant factor in shaping Sukarno's political agendas for his nation, it also played a part in augmenting the new system with a new type of social engineering. Sukarno's attempt to mobilize the people from 1959 to 1965 was similarly influenced by Chinese methods of generating social change from the top down. The launching of the New Life Movement (*Gerakan Hidup Baru*) presents a case in point.

In his August 1957 National Day speech, Sukarno announced a national effort of austerity, discipline and hard work. The concept of this movement was formulated earlier, and was perhaps partly modelled after the New Life Movement initiated by the Japanese in Java during World War II.[78] The immediate inspiration, however, stemmed from Sukarno's admiration for the extraordinary discipline and assiduousness displayed by the Chinese people. In April 1957, Sukarno called for "self-discipline and self-correction",[79] a formulation reminiscent of his praise for China's approach of "realizing unity through criticism and self-criticism". This appeal may be seen as a starting point of the New Life Movement, but the specific content of the movement remained unclear until the return of Colonel Sumarno from a trip to China. As vice-president of Indonesia's

---

his talk with this remark: "With the defeat of U.S. imperialism, the time will come when imperialism and colonialism will be really liquidated throughout the world. The ideal is bound to come true when the world truly becomes a community of nations with different social systems coexisting peacefully. China is ready to make all the necessary sacrifices for this noble ideal". For the full text of Chen Yi's speech, see Harold C. Hinton, ed., *The People's Republic of China, 1949–1979: A Documentary Survey*, vol. 2 (Wilmington, DE: Scholarly Resources Inc., 1980), pp. 1247–53.

[78] The New Life Movement in early 1945 included exhortations such as "respect your parents", "do not tell lies", "learn reading and writing", and "get up early and start working early in the morning". Shigeru Sato, *War, Nationalism, and Peasants: Java under the Japanese Occupation, 1942–1945* (Armonk, NY: M.E. Sharpe, 1994), pp. 77–9.

[79] *Sin Min*, 27 April 1957.

Red Cross organization and the director of the Health Department of the Army,[80] Sumarno was the vice-head of a military delegation that visited the PRC in May 1957; the group was led by General Gatot Subroto, vice-chief-of-staff of the army. During the 40-day trip, they travelled extensively to various regions and came back with positive impressions, not only of the integration of the military with society at large, but of China's economic progress and social dynamics.[81]

Shortly after the delegation's return in June, Sumarno delivered a public speech in Jakarta to government officials, in which he commended China's annual nationwide cleanliness movement, the government's initiatives in educating its citizens, and the leadership's efforts in serving as role models for the people. Sumarno then suggested that the Indonesian government and people should employ the PRC example in launching the New Life Movement.[82] In early August, the Indonesian-China Friendship Association further promoted the idea,[83] and in mid-August Sukarno formally announced the beginning of the New Life Movement, whose central tenets were basically in line with his own favourable observations of China and Sumarno's recommendations. The goals promoted by this movement were, among others, sober living, health and cleanliness, and literacy. Sukarno challenged "the upper classes" to live a "simpler life" and to set an example for the people.[84]

Although this movement was short-lived,[85] it clearly demonstrated Sukarno's determined intention to transform society by utilizing the state as a central catalyst. The rationale behind this movement was in accordance with Sukarno's strong conviction in leadership and in people's initiatives for generating political change. Similar efforts at social engineering were

---

[80] Sumarno was appointed by Sukarno in 1960 as the head of region (governor of Jakarta), who reported directly to the president. See McIntyre, "Sukarno as Artist-Politician", p. 182.
[81] *Seng Hwo Pao*, 27 June 1957; and Xia Minzhi, "Yindunixiya de Jiangjunmen zai Beijing" [Indonesian generals in Beijing], *Minzhu Ribao* (Medan), 28 June 1957.
[82] Kol. Dr. Sumarno, "'New Life Movement' di RRT Dapat Tjontoh di Indonesia", *Sin Min*, 29 July 1957.
[83] *Sin Min*, 6 August 1957.
[84] Sukarno, "1957, a Year of Decision in Indonesian History", *Indonesian Spectator* (Jakarta), 1 September 1957, pp. 14–5.
[85] On the evolution of this movement, see Van der Kroef, "Indonesia's 'New Life' Movement", *Eastern World* 11 (1957): 16–9.

undertaken during the Guided Democracy period, and they too reflected Chinese influence. In the sphere of education, for instance, the PRC's approach of integrating intellectuals with the masses was introduced to Indonesia. College students were urged to go from "the ivory tower to the village", to spend at least one to two months each year in the countryside, working and living with the peasants, as Chinese students did. By really understanding the life of the masses, they could narrow the difference between "manual workers" and "mental workers" and thus help forge national unity.[86] In early 1965, Marshal Surjadi Surjadarma, the first chief-of-staff of the Air Force who also served as Sukarno's military adviser, applauded China's example of sending students to the countryside as a way of strengthening social solidarity.[87] More broadly, in Sukarno's call for completing the Indonesian revolution, he attempted to bridge the gaps between the elite and the masses partly by employing the Chinese mass line, "going to the lower level" (*TURBA*, or *gerakan turun kebawah*). As Peter Hauswedell has pointed out, although this approach was interrupted by the 1965 coup, "in the context of Javanese *prijaji* (elite) politics the very idea of learning from the masses, not to mention actually going down to the masses, already had revolutionary cultural implications".[88] Indeed, the idea of "going to the lower level" also influenced the cultural and political views of left-leaning Indonesian writers; for example, Pramoedya Ananta Toer enthusiastically expounded this approach during the first half of the 1960s (see next chapter).

## CONCLUSION

It is evident that China provided both conceptual and practical inspiration to Sukarno in his efforts to transform Indonesia's sociopolitical system from 1956 to 1965. When asked in 1959 whether Indonesia's social and political systems emulated those of some nations that already had Guided Democracy, Sukarno replied that "an exact example is not to be found overseas". Nevertheless, he did concede,

> If it is a matter of *somewhat* the same, then what is *somewhat* the same is, for example, in the People's Republic of China. There is a people's representative body there called Congress. And there is something, a

---

[86] "'Turun ke Desa' dari 'Ivory Tower'", *Suluh Indonesia*, 17 January 1964.
[87] *Mingguan Seng Hwo Pao* (Jakarta), 1 January 1965.
[88] Peter C. Hauswedell, "Sukarno: Radical or Conservative? Indonesian Politics, 1964–5", *Indonesia* 15 (1973): 136.

stirring, a vibration, a movement (look at the motions of right hand!) There is a combination there — accidentally, it is said — of the communist party with the intelligentsia, with the armed forces, with the farmers, with the workers.[89]

Sukarno's adaptation of Chinese practices did not escape the attention of the Indonesian observers of the time. An editorial of the newspaper *Merdeka*, for instance, pointed out that Sukarno's new concept might have been inspired by what he had observed in China.[90] Colonel Zulkifli Lubis, who staged two coup attempts in late 1956, accused Sukarno of bringing China's People's Congress system to Indonesia.[91] Minister of Foreign Affairs Ide Anak Agung Gde Agung also acknowledged that "in formulating his system of guided democracy President Sukarno was much influenced by what he had seen in China".[92]

How do we explain the attraction of the practices of Communist China for Sukarno, an ardent nationalist? Part of the answer lies in his eclecticism, which is vividly illustrated by the following account:

When interviewed by the French correspondent Tibor Mende, he [Sukarno] said: "My philosophy is composed of nationalism, religious belief and Marxist historical analysis." When the journalist suggested to the President that his Moslem faith and Marxist historical analysis were rather strange bedfellows, he looked at him with a friendly mixture of pity and scorn and said: "You Westerners do not understand us. It's just that I am a complex individual".[93]

Sukarno was indeed a complex individual; and the images of China presented by him were similarly marked by this complexity. While he made a conscious effort to incorporate some of China's conceptual and practical devices into his own agenda, he did not see any incompatibilities between these ideas and his own views. The reason was at once obvious and complicated: his China was very much different from the China that existed in the minds of Western observers, who tended to portray China as

---

[89] *The Indonesian Revolution: Basic Documents and the Idea of Guided Democracy* (Jakarta: Department of Information, Republic of Indonesia, 1960), p. 90 (emphasis is original).
[90] *Merdeka*, 30 October 1956.
[91] *Keng Po* (Jakarta), 14 December 1956.
[92] Ide Anak Agung Gde Agung, *Twenty Years Indonesian Foreign Policy*, p. 414.
[93] Soekarno, *Leader of the Indonesian People: A Short Biography* (issued by the Embassy of the Republic of Indonesia in Beijing, 1956), p. 14.

an oppressive and ruthless Communist state. The China imagined by Sukarno, on the other hand, was essentially a populist regime supported by the people and working for the people's interests. In this China, social harmony and national unity reigned supreme.[94] Sukarno's perception of China, which in effect separated China from Communism, prompted him to downplay or simply ignore the ideological dimension when he took China as an inspiration for his country. He repeatedly emphasized that ideological differences were not a problem when Indonesia attempted to learn from the PRC.[95] This explains why he would typically add that not every Chinese was a member of the Communist Party when praising China's achievements. (Soong Ching Ling was not a Communist, Sukarno liked to remind his Indonesian audiences.[96])

Despite the fact that Sukarno often mentioned China and the Soviet Union in the same context, he apparently found the China example more appealing, as evidenced by the frequently used phrase, "especially in China".[97] Furthermore, he was inclined to disassociate China from the Soviet camp. While he felt that there was no freedom of speech in the Soviet Union, Sukarno appeared to believe that the Chinese did enjoy

---

[94] This emphasis on the theme of unity and harmony was a central characteristic of Sukarno's thinking. In the words of Mohammad Hatta, who had known Sukarno for over 30 years, "As a lover of art, Sukarno looks at everything from its beautiful side, in its harmonious surroundings and in its perfect unity. That is why unity has become for him the most important thing and the end of all his efforts". *Antara News Bulletin*, 8 March 1957.

[95] Sukarno, *Indonesia, Pilihlah*, p. 21; and his 9 November 1956 Bandung speech, in *New China News Agency*, 14 November 1956.

[96] Sukarno, *Marhaen and Proletarian*, p. 19.

[97] This observation was confirmed by Hugh S. Cumming, Jr., American ambassador to Indonesia, who reported that "Sukarno was especially impressed by confidence displayed by top Red Chinese in their leadership, and by outward appearance of economic progress in Communist China". The Indonesians' enthusiastic reactions to the PRC, he said, were partly the result of "an Indonesian sense of kinship with Communist China as fellow Asian country in alleged struggle against 'colonialism and imperialism'". See "Telegram from the Embassy in Indonesia to the Department of State" (27 October 1956), Robert J. McMahon *et al.*, eds., *Foreign Relations of the United States, 1955–1957*, vol. 22 (*Southeast Asia*) (Washington, DC: Government Printing Office, 1989), pp. 316–7. On another occasion, Cumming suggested that "Sukarno saw, particularly in China, conditions were more obtainable to him than those in the Soviet Union". See "A Transcript of a Recorded Interview with Ambassador Hugh S. Cumming, Jr.", p. 24.

"freedom of speech", though it came after "freedom from want". He repeatedly informed his compatriots that there was no forced labour and no regimentation in the PRC.[98] This is another indication that, in Sukarno's mind, China was not primarily a Communist regime. This perception, together with Sukarno's long-held pan-Asianism, played a significant part in his romanticization of — and identification with — China.

It would be an overstatement to say that the mode and substance of Sukarno's political thinking were determined by his views of China. Nevertheless, he saw the PRC as an important source of inspiration in reformulating his own vision for Indonesia. In fact, his attraction to China had some historical foundation. As he viewed Mao Zedong's New Democracy as a continuation of the Three People's Principles expounded by Sun Yat-sen, whom Sukarno had long admired, he must have felt a certain degree of affinity with the Chinese leadership. His 17-day tour of China provided him with the opportunity to witness the process of nation-building in a newly established Asian country. As a nationalist who rejected class struggle theory and tirelessly sought to achieve national unity, Sukarno was inclined to interpret China as a harmonious and unified social entity. In other words, he was convinced that there was a significant degree of confluence between Chinese ideas of nation-building and his own agenda for Indonesia. It was exactly this conviction that led him to declare that he saw China's guided democracy as a realization of the ideals he had been advocating after 1929. It was also this belief that prompted him to propose that Indonesia should — and could — learn from China. In addition, the inclusion of Chinese concepts in Sukarno's thinking stemmed from the characteristics of his own political personality. As John Legge has convincingly demonstrated, Sukarno was not a particularly original thinker, and his political thinking was "accumulative rather than systematic".[99] Sukarno's cumulative knowledge about China, developed after the 1920s, together with his long-standing admiration for Sun Yat-sen and the new China's socio-economic progress, reinforced the tendency to incorporate China's experiences into his own thinking and blueprint for reform. By transforming his perception of the PRC into a China metaphor, Sukarno thus found crucial conceptual and practical inspirations for his efforts to end parliamentary democracy and to establish Guided Democracy.

---

[98] Cumming, "A Transcript", pp. 19–20; Brackman, *The Communist Party of Indonesia*, p. 227; and *The Indonesian Revolution*, pp. 90–1.
[99] Legge, *Sukarno*, p. 338.

CHAPTER 8

# Pramoedya, the China Metaphor and Cultural Radicalism

*Frankly, I admire the tenacity, skillfulness, industriousness, honesty, and revolutionary characteristics of the Chinese People. Indonesian people, not bourgeois, can learn a great deal from China, especially in terms of nation building. Never in history has such a gigantic construction happened within so short a time. Such a revolution has changed the face of the earth and human beings! And this is the People's Republic of China.*

Pramoedya Ananta Toer (1960)[1]

*Chinese writers occupy a high position and their voices are heard by the society. Together with politicians they constitute the country's spiritual leaders, who hold an extremely important role in nation building of today.*

Pramoedya Ananta Toer (1957)[2]

*China's revolutionary writers and artists, writers and artists of promise, must go among the masses.... Literature and art are subordinate to politics.*

Mao Zedong (1940)[3]

*The Manifesto was a statement openly refusing the validity of the slogan, "politics is the commander".*

Goenawan Mohamad (1988)[4]

---

[1] Pramoedya Ananta Toer, *Hoakiau di Indonesia* (Jakarta: Bintang, 1960), p. 37.
[2] Pramoedya Ananta Toer, "Sedikit tentang Pengarang Tiongkok", *Mimbar Indonesia* 3 (1957): 22.
[3] Mao Zedong, *Talk at the Yenan Forum on Literature and Art* (Beijing: Foreign Language Press, 1965), pp. 19, 26.
[4] Goenawan Mohamad, "The 'Manikebu Affair': Literature and Politics in the 1960s", *Prisma* 46 (1988): 82.

The previous chapter has established that Sukarno's favourable perception of China helped shape his vision for Indonesia, which in turn contributed to the country's profound political changes between 1956 and 1965. This chapter shifts our attention to the cultural arena and analyses China's role in perpetuating Indonesian cultural radicalism during the same period. The centre of discussion is Pramoedya Ananta Toer (1925–2006); there are two major reasons for this focus. In the first place, he has been widely regarded, within and without Indonesia, as one of the country's most influential intellectuals.[5] Pramoedya's attraction to China and his attempt to utilize its politico-cultural concepts was a key factor in shaping his thought and actions during the crucial years between 1956 and 1965. Second, the change of Pramoedya's political and cultural visions was not merely a personal matter; instead, it had greater significance. Pramoedya was one of the most important writers behind the trend of cultural radicalization in the late Sukarno era (1959–65). As Boen Oemarjati puts it, "his role in the Lekra [the Institute of People's Culture] in the early sixties gave rise to a counter-literary movement that marked the history and development of modern Indonesian literature with yet another milestone".[6]

There are a number of important studies regarding Pramoedya's intellectual journey and his place in modern Indonesian culture. It has been generally agreed that the year 1956 marked a turning point in his intellectual and political life, and his central role in the cultural radicalization process has been carefully documented. Nevertheless, existing studies pay little attention to Pramoedya's perception of China and its implications. The only English-language, dissertation-length study of Pramoedya devotes merely a few sentences to his views of China and their relevance to his changing insight about Indonesia.[7] A. Teeuw, a leading scholar on modern Indonesian literature, is a major exception. He suggests that Pramoedya's

---

[5] Benedict Anderson, *Language and Power: Exploring Political Cultures in Indonesia* (Ithaca: Cornell University Press, 1990), p. 10; Jamie James, "The Indonesiad", *New Yorker* (May 1996): 40–8, 93. For a useful website on studies about Pramoedya, see <http://www.radix.net/~bardsley/prampage.html>

[6] Boen Oemarjati, "The Development of Indonesian Literature", in *Dynamics of Indonesian History*, ed. H. Soebadio and C.A.M. Sarvaas (Amsterdam: Elsevier/North Holland, 1978), p. 328.

[7] Savitri Scherer, "From Culture to Politics: The Writings of Pramoedya Ananta Toer" (Ph.D. dissertation, Australian National University, 1981).

1956 trip to China represented a milestone: "It was on his return from Peking that the dream of the poet was exchanged for the action of the social fighter."[8] However, Teeuw does not examine in any detail why his China trip was so significant and how his views of China affected his vision for Indonesian culture and society.[9] The gap on Pramoedya's complex perception of the PRC impedes a better understanding of him as an intellectual and of Indonesian cultural history during the first half of the 1960s. By analysing Pramoedya's attitude toward China and its intimate connections to his cultural thinking, this chapter attempts to fill this gap. More importantly, by using the case of Pramoedya, this chapter will demonstrate that the discourses about China and the subsequent formation of the China metaphor had an important impact on the cultural politics of postcolonial Indonesia.

## PRAMOEDYA BEFORE 1956: THE EVOLUTION OF A CULTURAL INTELLECTUAL

### Pramoedya as a Writer of "Universal Humanism"

Pramoedya Ananta Toer was born on 6 February 1925 in Blora, a small town in north-central Java.[10] While his maternal grandmother "appeared to

---

[8] A. Teeuw, *Modern Indonesian Literature*, 2nd ed. (The Hague: Martinus Nijhoff, 1979), vol. 1, p. 167. Boen Oemarjati concurs, "Before it [the 1956 trip] Pramudya may be regarded to have written a kind of *engagée* literature... After his Peking visit he seemed to have developed himself to a kind of *enragé* writer". See her "The Development", pp. 327–8; According to Harry Aveling, Pramoedya was "captivated by the social and economic progress made by China. From that time [October 1956] on, Pramoedya became increasingly involved with left-wing cultural and literary activities in Indonesia". See Aveling, "Introduction", in Pramoedya, *The Girl from the Coast* (Singapore: Select Books, 1991), p. vi. But none of the authors elaborates this argument.

[9] In his book devoted to studying Pramoedya, Teeuw makes no mention of his 1956 trip and its implications. See Teeuw, *Pramoedya Ananta Toer de Verbeelding van Indonesie* [Pramoedya Ananta Toer and the Imagining of Indonesia] (Breda: De Geus, 1993).

[10] The biographical data is drawn from Pramoedya Ananta Toer, "*Perburuan* 1950 and *Keluarga Gerilya* 1950", trans. Benedict Anderson, *Indonesia* 36 (1983): 25–48; and Boen Oemarjati, "The Development"; see also Teeuw, *Modern Indonesian Literature*, pp. 163–75.

be at least partially Chinese",[11] his father was headmaster of a *Budi Utomo* (a nationalist organization) school. After completing elementary school, Pramoedya went to Surabaya to study at the Radio Vocational School in 1940. During the Japanese occupation (1941–45), he attended an adult school while working at the Japanese Domei press agency. When the revolution broke out in 1945, he joined a *pemuda* (youth) paramilitary organization before entering the Siliwangi Division in East Java. Between July 1947 and December 1949, Pramoedya was imprisoned by the Dutch. After 1950, he became editor of the modern literature section at the Balai Pustaka, a government-owned publishing house, and of the magazine *Indonesia*, a prominent cultural journal. At the end of 1951, he left the Balai Pustaka and founded the DUTA, the Literary and Features Agency, of his own.

Nationalism and universal humanism were central to Pramoedya's thinking prior to 1956. These characteristics were evident in his *Perburuan* (*The Fugitive*) and *Keluarga Gerilya* (*The Guerrilla Family*), novels about the anti-Japanese and anti-Dutch revolutionary movements. In addition to their patriotic and nationalist orientations, these two novels had a deep humanistic underpinning, reflecting the prevailing universal humanism of the time. The key dimension of this literary stream was the belief that Indonesian writers were "the true heirs of world culture". The 1950 *Testimonial of Beliefs* (*Gelanggang*) declared, "Indonesian culture is determined by the combination of all sorts of stimulating voices which are caused by voices hurled from all corners of the world, to be hurled back later in the form of our own voice."[12] As Pramoedya himself acknowledged later, "this novel [*Keluarga Gerilya*] too was inspired by patriotic *semangat*, and from another angle, by humanity [*humanitas*] — a utopian idealism that lives and dies by its rejection of existing reality".[13] This humanistic concern was

---

[11] Pramoedya Ananta Toer, *The Mute's Soliloquy: A Memoir*, trans. by Willem Samuels (New York: Hyperion East, 1999), p. 107.

[12] Teeuw, *Modern Indonesian Literature*, p. 127. See also Savitri Scherer's discussion of the influence of universal humanism on Pramoedya, in her "From Culture to Politics", pp. 130–1.

[13] Pramoedya, "*Perburuan*", p. 38. On Pramoedya's early novels, see the provocative analyses in Benedict Anderson, "Reading 'Revenge' by Pramoedya Ananta Toer (1978–1982)", in *Writing on the Tongue*, ed. A.L. Becker (Ann Arbor: Center for South and Southeast Asian Studies, University of Michigan, 1989), pp. 13–94; and Keith Foulcher, "The Early Fiction of Pramoedya Ananta Toer, 1946–1949", in *Text/Politics in Island Southeast Asia*, ed. D.M. Roskies (Athens: Ohio University Southeast Asia Series, 1993), pp. 191–220.

partly responsible for Pramoedya's antagonism toward Indonesian Communists. His *Keluarga Gerilya*, for example, condemned not only the Dutch and the English (for bombing Surabaya), but the Communists for staging the bloody Madiun Rebellion. His other novels and short stories written in the early 1950s continued the frustrating theme of "the universal loneliness of man".[14]

Amid turbulent political and cultural transformation, Pramoedya left for Holland in June 1953. Perhaps he intended to escape the gloomy scene at home and to look for inspiration from the outside world. His six-month stay in Amsterdam as a guest of the Sticusa (Dutch Foundation for Cultural Cooperation), however, turned out to be a disappointment, partly because he came to believe that the two countries were simply too different. Holland reminded him of a coffin, and he was particularly sensitive to "the contrast between his own country, in the process of establishing itself and seeking an identity, and Holland which had already been established".[15] He was unhappy about the attitudes of many Dutch officials he encountered — "they often seemed to act like teachers toward Indonesians".[16] He became more critical of the West and charged that the Sticusa was a "colonial brain trust" that only intended to "import Western culture into Indonesia".[17] While in the Netherlands, he was deeply influenced by a prominent Dutch scholar, W.F. Wertheim, who was convinced that the root of confusion in Indonesian literature lay in "the failure of the Indonesian revolution as a social revolution".[18]

After returning home, Pramoedya's disillusionment was aggravated by the rampant corruption, economic stagnation and social chaos that

---

[14] Anthony Johns, "Pramudya Ananta Tur: The Writer as Outsider: The Indonesian Example", in his *Cultural Options and the Role of Tradition* (Canberra: Australian National University Press, 1979), pp. 96–108.

[15] Cited in Teeuw, *Modern Indonesian Literature*, p. 166.

[16] Pramoedya, *The Mute's Soliloquy: A Memoir*, p. 205.

[17] "Pramoedya tentang STICUSA", *Kompas* 5, 6 (1954): 55. According to Willard Hanna, Pramoedya's disappointment in Holland was mainly the result of personal problems: "He did not receive sufficient financial support to enable him live or travel as he wished; he did not meet many Dutch persons of prominence, literary or otherwise; and he did not find any appropriate opportunity for study." See Hanna, "Guerrilla Family: A Novel of the Indonesian Revolution", *American Universities Field Staff*, Southeast Asia Series (September 1957), p. 8.

[18] Pramoedya, "Prof. Dr. Wertheim tentang Kesasteraan Indonesia Modern", *Medan Bahasa* 3, 11 (1953): 39–43.

prevailed. As he later recalled of those days, "I saw that all the promises of the revolution had been left unfulfilled".[19] His literary probing to penetrate to the heart of human problems appeared to have taken him nowhere. In mid-1956, he published a story entitled *Silence at Life's Noon*, which vividly depicted the themes of intellectual alienation and resentment of Western cultural intrusion. According to Teeuw, this novel had symbolic meanings,

> In this story, the writer seemed to have reached a stage where he is ready to replace his dreams with action — he has reached this stage because of his embitterment with the world around him, and also because of his disappointment at the futility of his own life, at the failure of his writing and the insufficiency of his humanity.[20]

The break with the past, however, did not necessarily mean the finding of a new direction. In mid-1956, Pramoedya remained undecided as to what he could do as an intellectual amidst the baffling process of nation-building and quest for new identities. It was at this critical conjunction that he embarked on a trip to China — a trip that would profoundly change his life.

## Pramoedya's Knowledge of China: The Initial Stage

Prior to his trip to China, Pramoedya had acquired some knowledge about China and its cultural doctrines. By his own account, the activities of the Chinese red, Mao Zedong and Zhou Enlai had been widely covered in Indonesia's "revolutionary newspapers" before independence.[21] In 1948, when he was jailed in Bukitduri, Pramoedya met a Dutch prisoner who was a former officer in the Royal Netherlands Indies Army (KNIL). The Dutchman told Pramoedya that he had been sentenced to death. "However," he reportedly said, "I still have a gleam of hope; if the Chinese Red Army

---

[19] Cited in Margaret Scott, "Waging War with Words", *Far Eastern Economic Review*, 9 August 1990, p. 27. According to Patricia Henry, one of the major concerns in Pramoedya's writings in this period is the question "How did we get into this mess?" See Henry, "The Writer's Responsibility: A Preliminary Look at the Depiction and Construction of Indonesia in the Works of Pramoedya Ananta Toer", *Crossroads* 6 (1991): 59–72.
[20] Teeuw, *Modern Indonesian Literature*, p. 178.
[21] Pulamudiya Ananda Duer [Pramoedya], "Jiaqiang Yin Zhong Youyi, Fensui Mei Ying Qinlue" [Strengthening Sino-Indonesian friendship, smashing American and British aggression], *Warta Bhakti* [*Zhong Cheng Bao*] (Jakarta), 1 October 1964.

comes southward, I will be saved." Since that time, Pramoedya recalled, "I have an impression that the influence of the Chinese Red Army has been so far-reaching that it even penetrates to the minds of Dutch soldiers".[22] In his 1952 essay, "Literature as a Tool", Pramoedya cited Mao Zedong's work to support his own view that literature was nothing but a tool people used to achieve their desired ends. However, he had an ambivalent attitude toward Mao's principle, "art should serve the people, especially the workers, peasants, and soldiers". He contrasted this position with the aristocratic view that art was for those who understood (which he did not reject). Pramoedya found merits and deficiencies in these two opposite views: the first (aristocratic) view was capable of preserving creative integrity, whereas the second (Mao's) view had the power to eradicate a possible decadent creation that might imperil social unity.[23] In 1954, he translated, from a Dutch or English source, an article by Zhou Yang (Tjau Jang). Entitled "Socialist Realism — The Way Forward for Chinese Literature",[24] this essay argued that Chinese literature needed its own national character and to be open to all progressive influences. Pramoedya had developed a certain degree of admiration for the high social status of writers in the socialist nations, "where literature is considered to be one of the political and economic forces" and where writers were paid generously for their publications, presenting a stark contrast to the situation at home.[25]

During the 1955 Bandung Conference, Pramoedya had some contact with the Chinese delegation, which may be taken as an indication of his increasing interest in the PRC.[26] In early 1956, Pramoedya translated a long article by Ding Ling (Ting Ling), one of the most prominent writers in the PRC. Entitled "Life and Creative Writing", this essay appeared in the leading cultural journal *Indonesia*.[27] Central to Ding Ling's idea was

---

[22] Ibid. There are perhaps some factual bases for the Dutchman's assertion. In 1948–49, a few Pesindo units in East and West Java named themselves "Mao Tse-tung Brigades" and wanted to be united with the Red Army of China. See Jacques Leclerc, "Aidit dan Partai pada tahun 1950", *Prisma* 7 (1982): 61–78.
[23] "Kesusteraan sebagai Alat", *Indonesia* 3, 7 (1952).
[24] "Realisme Sosialis — Jalan Kemajuan bagi Kesusastraan Tionghoa", *Harian Rakjat*, 8 May 1954.
[25] Pramoedya, "Hidup dan Kerdja Sasterawan Indonesia Modern", *Seni* 1, 1 (1955): 22–36.
[26] Interview with Chen Xiaru (New York).
[27] "Hidup dan Penulisan Kreatif", *Indonesia* 7, 3 (1956): 102–10.

that good literary and artistic work came from concrete life experience; in order to create valuable writings, writers must "go into life" and to "live with the people". Only after understanding that they were "writing for workers, peasants and soldiers", Ding Ling argued, could writers truly be integrated with the masses. Pramoedya seemed to be partially convinced by Ding's argument. In an essay published three months later, he echoed Ding's views by suggesting that writers should go and live among the people and that the government should support this endeavour.[28] Pramoedya's writing prior to October 1956 indicated that he had read widely concerning literary and cultural development in the PRC and was familiar with the works of major PRC writers (such as Guo Moruo, Ding Ling and Mao Dun [Mao Tun]). In a July 1956 essay, he praised the Chinese government for its attention to culture and education and highlighted the work of Mao Dun and Lu Xun (Lu Hsun), who were regarded as "two of the best and most famous writers in China, because they belonged to the new generation who are conscious of their social responsibility".[29] By mid-1956, Pramoedya had also translated portions of *Diary of a Mad Man* (*Catatan Orang Gila*), a novel by Lu Xun.[30]

Pramoedya in the mid-1950s was at a crossroads. His conviction that the Indonesian revolution had failed, together with the gloomy national realities, was a major cause behind his frustration and disillusionment. The universal humanist belief had proven to be ineffectual in his attempt to confront the enormous problems facing the nation; he longed for greater social recognition and a more active role for intellectuals, yet he was deeply disappointed at the lack of organization and poor financial conditions of writers.[31] His generally hostile attitude toward Communism prevented him from joining the leftist cultural organization, Lekra. As a consequence, Pramoedya in the pre-1956 years remained a detached and frustrated intellectual. Furthermore, his experience in Holland convinced him that the West could not provide any useful solutions for Indonesia's problems. He began to look elsewhere for answers. His translation of Chinese literary

---

[28] Pramoedya, "Meninggalkan Negativisme", *Mimbar Indonesia*, 9 June 1956; cited from Scherer, "From Culture to Politics", pp. 160–1.
[29] Pramoedya, "Manakah Pengarang dari Golongan Keturunan Tionghoa", *Pendorong*, 13 July 1956.
[30] "Interview with Pramoedya", *Hsin Pao*, 17 November 1956.
[31] Pramoedya, "Kegiatan Seni dalam Bulan September di Ibukota", *Pudjangga Baru* 14, 3 (1952): 65–7.

work indicates that he was somewhat interested in the PRC's cultural practices. In fact, he might have found some convergence between his own outlook and Chinese cultural principles. For example, both shared a concern for the fate of the masses, though for Pramoedya, the "masses" represented undifferentiated "little people", while for the Chinese writers, the masses were members of the working class and peasants.

## PRAMOEDYA IN CHINA: THE POLITICS OF A TRANSNATIONAL ROMANCE

### The Politics of Invitation

In October 1956, Pramoedya embarked on a month-long trip to the PRC. The invitation was issued by three prominent cultural and political figures: Guo Moruo, chairman of the All-China Federation of Literary and Art Circles (AFLAC) and president of the Chinese Academy of Sciences; Mao Dun, chairman of the Writers' Union; and Cu Tunan, head of the Association of the Chinese People's Cultural Exchange with Foreign Countries, which was a major arm of China's public diplomacy. Pramoedya was invited to attend the conference commemorating the 20th anniversary of Lu Xun's death, followed by visits to several industrial cities.

Why was Pramoedya invited to China? Although one of Indonesia's most renowned writers, he was by no means pro-Communist in terms of his political and cultural orientations. In fact, his negative description of the Communist terror in his earlier work might have alienated some Communist Party members. According to an internal document compiled from the materials provided by the Chinese embassy in Jakarta, Pramoedya in the mid-1950s, together with writers such as Rivai Apin and Utuy Sontani, was classified as a "petit-bourgeois centrist writer". Unlike the rightists (e.g., Takdir Alisjahbana and Trisno Sumardjo) or the leftists (e.g., Lekra-associated writers), "the centrist writers" accounted for the largest group among Indonesian writers and they were characterized by

> a sense of frustration and aimlessness. They are unwilling to throw in their lot with the imperialists; yet they are not courageous enough to join in the people's struggle and be part of the Indonesian revolutionary cause. They are dissatisfied with the realities, corruptions and flaws of the capitalist regime; and they demand for the change of the *status quo*. However, they lack clear awareness of the arduous and prolonged nature of the national revolution and do not have adequate confidence in this

revolution. As a consequence, they display harsh and extreme sentiments toward the existing social conditions.³²

There were two major reasons behind Pramoedya's invitation. First, it was a principle of the Chinese cultural exchange policy to invite foreign intellectuals with centrist or rightist orientations to visit China. The rationale was that their favourable observations of the PRC would in turn produce greater effects upon public opinion in their home countries.³³ The second reason should be discussed within the Indonesian domestic context. By the mid-1950s, political conflict in the cultural sphere had been intensified, primarily as a result of Lekra's expansion. Established in 1950 and closely associated with the Communist Party of Indonesia (PKI), Lekra advocated the cultural principle of "art for the people". By 1956, the Lekra leadership had been "working on" Pramoedya, hoping to gain his support and sympathy for the left-leaning cultural movement.³⁴ In fact, it was Lekra that first suggested to the Chinese embassy in Jakarta that Pramoedya be invited to visit China. The embassy subsequently made the recommendation to the respective authorities in Beijing.³⁵

---

³² Duiwai Wenhua Lianluo Weiyuanhui Ersi [Second Office of the Committee of Cultural Exchanges with Foreign Countries], ed., *Yindunixiya Wenhua Gaikuang* [A survey of Indonesian culture] (Beijing, for internal circulation, 1962), pp. 5–6.

³³ This practice was confirmed by a document later sent by the Ministry of Foreign Affairs to the Chinese embassy in Jakarta, which suggested that "the invitation of prominent figures of centrist and centrist-rightist orientations to China ... would be of significant help to the strengthening of Sino-Indonesian friendly relations and expanding our influences in Indonesia". "Yaoqing Yindunixia Shehui Mingliu Fanhua Shi" [Matters pertaining to the invitation of prominent Indonesians to visit China] (8 August–27 September 1958), file no. 105-00862-02, Archives of the Ministry of Foreign Affairs, PRC.

³⁴ Interview with Shannu (Beijing), an Indonesian-Chinese writer who knew Pramoedya personally. He said that the PKI politburo member Njoto personally talked to Pramoedya. According to a Chinese official working in the cultural section of the Chinese embassy in Jakarta (who wishes to be anonymous), Joebaar Ajoeb, secretary-general of Lekra, mentioned a number of times that they "were making efforts" on Pramoedya (interview in Beijing). In an interview with Salim Said, Pramoedya also revealed that Lekra started approaching him in 1956. See "Saya Lebih Percaya Kepada Kemanusiaan", *Tempo*, 31 December 1977, pp. 8–11.

³⁵ Interviews in New York with Chen Xiaru (an Indonesian-language interpreter for the Chinese Writers' Union, which was one of the host organizations of Pramoedya); and in Washington, DC with Huang Shuhai (an official in the Jakarta Chinese embassy

## Pramoedya in China: 1956

Pramoedya arrived in Beijing in mid-October 1956, when the Sukarno delegation had just left the country. Before leaving for China, he had conceived of this trip as an important opportunity for developing his thought not only about China but, more significantly, about Indonesia. As he said later,

> When visiting a foreign country, I had to pay attention to two things. If I went to a developed country, there was no question. But in a new nation, I had to study, because there were certainly similarities in terms of how to better the fate of the nation and the people. China was one such new nation. If I was influenced by the PRC, it was because she was a new nation that had already been organized. Indonesia was also a new nation.... There must be certain resemblances between new nations. There was something to be learned from and some good examples could be taken. Indeed, just look at the PRC at that time, it was much more successful than Indonesia.[36]

Although Pramoedya remarked later that "there is little to say" about his China trip,[37] a number of important episodes did occur and they had significant implications. His first major activity was participating in the conference commemorating the 20th anniversary of Lu Xun's death, a well-publicized event attended by writers from more than 20 countries. This international gathering would likely reinforce Pramoedya's admiration for Lu Xun. Unmistakably aware of the appeal of Lu Xun to intellectuals of newly independent nations, both Guo Moruo and Mao Dun emphasized in their keynote speeches that the greatness of Lu Xun stemmed from "his revolutionary thinking and from his devotion to the people". Guo reassured his foreign guests that the PRC intellectuals would "live up to

---

and later in the Ministry of Foreign Affairs); and in Beijing with an anonymous Chinese official who worked in the Cultural Section of the Chinese embassy in Jakarta. The account by Promoedya himself, however, is different: he received "a surprise visit in July 1956 from an official from the embassy of the PRC", inviting him to go to China. This invitation, according to Pramoedya, was initiated by Prijono, Indonesian minister of education and culture. See Pramoedya, *The Mute's Soliloquy*, pp. 230–1.

[36] "Wawancara: Pramoedya, Bakal Pemenang Hadiah Nobel", *Nadi Insan* (Kuala Lumpur) 24 (1981): 8.

[37] Pramoedya, *The Mute's Soliloquy*, p. 231.

the expectations of cultural workers of other countries — that is, the new culture in the PRC would make greater contributions to world culture and China would produce more Lu Xuns".[38] As one of the foreign guests invited to speak to the conference, Pramoedya praised Lu Xun as a great writer whose contributions lay not only in his insightful observation of Chinese society but, more importantly, in his willingness and capacity to lead the struggle to improve the lot of the masses. "Lu Xun was the voice of his nation and his people", Pramoedya continued, "Lu Xun was the embodiment of a moral awakening which was full of noble hopes for human beings. He did not merely hope, he employed the best and most appropriate means — literature — in the struggle to realize his ideals."[39] This Lu Xun in Pramoedya's mind clearly re-ignited his own hope for Indonesian intellectuals,

> Every writer has responsibilities, and it is because of these responsibilities that choices have to be made. Lu Xun chose to be on the side of the people who suffered from hardship and misery.... He not only made choices, but also fought to ensure his ideals be realized in real life. He was a realist in thinking and a realist in action.[40]

This idea of combining thinking and action provided the most pertinent model in Pramoedya's passionate search for effective solutions to Indonesia's social problems. After returning home, he characterized Lu Xun not only as a great cultural intellectual, but as a fighter who was "the father of China's socialist realism in the literary realm".[41]

After the conference in Beijing, Pramoedya visited Shanghai, Nanjing and Guangzhou. He told an Indonesian reporter that, compared with his previous experience in Europe, he felt it was much easier to establish contact with the Chinese.[42] He met with a number of prominent writers, among them Zhou Yang, Mao Dun, Ba Ren (Wang Renshu, who was the first Chinese ambassador to Indonesia and then the head of the People's

---

[38] See the texts of their speeches in *Wenyi Bao* 20 (1956): 4–10.
[39] Pulamudiya Ananda Duer [Pramoedya], "Zai Lu Xun Xiansheng Shishi Ershi Zhounian Jinian Dahuishang de Jianghua" [Speech at the conference in commemorating the 20th anniversary of the death of Mr. Lu Xun], *Wenyi Bao* 20 (1956): 15–6.
[40] Ibid., p. 16.
[41] Pramoedya, "Sedikit tentang Kesasteraan Tionghoa di Indonesia", *Pantja Warna* 113 (1957): 86.
[42] "Pramudya Ananta Tur di RRT", *Sin Tjun* 2 (1957): 107.

Pramoedya speaking at the conference commemorating the 20th anniversary of Lu Xun's death, Beijing, 1956 (Photograph by Tu Xiuxian, by permission of the Xinhua News Agency, ID: 12494068).

Publishing House), Yang Shuo, Liu Baiyu and Liu Zixia.[43] These meetings took place in an amiable atmosphere and a line of communication between Pramoedya and his hosts was quickly established. Two major themes were constantly highlighted in these meetings and discussions.[44] The first was the PRC literary doctrine of "socialist realism", which originated in the Soviet Union but had been largely Sinicized by Mao and his cultural theoreticians. (Lu Xun, for example, was hailed as "a great pioneer and representative of socialist realism".) Central to this literary doctrine was the

---

[43] *Hsin Pao*, 17 November 1956; and interview with Chen Xiaru.
[44] Interview with Chen Xiaru.

idea that artistic works should reflect social realities and people's lives. The second theme, "art should serve the people", had been systematically elaborated by Mao in his 1940 *Talk at the Yenan Forum on Literature and Art*. As demonstrated earlier, Pramoedya had a certain degree of familiarity with and ambivalent admiration for both literary doctrines. His discussions with their Chinese architects enhanced his understanding and appreciation of these central tenets of the PRC's literary doctrines.

Pramoedya's impression from his first trip to China was overwhelmingly and profoundly favourable. He was amazed by the country's rapid social and economic progress, attributed to the Chinese people who "are making history".[45] What was important for the people was "not money, profit, loss and gain", Pramoedya remarked, "but sincerity, consciousness and work". He was fascinated by the Chinese, who possessed simultaneously the spirit of "romanticism and pragmatism" and who worked not for the interests of individual but those of the nation.[46] He described China as "an epic in the making" and the Chinese revolution as "a total revolution" instead of a reform.[47] Like many other observers of the time, Pramoedya's China was constructed as a stark contrast to Indonesia: "In Indonesia, people only think of themselves; over there, everyone thinks of others. Here in Indonesia, people have to be greedy in order to survive; over there, the greedy instinct has been totally eliminated".[48] As a writer, Pramoedya was particularly concerned with the relationship between intellectuals and society, one of the central issues he had tried to come to grips with. The Chinese practice provided him not only a mirror for reflecting what had gone wrong at home, but a viable model for what could be done. One of Pramoedya's favourable impressions was of the high social and political status of writers and artists:

> Chinese writers function as the spiritual engineers of the nation. With this in mind, we will have no difficulty in understanding why they occupy a high place and why their voices are heard by the society.

---

[45] Pramoedya, "Suatu Kali di Tiongkok", *Tiongkok Rakjat* 7 (1958): 40–1.
[46] Bahrum Rangkuti, *Pramoedya Ananta Toer dan Karja Seninja* (Jakarta: Gunung Agung, 1963), p. 21; "Pramudya Ananta Tur di RRT", *Sin Tjun*, p. 107; and Pramoedya, "Suatu Kali", p. 41.
[47] Pramoedya Ananta Toer, "Djiwa Revolusioner di Tiongkok Tetap Bergolak", *Sin Po*, 5 January 1957.
[48] Ibid.

Together with politicians, they constitute the spiritual leaders whose role is very important in the nation-building process. This also helps explain why writers are very well looked after by the society.[49]

According to Pramoedya, one indication of writers' high social status was the generous material reward they received for their work. "One thing that attracts much of my attention as a writer is the security of life enjoyed by writers in the new China", he commented, "Over there, a writer can lead a decent life from his pen."[50] He reported that Liu Zixia (Liu Tje Sie) was paid RMB400,000 as the remuneration for his novel *Railway Guerrilla*. This was certainly no small sum: "It is approximately 240 times a Chinese cabinet minister's monthly salary", Pramoedya marvelled, "In other words, Liu can enjoy the living standard of a cabinet minister for 20 years, just because of one novel." This generous material reward indicated that "Chinese culture is supported by the highest authorities".[51]

Underlying Pramoedya's enthusiastic description of Chinese writers' enviable social and financial status was the implicit acknowledgement that the PRC practice was in effect a realization of his own ideals for Indonesia. Pramoedya had complained repeatedly about the low financial rewards Indonesian writers received from their creative work after 1952,[52] and had called for greater respect for writers who should be rewarded in accordance with their creative contributions. The PRC practice made Pramoedya realize that the social and political status of intellectuals was contingent upon their contributions to the nation. He was convinced that Chinese writers' respectability was a direct result of their participation in nation-building, which led to a critical understanding that, in order to raise their status, intellectuals should first actively participate in the social and political

---

[49] Pramoedya, "Sedikit tentang Pengarang Tiongkok", p. 21. The term "engineers of human souls" was first applied by Joseph Stalin to refer to writers and other cultural workers in the 1930s.

[50] "Pramudya Ananta Tur di RRT", p. 107.

[51] Ibid.; see also *Hsin Pao*, 17 November 1956.

[52] Pramoedya noted that while the Chinese writers were paid Rp. 1,000–3,000 for every three pages of their writing, Indonesian writers got only Rp. 30 per short story. In order to barely survive, Indonesian writers had to publish at least ten stories every month and they often had to seek other part-time employment. Pramoedya, "Hidup dan Kerdja"; and Pramoedya, "Keadaan Sosial Para Pengarang: Perbandingan Antarnegara", *Siasat* 11, 506 (1957): 28.

process. The attitude of a detached bystander could only further jeopardize writers' place in society.⁵³

The China trip also provided Pramoedya with practical methods of organizing writers to participate in the nation-building process. He had argued previously that writers needed to be organized to combat against the decadent social atmosphere (such as corruption). Yet he was very disappointed by the lack of effective organization, which he thought was a major difficulty facing intellectuals.⁵⁴ His meetings with Chinese cultural officials, especially Mao Dun, chairman of the Chinese Writers' Union, might have given him some concrete approaches on how to organize writers. Shortly after returning home, he published an essay giving a detailed description of the Writers' Union and its organizing structure. Pramoedya highlighted its five major functions and means of achieving its goals; these functions ranged from organizing writers to "participating in and experiencing life" and "undertaking cultural exchanges with progressive countries".⁵⁵ Pramoedya's admiration for the integration of writers into society had a bearing on his evaluation of Chinese literary works. As noted earlier, Pramoedya's previous view of the two opposite cultural perspectives — "art for the art's sake" and "art for the people" — was ambivalent. However, he came to develop a clear preference for the latter after the end of 1956:

> Seen from the standpoint of international literature, China's literary works are somewhat formalistic. However, seen from the perspective of the Chinese state, there is no ground for criticism; because China is now in the process of massive construction; writers write for the purpose of educating the masses rather than for money.⁵⁶

## Pramoedya in China: 1958

Pramoedya made his second China trip in October 1958. By this time, it was a new Pramoedya, mainly as a result of his transformation after returning from China in 1956 (see below). It was also a different China by then; the start of the Great Leap Forward and the People's Commune

---

⁵³ Pramoedya, "Kearah Sastera Revolusioner", *Star Weekly*, no. 574 (29 December 1956), pp. 6–7.
⁵⁴ Pramoedya, "Kegiatan Seni".
⁵⁵ Pramoedya, "Sedikit tentang Pengarang Tiongkok", pp. 20–1.
⁵⁶ "Interview with Pramoedya", *Hsin Pao*, 17 November 1956.

movement had fundamentally changed the country's geographical and political landscape. Consequently, Pramoedya looked at this new China from a new political and cultural vantage point; China continued to be a source of inspiration, and his second trip accelerated the process of his move to cultural radicalism.

Pramoedya's second visit was in conjunction with the Asian and African Writers' Conference held in Tashkent, the Soviet Union. After the conference, Pramoedya, who was the head of the Indonesian delegation, returned home via China. In addition to Beijing, he visited the cities of Wuhan, Chengdu and Kunming. By this time, China no longer considered Pramoedya a "directionless and frustrated writer". Instead, he was regarded as a representative of those former "centrist writers" who had disassociated themselves from "the camp of illusionalists" and joined in the leftist "nationalist and democratic front".[57] Prior to his arrival, it had been decided by the Writers' Union that there would be three central themes in the meetings with the Indonesian visitors.[58] The first was that "the American imperialists are just paper tigers", who would be defeated if people in the world united in their struggle against imperialism. The second was the promulgation of China's experiences and achievements in carrying out economic construction. The third theme was the principle of "politics is commander" in the cultural sphere. Other topics also emerged in Chinese writers' and cultural officials' meetings with Pramoedya. Zhou Yang, for instance, spoke of the new cultural doctrine of "revolutionary romanticism",[59] while others emphasized that "writers must follow Mao Tse-tung's road". Pramoedya took these topics seriously and appeared to agree with his host on the major issues discussed.[60]

By 1958, Pramoedya was no longer a detached spectator but an active participant. During his first China trip, his attitude toward art and

---

[57] Duiwai Wenhua, *Yindunixiya*, p. 7.

[58] Interview with Chen Xiaru in New York (who was Pramoedya's interpreter throughout his second trip).

[59] This combination of "revolutionary realism and revolutionary romanticism and socialist realism" was first elaborated by Zhou Yang in mid-1958 and represented the Chinese attempt to replace the Russian-originated concept of "socialist realism". It was also a reflection of the widening Sino-Soviet rift of the time. D.W. Fokkema, *Literary Doctrine in China and Soviet Influence, 1956–1960* (The Hague: Mouton, 1965), pp. 196–201.

[60] Interview with Chen Xiaru.

intellectuals' social role had been ambivalent, his perception of China primarily characterized by the sense of amazement and admiration. The second China trip evoked profound political feelings and he explicitly expressed his political views on a variety of issues. In other words, Pramoedya's China had become a political instead of just a cultural symbol. While he continued to praise Chinese writers as "engineers of the human spirit", he talked more frequently about politics and the political ramifications of China's experience. In addition to openly rejecting Western influences, he called for establishing a united front centred in Beijing ("a symbol of Asia and Africa") in the struggle against imperialism and colonialism.[61] Pramoedya's view of art and its relation to society was no longer ambiguous; he stated unmistakably that art should be responsible to the people. Writers should be not only the society's conscience, but also participants in the battle on the front line.[62]

As an active participant, Pramoedya attempted to draw certain practical examples from Chinese writers' involvement in social and political change. His participation in the "steel-making" process presents a case in point. The year 1958 was the beginning of China's Great Leap Forward movement that was characterized by frenetic over-optimism nationwide. One of its goals was to produce 3,000,000 tonnes of steel the next year, a component of the ambition of "surpassing the British and catching up with the Americans" in the industrial field. Chinese intellectuals enthusiastically partook in this primitive steel-making process (which resembled backyard blast furnaces).[63] Pramoedya too was excited about this practice. "This [steel-making] is also an urgent issue facing Indonesia. I myself once suggested to the government that the efforts of steel-making and iron-making should be spread", Pramoedya wrote, three days after arriving in Beijing. "Therefore, I told my Chinese host, on short notice, that I too

---

[61] Pramoedya, "Tasjkent — Peking", *Tiongkok Rakjat* 1 (1959): 48–50.
[62] Ibid.
[63] What follows is a description of the typical scene of "steel-making": "Small red flags fly overhead indicating the sections belonging to the various companies and squads of farmer-steel workers, who are organized like militia units. The air is filled with the high-pitched melodies of local operas pouring through amplifier above the site and accompanied by the hum of blowers, the panting of gasoline engines, the honking of heavily-laden lorries, and the bellowing of oxen hauling ore and coal." Cited from Mark Selden, *The People's Republic of China: A Documentary History of Revolutionary Change* (New York: Monthly Review Press, 1979), p. 413.

would like to participate in steel-making. In future I may extend this new experiment to Indonesia".[64] He proved to be sincere — on site, he was drawing charts and writing notes on specific procedures.[65] His participation in this process had a broader symbolic implication. It was that Pramoedya had gone beyond the stage of detachment and disillusionment; he had started the endeavour to change society not only by pen but, more significantly, by action.

During his second trip to China, a significant episode happened in Pramoedya's personal life. According to Bahrum Rangkuti, he had a romantic relationship with his Chinese interpreter, Chen Xiaru. Bahrum Rangkuti wrote:

> One thing that is no less important, which can clarify other aspects of Pramoedya's preference, is his close friendship with a Chinese woman who was fluent in Indonesian and a university graduate. It was this woman who translated his speeches and lectures while he was in China. For weeks both of them were in close contact, which turned friendship into love. But in the end, both of them recognized that their respective interests must take a back seat for the sake of the family and nation. This kind of situation resulted in extraordinary activities in their correspondence, which contains extensive treatment of literature, culture and the meaning of life.[66]

Pramoedya had met Chen Xiaru during his first trip in 1956, when Chen was the Indonesian-language interpreter affiliated with the Writers' Union. Pramoedya appeared to have a very good impression of her and marvelled that Chen was able to translate Abdul Muis's *Salah Asuhan* (*A Wrong Upbringing*) into Chinese, even though she had graduated from the Department of Oriental Languages of Peking University only two years earlier and had never been to Indonesia.[67] In his essay about Chinese writers, appearing in a prominent literary journal, Pramoedya inserted a picture of Chen Xiaru.[68]

---

[64] Pulamudiya Ananda Duer [Pramoedya], "Liangan Luqian" [In front of a melting furnace], trans. Chen Xiaru, *Renmin Wenxue* 12 (1958): 16.
[65] Interview with Chen Xiaru.
[66] Bahrum Rangkuti, *Pramoedya*, p. 23.
[67] *Hsin Pao*, 17 November 1956.
[68] Pramoedya, "Sedikit tentang Pengarang Tiongkok".

Pramoedya's short-lived romantic involvement with Chen Xiaru might have partly contributed to his romanticization of the PRC.[69] It perhaps had an impact on his creative writings as well. As Boen Oemarjati has pointed out, Pramoedya's work had "a very strong autobiographical strain and his books are his personal experiences molded into literature".[70] Chen Xiaru's image may be revived in his *Footsteps*, the third volume of his highly acclaimed Buru quartet. Although these novels are based on the experiences of the Indonesian nationalist Tirto Adi Suryo (who is the fictional Minke, the novels' central character), there are confluences between the views of Minke and those of Pramoedya himself.[71] An important segment of *Footsteps* is devoted to a romantic relationship between Minke and Ang San Mei, a revolutionary youth from China who was fluent in English and French, after her graduation from college. Minke's affection and admiration for Ang San Mei leads him to propose to her. It is, however, a tragic and short-lived marriage: Ang San Mei dies of disease one year after they marry. It has been speculated that Chen Xiaru may well be the prototype of Ang San Mei.[72]

## THE TRANSFORMATION OF PRAMOEDYA: THE CRITICAL YEARS, 1956–59

Pramoedya went through a critical transformation in his cultural outlook and political affiliation immediately after his return from China in November 1956. In reformulating his vision for Indonesia, he persistently drew upon inspirations acquired from China and his understanding of PRC cultural doctrines. After the end of 1956, Pramoedya changed from a detached writer to an active fighter; his universal humanism was replaced by devout socialist realism.

---

[69] According to Chen Xiaru (interview), Pramoedya wanted to visit China again after 1958. A letter appearing in the anti-Communist newspaper *Abadi*, which was highly critical of Pramoedya, alleged that "Pramoedya is crazy for going back to China" ("setiap kali gila hendak kembali ke Tiongkok"), *Abadi*, 6 January 1960.
[70] Oemarjati, "The Development", p. 323.
[71] See, for example, Patricia Henry, "The Writer's Responsibility", pp. 63–70.
[72] Interview in Beijing with Professor Ju Sanyuan of Peking University, co-translator of the Chinese version of *Footsteps*.

## From Detachment to Involvement

The first conversion of Pramoedya was political; he was transformed from a detached intellectual to a political activist. Before the end of 1956, he was disappointed at the results of the country's post-independence evolution. He not only disassociated himself from any political organizations, but also ruled out ideological and political means for solving Indonesia's problems. The best way of achieving a just society, Pramoedya believed, was through cultural or social adjustment rather than through reforms in political institutions.[73] The end of 1956 saw a fundamental shift in his outlook. He was no longer preoccupied with the cultural approach to sociopolitical change. Instead, he came to the conclusion that political restructuring was essential not only for solving political problems, but for coping with the cultural quandary.

The new Pramoedya had an unambiguous political stance. In February 1957, three days after Sukarno formally announced his "Conception" for Guided Democracy, Pramoedya wrote his first political essay, entitled "Djembatan Gantung dan Konsepsi Presiden" (The Suspension Bridge and the President's Conception). It appeared in the *Bintang Merah* (Red Star) and the *Harian Rakjat* (*The People's Daily*),[74] both official publications of the PKI. The significance of this essay lay not only in its timing and venues of publication, but in its manifestation of the author's political allegiance. In addition to acknowledging his new understanding of the PKI and its role in Indonesian history, Pramoedya expressed his firm support for Sukarno's concept of political restructuring. He admitted that in the past he had misunderstood the PKI; his anti-Communist attitude was formulated through reading economic and sociopolitical accounts by Westerners. After independence, Pramoedya pointed out, many political parties had betrayed the ideals of the revolution and the people. The only exception was the Communist Party, which not only held firmly to the

---

[73] See Savitri Scherer, "From Culture to Politics: The Development of Class Consciousness in Pramoedya Ananta Toer's Writings", in *Writers and Society*, ed. Wang Gungwu (Canberra: Australian National University Press, 1981), pp. 239–61. Pramoedya wrote: "I had been fairly apolitical up until that time [1955]. In fact, I had consciously avoided involving myself in any activity that could be described as political". Pramoedya, *The Mute's Soliloquy*, p. 228.

[74] Pramoedya Ananta Toer, "Djembatan Gantung dan Konsepsi Presiden", *Harian Rakjat*, 28 February 1957; also in *Bintang Merah* 13, 1/2 (1957): 69–75.

revolution and distanced itself from rampant corruption, but served as the sole and true representative of the people's interests. Here Pramoedya redefined the meaning of the people. They were no longer faceless, undifferentiated and passive "little guys". Instead, they were "workers and peasants who have provided us with food, clothing, and housing. Over the past centuries, it has also been workers who built roads and created national wealth. However, since the transfer of sovereignty, they have been abandoned ... even slandered, betrayed, exploited and trampled upon".[75] This newfound meaning of the people and its political representative, the PKI, was to become a "suspension bridge" by which Pramoedya entered the volatile and intriguing political scene of the late 1950s and early 1960s. He ceased to be a disengaged intellectual who used his pen only to attempt to reflect society's sentiments; rather, he started to be directly involved in the process of cultural politics by being a leader himself.

The February 1957 essay represented the point of no return in Pramoedya's career as an intellectual. In March 1957, together with the painter Henk Ngantung and film director Kotot Sukardi, he led a delegation of 67 artists and writers to meet with Sukarno in the National Palace, where they expressed their enthusiastic support for Sukarno's "Conception".[76] Considering the fact that this controversial concept of Guided Democracy was still being heatedly debated and that the PKI was the first political party to endorse the plan, Pramoedya's stance had broader significance. It was a political statement for him in formally siding with the left-wing political and cultural movement. From that time onwards, until his arrest in 1965 and subsequent imprisonment, Pramoedya was closely associated with Lekra. In January 1959, immediately after returning from his second China trip, Pramoedya was elected to Lekra's central leadership. He also became editor of the *Lentera*, a literary forum of the daily *Bintang Timur*, the major cultural apparatus in battles with non-Lekra intellectuals between 1963 and 1965.

In the transition from detached writer to devoted fighter, Pramoedya was deeply influenced by what he had observed in China. His admiration for and identification with the PRC facilitated his shift to the left. It was not a coincidence that Pramoedya had formulated his new vision for Indonesia at the same time when he wrote extensively about cultural practices and the role of intellectuals in China. He employed the Chinese

---

[75] Pramoedya, "Djembatan Gantung", *Bintang Merah*, p. 72.
[76] *Harian Rakjat*, 9 March 1957.

expression (imported initially from the Soviet Union) "writers are the engineers of human souls" as a metaphor for demonstrating the need for intellectuals to be responsible to the nation. In a 1958 speech to school teachers in Padang, apart from attacking Western individualism and calling for support for Guided Democracy, Pramoedya stated, "artists are architects and engineers of the nation who occupy an important place in society and in shaping the national spirit".[77] He then gave the example of Lu Xun as a model of an involved writer. In his report to Lekra about the Tashkent Asian-African Writers Conference, Pramoedya reiterated some of the central themes he first expounded in February 1957. He admitted that in the past he had considered literature merely as an expression of personal thinking without realizing that the individual was a social entity. After acknowledging Lekra's help in shaping his views of the people, he went on to declare that writers had a vital responsibility in changing society.[78]

As a consequence of the transformation in his political and cultural outlook after 1956, Pramoedya became more and more occupied with political rather than cultural issues. In 1955, he had planned to spend the next ten years writing a major creative work and had started library research for it.[79] Nevertheless, from his return from China until 1965, Pramoedya wrote primarily political and social commentaries rather than creative works. The publication of *Hoakiau di Indonesia* (The Chinese in Indonesia) in 1960 is a case in point. This 200-page, thoroughly documented book was written in late 1959, at the height of anti-Chinese sentiment in the Sukarno era. It was composed of nine lengthy letters to Chen Xiaru, which first appeared in the weekly *Bintang Mingguan*. In this book, dedicated to Chen Xiaru, Pramoedya came to the defence of the *Hoakiau* (or *huaqiao*, overseas Chinese). He argued that those who initiated the anti-Chinese movement were motivated by their own political agendas and supported by the imperialists. By quoting extensively from Dutch, Indonesian and English materials, Pramoedya demonstrated that the ethnic Chinese should not be viewed as foreigners, as they had long been integrated with the Indonesian people. Furthermore, he contended that the *Hoakiau* had made significant contributions to the nation's economic, social

---

[77] Pramoedya, "Seniman adalah Insinjur Pembentuk Djiwa Bangsa", *Pikiran Rakjat*, 19 June 1958.
[78] Pramoedya, "Lekra telah Mendidik Saja Mentjintai Rakjat", *Zaman Baru* (30 January–10 February 1959), pp. 7–10.
[79] Savitri Scherer, "From Culture to Politics", p. 23.

and cultural development; they should therefore be taken as "comrades-in-arms" of the Indonesian people. This book was very influential and reportedly became a bestseller of the time. The adapted Chinese translation of this book appeared in Indonesia, China and other Southeast Asian countries; the PRC government praised Pramoedya's courage in seeking justice for the overseas Chinese.[80] Pramoedya himself, however, paid a high price for writing this book, which was banned soon after its publication; he was detained by the military authorities for nine months.

## From Universal Humanism to Socialist Realism

Pramoedya's cultural thought prior to 1956 had been within the framework of universal humanism. While he had genuine concerns for the disadvantaged members of the society, "the people" in his creative writings tended to be undifferentiated; he did not see Indonesian society through the lenses of class. He also accepted the basic, elite cultural tenet that *priyayi* (elite), no matter how imperfect, were "superior" to the *wong-cilik* (little guys). According to this view, "it is the *priyayi* who are depicted to be ones with idealism and dedication, while the *wong-cilik* (when they are not depicted as 'docile') are the ones who are capable of committing atrocious acts".[81]

The new Pramoedya displayed a very different perception regarding the people and how they ought to be portrayed in literature. He no longer viewed "the people" as undifferentiated and passive; instead, he saw them as workers and peasants who contributed greatly to society and should be portrayed positively in literature. The PRC cultural doctrine of "art should serve the people" reinforced Pramoedya's conviction that the people

---

[80] See, for example, *Tay Kong Sian Po* (Surabaya), 4–15 January 1960; *Yinhua Jinji* (Jakarta), 7 January 1960; *Xinyanguang Bao* (Rangoon), 3 May 1960; *Mianghua Ribao* (Phnom Penh), 26 April 1960; *People's Daily* (Beijing), 23 June 1960; and *Dongnanya Yanjiu Ziliao* (Guangzhou), nos. 1–2 (1960), pp. 2–10, 87–95. In a letter to the Association of the Chinese People's Cultural Exchange with Foreign Countries, the Chinese embassy in Jakarta reported that Pramoedya "has performed marvellously in the campaign to counterbalance the anti-China and anti-Chinese movement ... and his book on the Chinese in Indonesia, which has directly confronted the biases of counter-revolutionaries, has been very influential". File no. 105-0098-01 (28 May–28 July 1960), Archives of the Ministry of Foreign Affairs, PRC.
[81] Savitri Scherer, "From Culture to Politics", p. vii.

were not idle objects of oppression. He started attaching great importance to the theme of class differentiation in society and its cultural ramifications. This shift of attention began while he was still in the PRC. Toward the end of his first visit, Pramoedya gave a talk about Indonesian literature in Guangzhou and a few new themes surfaced in this speech.[82] For example, he thought it was unfortunate that, before World War II, no intellectuals had represented the spirit and consciousness of the peasant and working classes. He considered Armijn Pane's *Belenggu* (*Shackles*, 1940) and Takdir Alisjahbana's *Layar Terkembang* (*With Sails Unfurled*, 1936) as reflecting "the spiritual life of the bourgeois and petit-bourgeois". Faulting Indonesian intellectuals for their lack of connection with the people, Pramoedya declared that "in our time, there is a greater urgency in producing writers like Lu Xun, a thinker with firm convictions". His attitude toward the cultural leftists who advocated the doctrine of "art serving the people" had also changed: "With the founding of the People's Institute of Culture (Lekra), it has become the dynamic in pushing forward the development of culture in society; the socialist stream has also gradually gained ground among writers".[83]

After the end of 1956, Pramoedya developed a new appreciation of the mass-elite relationship and how this relationship should be portrayed in literature. This change was evident in the first novel he wrote after returning from China, *Sekali Peristiwa di Banten Selatan* (*An Event in Southern Banten*). Acknowledging the importance of "living with peasants and workers" in order to accurately interpret their life, Pramoedya "went down" to the countryside of the Banten area, where he met peasants and miners at the end of 1957.[84] The novel had a strong political undertone, depicting class confrontations between the oppressed and the exploiters. An underlying implication was that the little guys were not mere objects of exploitation; their fate could be changed for the better if they united and fought against injustice. Although this novel has been criticized as "shabbily written",[85] its political implication shadowed its literary imaginativeness.

---

[82] Pramoedya, "Tantan Yindunixiya Wenxue" [A talk on Indonesian literature], *Wenyi Yuebao* 11 (1958): 20–2.

[83] Ibid., p. 22.

[84] Savitri Scherer, "From Culture to Politics", p. 181. For a more systematic discussion of Pramoedya's views of socialist realism, see Eka Kurniawan, *Pramoedya Ananta Toer dan Sastra Realisme Sosialis* (Yogyakarta: Yayasan Aksara Indonesia, 1999).

[85] Ibid., p. 184.

Shortly after the novel's publication, it was adapted by Dhalia (a playwright affiliated with Lekra) with the title of *Orang² Baru dari Banten* (*The New People from Banten*) and published by Lekra in 1959.[86]

The China connection, therefore, served as one of the most significant factors leading to the transformation of Pramoedya in his political orientation, literary practice and aesthetic understanding of society. By joining in the left-wing cultural movement, Pramoedya became a prototype of the Indonesian intellectuals who tried to generate cultural and political change through personal participation in the process. This new Pramoedya was a product of the complex political environment of the time. Sukarno's efforts at fundamentally restructuring the political system, also influenced by his own favourable views of the PRC model, provided him with a new domestic political framework within which his vision for the nation could be realized. In retrospect, October 1956 was a crucial turning point in Indonesia's political and cultural history, as evidenced by the fact that both President Sukarno and Pramoedya reached a critical transition through the vital intermediary of the PRC. Hence, it was not a coincidence that Pramoedya was among the first (former) centrist intellectuals who pledged their firm support for Sukarno's concept of Guided Democracy.

## CONCLUSION

Pramoedya's transition took place at a time of heightened cultural confrontation, when the debates on culture became increasingly politicized and polarized. Pramoedya himself was clearly aware of this development, as he put it in 1962,

> The birth of Lekra sounded the deathknoll [sic] for the 1945 Generation, already in a state of serious disorder after having been infected by Dutch cultural infiltration.... During the first years of its existence, Lekra was involved in a difficult struggle to evolve the correct forms for its easthetic [sic] expression to be welded with political or ideological consciousness ... at the present stage of Indonesian literatures, there are

---

[86] This play was reportedly very popular among peasants. See Liang Liji, "Pulamudiya Ananda Tuer jiqi Chuangzuo" [Pramoedya Ananta Toer and his writings], in *Dongfang Yanjiu Lunwenji* [Papers on Oriental studies], ed. Beijing Daxue Dongfang Yuyan Wenxhe Xi [Department of Oriental Studies, Beijing University] (Beijing: Beijing Daxue Chubanshe, 1983), pp. 206–24.

two contrary forces: on the one hand, progressive writers inside and outside Lekra, and on the other hand, the neutral or even reactionary writers who voice to [sic] the wishes of the Indonesian bourgeoisie now in the state of decay.[87]

Politically, Lekra writers were closely associated with the PKI and, to a lesser degree, with Sukarno, while many of the 1945 Generation writers aligned themselves with the right-wing army leadership and conservative Muslims. Culturally, these two groups held opposing aesthetic views. While Lekra writers firmly believed that art should serve the people and politics, the majority of the 1945 Generation writers insisted that art should have its own aesthetic criteria and be separated from politics. The clash of these political and cultural visions finally led to the Manikebu Affair in 1963–64, in which the anti-Lekra intellectuals associated with universal humanism, and espousing art for the sake of art, were effectively silenced.[88]

The incorporation of PRC cultural doctrines and practices by Lekra writers reinforced the tendency toward cultural radicalism and polarization. This integration was facilitated by a number of political and diplomatic factors. In the first place, the increasingly left-leaning trend in Indonesia's domestic and foreign policy was conducive in facilitating the appropriation of the China metaphor and its applicability in cultural politics. The influence of the PRC on Indonesia's domestic transformation increased remarkably. For instance, during the final years of Guided Democracy, the official Indonesian news agency (*Antara*) used the dispatches of the New China News Agency not only for information regarding China, but for its coverage of Indonesia's domestic events.[89] The second reason for the

---

[87] Pramudya Ananta Tur, "Introducing Indonesian Literature", *Harian Rakjat*, part 3, 5 September 1962 (originally in English).

[88] In September 1963, 16 intellectuals, including H.B. Jassin, Goenawan Mohamad and Wiratmo Sukito, issued the "Cultural Manifesto" (*Manifesto Kebudayaan*). In addition to reaffirming the values of "universal humanism", the Manifesto rejected the idea promoted by Lekra that artistic quality was better judged by social criteria than by self-referencing aesthetic notions. After extensive debates and fierce attacks by Lekra writers, the Manifesto was banned by Sukarno on 8 May 1964, and many of the Manifesto writers were subsequently removed from their jobs. See Goenawan Mohammad, "The 'Manikebu Affair'"; and Keith Foulcher, "A Survey of Events Surrounding 'Manikebu': The Struggle for Cultural and Intellectual Freedom in Indonesian Literature", *Bijdragen tot de Taal-, Land- en Volkenkunde* 125, 4 (1969): 429–65.

[89] Arnold C. Brackman, *The Communist Collapse in Indonesia* (New York: W.W. Norton, 1969), pp. 146–7.

Cover of Agam Wispi et al., *Dinasti 650 Djuta* (Jakarta: Lekra, 1961).

Cover of Chinese translation of Situmorang's *Collection of Poems*, translated by Chen Xiaru *et al.*

incorporation of Chinese cultural doctrines was China's growing attraction to Indonesian intellectuals, especially those with a leftist persuasion. Almost all the Lekra members, for instance, made at least one trip to the PRC, and they produced a significant number of literary romanticizations of the new China.[90]

Throughout the first half of the 1960s, Lekra's cultural doctrines had a clear Chinese imprint. The most important was the doctrine of "politics is the commander" (*politik adalah panglima*), which was the principle dominating all of Lekra's artistic works.[91] Other doctrines and working methods included *turun ke bawah* (going to the lower level) and *meluas dan meninggi* (going wide and high). They bore a clear parallel with the doctrines that first elaborated by Mao Zedong in his 1940 *Talk at the Yenan Forum on Literature and Art* (the essence of which was translated by Njoto in 1950). The expression "going wide and high", for example, was a variation of Mao's formulation of "raising art's standard and at the same time promoting its popularization".[92] "Going to the lower level", on the other hand, was the central thrust of socialist realism.[93] Influenced by this "going down" approach, Pramoedya himself organized some Lekra writers

---

[90] See, for example, Agam Wispi *et al.*, *Dinasti 650 Djuta* (Jakarta: Lekra, 1961); Sitor Situmorang, *Zaman Baru* (Jakarta: Madjalah Zaman Baru, 1961); and H.R. Bandaharo, *Dari Bumi Merah* (Jakarta: Pembaruan, 1963); see also Yahaya Ismail, *Pertumbuhan, Perkembangan dan Kejatuhan Lekra di Indonesia* (Kuala Lumpur: Dewan Bahasa dan Pustaka, 1972), pp. 57–9. Sitor Situmorang was the head of LKN (Lembaga Kebudajaan Nasional, cultural organization of the Indonesian Nationalist Party), which was close to Lekra.

[91] Pramoedya later recalled that "At that time, I did stand for the slogan Politics is the Commander, I believed then that a revolution would lead to the emancipation of the people." Margaret Scott, "Waging War with Words", p. 27.

[92] Mao Zedong, *Talk at the Yenan Forum*, pp. 16–8; Njoto, "Literatur Baru: Bagaimanakah Pendapat Mao Tse-tung tentang Literatur?" *Republik* 1, 4 (1950): 36–7; Mau Tje-tung [Mao Tse-tung], *Front Nasional dalam Pekerdjaan Kebudajaan*, trans. Njoto (Jakarta, 1959).

[93] As Mao wrote in 1953, "China's revolutionary writers and artists, writers and artists of promise, must go among the masses … go into the heat of the struggle … in order to observe, experience, study and analyse all the different kinds of people, all the classes, all the masses, all the vivid patterns of life and struggle, all the raw materials of literature and art." Cited in Julie Shackford-Bradley, "Mao's Ghost in Golkar", *Inside Indonesia* (January–March 2000), p. 27.

to live among the common people and study them.⁹⁴ The China-originated "revolutionary romanticism" was also gradually incorporated into the Lekra cultural movement.⁹⁵

Therefore, the PRC cultural doctrines — which were peripheral to the Indonesian intellectual and literary tradition — became a centre of cultural polemics in the late Sukarno era. Writers espousing "universal humanism" fiercely opposed the inclusion of these PRC cultural doctrines. Goenawan Mohamad, one of the younger Manifesto members, wrote an essay in 1963 disputing the PRC cultural concepts by rejecting the Chinese poet Feng Zhi (Feng Chih)'s contention that "a [political] slogan is a powerful poem" and argued that poetry was a free statement that made it impossible to compare with "the hypocrite".⁹⁶ The anti-Lekra movement had a definite anti-PRC overtone; as Goenawan put it, "The Manifesto was a statement openly refusing the validity of the slogan, politics is the commander".⁹⁷

There was a similar trend of politicization in the arena of education whereby China-originated principles also became a focal point of controversy. The contest for education during the first half of the 1960s was centred on the largely China-originated *Panca Cinta* (Five Loves), the five principles that should be inculcated in all students: patriotism, the love of knowledge, world peace and international understanding, the study of

---

⁹⁴ Scherer, "From Culture to Politics", Chapter 8. This view of "*turba*" continues to influence Pramoedya's creative writings in the 1980s. According to Keith Foulcher, "*Anak Semua Bangsa* [*Child of All Nations*] is the fullest and most powerful statement ever to appear of the notion of *turun ke bawah* (*turba*) enunciated as a political and cultural principle by the PKI in the early 1960s … Minke's self-discovery, through *Anak Semua Bangsa*, rests decisively on the exercise of this principle". See Foulcher, "*Bumi Manusia* and *Anak Semua Bangsa*: Pramoedya Ananta Toer Enters the 1980s", *Indonesia* 32 (1981): 14–5. See also Razif Bahari, "Remembering History, W/righting History: Piecing the Past in Pramoedya Ananta Toer's Buru Trilogy", *Indonesia* 75 (2003): 61–94.
⁹⁵ Keith Foulcher, *Social Commitment in Literature and the Arts: The Indonesian "Institute of People's Culture", 1950–1965* (Clayton, Victoria: Centre of Southeast Asian Studies, Monash University, 1986), pp. 110–1.
⁹⁶ Mohamad, "Seribu Slogan dan Sebuah Puisi" (1963), in his *Potret Seorang Penjair Muda Sebagai Si Malin Kundang* (Jakarta: Pustaka Jaya, 1972), pp. 31–2.
⁹⁷ Mohamad, "'The Manikebu Affair'", p. 82.

Cover of the *Sastra* magazine (1964) which was closely associated with the "Manifesto" members.

the physical sciences, and appreciation of manual work.[98] Together with land reform and the restructuring of the party system, the educational principles constituted one of the three central issues dividing an already polarized Indonesia. On the one side were the PKI and its alliance, who argued that *Panca Cinta* served as the moral basis for implementing Sukarno's new vision for Indonesia. At the other end of the spectrum, non-Communists, especially the Muslim groups, were critical of *Panca Cinta*'s atheistic stance. The two sides heatedly and emotionally exchanged views in the newspapers and a number of well-publicized seminars. As in the case of the Manikebu affair, Sukarno intervened in June 1964 and the outcome was in favour of the *Panca Cinta*. As Sukarno declared,

> I want *ke-Binneka Tunggal Ika-an* ["unity in diversity", the nation's motto] to produce as many ideas, conceptions, and creations as possible; and to produce youths, patriots, intellectuals, artists, writers, experts and indeed even craftsmen whom we can be proud of. In the People's Republic of China, Chairman Mao Tse Tung taught "Let a hundred flowers bloom together". Here I would use the slogan "Let the *melati* and the *mawar* and the *kenanga* and the *cempaku* bloom together in the Indonesian garden.[99]

In short, Pramoedya and other Lekra-associated writers were the driving force behind Indonesia's trend of cultural radicalism between 1963 and 1965, which was significantly facilitated by an extensive and systemic incorporation of PRC cultural doctrines and working methods. With the transformation of favourable China perceptions into actions, the China metaphor thus became a major factor shaping the cultural politics of the Guided Democracy era.

---

[98] Lee Kam Hing has pointed that there was a similarity between *Panca Cina* and the educational principles of China, which included "love for the fatherland and the people, lover of labor, and love of science". He suggested that "it is likely that the PKI adopted the set of five loves contained in Chinese education and then employing the evocative Javanese term of *Panca*". Lee, *Education and Politics in Indonesia*, pp. 220–2.

[99] Cited in Lee, *Education and Politics in Indonesia*, p. 332. For a detailed account of the controversy and political manoeuvres centring on *Panca Cinta*, see pp. 299–346.

## CONCLUSION

# China as an Alternative Modernity

> *Not finding anything about them which seemed to confirm to their ideals, they [the Physiocrats] went to search for it in the heart of Asia. It is no exaggeration to say that everyone of them in some part of his writings passes an emphatic eulogy on China ... That imbecile and barbarous government ... appeared to them the most perfect model for all of the nations of the world to copy.*
>
> Alexis de Tocqueville (1865)[1]

> *The struggle to understand China became part of a struggle by Americans to understand themselves as a national community of democratic citizens committed to the universal good of freedom.*
>
> Richard Madsen (1995)[2]

> *Modernity and Westernization are not identical; Western patterns of modernity are not the only 'authentic' modernities, though they enjoy historical precedence and continue to be a basic reference point for others.*
>
> S.N. Eisenstadt (2000)[3]

This study has examined in detail Indonesian representations of China in the political, socio-economic and cultural arenas that led to the emergence of three sets of master narratives, each with a series of interconnected sub-narratives. They depicted China as a purposeful and harmonious society experiencing rapid economic progress, a nationalistic and populist regime

---

[1] Alexis de Tocqueville, *L'ancien Regime et la Revolution*, quoted in Lewis A. Coser, *Men of Ideas: A Sociologist's View* (New York: Free Press, 1965), p. 227.
[2] Richard Madsen, *China and the American Dream: A Moral Inquiry* (Berkeley: University of California Press, 1995), pp. 211–2.
[3] S.N. Eisenstadt, "Multiple Modernities", *Daedalus* 129 (2000): 1–29.

profoundly different from the Soviet Union, and a nation characterized by a vibrant cultural and intellectual renaissance. Let us recapitulate the substance of these narratives before deciphering their contextualization and significance.

(1) *China as a purposeful and harmonious society.* The dominant theme in this master narrative characterized Chinese society with catchwords such as purposefulness, harmony, newness and the unity of people, who worked indigenously for the collective social good in which national interests always reigned supreme. Rapid economic progress and equable social distributions of wealth was one of the two sub-narratives under this master narrative, while the other sub-narrative extolled the disciplined and altruistic nature of the people.

(2) *China as a participatory and populist polity.* The second master narrative was concerned with polity, with many intellectuals holding the notion that China was a populist regime supported "by the people, for the people and of the people". Implicit in this interpretation was a persistent penchant for separating China from Communism (and vice versa) and for emphasizing its nationalistic characteristics. This master narrative was composed of three sub-narratives, portraying China's political system ("New Democracy") as essentially a continuation of the country's long-standing tradition dating back to Confucian times; it regarded Mao as a benevolent philosopher-king who was the genuine heir to Sun Yat-sen, the founding father of modern Chinese nationalism. China was, furthermore, depicted as a country pursuing peaceful international diplomacy in Southeast Asia.

(3) *China as a vibrant culture imbued with great intellectual creativities.* As creators of cultural norms, China observers in Indonesia were naturally attracted by the role of culture and the intelligentsia in the processes of socio-economic development. Cultural renaissance was in the centre of discourse on Chinese intellectual life, which not only derived its vitality from a rich tradition, but from the spontaneity of the people and the exciting nation-building process. Chinese intellectuals' energetic participation in sociopolitical change, which earned them a respected place in the society, was admired by a significant segment of observers in Indonesia.

To be sure, in a highly politicized and plural society such as Indonesia during the 1950s and the early 1960s when a significant degree of press freedom existed, China did not have an undifferentiated and unified image; instead, it was fervently contested and constantly refashioned. While the above master narratives were largely expounded by prominent political and cultural intellectuals and appeared in the mainstream mass media (especially newspapers and leading political and cultural magazines) consumed by the political public, some dissenting and critical perceptions of China were presented by other intellectuals, especially those with anti-Communist and strong religious persuasions. They portrayed China as the Soviet's satellite state under Communist dictatorship, a regimented society stringently controlled by the Communist Party, and a people degenerated into slaves who blindly worshipped ruthless rulers such as Mao. They held negative views pertaining to the relationship between the arts and politics in the PRC, and believed that art in China had become "pure propaganda". By placing political allegiance and social commitment above aesthetic sensitivity and artistic standards, intellectuals had become "tools of propaganda". In comparison with the master narratives, however, these critical perceptions were in the minority in terms of the relative number of their proponents and their impact, and their voices were effectively silenced toward the end of the Sukarno regime, when China emerged as Indonesia's most vital diplomatic ally. In other words, while the multiplicity of China perceptions reflected the pluralist nature of Indonesian society and value systems, the increasing ascendancy of these master narratives symbolized a hegemonic turn in the turbulent search for alternative models of governance, which ended with the (temporary) triumph of the political and cultural visions of Sukarno and Pramoedya — in turn significantly shaped by their interpretations of the Chinese model of development. Beijing's escalated efforts, through both formal and informal diplomacy, to shore up its affirmative image further facilitated the tendency of interpreting and presenting the Chinese experiences mainly in a positive light.

Throughout the process of articulating, presenting and contesting these master narratives, Indonesian political and cultural intellectuals — who constituted the core of the nation's China observers — were inevitably and repeatedly confronted with a perplexing question: Why was the People's Republic, as a new nation founded at the same time as their own country, able to accomplish so much in such a short span of time? While some attributed the reason to China's political system and Communist ideology, which allowed for mass mobilization in production and social control, the majority of observers evoked Oriental and cultural characteristics as the key explanatory factor. According to this perspective, which appeared to be dominant in the public and policy discourses throughout the period under discussion, the change of political system only provided an environment for development. It was the so-called Chinese character (hardworking, discipline, thrifty, loyalty, and pragmatism, etc.) that was ultimately responsible for that country's social and economic progress. As Mohammad Hatta, a staunch anti-Communist, stated unambiguously: "It has mainly been the Chinese people's own characteristic talent that made those achievements possible". In the meantime, as a long-time advocate of the ideal and powers of pan-Asianism and immensely frustrated by political predicaments at home, Sukarno became attracted by the Chinese example of coalescing strong leadership and mass mobilization, which fitted nicely into his conviction that Asia's problems should and could only be resolved by "Asian formulas". It was through a series of critical conjunctions that China entered the realms and structures of Indonesian discourse as an imitable sociopolitical entity, a cherished cultural symbol and, above all, an intriguing metaphor with "a stratification of meaning" that "produce[d] an influx of significance", to paraphrase Clifford Geertz's eloquent expression.[4]

It should be clear by now that narratives about the PRC *per se* did not necessarily constitute the China metaphor; it was only when the narratives were presented by political and cultural intellectuals *in conjunction with* their respective, sometimes competing, visions and blueprints for the already polarized domestic scene that perceptions of China were transformed into the China metaphor. As I have demonstrated, the China metaphor reflected not only Indonesians' disillusionment about what had gone wrong at home but, more importantly, their aspirations for what could be achieved. In both contexts, China served as a reflective mirror and constituted a viable model — or the opposite — of social engineering, political activism, economic dynamism and cultural/intellectual vibrancy. In so doing, the exhaustive attempts at fusing culture with politics, literature with nation-building, intellectuals with the masses contributed to the debates about the nation/society's destiny. It was in this sense that the China metaphor constituted an embedded component of the sociocultural process/practice in Sukarno's Indonesia and that China — as a polity and as an imagination — played a significant part in shaping its political and cultural trajectories.

This study on the changing representations and implications of China can be viewed in the broader framework of Indonesia's unremitting search for identity and modernity at a rapidly changing time in the postcolonial world. While the "process to modernity" has often been defined, in the Southeast Asian context, as "sharing in the institutions and economic prosperity of the industrialized countries",[5] the complex (re)presentations

---

[4] Clifford Geertz, "Ideology as a Cultural System", in his *The Interpretation of Cultures* (New York: Basic Books, 1972), p. 210.
[5] Cited in Ruth McVey, "Change and Continuity in Southeast Asian Studies", *Journal of Southeast Asian Studies* 26, 1 (1995): 1–9.

of China in Indonesia alert us to the necessity of taking the modernity project beyond the conventional binary that sees Southeast Asian experiences through the monocular lens of the West. S.N. Eisenstadt has argued that the idea of "multiple modernities" needs to be seen as a refutation of theories of modernization and that the "homogenizing and hegemonic assumptions of this Western program of modernity" were not realized. "One of the most important implications of the term 'multiple modernities'", he contends, "is that modernity and Westernization are not identical; Western patterns of modernity are not the only 'authentic' modernities, though they enjoy historical precedence and continue to be a basic reference point for others ... The idea of multiple modernities presumes that the best way to understand the contemporary world — indeed to explain the history of modernity — is to see it as a story of continual constitution and reconstitution of a multiplicity of cultural programs".[6] With full recognition of the internal dynamisms and complexities and the co-existence of multiple modernities, this book argues that China served as an important and viable alternative to Western-dominant notions of the modernity project in Indonesia, which in turn has significant ramifications for an understanding of the new regional order in 21st-century Asia.

Arjun Appadurai has pointed out, "It has now become something of a truism that we function in a world fundamentally characterized by objects in motion. *This is a world of flows.*"[7] As a matter of fact, Asian modernities — since the turn of the 20th century — have been characterized by a tremendous scale and intensity of flows of ideas and people in the transnational and intraregional contexts, which include the contact zones connecting China with Southeast Asia through migration, cultural exchanges and long-distance nationalism, or a "network" linking intellectuals between Japan, China and Southeast Asia on the articulations and implementation of concepts such as Asianism, to name just a few examples.[8]

---

[6] S.N. Eisenstadt, "Multiple Modernities".

[7] Arjun Appadurai, *Modernity at Large: Cultural Dimensions in Globalization* (Minneapolis: University of Minnesota Press, 2001), p. 5 (emphasis added).

[8] See, for example, Hong Liu, "Sino-Southeast Asian Studies: Toward an Alternative Paradigm", *Asian Studies Review* 25, 3 (2001): 259–83; Caroline S. Hau and Takashi Shiraishi, "Daydreaming about Rizal and Tetchō: On Asianism as Network and Fantasy", *Philippine Studies* 57, 3 (2009): 329–88; Rebecca E. Karl, *Staging the World: Chinese Nationalism at the Turn of the Century* (Durham, NC: Duke University Press, 2002); and Wang Hui, *The Politics of Imagining Asia* (Cambridge: Harvard University Press, 2011).

The spread of ideas, in fact, has been precipitated by the constructions of mutual representations and contributes to the making of modernity in the Asian context. As an alternative modernity, China was taken seriously and simultaneously as an idea and an institution in postcolonial Indonesia. For the former, the ideas of equitable progress, human initiatives, freedom from want (placed above freedom of expression), cultural vivacity and boundless optimism for a brighter future were all attractive to Indonesians. At the institutional level, an important segment of politicians and intellectuals regarded China's practices of industrialization and collectivization, social engineering in integrating elite and the masses, and political control through effective leadership as potential ways forward. The introduction and implementation of China as an alternative form of modernity, to be sure, were not without contestation. Nevertheless, during the Sukarno era, its closing years in particular, dissenting voices and competing models did not represent a substantial challenge to an internalization of the China examples. It was only after 1965, when the anti-Communist and pro-Western Suharto regime took over that China was completely (but temporarily) removed from the country's political scene, cultural imagination, and historical memory.

The fading of China in Indonesia, however, proved to be short-lived. The introductory chapter has already highlighted a warm relationship that resurfaced soon after the fall of Suharto in 1998. President Abdurrahman Wahid stated in Beijing in late 1999 that he was delighted to have a "Confucian brother", and he made it clear that the new Indonesia would build stronger relations with its Asian neighbours, particularly China.[9] In 2001, an editorial of the influential daily, *Kompas*, urged Indonesians to "learn from China's example in development".[10] Dahlan Iskan, the CEO of the *Jawa Pos* Group, advocated in 2008 that not only Indonesia should learn from the Chinese model in his book, *Teachings from China*, but America could learn something from China, too.[11]

---

[9] "China Tops Indonesian Head's Agenda", *New York Times*, 24 October 1999; *Lianhe Zaobao* (Singapore), 6 December 1999.

[10] "Kita Bisa Mendengar Langsun Kisah Sukses Pembangunan Cina", *Kompas*, 7 November 2001.

[11] Dahlan Iskan, *Pelajaran dari Tiongkok* (Surabaya: JP Books, 2008); Iskan, "Amerika Harus Belajar Langkah-Langkah Tiongkok", *Jawa Pos*, 19 November 2008. For a scholarly discussion of the Chinese model and the implications for Indonesia, see I. Wibowo, *Belajar dari Cina: Bagaimana Cina Merebut Peluang dalam Era Globalisasi* (Jakarta: Kompas, 2004).

At the regional level, China's development model (the so-called Beijing Consensus) has become increasingly attractive in Southeast Asia as an effective alternative to the Washington Consensus (a series of neoliberal policies emphasizing fiscal discipline, trade liberalization, privatization and deregulation). Characterized as "driven by a desire to have equitable, peaceful high-quality growth", China's new development approach "turns traditional ideas like privatization and free trade on their heads. It is flexible enough that it is barely classifiable as a doctrine. It does not believe in uniform solutions for every situation.... Change, newness and innovation are the essential words of power in this consensus".[12] Apart from the resurfacing of catchwords widely used in Indonesia during the 1950s and 60s, such as *pragmatism*, *equitable development* and *newness*, the past decade has also witnessed the rapid ascendance of China's soft power in neighbouring countries that is not substantially dissimilar to its historical practices described in this study. For example, in Vietnam, where novels by Chinese writers now account for about half of all foreign literary books translated in the country, younger policy-makers have adopted what they call a "Chinese model" of slowly opening up the economy while retaining control of the political system. To Laotians, "China kind of symbolizes modernity".[13]

The dynamic (and to some observers, problematic) resurgence of the Chinese model of development in Southeast Asia and beyond poses important questions on how to comprehend and conceptualize a changing Asia

---

[12] The term "Beijing Consensus" was first coined by Joshua Ramo, the former foreign editor of *Time* magazine in his *The Beijing Consensus* (London: Foreign Policy Centre, 2004). For a more detailed analysis of the Chinese model of development and relevant intellectual debates, see Huang Ping and Cui Zhiyuan, *Zhongguo yu Quanqiuhua: Huashengdun Gongsi haishi Beijing Gongsi?* [China and globalization: Washington Consensus or Beijing Consensus?] (Beijing: Shehui Kexue Wenxian Chubanshe, 2005); Tianyu Cao, ed., *The Chinese Model of Modern Development* (London: Routledge, 2005); and Mark Leonard, *What Does China Think?* (London: Fourth Estate, 2008). Stefan Halper, *The Beijing Consensus: How China's Authoritarian Model Will Dominate the Twenty-first Century* (New York: Basic Books, 2010) presents critical views on China's expanding influence and its challenges to the American vision of liberalism and freedom.

[13] Joshua Kurlantzick, *Charm Offensive: How China's Soft Power Is Transforming the World* (New Haven: Yale University Press, 2007), pp. 119, 133, 138; See also David C. Kang, *China Rising: Peace, Power and Order in East Asia* (New York: Columbia University Press, 2007).

as well as China's increasingly prominent place in it. For better or for worse, this is not entirely uncharted territory; a transnational perspective embedded within a nuanced sense of the historicity of knowledge and power will contribute to our explorations. This study on China's intriguing role in postcolonial Indonesia's assiduous search for alternative modernities, I hope, may provide a revealing case in understanding and deciphering the complex interplay between imagination, power, diplomacy, ethnicity and intellectuality that will unquestionably be an integral component of the region's uncertain, yet exciting, future trajectories.

# APPENDIX

# Biographical Notes on Major China Observers in Indonesia, 1949–65

*A & S: Apa dan Siapa Sejumlah Orang Indonesia, 1985–1986* (Jakarta: Tempo, 1986).
*ENI: Ensiklopedia Nasional Indonesia* (Jakarta: Cipta Adi Pustaka, 1988).
*EI: Ensiklopedia Indonesia* (Jakarta: Ichtiar Bara-Van Hoeve, 1980).

**Abdulgani, Roeslan** (1914–2005). Born in Surabaya, Abdulgani was the secretary-general of the Ministry of Information between 1947 and 1954; secretary-general of the Afro-Asian Conference in 1955 (in which capacity he had extensive contacts with the Chinese delegation headed by Zhou Enlai); minister of foreign affairs, 1956–7; and vice-chairman of the National Council, 1957–9. He visited China with Sukarno in 1956 and was the author of a number of books on Indonesian politics and foreign policy. [O.G. Roeder, *Who's Who in Indonesia* (Jakarta: Gunung Agung, 1971), p. 4; A & S, pp. 3–4]

**Adjitorop, Jusuf** (?–). Elected to the central committee secretariat of the PKI in 1956, he became a candidate member for the politburo two years later and acquired full membership in 1963. He was in Beijing when the 30 September 1965 coup took place and has remained there since then. Adjitorop is the author of *Integrasi Kekuasaan Politik dan Sistim Hukum dengan Revolusi di Tiongkok Rakjat* (Jajasan Pendidikan dan Kebudajaan Baperki, 1964), a study of the PRC's political and legal systems based upon his personal observations in China during the early 1960s. [Donald Hindley, *The Communist Party of Indonesia, 1951–1963* (Berkeley: University of California Press, 1964), pp. 65–7]

**Adinegoro, Djamaluddin** (1904–68). Born in West Sumatra, he was educated in Jakarta and studied journalism and geography in Germany and Holland from 1926 to 1930. After returning to Indonesia, he became the editor-in-chief of the *Pandji Poestaka* and moved to Medan in 1932 to join the daily *Pewarta Deli* and became the newspaper's "leading expert on foreign countries". He was appointed by Sukarno as head of the Indonesian National Committee in Sumatra in 1945 and subsequently worked for the official news agency *Antara* in Java. Adinegoro co-founded the influential weekly, *Mimbar Indonesia*, and was the head of Persbiro Indonesia Aneta in the 1950s. He visited China in the 1930s and 1956, and authored more than 25 books, including *Tiongkok: Pusaran Asia* (Jakarta and Amsterdam, 1951). [I.N. Soebagijo, *Adinegoro: Pelopor Jurnalistik Indonesia* (Jakarta: Haji Masagung, 1987); Soebagijo, *Jagat Wartawan Indonesia* (Jakarta: Gunung Agung, 1981), pp. 438–43]

**Agung, Ide Anak Agung Gde** (1919–99). Born in Bali, he attended law school in Jakarta. He was ambassador to Belgium, Luxembourg and France (1950–5), and minister of foreign affairs (1955–6). Imprisoned for four years (1962–6) for political reasons, he became a senior specialist at the East-West Center in Honolulu between 1967 and 1968, when he wrote *Twenty Years Indonesian Foreign Policy, 1945–1965* (1971), which contains an extensive treatise on the Sino-Indonesian relationship during the Sukarno era. [Zainal Rasjid, *Riwajat Orang-Orang Politik* (Medan: Bakti, 1952), pp. 31–4; *Who's Who in Indonesia*, p. 18]

**Ahmad, Zainal Abidin** (1911–?). Born in West Sumatra, he started his career as a journalist working for various magazines and dailies before 1942 and was deputy head of Indonesian Information Services in 1946. After 1947 he was a member of parliament and was appointed third vice-speaker in 1956; Ahmad was also the president of the School of Journalism and Political Science in Jakarta after 1956 and author of numerous books on Islam, politics and education. He visited China in 1956. [*The Asia Who's Who 1958* (Hong Kong: Pan-Asia Newspaper Alliance, 1958), p. 203]

**Aidit, Dipa Nusantara** (1923–65). Born in Medan, he worked in 1946 at the Solo headquarters of the PKI, which he joined in 1943. On the eve of the 1948 Madiun revolt, he was elected to the politburo and following its suppression fled abroad, spending much of 1949 and 1950 in China. After returning from China ("with prestige"), Aidit and a group of young leaders took over control of the PKI from the older leaders, Alimin and Tan

Ling Djie. He became secretary-general of the party in 1953 and its first chairman in 1959. Aidit was killed in the aftermath of the 30 September 1965 coup. He visited China a number of times between 1949 and 1965, and his numerous speeches and pamphlets were translated into English and Chinese, including *Problems of the Indonesian Revolution* (Bandung, 1963) and two volumes of *Aidi Xuanji* [*Selected Writings of Aidit*] (Beijing, 1960, 1963). [Herbert Feith and Lance Castles, eds., *Indonesian Political Thinking, 1945–1965* (Ithaca: Cornell University Press, 1972), p. 473; Jacques Leclerc, "Aidit dan Partai pada Tahun 1950", *Prisma* 7 (1982): 61–78]

**Anantaguna, S.** (1930–). One of the members of Lekra's central leadership (1959–65), he visited China more than twice and published a number of accounts of his trips. His other writings included *Jang Bertanah Air tapi tidak Bertanah* (Jakarta: Lekra, 1962). [*Authority Files: Names of Indonesian Authors* (Jakarta: Kantor Bibliografi Nasional, 1975), p. 26]

**Ang Goan Jan** (1894–1984). Born in Bandung, Ang joined the editorial board of the *Sin Po* in 1922 and became its director three years later, a position he held until the newspaper's closure in 1959. In 1960 he established the Surya Prabha publishing company, which published *Warta Bhakti* (*Zhong Cheng Bao*), a left-wing daily in Jakarta. A speaker of Malay, Dutch, English and some Chinese, Ang was a leading figure in the Indonesian Chinese community and was active in promoting the Sino-Indonesian relationship. [Leo Suryadinata, *Eminent Indonesian Chinese: Biographical Sketches*, revised edition (Singapore: Institute of Southeast Asian Studies, 1981), p. 2; Hong Yuanyuan [Ang Goan Jan], *Hong Yuanyuan Zizhuan* [An autobiography of Ang Goan Jan], trans. Liang Yingming (Beijing: Zhongguo Huaqiao Chuban Gongsi, 1989)]

**Arifin, Zainul** (1909–63). Born in Jakarta, he was a founding member of the Nahdatul Ulama. He worked in the Department of Education and Culture in the early 1950s and was the second vice-speaker of parliament between 1956 and 1959. Arifin visited China in 1956. [E.K. Siahaan, *Pahlawan Nasional: K.H. Zainul Arifin* (Jakarta: Departemen Pendidikan dan Kebudayaan, 1978/79)]

**Aziz, H.A.** (1922–84). Born in Madura, Aziz was educated in a technical high school and worked for the daily *Suara Asia* during the Japanese occupation. When the Revolution began, he took over the newspaper's Malang edition, in addition to establishing the daily *Suara Rakjat* and the biweekly

*Tinjauan*. During the 1950s he was the publisher and editor-in-chief of the *Surabaya Post* and chairman of the Indonesian Journalists Association (PWI) between 1953 and 1955. Aziz visited China in 1956. [*Ensiklopedi Nasional Indonesia* (hereafter *ENI*) (Jakarta: Cipta Adi Pustaka, 1988), vol. 2, pp. 459–60; Soebagijo, *Sejarah Pers Indonesia* (Jakarta: Dewan Pers, 1977), pp. 97–8]

**Bafagih, Asa** (1915–78). Born in Jakarta to a modest Muslim family, Bafagih taught in small Muslim schools and wrote regularly for the *Pemandangan* (Jakarta) and *Pandji Islam* (Medan). He became closely associated with Sukarno, Hatta and Natsir and was appointed foreign news editor of the *Pemandangan* before World War II. He was a journalist with the *Antara* news agency during the Indonesian Revolution. In 1948 he assumed the editorship of the *Merdeka* and became editor-in-chief of the new Nahdatul Ulama daily, *Duta Masjarakat*, in 1953. He was elected to the People's Representative Council in 1959 and appointed as Indonesia's ambassador to Sri Lanka between 1960 and 1964. Bafagih travelled widely and visited the PRC three times during the 1950s. His *RRT dari Luar dan Dalam* (Jakarta, 1955) was based on his first China trip in 1954. [Soebagijo, *Jagat Wartawan*, pp. 361–5; Willard Hanna, "The Case of the Forty Million Missing Muslims", *American Universities Field Staff* (Southeast Asian Series), September 1956, pp. 4, 15]

**Bandaharo, H.R.** (1917–93). Born in Medan, he was a Batak by ethnic origin. He took an active role in the national revolution in East Sumatra between 1945 and 1949, and moved to Jakarta after Independence. From the early 1950s, he became known as a prominent member of Lekra and published widely in cultural journals such as the *Zaman Baru*, *Zenith* and *Kebudayaan*. In 1959 he was elected to the Lekra central leadership and travelled overseas as a Lekra representative on delegations to Eastern bloc countries (including China). In 1965 he suffered arrest and imprisonment without trial and was released in the late 1970s. He was the author of *Dari Bumi Merah* (Jakarta: Pembaruan, 1963), a collection of poems recording his impressions of China and North Korea. [Keith Foulcher, "In Memoriam: H.R. Bandaharo (1917–1993)", *Inside Indonesia*, September 1993, pp. 35–6]

**Barioen A.S.** (?–?). An educator from Sumatra, he visited China in 1951 and published a widely read book, *Melihat Tiongkok Baru*. During the 1950s he was a member of the Indonesian-China Friendship Association, while his wife, Rasuna Said, was its chairperson from the mid-1950s to early 1960s. [*Perkenalan Lembaga Persahabatan Indonesia-Tiongkok* (Jakarta: Rada, 1956), p. 61]

**Bey, Arifin** (1925–). Born in Padang Panjang, Bey went to school in Bandung and studied Japanese in Bukittinggi, Singapore and Tokyo. After World War II, he worked as a translator for various news agencies in Japan before returning to Indonesia in the early 1950s as an employee for the UN's International Civil Services in Jakarta. In 1954 he became an assistant programme officer in the Indonesian Department of Information and was assigned to the UN's New York headquarters. Bey obtained a Ph.D. in international politics from Georgetown University in 1961 and returned to Jakarta to work as an editor of the *Indonesian Herald*, a post he held until 1965. Arifin Bey published widely in Indonesian, Japanese and English and is the author of a book on modern China entitled *Dari Sun Yat-sen Ke Mao Tse-tung* (1953). [Arifin Bey, *Peranan Jepang dalam Pasca "Abad Amerika"* (Jakarta: CV Antarkarya, 1990), pp. 350–1]

**Djawoto** (1906–92). Born in East Java, he was educated at a Dutch-language high school. At the end of the 1920s he joined the Hatta-Sjahrir wing of the *PNI-Pendidikan* (or the New PNI) and contributed regularly to the Jakarta daily *Pemandangan*. He joined the Indonesian news agency *Antara* in 1942 and became its head in 1946. He was elected president of the Indonesian Journalists' Association (Persatuan Wartawan Indonesia) in 1961 and later became secretary-general of the Asian-African Journalist Association. Djawoto was the chairman of the Indonesia-China Friendship Association in the early 1960s and was appointed ambassador to China in 1964 (and remained in China until 1979, when he left for the Netherlands). His publications include *Djurnalistik dalam Praktek* (Jakarta, 1960). [Soebagijo, *Jagat Wartawan*, pp. 538–42]

**Hatta, Mohammad** (1902–80). Born in West Sumatra, Hatta was active in the nationalist Indonesian Association when he was a student at the Economic University of Rotterdam. On his return to Indonesia, Hatta became chairman of the New PNI, or the Nationalist Education Association. He was vice president of Indonesia from 1945 to 1956. After 1950 he became increasingly associated with the Masyumi and Socialist parties in opposition to President Sukarno and the parties supporting him. He visited China as a state guest in 1957, shortly after his resignation from the vice-presidency. [Feith and Castles, eds., *Indonesian Political Thinking*, pp. 474–5]

**Karim, Abdul Daeng Patombong** (1926–). A journalist associated with the *Sin Po* and its successor *Warta Bhakti*, Karim was elected general chairman of the Indonesian Journalists' Association (PWI) between 1963 and 1965. He visited China in 1956. [Indonesian Journalists' Association, *Indonesian Journalists' Association (Persatuan Wartawan Indonesia)* (Jakarta, 1986), p. 22; Oey Hong Lee, *Indonesian Government and Press during Guided Democracy* (Hull: Hull University Centre for Southeast Asian Studies, 1971), p. 183]

**Koentjaraningrat** (1923–99). Born in Yogyakarta, he obtained his M.A. from Yale University and Ph.D. from the University of Indonesia. Between 1956 and 1961 he was a lecturer in anthropology at the University of Indonesia and Gadjah Mada University and was promoted to professor at the University of Indonesia in 1962. He visited China as a member of the Department of National Research delegation in 1965. His many publications include *Ke Mode² Anthropologi dalam Penjelidikan Masjarakat dan Kebudajaan di Indonesia* (1958) and *Javanese Culture* (1985). [*Who's Who in Indonesia*, pp. 184–5; *A & S*, pp. 407–8; <http://tokohindonesia.com/ensiklopedi/k/koentjaraningrat/index.shtml>]

**Kussudiardjo, Bagong** (1928–2004). Born in Yogyakarta, one of the best-known painters, dancers and choreographers in Indonesia, he studied at the Indonesian Arts Academy in Yogyakarta. In the early 1950s he was a member of the People's Painters group. However, he left the group when it united with Lekra. He established the Bagong Kussudiardjo Dance Training Center in 1958. Kussudiardjo visited China in 1954. [*ENI*, vol. 9, p. 245]

**Kwee Kek Beng** (1900–75). Born in Jakarta and educated in the Dutch-Chinese Teachers College, Kwee was the editor-in-chief of the *Sin Po* from 1925 to 1947. Although he advocated that *peranakans* should remain Chinese and hold Chinese citizenship, he was sympathetic to Indonesian nationalism and served as an assistant to the PNI journal, *Soeloeh Indonesia Moeda*, during the 1930s. He became an Indonesian citizen in 1950 and continued to edit a number of journals (among them *Sin Tjun*). After his two visits to China, Kwee published two books on China, *Ke Tiongkok Baru* (Jakarta: Kuo, 1952); and *50,000 Kilometer dalam 100 Hari* (Palembang: Lauw Putra, 1965). He was also the author of *Pendekar-pendekar R.R.T (Who's Who in the New China)* (Jakarta: Kuo, 1953). [Leo Suryadinata, *Eminent Indonesian Chinese*, pp. 54–5]

**Liem Koen Hian** (1896–1952). Born in Kalimantan, Liem was the editor-in-chief of a number of China-oriented newspapers before World War II, including the influential *Sin Jit Po* (Surabaya, 1929–32, 1939). In 1932 he founded the Partai Tionghoa Indonesia (PTI), a *peranakan* Chinese organization that sided with the Indonesian nationalists in pursuing independence. In 1946 Liem was appointed a member of the Indonesian Central National Committee. He translated Günther Stein's book *The Challenge of Red China* into Indonesian and published it in 1949. Liem was arrested by the Sukiman government on the suspicion of being a Communist. Upon his release he repudiated Indonesian citizenship and became a PRC citizen. [Suryadinata, *Eminent Indonesian Chinese*, pp. 74–5; Mary Somers, "Peranakan Chinese Politics in Indonesia" (Ph.D. diss., Cornell University, 1965, p. 231]

**Mononutu, Arnold** (1898–1983). Born in Manado, he was educated in the Hague, University of Leiden and Paris, where he studied politics. He was the editor-in-chief of the *Menara Merdeka* in 1945 and became a member of parliament in 1947. In the early 1950s he was the minister of information and served as the first ambassador to China from 1953 to 1955. Afterwards he was the head of the American-Pacific Division, Ministry of Foreign Affairs. Mononutu was the president of Hanssanudin University between 1960 and 1965 [Zainal Rasjid, *Riwajat Orang-Orang Politik* (Medan: Bakti, 1951), p. 24; R. Nalenan, *Arnold Mononutu: Potret seorang Patriot* (Jakarta: Gunung Agung, 1981)]

**Ngantung, Henk** (1921–91). Born in Manado, he studied painting in Bandung and worked as an illustrator for the *Yomiuri Shimbun* during the Japanese occupation. As one of the leading realist painters in Indonesia, Ngantung's many paintings were deposited in the National Palace. In the 1950s he participated in the artists' delegation to China and became a member of Lekra's central leadership (1959–65). He was appointed by President Sukarno as head of the Special District of Jakarta (1960–64) and Governor of Jakarta (1964–65) [*EI*, p. 2374; *ENI*, vol. 11, p. 113]

**Nio Joe Lan** (1904–73), born in Jakarta, he was a journalist for the newspapers *Keng Po* (1924–27), *Sin Po* (1935–42, 1945–58), and editor-in-chief of the periodical *Panca Warna* during the 1950s. His writings included *Peradaban Tionghoa Selajang Pandang* (1961) and *Sastra Indonesia-Tionghoa* (1962). [Pamusuk Eneste, *Leksikon Kesusastraan Indonesia Modern*, 3rd ed. (Jakarta: Djambatan, 1990), p. 126]

**Njoto** (1925–65). He was active in the underground movement during the Japanese occupation. In mid-1948 he became a member of both the central committee and politburo of the PKI, a position he held until his death in 1965. Njoto was the PKI's "guiding hand" in the central leadership of Lekra. He visited China a number of times, writing and speaking extensively about Chinese politics and culture. [Hindley, *Indonesian Communist Party*, pp. 23–4, 184]

**Ong Hok Ham** (1933–2007). Born in Surabaya, his family was hybrid Chinese-Dutch Indies. He started studying law at the University of Indonesia, but by 1957 had given up on his studies to work as an assistant for the Cornell professor Bill Skinner, researching the Chinese in Indonesia. This led to writing historical articles for the influential *Star Weekly*, 1958–61, when he became well known as an advocate for the assimilation of the Chinese into Indonesian society. Ong studied for a doctoral degree at Yale University in the late 1960s and early 1970s and became a well-known historian and public intellectual. [David Reeve, "Ong Hok Ham, 1933–2007: Intellectual, Chinese, Atheist, Gay — and Wholly Indonesian", *Inside Indonesia*, no. 90, Oct.–Dec., 2007]

**Pane, Armijn** (1908–70). Born in northern Sumatra and educated in Dutch-language schools in Jakarta, Surabaya and Solo, Pane was the editor of the *Pujangga Baru* between 1933 and 1938. He became the secretary of the Consultative Committee on National Culture (BMKN, 1950–55) and editor of the *Indonesia* magazine (1948–55). His *Belenggu* is considered as one of the most important novels in modern Indonesian literature. Pane visited China in 1951 and published a book on Chinese history and politics two years later. [*EI*, p. 270; Eneste, *Leksikon*, pp. 26–7]

**Pramoedya Ananta Toer** (1921–2006). Born in Central Java, Pramoedya's early writings from the 1940s show a terse, personal style and a cynical view of the Revolution. He shifted to the left in the 1950s, arguing for popular commitment in literature and becoming a major figure in Lekra. He helped formulate the doctrine of socialist realism as it applied to Indonesia in the 1960s. Pramoedya was jailed without trial between 1965 and 1979. While in detention he wrote a series of historical novels based on the emergence of Indonesian national consciousness in the early 20th century. These novels have been translated into English (winning him nominations for the Nobel Prize in Literature): *This Earth of Mankind*, *Child of All Nations*, *Footsteps* and *House of Glass*. Pramoedya visited China twice in the 1950s. [Robert Cribb, *Historical Dictionary of Indonesia* (Metuchen, NJ: Scarecrow Press, 1992), pp. 384–5; Eneste, *Leksikon*, pp. 139–40]

**Prijono** (1907–69). Born in Yogyakarta, he obtained his Ph.D. from Leiden University and was the dean of the arts faculty of the University of Indonesia from 1950 to 1957. Though generally classed with the Murba Party, Prijono received the Stalin Peace Prize for his activities as a member of Indonesian Committee of World Peace Movement in 1955 and was the chairman of Indonesian-China Friendship Association (1955–57). He became minister of education in 1957 and retained major though not sole responsibility for that field throughout the Guided Democracy period. He visited China in 1954. [Feith and Castles, eds., *Indonesian Political Thinking*, pp. 477–8]

**Ramadhan K.H.** (1927–2006). Born in Bandung from a Sundanese background, he took classes at the Bandung Technical Institute. During the Sukarno era he was the editor of the *Kisah*, *Siasat* and *Siasat Baru*. Ramadhan served as the editor of the *Budaya Jaya* (1972–79) and a member of the Jakarta Arts Council (1971–74). He was the author of *Priangan si Jelita*, which won him the National Prize of Literature from the BMKN (Consultative Committee on National Culture) in 1957/58, and co-editor of *Soeharto: Pikiran, Ucapan, dan Tindakan Saya* (1988). He visited China in 1956. [Eneste, *Leksikon*, pp. 148–9; A. Teeuw, *Modern Indonesian Literature* (The Hague: Nijhoff, 1979), vol. 2, pp. 172–3]

**Said, Rasuna** (1910–65). Born in West Sumatra, she was educated at the Islamic College in Sumatra. Said moved to Medan in 1937, where she published a nationalist weekly, *Menara Poeteri*. She was a Sumatra member for the KNIP during the Indonesian Revolution and subsequently a member of parliament during the 1950s. In 1957 she was selected by Sukarno as a National Council member, representing women's organizations. Both Rasuna Said and her husband, Barioen A.S., were active in promoting Sino-Indonesian relationships; Said was the president of the Indonesia-China Friendship Association from 1957 to the early 1960s. She led a delegation to China in the 1950s. [Soebagijo, *Jagat Wartawan*, pp. 502–6; Hong Yuanyuan, *Hong Yuanyuan Zizhuan*, pp. 231–3]

**Sakirman** (1911–67?). A member of the PKI central committee from 1951 and of the politburo from 1954, he was chairman of the Communist group in the provisional parliament (1950–56) and a PKI spokesman on economic and defence questions. After the 1965 coup he went into hiding and was reported killed in 1967. He was the author of *Pembangunan Ekonomi Raksasa Tiongkok Rakjat* (Jakarta: Pembaruan, 1960). [Feith and Castles, eds., *Indonesian Political Thinking*, p. 480; *ENI*, vol. 14, p. 335]

**Saleh, Buyung** (1923–89). Saleh was the son of a village clerk at a so-called "native school" who was a member of the PKI. After the proclamation of Indonesian independence, Buyung Saleh began working at the daily *Bintang Merah*, a PKI-affiliated newspaper. In the 1950s he moved to the literary world, publishing short stories and essays. In addition to being closely involved in the debate on Indonesia's nationality problem, Saleh was appointed by the minister of education, Prijono, as a lecturer in Indonesian literature at the University of Indonesia in the mid-1950s. His publications included sympathetic accounts of the Indonesian Chinese and *Beberapa Pandangan tentang Kebudajaan Indonesia* (1954). As one of Lekra's central leaders, Saleh was imprisoned for ten years after 1965. [Suparna, "Buyung Saleh: Trade Unionist and Writer", *Inside Indonesia*, March 1990, pp. 9–10]

**Sartono** (1900–68). Born in Solo, he was educated in law at Leiden University and was secretary of the Perhimpunan Indonesia, an Indonesian student organization in the Netherlands. He was chairman of the National Committee of the provisional parliament in 1950 and was re-elected member of parliament (PNI) and speaker between 1956 and 1959. He visited China in 1956. [Zainal Rasjid, *Riwajat Orang-orang Politik* (Medan: Bakti, 1952), pp. 28–31; *ENI*, vol. 14, pp. 428–31]

**Sastroamidjojo, Ali** (1903–76). Born in Central Java, he obtained his law degree from Leiden University, where he was active in the nationalist movement. His many activities prior to World War II included editing PNI's *Suluh Indonesia Muda* magazine. He was Indonesia's first ambassador to the USA (1950–53) and two-time prime minister (1953–55, 1956–57). During his first term he presided over the Bandung Conference in 1955. He was twice elected general chairman of the PNI and deputy chairman of the MPRS (People's Deliberative Assembly) from 1960 to 1966. Sastroamidjojo visited China in 1955 at the invitation of Zhou Enlai. [*Who's Who in Indonesia*, pp. 347–8; *EI*, 151–7]

**Satya, Graha (Satyagraha)** (?–?). A PNI member, he was vice editor-in-chief of the PNI daily, *Suluh Indonesia*, in addition to editing the *Berita*

*Minggu*, a popular journal during the 1950s. He was secretary-general of the Indonesian Journalists Association from 1959 to 1965. Satya Graha visited China three times between 1956 and 1965 and published widely about his impressions of the PRC. [*Indonesian Journalists Association*, p. 22; *ENI*, vol. 15, p. 352]

**Sayuti, Melik** (1908–89). Born in Yogyakarta, he was educated in the Faculty of Law and Social Sciences of the University of Indonesia. Originally a Communist, he later converted to the national-communism of Tan Malaka and the radical nationalism of Sukarno. He founded the periodical *Pesat* in 1938 and was the person who typed the text of the Independence Proclamation on 17 August 1945. During the 1950s he was a member of the PNI and personal assistant to Sukarno, in addition to being a columnist (using the pen names of "Juti" and "Yuti") for several Jakarta newspapers (among them *Suluh Indonesia*). He was the author of several books, including *Antara Marhaenisme dan Marxisme* (1958). He visited China in 1956 and wrote a series of reports and commentaries about his trip. [Feith and Castles, eds., *Indonesian Political Thinking*, p. 479; *Who's Who in Indonesia*, revised edition (Jakarta, 1980), p. 241; Solichin Salam, *Wajah-wajah Nasional* (Jakarta: Pusat Studi dan Penelitian Islam, 1990), pp. 172–6]

**Siauw Giok Tjhan** (1914–81). Born in Surabaya, Siauw was educated in a Dutch secondary school and worked for the *peranakan* daily *Mata Hari* (1934–42). During the Revolution, in addition to publishing the periodicals *Liberty* and *Pemuda*, he was appointed a member of the BPKI (Indonesian Central National Committee) and the minister without portfolio for *peranakan* affairs. From 1950 to 1966 he was a member of parliament representing the Chinese minority. In 1954 he co-founded Baperki, the most influential *peranakan* sociopolitical organization during the Sukarno era, and was elected chairman of its central board, a position he held until 1965, when Baperki was banned and he was subsequently jailed by the Suharto regime. Siauw visited China in 1956. [Suryadinata, *Eminent Indonesian Chinese*, pp. 113–4; Zhou Nanjing, ed., *Dictionary of Overseas Chinese* (Beijing: Beijing University Press, 1993), pp. 706–7]

**Sie Boen Lian** (?–1971). Born in Madiun, he was educated in Dutch-language schools. He continued his advanced medical education in Jakarta and Prague, specializing in eye diseases. During the Sukarno era, Sie served as the president's private doctor. He visited China in the late 1950s and wrote about China's economic and social progress. [Suryadinata, *Eminent Indonesian Chinese*, p. 115]

**Siregar, Bakri** (1922–94). Born in Aceh, he was the editor of the daily *Pendorong* and the *Arah* magazine and a lecturer of Indonesian language at Northern Sumatra University in Medan (1957–59). A member of Lekra's central leadership (1959–65), Siregar was its leading theoretician and a visiting professor of Indonesian literature at Beijing University from 1959 to 1962. Siregar was jailed between 1965 and 1977. His publications include *Jejak Langkah* (1953) and *Sejarah Sastra Indonesia Modern I* (1964). [Eneste, *Leksikon*, p. 35; *EI*, p. 3201; <http://acehpedia.org/Bakri_ Siregar>]

**Situmorang, Sitor** (1924–). Born in North Sumatra, he received a Dutch-language education before World War II and spent an extended time studying and writing in Amsterdam, Paris and the USA during the 1950s. From 1959 to 1965 he was the head of the Indonesian Cultural Institute (Lembaga Kebudayaan Nasional) and vice-head of the 1961 cultural delegation to China. Situmorang's *Zaman Baru* (1962) is a collection of poems recording his impressions of China. His other writings include *Surat Kertas Hijau* (1953), *Sastra Revolusioner* (1963) and *Sitor Situmorang: Seorang Sastrawan 45* (1981). [Eneste, *Leksikon*, pp. 166–7; *EI*, p. 3211]

**Sjahrir, Soetan** (1909–66). Born in West Sumatra, he studied in Medan and Bandung, and at Leiden University. In Holland he gained an appreciation for socialist principles, and was a member of several labour unions. He was briefly the secretary of the Indonesian Association (Perhimpunan Indonesia), an organization of Indonesian students in the Netherlands. He was appointed prime minister by Sukarno in November 1945 and served until June 1947. Sjahrir founded the Indonesian Socialist Party in 1948, which was small but influential in the early post-independence years, because of the expertise and high education levels of its leaders. But the party performed poorly in the 1955 elections and was banned by Sukarno in 1960. [Rudolf Mrazek, *Sjahrir: Politics and Exile in Indonesia* (Ithaca, N.Y. Southeast Asia Program, Cornell University, 1994)]

**Soemardjan, Selo** (1915–2003). Born in Yogyakarta, he was educated in MOSVIA (School for Native Government Executives) in Magelang during the 1930s and obtained his Ph.D. in sociology from Cornell University in1959. He served as an official of Yogyakarta Sultanate (1934–49); head of the Secretariat of Security Staff, Prime Minister's Cabinet (1950–56); secretary of BAPEKAN (Institute for Controlling the Activities of the State Apparatus, 1959–62); and general secretary of BAPEKAN (1962–66). Soemardjan is the author of *Social Changes in Yogjakarta* (Cornell University

Press, 1962) and visited China in 1965 as a member of the Department of National Research Delegation. [*Who's Who in Indonesia*, p. 409; *EI*, pp. 3241–2]

**Soenarjo, Raden Haji Achmad** (1910–?). Born in Surakarta, he was educated at the Law Faculty of the University of Indonesia and became a professor at the Perguruan Tinggi Agama Islam Sunan Kalijaga/IAIN Yogyakarta. He served as the secretary-general of the Department of Religious Affairs (1950–54); minister of domestic affairs (1958–59); minister of agriculture (1960–72); and president of the National Institute of Islamic Religion in Yogyakarta (1972–75). Soenarjo was the author of *Pengantar Ilmu Kriminologi* and visited China in the early 1960s. [*EI*, p. 3244]

**Soeharto, R.** (1908–?). He studied medicine in Jakarta before World War II and was President Sukarno's private doctor from 1950 and 1965. He visited China in the 1950s and wrote about China's achievements in public health. [Solichin Salam, *Wajah-wajah Nasional*, pp. 260–6]

**Soeto Meisen (Situ Meisheng; Sze Tu Mei Sen)** (1928–2010). Born in the Western Java town of Sukabumi, Soeto Meisen was educated in Chinese schools in Jakarta and joined in 1947 the *Harian Thien Sung Yit Po* (Tiansheng Ribao), a newspaper associated with the Kuomintang (KMT), and became acquainted with President Sukarno. He joined the Chinese newspaper *Hsin Po* (Sin Po) in the early 1950s as a journalist and politics editor. He was engaged by Sukarno as an informal personal assistant dealing with China affairs and accompanied the President in his historic visit to China in October 1956 during which Soeto Meisen served as an interpreter on some occasions. Soeto Meisen resigned from the *Hsin Po* in the end of 1959 to become Sukarno's personal assistant, drawing a stipend from the government. From 1963 to 1965, he served as the director of the *Shoudou Ribao*, a semi-official Chinese-language newspaper published in Jakarta. In the early 1960s, he accompanied Sukarno for two further state visits to China and took part in activities relating to Indonesia-China diplomacy. Soeto Meisen left Indonesia in the end of 1965 and had resided in Macau till his death in 2010. [Hong Liu, "Soeto Meisen", in *Prominent Chinese of Southeast Asia*, ed. Leo Suryadinata, forthcoming]

**Suaidy, Hadji Muhammad Saleh** (1913–?). Born in West Sumatra, he was educated in Al-Irsjad School in Surabaya and became a PNI member in 1930. From 1935 to 1941 he was editor-in-chief of the *Al-Islaah* magazine.

Suaidy was the head of the Press and Radio Section, Ministry of Religious Affairs from 1950 to 1956. He visited China in 1956. [*Who's Who in Indonesia*, pp. 376–7]

**Subandrio** (1914–2004). Born in Malang, a graduate of the Jakarta Medical School, he was the head of the Central Java Division, Ministry of Information in 1945, ambassador to the UK (1950–54), and to the USSR (1954–56). He became minister of foreign affairs in 1957, a position he held until 1965 (during his tenure he visited China a number of times). Subandrio was particularly powerful in the last two years of Guided Democracy (1963–65) when, as first deputy prime minister, he was President Sukarno's senior minister and often regarded as his likely successor. After the 1965 coup he came under heavy attack from the army, student and Muslim groups as pro-Communist and pro-Chinese. He was arrested and sentenced to death in 1966. Two volumes of his speeches were published under the title *Indonesia on the March*. [Feith and Castles, eds., *Indonesian Political Thinking*, pp. 483–4]

**Sudiro, Raden** (1911–?). Born in Yogyakarta, he was educated in the Dutch Native School and was active in the Taman Siswa movement before World War II. A PNI member, Sudiro was the governor and mayor of Greater Jakarta between 1953 and 1960. Sudiro visited China at the invitation of the mayor of Beijing in 1956. [Soebagijo, *Sudiro: Pejuang Tanpa Henti* (Jakarta: Gunung Agung, 1981); *EI*, pp. 3327–8]

**Sugardo** (?–?). He visited China in the early 1950s and was the author of *Si Djembel Mentjari Keadilan Sosial* (Jakarta: Dharma, 1952) and *Tiongkok Sekarang: Terra Incognita (Tanah tak dikenal)* (Jakarta: Endang, 1953), as well as numerous articles about China. [*Bibliografi Nasional Indonesia (1945–1963)* (Jakarta, 1965), vol. 2]

**Sukarno** (1901–70). Brought up in the small Javanese towns of Blitar and Sidoardjo, Sukarno in 1920 was among the first 12 students enrolled in the architecture course at the Bandung Technical University, one of the first institutions of higher learning in Indonesia. He was the founder of the Indonesian Nationalist Party (PNI) in 1927 and became president of the Republic of Indonesia in 1945, a position he held until 1967. He visited China for two weeks in October 1956, and had two short trips to China during the first half of the 1960s. [Feith and Castles, eds., *Indonesian Political Thinking*, pp. 485–6]

**Sukiman** (1887–?). Born in Solo, he studied in STOVIA (School for the Training of Native Physicians) in Jakarta before going to the University of Amsterdam. Sukiman returned in 1925 and was active in the nationalist movement. During the Japanese occupation he was vice-chairman of the PUTERA and a founding member of the Masyumi Party. He was the prime minister in 1951/52, when an infamous anti-Communist raid took place. Sukiman visited China in 1956 [Zainal Rasjid, *Riwajat Orang-Orang Politik* (Medan: Bakti, 1951), pp. 12–3]

**Sumardjo, Trisno** (1916–69). Born in Surabaya, Sumardjo was educated in the AMS (General Secondary School) in Yogyakarta, where he studied Western classics. He started writing and painting in 1946 in Madiun, and served as editor of the *Seniman* (1947–48), *Indonesia* (1950–2), and *Seni* (1954). Expounding the views of universal humanism, Sumardjo was the secretary of the Indonesian Cultural Institute (Lembaga Kebudayaan Indonesia) and secretary-general of the BMKN (Consultative Committee on National Culture) during the 1950s. He led a cultural delegation to China in 1957. One of the signatories of the Cultural Manifesto in 1963, Sumardjo's creative writings included *Kata Hati dan Perbuatan* (1952), *Cita Teruna* (1953), and *Rumah Raya* (1957). [*EI*, p. 3350; Eneste, *Leksikon*, pp. 192–3]

**Tabrani, Mohammad** (1904–84). Born in Pamekasan, he was educated in OSVIA (School for the Training of Native Civil Servants) in Bandung from 1918 to 1925, when he took the editorship of the newspaper *Hindia Baru*. Between 1927 and 1930 he studied journalism in Berlin, and subsequently became the editor-in-chief of the daily *Pemandangan* and helped edit the PNI daily, *Suluh Indonesia*, from 1936 to 1940. Shortly before World War II, he and Wilopo founded the Institute of Journalism and General Knowledge. Between 1945 and 1951, Tabrani was a KNIP and PNI member and served as an adviser to the government on ethnic policy. In 1953 he was in charge of the Jakarta daily *Suluh Indonesia*. Together with Armijn Pane and Barioen A.S., Tabrani visited China in 1951, and wrote extensively in newspapers about his China trip. Tabrani is the author of *Soal Minoriteit dalam Indonesia Merdeka* (Yogyakarta, 1950) [Mohammad Tabrani, *Anak Nakal Banyak Akal* (Bandung: Aqua Press, 1979); Soebagijo, *Jagat Wartawan*, pp. 85–90; and *EI*, pp. 3414–5]

**Tan Malaka** (c. 1894–1949). Born in West Sumatra, Tan Malaka converted to Marxism while studying in the Netherlands. In 1921 he became chairman of the Indonesian Communist Party for two months before the first of his many imprisonments. He spent more than ten years in China as the director of Comintern activities for Southeast Asia and Australia. Returning to Indonesia during the Japanese occupation, he quickly rose to prominence after 1945 and led an opposition coalition against the leadership of Sukarno as president and Sjahrir as prime minister, criticizing their policy of negotiation with the Dutch. He was executed after the 1948 Communist Madiun rebellion. Tan Malaka's extensive autobiography, *From Jail to Jail*, has been translated and published in English (1993). [Feith and Castles, eds., *Indonesian Political Thinking*, p. 488]

**Thaib, Maisir** (?–?). Born in West Sumatra, he was a member of the Sarikat Islam in the 1920s and was active in the nationalist movement. Later on he became the commissioner of Partai Serikat Islam in Sumatra. He went to Jakarta in 1945, where he joined the Indonesian militia in the anti-Dutch war. He was the author of *Sjahrir Pegang Kemoedi* (1946?), *Tiongkok Merah* (1949?), and co-author (with A. Moeis), *Sejarah Indonesia* (1962). [*Autobiografi/ Biografi Perintis Kemerdekaan* (Jakarta: Proyek Pembinaan Kepahlawanan dan Keperintisan, Departmen Sosial RI, 1990/91), pp. 81–97; *Bibliografi Nasional Indonesia (1945–1963)*, vol. 2]

**Thung Liang Lee (Tirtawidjaja)** (1901–70?). Born into a landowning family in Bogor, he was educated at the universities of London and Vienna, where he studied economics. During the 1930s he was the *New York Times* correspondent in Beijing and managing director for the China United Press. After returning to Indonesia he formed the Persatuan Tenaga Indonesia with Liem Koen Hian and then worked for the Ministry of Information, Republic of Indonesia. After the 1965 coup he and other intellectuals established the Indonesian Institute of International Affairs (Jakarta). His publications include *China in Revolt* (London, 1927) and *The New Social Order in China* (Shanghai, 1936). During the 1950s he advocated an Indonesian Chinese identity and the cessation of loyalty to China. [Suryadinata, *Eminent Indonesian Chinese*, pp. 168–9; Thung Liang Lee, "The Unreality of Chinese Nationalism in Indonesia: An Apologia and a Reorientation", *Indonesian Review* 2, 1 (1954): 69–75]

**Tirtodiningrat, Djoko Marsaid** (1903–?). He was educated in the Netherlands and Germany before World War II. In 1957, at the request of Sukarno, he accepted the appointment as president of Hassanuddin University, a post he held until 1959, when he paid a visit to China. Tirtodiningrat was the author of *Ichtisar Hukum Perdata dan Hukum Dagang* (1956). [Duiwai Wenhua Lianluo Weiyuanhui Ersi [Research office of the Committee of Cultural Exchanges with Foreign Countries], ed., *Yindunixiya Wenhua Gaikuang* [A survey of Indonesian culture] (Beijing, for internal circulation, 1962), p. 124]

**Wardhana, Wisnoe** (1937–). Born in Yogyakarta, he established the contemporary dance school Wisnoe Wardhana in 1958 and the Dance Academy in 1963. He participated in numerous artists' delegations to Europe, the United States and Asia. His many creative dances including *Yogaprana* (1953), *Pekan Olah Raga* (1956), *Seeking the Truth* (1957) and *The Devil* (1959). Wardhana visited China in the 1950s. [*EI*, p. 3876]

**Wilopo** (1909–81). A native of Central Java, Wilopo graduated from the Law School in Batavia in 1942. Before the war he was a founder of the nationalist party Gerindo; after independence he was one of a group of younger leaders of the PNI who were close to the democratic socialists in many of their ideas. After holding several cabinet posts in the fields of labour and economic affairs, he became prime minister in 1952/53. He served as chairman of the Constituent Assembly (1956–9). In 1956 Wilopo visited China to study the country's experience of constitution-making. [Feith and Castles, eds., *Indonesian Political Thinking*, p. 489; *EI*, p. 3926]

**Wirjopranoto, Sukardjo** (1903–62). Born in Central Java, he was educated in the Dutch-language school in Surabaya and joined the PNI. During the Japanese occupation he worked for the newspaper *Asia Raya*. As a KNIP member in the early years of the Revolution, Wirjopranoto and Adinegoro founded the weekly *Mimbar Indonesia* in 1948. He was appointed ambassador to Italy (1952–3); head of the Asian-Pacific Division, Ministry of Foreign Affairs (1954–6); ambassador to China (1956–60); and Indonesian representative to the United Nations (1960–2). [*EI*, p. 3933]

**Wispi, Agam** (1930–2003). Born in Aceh, he was a member of Lekra's central leadership between 1959 and 1965 and visited China a number of times. His collections of poems include *Sahabat* (1959) and *Matinya Seorang Sahabat* (1962). [Eneste, *Leksikon*, p. 9]

# BIBLIOGRAPHY

## Newspapers and Periodicals

(1) Published in Indonesia

*Bahasa dan Budaja*, 1952–64.
*Basis*, 1951–65.
*Berita Indonesia*, 1961–5.
*Berita Minggu*, 1962–5.
*Bintang Merah*, 1945–65.
*Budaja*, 1951–64.
*Djakarta Press Summary*, 1961–5.
*Djiwa Baru*, 1951–65.
*Dunia Internasional*, 1950–9.
*Duta Masjarakat*, 1956–65.
*Editorials from Djakarta Press*, 1961–5.
*Forum*, 1954–9.
*Gadjah Mada*, 1950–60.
*Harian Rakjat*, 1952–65.
*Hsin Pao* [in Chinese], 1951–9.
*Indonesia: Madjalah Kebudajaan*, 1950–65.
*Indonesian Spectator*, 1956–9.
*Indonesian Affairs*, 1951–4.
*Kompas untuk Generasi Baru*, 1951–4.
*Konfrontasi*, 1954–60.
*Liberty*, 1945–65.
*Madjalah Merdeka*, 1963–65.
*Merdeka*, 1945–65.
*Mimbar Indonesia*, 1947–66.
*Nasional*, 1957–65.
*Pantjawarna*, 1963–5.
*Pedoman*, 1948–65.
*Pesat*, 1949–65.
*Pikiran Rakjat*, 1951–60.
*Pudjangga Baru*, 1950–3.
*Republik*, 1949–55.

*Seng Hwo Pao* [in Chinese], 1952–8.
*Seng Hwo Pao Xinnian Tekan* [in Chinese], 1952–5.
*Siasat*, 1947–61.
*Sikap*, 1948–59.
*Sin Po*, 1953–9.
*Sin Min*, 1947–58.
*Sin Tjun*, 1956–60.
*Star Weekly*, 1946–61.
*Suara Marhaenis*, 1955–8.
*Suara Guru*, 1950–65.
*Suara Masjumi*, 1950–7.
*Suluh Indonesia*, 1953–65.
*Ta Hsueh Tsa Chih*, 1949–54.
*U.S. Information Service: Media Study*, 1958–9.
*U.S. Information Service: Indonesian Press Review*, 1953–5.
*Warta Bhakti [Zhong Cheng Bao]* [in Chinese], 1963–5.
*Zaman Baru*, 1955–65.
*Zenith*, 1951–4.

(2) Published in China

*Dongnanya Yanjiu Ziliao* [Research Materials on Southeast Asia], 1959–64.
*Nanyang Wenti Ziliao Yicong* [Translations of Materials on Nanyang], 1957–65.
*Peking Review*, 1957–65.
*Renmin Ribao* [People's Daily], 1946–65.
*Shijie Zhishi* [World Affairs], 1950–65.
*Tiongkok Rakjat*, 1958–65.
*Xinhua Yuebao* [New China Monthly Bulletin], 1950–65.

## Archives

Archives of the Ministry of Foreign Affairs, the People's Republic of China, Beijing (Declassified archives pertaining to China's interactions with Indonesia, 1949–65)

## Indonesian Writings about China and Other Works

Abdulgani, Ruslan. "Di Peking Hidup Vitalitet". *Suluh Indonesia*, 15 October 1956.
———. *Laporan Menteri Luar Negeri kepada Dewan Perwakilan Rakjat R.I. tentang Perdjalanan Presiden R.I. ke Sovjet Uni, Yugoslavia, Austria, Czechoslovakia, Mongolia, dan Republik Rakjat Tiongkok (26 Agustus–16 Oktober 1956)*. Jakarta: Kementerian Luar Negeri, 1956.
———. "In Search of an Indonesian Identity". *Indonesian Spectator*, 1–15 August 1957, pp. 9–10.

―――――. "Luetang Zhonghua Renmin Gongheguo Yu Yindunixiya Guanxi de Jichu" [A brief discussion on the foundation of the Sino-Indonesian relationship]. *Seng Hwo Pao*, 1 January 1958.

―――――. "Kesan tentang Tiongkok". *Merdeka*, 3 November 1979.

―――――. "Spekulasi Sekitar Normalisasi Hubungan Indonesia-RRT: 'The China Syndrome'". *Merdeka*, 23 November 1979.

―――――. *The Bandung Connection: The Asian-African Conference in Bandung in 1955*. Singapore: Gunung Agung, 1981.

Adinegoro. *Tiongkok: Pusaran Asia*. Jakarta and Amsterdam: Djambatan, 1951.

―――――. "Xin Shijie: Suitong Zongtong Chuguo Fanwenji" [A new world: Accounts of visiting foreign countries with the president]. *Hsin Pao*, 23 October–1 November 1956.

Adiputra. "Overseas Chinese dan Indonesia". *Mimbar Indonesia* 6, 30 (1952): 8, 27.

―――――. "Tiongkok Merah dan Indonesia". *Mimbar Indonesia* 7, 30 (1953): 6.

Adjitorop, Jusuf. *Integrasi Kekuasaan Politik dan Sistim Hukum dengan Revolusi di Tiongkok Rakjat*. Jakarta: Jajasan Pendidikan dan Kebudajaan Baperki, 1964.

Agung, Anak Ide Agung. *Twenty Years Indonesian Foreign Policy, 1945–1965*. Yogyakarta: Duta Wacana University Press, 1990 [1972].

Ai Lan. "Zhongguo he Yindunixiya de Youhao Guangxi" [Friendship between China and Indonesia]. *Shijie Zhishi* 11 (1955): 4–5.

Aidit, D.N. "Persahabatan Tiongkok-Indonesia". *Bintang Merah* 15, 3 (1959): 94–8.

―――――. *Selected Works*. 2 volumes. Washington, DC: JPRS, 1961.

―――――. "RRT akan Mentjapai Kelimpahan Produksi Komune Rakjat". *Harian Rakjat*, 1 October 1963.

―――――. *Aidi Xuanji* [Selected writings of Aidit]. Beijing: Renmin Chubanshe, 1963.

Ajoeb, Joebaar. "Manifesto Politik dan Kebuajaan". In *Pleno Agustus, Pimpinan² Pusat Lekra*. Jakarta: Lekra, 1960.

―――――. "Djembatan Persahabatan Indonesia-Tiongkok semakin Kokoh". *Tiongkok Rakjat* 7 (1961): 37–8.

Ambekar, G.V., and V.C. Divekar, eds. *Documents on China's Relations with South and Southeast Asia (1949–1962)*. Bombay: Allied Publishers, 1964.

Anantaguna, S. "Tiongkok Baru selalu Baru". *Harian Rakjat*, 15 November 1958.

Anderson, Benedict R. O'G. *Language and Power: Exploring Political Cultures in Indonesia*. Ithaca: Cornell University Press, 1990.

―――――. *Spectre of Comparisons: Politics, Culture and the Nation*. London: Verso, 1998.

―――――. "Bung Karno and the Fossilization of Soekarno's Thought". *Indonesia* 74 (2002): 1–19.

Anderson, Benedict R. O'G. and Audrey Kahin, eds. *Interpreting Indonesian Politics: Thirteen Contributions to the Debate*. Ithaca: Cornell Modern Indonesian Project, 1982.

Ang Hong To. "Dari Perdjalanan jang Membawa Tjeritera Komune Rakjat". *Pantjawarna* 2, 59 (1963): 5–7.

Anwar, Rosihan. "Menindjau Sepoetar Daerah Tanggerang". *Merdeka*, 13–14 June 1946.

———. "Persuratkabaran Indonesia Sekarang". *Konfrontasi* 3 (1954): 19–30.

———. *Sebelum Prahara: Pergolakan Politik Indonesia, 1961–1965*. Jakarta: Sinar Harapan, 1981.

"Apa Artinja Kemenangan Mao Tse Tung di Tiongkok?" *Siasat* 3 (1949): 11.

Ash, Robert David Shambaugh, Seiichiro Takagi, eds., *China Watching: Perspectives from Europe, Japan and the United States*. London: Routledge, 2006.

Asmudji. *Genderang Tiongkok Baru*. Bodjonegoro: Suara Pemuda, 1950.

Assaat. "Perlindungan Chusus". In *Kensi Berdjuang*, ed. Badan Pekerdja Kensi Pusat. Jakarta: N.V. Seno, 1957, pp. 51–62.

Ba Ren (Wang Renshu). *Yinni Shehui Fazhan Gaikuang* [A survey of Indonesian social development]. Shanghai: Shenghuo Shudian, 1948.

———. "Yindunixiya Geming Guangan" [Relections on the Indonesian revolution]. *Nanya yu Dongnanya Yanjiu* (Beijing) 5 (1983): 1–89.

Bafagih, Asa. *RRT dari Luar dan Dalam*. Jakarta: Pengurus Besar Nahdlatul Ulama, 1955.

"Bahaja Komunisme". *Suara Masjumi* 10 (1955): 6–7.

Bandaharo, H.R. *Dari Bumi Merah*. Jakarta: Pembaruan, 1963.

Barnett, Doak. "Chou En-Lai at Bandung". *American Universities Field Staff* (Southeast Asian Series), 4 May 1955.

———. "Echoes of Mao Tse-Tung in Djakarta (An Interview with D.N. Aidit)". *American Universities Field Staff* (Southeast Asian Series), 21 May 1955.

Barioen, A.S. *Melihat Tiongkok Baru: Negara Merdeka, Pandai Merdeka, Sanggup Merdeka*. Jakarta: Rada, 1952.

"Bersatu dibelakang Pemerintah dalam Konflik dengan RRT". *Star Weekly*, no. 729 (19 December 1959), pp. 1–2, 7.

Bertrand, Jacques. *Nationalism and Ethnic Conflict in Indonesia*. Cambridge: Cambridge University Press, 2004.

Bey, Arifin. *Dari Sun Yat Sen ke Mao Tze Tung*. Jakarta: Tintamas, 1953.

Biro Research Umum, Departemen Luarnegeri. *Documenta Diplomatik No. 04, Thn 1967 (Hubungan Republik Indonesia dengan Republik Rakjat Tjina dalam Masa sesudah G-30-S/PKI)*. Jakarta, 1968.

Boediono, J.A. Lie. "Asimilasi Total". *Suluh Indonesia*, 25–26 September 1963.

Bourchier, David, and John D. Legge, eds. *Democracy in Indonesia: 1950s and 1990s*. Clayton: Centre of Southeast Asia Studies, Monash University, 1994.

Brackman, Arnold C. "The Malay World and China: Partner or Barrier?" In *Policies toward China: Views from Six Continents*, ed. A.M. Halpern. New York: McGraw-Hill, 1965, pp. 262–302.

Brotokusumo, Martono. *Sedjarah Tiongkok*. Semarang: Abede, 1951.

Browidjojo. "Lembaga-lembaga Persahabatan di Tiongkok". *Mimbar Indonesia* 9, 25 (1955): 5–6, 28.

"Bung Karno Menemukan diri sendiri". *Harian Rakjat*, 18 October 1956.

Bunnell, Frederick P. "Guided Democracy Foreign Policy, 1960–1965: President Sukarno Moves from Non-alignment to Confrontation". *Indonesia* 2 (1966): 37–76.

"Buku² Tionghoa jang Dilarang oleh Pemerintah untuk Dipakai disekolah dan sebagainja". *Almanak Umum Nasional 1955* (Jakarta: Endang, 1956), pp. 147–9.

Carey, Peter. "Changing Javanese Perceptions of the Chinese Communities in Central Java, 1755–1825". *Indonesia* 37 (1984): 1–48.

Central Comite Partai Komunis Tiongkok. "Beberapa Masalah Komune Rakjat". *Pesat* 15, 17 (1959): 1.

Chen Lou-wie. *Kundjungan Madame Soong Ching Ling ke Indonesia*. [Jakarta?], 1956.

Chen Luwei, ed. *Yafei Huiyi Shilu*. [A historical account of the Asian-African Conference]. Jakarta: Yinhua Jingji Chubanshe, 1955.

Chen Qimin. "Yinni Huaqiao Yinyou de Juexing" [A wake-up call for the Indonesian Chinese]. *Chung Hua Hsies Hui Hui Khan* (Jakarta), no. 12 (1949).

Chen Jian, "China and the Bandung Conference: Changing Perceptions and Representations". In *Bandung Revisited: The Legacy of the 1955 Asian-African Conference for International Order*, ed. See Seng Tan and Amitav Acharya. Singapore: NUS Press, 2008, pp. 132–59.

Cheng Hsueh-chia. *Whither Indonesia? PKI and CCP*. Taipei: Asian People's Anti-Communist League, 1960.

Cheng Lim Fei. "Saja Pernah Sekolah di Tiongkok". *Gadjah Mada* 9, 2 (1959): 92–6.

*Chinese Communist Propaganda Activities in Indonesia* (*Research Backgrounder*). Hong Kong: Union Research Institute, 1960.

Christie, Clive. *Ideology and Revolution in Southeast Asia, 1900–1980: Political Ideas of the Anti-Colonial Era*. Richmond, Surrey: Curzon Press, 2001.

Chu Tunan. "Zhongguo he Yafei Geguo Wenhua Jiaoliu de Xiangzhuan he Qiangjing." [Current status and future prospect of cultural exchanges between China and Asian and African countries]. *Shijie Zhishi* 14 (1956): 13–5.

Chungkuo-Jen. *General Mao Tse Tung: Presiden RRT*. Surabaya: Gwie Hong Publishing Company, 1950.

*Cina: Semilyar Wajah*. Jakarta: Kumpulan Selingan MBM TEMPO, 1985.

"'Cold War' Indonesia-RRT: Kalau ada Asalnja tidak dari Indonesia". *Pikiran Rakjat*, 9 August 1951.

Coppel, Charles A. *Indonesian Chinese in Crisis*. Kuala Lumpur: Oxford University Press, 1983.

Coppel, Charles A. and Leo Suryadinata. "The Use of the Terms 'Tjina' and 'Tionghoa' in Indonesia: An Historical Survey". In *The Chinese Minority in Indonesia: Seven Papers*, ed. Leo Suryadinata. Singapore: Chopmen, 1978, pp. 113–28.

Curley, Melissa and Hong Liu, eds. *China and Southeast Asia: Changing Socio-cultural Interactions*. Hong Kong: Centre of Asian Studies, University of Hong Kong, 2002.

Dahm, Bernhard. *Sukarno and the Struggle for Indonesian Independence*. Trans. Mary F. Somers-Heidhues. Ithaca: Cornell University Press, 1969.

Dake, Antonie C.A. *In the Spirit of the Red Banteng: Indonesian Communists between Moscow and Peking, 1959–1965*. The Hague and Paris: Mouton, 1973.
Damunik, E.W. "Koperasi di RRT". *Dunia Internasional* 2, 12 (1952): 718–21.
Danubroto. "Tiongkok Laksana Sarang Labah: Setiap Orang Bergerak dan Bekerdja". *Sin Po*, 11 July 1956; *Seng Hwo Pao*, 12 July 1956.
Department of Foreign Affairs. *New Forces Build A New World* (Indonesian Policy Series). Jakarta: Department of Foreign Affairs, 1965.
Dijk, Cornelis Van. *The Indonesian Communist Party and Its Relations with the Soviet Union and the People's Republic of China*. The Hague: Interdoc, 1972.
Djawoto. "Sekali Lagi di Tiongkok". *Tiongkok Rakjat* 7 (1962): 7–9.
Duiwai Wenhua Lianluo Weiyuanhui Ersi [Second Bureau of the Committee of Cultural Exchanges with Foreign Countries], ed. *Yindunixiya Wenhua Gaikuang*. [A survey of Indonesian culture]. Beijing, for internal circulation only, 1962.
"Editorial: Kundjungan Hatta ke RRT". *Merdeka*, 19 September 1957.
"Editorial: Indonesia-Tiongkok". *Zaman Baru* 7 (1961): 1.
"Editorial: Perlawatan Kesenian ke RRT". *Budaya* 3, 7 (1954): 1.
Elson, Robert. *The Idea of Indonesia: A History*. Cambridge: Cambridge University Press, 2008.
"Emansipasi Wanita RRT Sangat Madju". *Sin Min*, 15 October 1957.
Eisenstadt, S.N. "Multiple Modernities". *Daedalus* 129 (2000): 1–29.
Feith, Herbert. *The Decline of Constitutional Democracy in Indonesia*. Ithaca: Cornell University, 1962.
———. "The Dynamics of Guided Democracy". In *Indonesia*, ed. Ruth McVey. New Haven: HARF, 1963, pp. 309–547.
———. "Indonesia's Political Symbols and Their Wielders". *World Politics* 16, 1 (1963): 79–97.
———. "Democracy, A Recurring Challenge: An Interview with Herbert Feith". *Prisma* 10 (1978): 68–76.
Feith, Herbert, and Lance Castle, eds. *Indonesian Political Thinking, 1945–1965*. Ithaca: Cornell University Press, 1970.
Feng Ting. "Bagaimana Bentuk 'Keluarga Baru' Model RRT?" *Siasat Baru* 13, 623 (1959): 9–11.
Fic, Victor. *Anatomy of the Jakarta Coup, October 1, 1965: The Collusion with China Destroyed the Army Command, President Sukarno and the Communist Party of Indonesia*. New Delhi: Abhinav Publications, 2004.
Fitzgerald, Stephen. *China and the Overseas Chinese: A Study of Peking's Changing Policy, 1949–1970*. Cambridge: Cambridge University Press, 1972.
Foulcher, Keith. "A Survey of Events Surrounding 'Manikebu': The Struggle for Cultural and Intellectual Freedom in Indonesian Literature". *Bijdragen tot de Taal-, Land- en Volkenkunde* 125, 4 (1969): 429–65.
———. *Social Commitment in Literature and the Arts: the Indonesian "Institute of People's Culture" 1950–1965*. Clayton: Monash University Center of Southeast Asian Studies, 1986.

———. "Politics and Literature in Independent Indonesia: The View from the Left". *Southeast Asian Journal of Social Science* 15 (1987): 83–103.

———. "On a Roll: Pramoedya and the Postcolonial Transition", Indonesian Studies Working Paper (January 2008), University of Sydney.

Frederick, William H. "Dreams of Freedom, Moments of Despair: Armijn Pane and the Imagining of Modern Indonesian Culture". In *Imagining Indonesia: Cultural Politics and Political Culture*, ed. Jim Schiller and Barbara Martin-Schiller. Athens: Ohio University Center for International Studies Southeast Asian Series, 1997, pp. 54–89.

"Gambaran Komunisme jang sebenarnja (I)". *Suara Masjumi* 10 (1955): 5–6.

"Gambaran Komunisme jang sebenarnja (II)". *Suara Masjumi* 10 (1955): 6–7.

Geertz, Clifford. *The Interpretation of Cultures*. New York: Basic Books, 1973.

"Gerakan Wanita di Tiongkok Baru". *Dunia Internasional* 3, 3 (1952): 1029–36.

Gordon, Bernard K. "The Southeast Asian View of China". *Current History* 55, 325 (1968): 165–70, 180–1.

Gouw Soei Tjiang. "Status Golongan Peranakan Tionghoa di Indonesia Berhubung dengan Berdirinja Republiek Rakjat Tiongkok". In *Kongres 1950 Persatuan Tiongkok* (Jakarta: Pusat Persatuan Tionghoa, 1950), pp. 19–21.

Graha, Satya. "Melihat Komune Rakjat dari dekat". Parts 1–2. *Pesat* 15, 14–15 (1959): 5–7; 7–8; *Suluh Indonesia*, 16–19 March 1959.

———. "Fanwen Zhongguo Tongxun". [Newsletter from China]. *Warta Bhakti* [*Zhong Cheng Bao*], 2–5 November 1963.

———. "Tantan Renmin Gongshe" [On the People's Commune]. *Warta Bhakti* [*Zhong Cheng Bao*], 10–11 November 1963.

———. "Zaitan Renmin Gongshe [II]" [On the People's Commune, part II]. *Warta Bhakti* [*Zhong Cheng Bao*], 14–15 November 1963.

———. "Zhongguo Shixianle Sifenzhiyi Renlei de Tuanjie" [The solidarity of a quarter of the world population]. *Warta Bhakti* [*Zhong Cheng Bao*], 2–7 November 1963.

Groeneveldt, W.P. *Historical Notes on Indonesia and Malaya: Compiled from Chinese Sources*. Jakarta: Bhratara, 1960 [1880].

Hadiz, Vedi. "The Left and Indonesia's 1960s: The Politics of Remembering and Forgetting". *Inter-Asia Cultural Studies* 7, 4 (2006): 554–69.

Halpern, A.M. "The Foreign Policy Use of the Chinese Revolutionary Model". *China Quarterly* 7 (1961): 1–16.

Hamid, Amarzan Ismail. "Melihat RRT sesudah 15 tahun: Revolusi Menempa Manusia Baru". *Harian Rakjat*, 12 November 1964.

Hanna, Willard A. "The Case of the Forty Million Missing Muslims". *American Universities Field Staff* (Southeast Asian Series), September 1956.

———. "Moscow Comes to Bung Karno — and So Does Peking". *American Universities Field Staff* (Southeast Asian Series), 30 November 1956.

———. *Bung Karno's Indonesia*. New York: American Universities Field Staff, 1959.

———. "Of Mao, Sukarno, and Ali Baba". *Reporter*, 3 March 1960, pp. 36–8.

Hanssens, Van. "The Campaign against Nationalist Chinese in Indonesia". In *Indonesia's Struggle, 1957–1958*, ed. B.H.M. Vlekke. The Hague: Netherlands Institute of International Affairs, 1959, pp. 56–76.
Hardjo. "Arti Revolusi Oktober dan Revolusi Tiongkok bagi Indonesia". *Bintang Merah* 8, 3/4 (1952): 124–7.
*Hasil Ekonomi Tiongkok Baru, 1949–1952*. Beijing: Pustaka Bahasa Asing, 1953.
Hatta, Mohammad. "Indonesia's Foreign Policy". *Foreign Affairs* 31, 3 (1953): 441–52.
―――. *Dasar Politik Luar Negeri Republik Indnonesia*. Jakarta: Tintamas, 1953.
―――. "Warganegara Indonesia Turunan Tionghoa". *Star Weekly*, no. 578 (26 January 1957), pp. 2–4.
―――. "Speech before the Chinese People's Political Consultative Conference". *Indonesian Spectator*, 1 November 1957.
―――. "Pembangunan RRT". *Pikiran Rakjat*, 20–21 November 1957.
―――. "Not Communism but Chinese Qualities Made People's China Rise". *Indonesian Spectator*, 1 December 1957, pp. 10–1.
―――. "Masalah Pembangunan dalam RRT". *Pikiran Rakjat*, 23–24 December 1957.
―――. "Indonesia between the Power Blocs". *Foreign Affairs* 36, 3 (1958): 480–90.
―――. "One Indonesian View of the Malaysian Issue". *Asian Survey* 5, 3 (1965): 139–43.
―――. *Portrait of a Patriot: Selected Writings*. The Hague and Paris: Mouton, 1972.
―――. *Bung Hatta's Answers*. Singapore: Gunung Agung, 1981.
―――. *Kumpulan Pidato, (vol. 2: dari tahun 1951 s.d. 1979)*, ed. I. Wangsa Widjaja and Meutia F. Swasono. Jakarta: Inti Idayu Press, 1983.
Hau, Carol and Takashi Shiraishi. "Daydreaming about Rizal and Tetcho: On Asianism as Network and Fantasy". *Philippine Studies* 57, 3 (2009): 329–88.
Hauswedell, Peter C. "The Anti-Imperialist International United Front in Chinese and Indonesian Foreign Policy 1963–1965: A Study of Anti-Status Quo Politics". Ph.D. dissertation, Cornell University, 1976.
Hefner, Robert. "Introduction: Multiculturalism and Citizenship in Malaysia, Singapore, and Indonesia". In *The Politics of Multiculturalism: Pluralism and Citizenship in Malaysia, Singapore, and Indonesia*, ed. Robert Hefner. Honolulu: University of Hawaii Press, 2001, pp. 1–58.
*Heping Waijiao he Mulin Zhengce de Dianfan: Liu Shaoqi Zhuxi Fangwen Yindunixiya, Miandian, Jianpuzai, Yuenan* [A model of peaceful co-existence policy: Chairman Liu Shaoqi visits Indonesia, Burma, Cambodia, and Vietnam]. Beijing: Renmin Chubanshe, 1963.
Hidajat, Z.M. *Masyarakat dan Kebudayaan Cina di Indonesia*. Bandung: Tarsito, 1977.
Hinton, Harold C. *China's Turbulent Quest: An Analysis of China's Foreign Relations since 1949*. Bloomington: Indiana University Press, 1972.
―――, ed. *The People's Republic of China, 1949–1979: A Documentary Survey*. 5 volumes. Wilmington, DE: Scholarly Resources, 1980.

Hollander, Paul. *Political Pilgrims: Travels of Western Intellectuals to the Soviet Union, China, and Cuba*. Lanham, MD: University Press of America, 1990 [1981].
Hong Yuanyuan [Ang Goan Jan]. *Hong Yuanyuan Zizhuan*. [An autobiography of Ang Goan Jan]. Trans. Liang Yingming. Beijing: Zhongguo Huaqiao Chuban Gongsi, 1989.
Nordholt, Henk Schulte, ed. *Indonesian Transitions*. Yogyakarta: Pustaka Pelajar, 2006.
Howie, R. "Sino-Indonesian Relations, October 1965 — April 1967". Ph.D. dissertation, University of London.
Hsu Chien. "Mengenai Republik Rakjat Tiongkok". *Suluh Indonesia*, 12 April 1963.
Huang Aling. *Zhongguo Yinni Guangxishi Jianbian*. [A short history of Sino-Indonesian relations]. Beijing: Zhongguo Guoji Guangbo Chubanshe, 1987.
Huang Dongping [Oey Tong Ping]. "Cong 'Haiwai Kuer' dao 'Zhuguo Xingshi'" (1951) [From "overseas orphanage" to "motherland's messengers"]. In Huang, *Tuan Gao E Ji* [Selected essays, vol. 2]. Singapore: Daoyu Wenhua Chubanshe, 1993, pp. 465–6.
Huang, P.C. "Tentara dan Produksi". *Republik* 1, 6 (1950): 29–33.
———. "Buruh Tiongkok Membangun". *Republik* 1, 7 (1950): 23–4.
"Hubungan Rakjat Indonesia-Rakjat Tiongkok". *Republik* 2, 2 (1951): 23–4.
*Indonesia: A Feature Bulletin*. Beijing: Embassy of the Republic of Indonesia, 1955.
*Indonesia Antara Dua Blok Raksasa*. Jakarta: New Nusantara, 1958[?].
"Indonesia dan RRT Punya Banyak Persamaan Pandangan". *Merdeka*, 29 December 1973.
Ingleson, John. "Mohammad Hatta: Cendekiawan, Aktivis dan Politikus". *Prisma*, January 1982, pp. 61–74.
"Interview J.M. P.M. RRT Chou En Lai dengan Wartawan-Wartawan Indonesia di Peking". *Mimbar Penerangan* 15, 3 (1965): 33–6.
"Islam di Tiongkok". *Sin Min*, 5–6 October 1956.
Iskan, Dahlan. *Pelajaran dari Tiongkok*. Surabaya: JP Books, 2008.
———. "Amerika Harus Belajar Langkah-Langkah Tiongkok". *Jawa Pos*, 19 November 2008.
Ismail, Yahaya. *Pertumbuhan, Perkembangan dan Kejatuhan Lekra di Indonesia*. Kuala Lumpur: Dewan Bahasa dan Pustaka, 1972.
Jahja, Hadji Junus, ed. *Nonpri di Mata Pribumi*. Jakarta: Yayasan Tunas Bangsa, 1991.
Jassin, H.B. "Kesusteraan Asing dalam Terdjemahan Indonesia". *Bahasa dan Budaja* 4, 4 (1956): 11–24.
———. *Surat-surat, 1943–1983*. Jakarta: PT Gramedia, 1984.
Juti [Melik Sayuti]. "Limabelas Hari di Tiongkok". *Suluh Indonesia*, 26–30 October 1956.
Kahin, George M. *The Asian-African Conference, Bandung, Indonesia, April 1955*. Ithaca: Cornell University Press, 1956.
———. "Indonesia". In *Major Governments of Asia*, ed. George M. Kahin. 2nd ed. Ithaca: Cornell University Press, 1963, pp. 535–700.

———. *Nationalism and Revolution in Indonesia*. Ithaca: Cornell University Press, 1970 [1952].
Kartowijono, Nj. S. "Keadaan Wanita di RRT". *Suara Guru* 14 (1959): 15–6, 19.
"Kalau Komunis Berkuasa". *Suara Masjumi* 10 (1955): 6–7.
Karim, A. "Dengan Bung Karno Melihat Dunia Baru: Perobahan Tjara Berpikir di RRT". *Sin Po*, 13–16 November 1956.
"Kata Pengantar [tentang Lu Hsun]". *Konfrontasi* 14 (September/October 1956).
"Keadaan Tiongkok dilihat dari Katja Mata satu Hoakiauw". *Star Weekly*, no. 219 (12 March 1950), pp. 24–5.
"Kehidupan dan Pikiran Lu Hsun: Pengarang dan Internasionalis Tiongkok". *Dunia Internasional* 3, 5 (1952): 1279–84.
"Kehidupan Seniman RRT Terdjamin". *Suluh Indonesia*, 14 November 1963.
"Kesan² Prof. Dr. Prijono tentang Kundjungannja ke RRT". *Merdeka*, 21–22 October 1954.
Koesnan. "Hubungan Indonesia-RRT Agar Dipererat". *Suluh Indonesia*, 13 October 1956.
Koh Young Hoon. *Pemikiran Pramoedya Ananta Toer dalam Novel-novel Mutakhirnya*. Kuala Lumpur: Dewan Bahasa dan Pustaka, 1996.
"Komune Rakjat di RRT". *Siasat Baru* 13, 622 (1959): 3–5.
"Komunisme dan Nasionalisme di Tiongkok". *Sikap* 4, 1 (1951): 9–10.
"Konfernas Pengarang dan Seniman Tiongkok". *Harian Rakjat*, 7 July 1963.
Kong Yuanzhi, *Zhongguo Yindunixiya Wenhua Jiaoliu* [Cultural exchanges between China and Indonesia]. Beijing: Peking University Press, 1999.
"Konsepsi: Lembaga Persahabatan Tiongkok-Indonesia". *Zaman Baru* 4, 22/23 (1953): 13–6.
Kristiatma. "Brainwashing di Tiongkok (II)". *Basis* 7, 3 (1957): 85–91.
Kroef, Justus M. Van der. "The Sino-Indonesian Partnership". *Orbis* 8, 2 (1964): 332–56.
Kurlantzick, Joshua. *Charm Offensive: How China's Soft Power Is Transforming the World*. New Haven: Yale University Press, 2007.
Kusno, Abidin. "From City to City: Tan Malaka, Shanghai, and the Politics of Geographical Imagining". *Singapore Journal of Tropical Geography* 24, 3 (2003): 327–39.
Kussudiardjo, B. "Kesan-kesan Perlawatan ke RRT". *Budaya* 4, 1 (1955): 2–12.
Kwee Kek Beng. *Ke Tiongkok Baru*. Jakarta: Kuo, 1952.
———. *Pendekar-pendekar R.R.T. (Who's Who in New China)*. Jakarta: Kuo, 1953.
———. *50,000 Kilometer dalam 100 Hari*. Palembang: Lauw Putra, 1965.
*Lahirnya Konsepsi Asimilasi*. 5th printing. Jakarta: Yayasan Tunas Bangsa, 1977 [1961]
*Laporan Kundjungan Delegasi Ilmiah Departemen Urusan Research Nasional ke Republik Rakjat Tiongkok, tanggal 25 April–17 Mei 1965*. Jakarta: n.p., 1965. [Note: Koentjaraningrat and Selo Soemardjan are among the co-authors of this report].
Latif, Yudi. *Indonesian Muslim Intelligentsia and Power*. Singapore: Institute of Southeast Asian Studies, 2008.

Leclerc, Jacques. "Aidit dan Partai pada tahun 1950". *Prisma* 7 (1982): 61–78.
Lee Kam Hing. *Education and Politics in Indonesia, 1945–1965*. Kuala Lumpur: University of Malaya Press, 1995.
Legge, John D. *Sukarno: A Political Biography*. Sydney: Allen & Unwin, 1990 [1972].
_____. *Intellectuals and Nationalism in Indonesia: A Study of the Following recruited by Sutan Sjahrir in Occupation Jakarta*. Ithaca: Cornell Modern Indonesia Project Publications, 1988.
Lembaga Pembinaan Kesatuan Bangsa. *Peristiwa "10 Mei" dalam Penelitian: Hasil Survey*. Jakarta: Seksi Penerangan Komando Operasi Tertinggi, 1965.
Lev, Daniel S. *The Transition to Guided Democracy: Indonesian Politics 1957–1959*. Ithaca: Cornell University Modern Indonesian Project, 1966.
Li Hua-yu. *Mao and the Economic Stalinization of China, 1948–1953*. Lanham, MD: Rowman & Littlefield, 2006.
Li Wei-Han. *Perdjuangan untuk Hegemoni Proletariat selama Masa Revolusi Demokrasi Baru Tiongkok*. Seri Gerakan Pembebasan Nasional. Jakarta: Akademi Ilmu Sosial Aliarcham, 1962.
Liang Liji. "Sastra Indonesia Populer di Tiongkok". *Madjalah Merdeka*, nos. 51/52 (26 December 1964), pp. 1, 3.
Lie Ping An. "Konfrontasi Sila-sila Tiongkok Lama dan Tiongkok Baru". *Sin Min*, 2 August 1956.
Lie Tek Tjeng. "Indonesia in China's Foreign Policy, 1949–1977: A Perspective from Jakarta". In *China: Development and Challenge*, vol. 3, ed. Lee Ngok and Leung Chi-Keung. Hong Kong: University of Hong Kong Press, 1979, pp. 331–40.
_____. "The Sinic East Asia Image in Southeast Asia as Seen from Jakarta". *Korean Journal of International Studies* 14, 4 (1983): 381–90.
_____. "The Meaning of 'Overseas Chinese'". *Jakarta Post*, 10–11 May 1994.
Lindbald, Thomas. "The Political Economy of Realignment in Indonesia during the Sukarno Period". In *Europe-Southeast Asia in the Contemporary World: Mutual Images and Reflections 1940s–1960s*, ed. Piyanart Bunnag, Franz Knipping and Sud Chonchirdsin. Baden-Baden: Normos Verlagsgesellschaft, 2000, pp. 149–72.
Liu, Hong. "Pramoedya Ananta Toer and China: The Transformation of a Cultural Intellectual", *Indonesia* 61 (1996): 119–43.
_____. "Constructing a China Metaphor: Sukarno's Perception of the PRC and Indonesian Political Transformation". *Journal of Southeast Asian Studies* 28, 1 (1997): 27–46.
_____. "Intellectual Representations and Socio-Political Implications: Comparative China-Imagining in Postcolonial Indonesia and Contemporary United States". *Asian Thought and Society* 26, 76 (2001): 29–50.
_____. "Sino-Southeast Asian Studies: Toward an Alternative Paradigm". *Asian Studies Review* 24, 3 (2001): 259–83.
_____. "Social Capital and Business Networking: A Case Study of Modern Chinese Transnationalism". *Southeast Asian Studies* (Kyoto University) 39, 3 (2001): 357–81.

———. "Introduction: The Historicity and Multi-dimensionality of Sino-Southeast Asian Socio-Cultural Interactions" (with Melissa Curley). In *China and Southeast Asia: Changing Social and Cultural Linkages*, ed. Melissa Curley and Hong Liu. Hong Kong: Centre of Asian Studies, Hong Kong University, 2002, pp. 1–10.

———. "Beyond Orientalism and the East-West Divide: China and Southeast Asia in the Double Mirror". *Stockholm Journal of East Asian Studies* 13 (2003): 45–65.

———. "Introduction: Toward a Multi-dimensional Exploration of the Chinese Overseas". In *The Chinese Overseas*, Vol. 1: *Conceptualizing and Historicizing Chinese International Migration*, ed. Hong Liu. London and New York: Routledge, 2006, pp. 1–30.

———. "The Transnational Construction of 'National Allegory': China and the Cultural Politics of Postcolonial Indonesia". *Critical Asian Studies* 38, 3 (2006): 179–210.

———. "The Historicity of China's Soft Power: The PRC and the Cultural Politics of Indonesia, 1949–65". In *The Cold War in Asia: The Battle for Hearts and Minds*, ed. Yangwen Zheng, Hong Liu and Michael Szonyi. Leiden and Boston: Brill, 2010, pp. 147–82.

———. "An Emerging China and Diasporic Chinese: Historicity, State, and International Relations". *Journal of Contemporary China* 20, 71 (2011).

Liu, Hong, Goenawan Mohamad, and Sumit Mandal. *Pram dan Cina*. Jakarta: Komunitas Bambu, 2008.

Liu Tsun-chi. "Pers di Tiongkok Baru". *Mimbar Penerangan* 2, 7 (1951): 20–3.

Liu Shao-chi. "Perkembangan Demokrasi di Tiongkok Baru". *Republik* 1, 23 (1951): 32–4.

Loe Tjin Soe. "Tiongkok Merah dan Indonesia". *Mimbar Indonesia* 7, 39 (1953): 8, 11.

Lydia. "Hari 4 Mei dan Huakiao". *Republik* 2, 3 (1951): 44–6.

Mackie, J.A.C., ed. *The Chinese in Indonesia: Five Essays*. Melbourne: Nelson, 1976.

Mao Tse-tung. "Democratic Centralisme". *Sin Min*, 9 October 1957.

———. "Sosialisme tak Bisa sekali Gus". *Merdeka*, 15 June 1958.

"Mao Tse Tung: Boekan Hamba dari Moskou". *Star Weekly*, no. 178 (29 May 1949), pp. 25–7.

McVey, Ruth. *The Development of the Indonesian Communist Party and Its Relations with the Soviet Union and the Chinese People's Republic*. Cambridge, MA: Center for International Studies, MIT, 1954.

———, ed. *Indonesia*. New Haven: HRAF Press, 1963.

———. "Indonesian Communism and China". In *China in Crisis*, vol. 2, ed. Tang Tsou. Chicago: University of Chicago Press, 1969, pp. 357–94.

"Melawat ke Sovjet Uni dan RRT". *Suara Guru* 12, 12 (1958): 19–22.

*Mengapa 600 djuta Rakjat RRT Bergerak Keselatan?* Seri Kewaspadaan Nasional. Jakarta: New Nusantara, 1960.

"Mengapa Presiden Ambil Tjontoh Pembangunan dari RRT?" 31 August 1957.

"Menjambut Ulang Tahun Republik Rakjat Tiongkok". *Zaman Baru* 4, 24 (1953): 1–5.

Mertodipuro, Sumantri. "Dunia tetap Ramai: Konflik Moskwa-Peking". *Madjalah Merdeka*, nos. 36–39 (September 1964).
Min Ying. "Jiaqiang Yin Zhong Liangguo Renmin Zhijian de Huxian Wanglai he Wenhua Jiaoliu – Fangwen Hu Yuzhi Xiansheng" [Strengthening cultural exchanges between the Chinese people and Indonesian people: An interview with Hu Yuzhi]. *Juexing Zhoukan* (Jakarta) 6, 33 (1959): 14–5.
"Missi Subandrio ke Peking". *Madjalah Merdeka*, nos. 3/4 (16 January 1965), p. 5.
Mizuno Kosuke and Pasuk Phongpaichit, eds. *Populism in Asia*. Singapore and Kyoto: NUS Press and Kyoto University Press, 2009.
Modelski, George. *The New Emerging Forces: Documents of the Ideology of Indonesian Foreign Policy*. Canberra: Department of International Relations, Research School of Pacific Studies, Australian National University, 1963.
Mohamad, Goenawan. "The 'Manikebu Affair': Literature and Politics in the 1960s". *Prisma* 46 (1988): 70–88.
Mortimer, Rex. *Indonesian Communism under Sukarno: Ideology and Politics, 1959–1965*. Ithaca: Cornell University Press, 1974.
Mozingo, David. *Chinese Policy toward Indonesia, 1949–1967*. Ithaca: Cornell University Press, 1976.
Muaja, A.J. *The Chinese Problem in Indonesia*. Jakarta: New Nusantara, 1958.
Mudjahid Islam Indonesia. *Supplement bagi Perdamaian Dunia: Pudji dan Kritik bagi Bangsa Tionghoa dan Republik Rakjat Tiongkok*. Jakarta, 1953[?].
Mundingsari, S. *Sastera dan Filsfat Tionghoa*. Medan: Gedung Pustaka, 1946.
Nassa, Gede. "Pengalaman Beladjar di RRT". *Tiongkok Rakjat* 12 (1962): 16–8.
Nasution, Zain. "Mengikuti Misi Persahabatan Tiongkok". *Harian Rakjat*, 27 September 1956.
Nio Joe Lan. *Tiongkok Sepandjang Abad*. Jakarta: Balai Pustaka, 1952.
⸻. "Perhubungan Kebudajaan Indonesia-Tiongkok". *Mimbar Indonesia* 8, 49 (1954): 5–6.
⸻. *Perabadan Tionghoa Selajang Pandang*. Jakarta: Keng Po, 1961.
Njoto. "Literatur Baru: Bagaimanakah Pendapat Mao Tse-tung tentang Literatur?" *Republik* 1, 4 (1950), pp. 36–7.
Noer, Zochara. "Surat dari Peking". *Tiongkok Rakjat* 7 (1965): 92–3; *Zhong Cheng Bao*, 27 August 1965.
Noerhadi. "Ho-Ping Kung-Ch'u (I & II)". *Mimbar Indonesia* 9, 1 (1955): 7–8; nos. 2/3 (15 January 1955), pp. 13, 23.
Notermans, Jef. "Apa Tiongkok Bisa Meroekoenkan Kapitalisme & Communisme?" *Star Weekly*, no. 196 (2 October 1949), pp. 21–2.
Nurhadi. "Politik Minoriteit RRT dan Politik Minoriteit Republik Indonesia". *Kompas (untuk Generasi Baru)* 4, 3 (1954): 8–12.
Oei Oe Ang. "Terbentuknja Republik Rakjat Tiongkok". *Ta Hsueh Tsa Chih* 19, 1/2 (1951): 11–2.
Oey Hong Lee. *Naga dan Tikus: Kisah Perang Tiongkok-Djepang (7 Djuli 1937–2 September 1945)*. Jakarta: Lucky, 1959.

———. *Naga Bangkit!*. 2nd printing. Jakarta: Jajasan Kebudajaan "Zamrud", 1962.
Oey Seng Oea, trans. *Riwajat Mao Tse-Tung Dituturkan oleh Sendiri*. Jakarta: Dunia, 1950.
Ouw Eng Liang, Prof. Dr. "Menindjau Tiongkok untuk Kedua Kali". *Tiongkok Rakjat* 8 (1962): 8–10.
Oyen, Meredith. "Communism, Containment and the Chinese Overseas". In *The Cold War in Asia: The Battle for Hearts and Minds*, ed. Yangwen Zheng, Hong Liu and Michael Szonyi. Leiden and Boston: Brill, 2010, pp. 59–94.
Pane, Armijn. "Indonesia di Asia Selatan: Sejarah Indonesia sampai 1600". *Indonesia* 1/2 (1951): 1–36.
———. *Tiongkok Zaman Baru: Sedjarahnja, abad ke-19-Sekarang*. Jakarta: Arbati, 1953.
Pangon, Sabdo. *Angkatan Muda Tiongkok*. Seri Kewaspadaan Nasional. Jakarta: New Nusantara, 1960[?].
Panitya Penulisan Sedjarah Departemen Luar Negeri. *Dua Puluh Lima Tahun Departemen Luar Negeri, 1945–1970*. Jakarta: Jajasan Kesedjahteraan Karyawan Deplu, 1971.
Parna, Ibnu. "Angin dari Utara: Laporan Perdjalanan ke RRT dan Korea-Utara". Parts 12–16. *Mingguan Pekerdja*, nos. 19–33 (1964).
Partokoesoemo, Moedjijoewono. "Beladjar, Persahabatan dan Setiakawan". *Tiongkok Rakjat* 4 (1962): 49–51.
Passin, Herbert. *China's Cultural Diplomacy*. New York: Praeger, 1963.
Pauker, Guy J. "Indonesian Images of Their National Self". *Public Opinion Quarterly* 22, 2 (1958): 304–24.
Peng Chen. *Speech in the Aliarcham Academy of Social Sciences in Indonesia, Jakarta, May 25, 1965*. Beijing: Foreign Language Press, 1965.
Peng Di, and Xing Qiang. "Hongdong Yindunixiya de Zhongguo Yishu de Yanchu" [Chinese artist performance caused a sensation all over Indonesia]. *Shijie Zhishi* 15 (1955): 27–9.
"Pengaruh Revolusi Tiongkok terhadap Seni Suara Rakjatnja". *Nasional* 5, 30 (1954): 9–10.
"Pergerakan 4 Mei di Tiongkok dan Perdamaian". *Republik* 2, 2 (1951): 29–32.
*Perhubungan Tiongkok-Indonesia dizaman Purbakala*. Surabaya: Sawahan Chung Hua Hui, 1951.
*Perkenalan Lembaga Persahabatan Indonesia-Tiongkok*. Jakarta: Rada [?], 1956.
"Pernjataan Bersama Himpunan Pengarang Tiongkok dan Delegasi Nasional Pengarang Indonesia". *Tiongkok Rakjat* 7 (1961): 34–5.
*Persahabatan dalam Perdjuangan*. Jakarta: Jajasan Kebudajaan Zamrud, 1963.
*Pertundjukan Delegasi Kebudajaan Republik Rakjat Tiongkok*. Jakarta: Embassy of the People's Republic of China, 1955.
*Perubahan Agraria Tiongkok Baru*. Jakarta: Penerbit Kebudajaan Rakjat, 1951.
Phan Hung. "Politik Ekonomi Tiongkok". *Republik* 1, 5 (1950): 16–20.

Philpott, Simon. *Rethinking Indonesia: Postcolonial Theory, Authoritarianism and Identity*. New York: St Martin's Press, 2000.

Pramoedya Ananta Toer. "Kesusasteraan sebagai Alat". *Indonesia* 3, 7 (July 1952).

———. "Lun Yinni Xiandai Wenxue" [On contemporary Indonesian literature]. *Huaqiao Daobao* (Jakarta) 16 (1953): 15–7.

———. "Manakah Pengarang dari Gelongan Keturunan Tionghoa?" *Pendorong*, 13 July 1956.

———. "Zai Lu Xun Xiansheng Shishi Ershi Zhounian Jinian Dahuishang de Jianghua" [Address at the conference in commemorating the 20th anniversary of Lu Xun's death]. *Wenyibao* 20 (1956): 15–6.

———. "Djiwa Revolusioner di Tiongkok Tetap Bergolak". *Sin Po*, 5 January 1957.

———. "Keadaan Sosial Para Pengarang: Perbandingan Antarnegara". *Siasat* 11, 506 (1957): 25, 28.

———. "Djembatan Gantung dan Konsepsi Presiden". *Harian Rakjat*, 28 February 1957. Also published in *Bintang Merah* 13, 1/2 (1957): 69–75.

———. "Kesusasteraan Indonesia Modern Dinegeri-negeri Timur". *Star Weekly*, no. 584 (9 March 1957), pp. 38–9.

———. "Pedoman Kehidupan Kesenian Indonesia". *Harian Rakjat*, 13 March 1957.

———. "Sedikit tentang Kesusasteraan Tionghoa di Indonesia". *Pantjawarna* 113 (1957): 1–2.

———. "Seniman adalah Insinjur Pembentuk Djiwa Bangsa". *Pikiran Rakjat*, 19 June 1958.

———. "Suatu Kali di Tiongkok Baru". *Tiongkok Rakjat* 7 (1958): 40–1.

———. "Tantan Yindunixiya Wenxue" [On Indonesian literature]. *Wenyi Yuebao* (Shanghai) 11 (1958): 20–2.

———. "Liangan Luqian" [In front of the melting furnace]. Trans. Chen Xiaru. *Renmin Wenxue* (Beijing) 12 (1958): 30–1.

———. "Tasjkent-Peking". *Tiongkok Rakjat* 1 (1959): 48–50.

———. "LEKRA telah Mendidik Saja Mentjintai Rakjat". *Zaman Baru*, 30 January–10 February 1959, p. 710.

———. "Fitnah terhadap Tasjkent". *Zaman Baru*, 20–30 February 1959, pp. 1, 4–5, 9–10.

———. "Paiyu Yundong yu Huaqiao" [Anti-Semitism and Overseas Chinese]. *Yihua Jingji* (Jakarta), 7 January 1960.

———. *Hoakiau di Indonesia*. Jakarta: Bintang, 1960 [Reprinted: Jakarta: Garba Budaya, 1998].

———. "Sastera Harus Militan Melawan Imperialisme dan Neo-Kolonialisme". *Harian Rakjat*, 17 February 1962.

———. "Introducing Indonesian Literature". *Harian Rakjat*, 3–5 September 1962.

———. "Jiaqiang Yin Zhong Youyi, Fensui Mei Ying Qinglue" [Strengthening Sino-Indonesian friendship, smashing the aggressive Americans and British]. *Warta Bhakti* [*Zhong Cheng Bao*], 1 October 1964.

_____. "Pengadjaran Sastra adalah Pengadjaran Ideologi". *Harian Rakjat*, 14 April 1965.

_____. "Wawancara: Pramoedya, Bakal Pemenang Hadiah Nobel". *Nadi Insan* (Kuala Lumpur) 24 (1981): 3–9.

_____. "*Perburuan* (1950) and *Keluarga Gerilya* (1950)". Trans. Benedict Anderson. *Indonesia* 36 (1983): 25–48.

_____. *The Mute's Soliloquy: A Memoir*. Trans. Willem Samuels. New York: Hyperion East, 1999.

"Pramudya Ananta Tur di RRT". *Sin Tjun* 2 (1957): 107–8.

"Presiden Sukarno di Peking". *Siasat* 10, 488 (1956): 11.

*Presiden Sukarno di Tiongkok*. Peking: Pustaka Bahasa Asing, 1956.

*Presiden Sukarno Mengundjungi Tiongkok*. Jakarta: Kedutaan Besar Republik Rakjat Tiongkok di Indonesia, 1956.

Pusponegoro, Sudjono D. "RRT Berdiri diatas Kaki Sendiri". *Berita Minggu*, 28 June 1964.

Qiu Zhengou. "Yinni Jinyong Zhongwen Wenti" [Issues regarding the ban on the use of Chinese in Indonesia]. *Yinni Qiaosheng (The Voice of Overseas Chinese from Indonesia)* (Taipei) 1, 4 (1961): 5–6, 11.

Ramadhan, K.H. "Serakan Bintang Sekitar Yang-Tse". *Konfrontasi* 4, 12 (1957): 60–72.

_____. "Kesan[2] Perdjalanan ke RRT: I-IX". Parts 1–9. *Siasat* 11, 545–53 (November 1957–January 1958).

Rangkuti, Bahrum. *Pramoedya Ananta Toer dan Karja Seninja*. Jakarta: Gunung Agung, 1963.

"Realpolitiker". "Soal Komunisme dan Nasionalisme di Asia". *Sikap* 3, 10 (1950): 1–3.

Reid, Anthony, ed. *Sojourners and Settlers: Histories of Southeast Asia and the Chinese*. Sydney: Allen & Unwin, 1996.

_____. "Writing the History of Independent Indonesia". In *Nation-Building: Five Southeast Asian Histories*, ed. Wang Gungwu. Singapore: Institute of Southeast Asian Studies, 2005, pp. 69–91.

"RI-RRT: 2 Kamerad dalam Perdjuangan". *Suluh Indonesia*, 13 August 1963.

Ricklefs, M.C. *A History of Modern Indonesia since c. 1200*. 3rd ed. Basingstoke: Palgrave, 2001.

Roosa, John. *Pretext for Mass Murder: The September 30th Movement and Suharto's Coup d'Etat in Indonesia*. Madison: University of Wisconsin Press, 2006.

"RRT Menghargai Kaum Muslim: Keterangan Duta Besar RRT". *Pikiran Rakjat*, 12 May 1951.

"RRT [Tentang Presiden Sukarno di Tiongkok]". *Dunia Internasional* 7, 7/8 (1956): 82–99.

Sakirman. *Pembangunan Ekonomi Raksasa Tiongkok Rakjat*. Seri Perdjalanan. Jakarta: Pembaruan, 1960.

Saleh, Bujung. "Orang[2] Tionghoa di Indonesia sebelum Kompeni (VOC)". *Sin Min*, 31 December 1956.

———. "Orang² Tionghoa di Indonesia sedjak Djaman Kompeni (VOC) hingga tahun 1800". *Sin Min*, 30 January 1957.

———. "Yindunixiya de Shaoshu Minzu Wenti" [Minority problems in Indonesia]. *Nanyang Wenti Ziliao Yicong* 3 (1957): 35–7.

———. "Yindunixiya Huayi Gongmin Dui Yindunixiya Xiandai Wenhua de Gongxian". [Contributions of the ethnic Chinese to modern Indonesian culture]. *Nanyang Wenti Ziliao Yicong* 4 (1957): 94–8.

Saleh, N.J. Siti Chairul. "Tiongkok Rakjat jang Kami Lihat: Kita Datang, Kita Lihat, Kita Beladjar..." *Pantjawarna* 2, 104 (October 1964).

———. "Bunga Rampai dari Tiongkok". *Tiongkok Rakjat* 1 (1965): 30–3.

Salmon, Claudine. *Literature in Malay by the Chinese of Indonesia: A Provisional Annotated Bibliography*. Paris: Éditions de la Maison des Sciences de l'Homme, 1981.

Samandjaja. "Naga Merah". *Zaman Baru* 4, 8 (1953): 41–4.

Samil, Suprapti. *Laporan Kundjungan dua Utusan "Perserikatan Perhimpunan² Mahasiswa Indonesia"*. N.p., May/June 1954.

———. "Melawat ke Republik Rakjat Tiongkok". *Forum: Madjalah Umum Mahasiswa* 1, 4 (1954): 13–30.

Samil, Suprapti and Sabam Siagian. "Mahasiswa Indonesia ke RRT". *Kompas untuk Generasi Baru* 4, 10 (1954): 11–26.

Samtiar. "Kesan² Menindjau RRT selajang Pandang: Kehidupan Baru di Tiongkok Baru". *Harian Rakjat*, 9 November 1964.

Sardjono, M.U. "Kami Diuniversitas Tiongkok". *Tiongkok Rakjat* 12 (1958): 49–52.

Sartono. "Kesan² tentang RRT". *Sin Min*, 16 August 1956.

Sastroamidjojo, Ali. *Milestones on My Journey*, ed. C.C.M. Penders. St. Lucia: University of Queensland Press, 1979.

Schiller, Jim, and Barbara Martin-Schiller, eds. *Imagining Indonesia: Cultural Politics and Political Culture*. Athens: Ohio University Research in International Studies Southeast Asia Series, 1997.

Schurmann, H.F. "Sendi² Organisasi Masjarakat RRT". *Siasat (Baru)* 13, 624 (1959): 3–6.

See Seng Tan and Amitav Acharya, eds. *Bandung Revisited: The Legacy of the 1955 Asian-African Conference for International Order*. Singapore: NUS Press, 2008.

Setianegara. *Sedikit tentang Komune-Komune Rakjat di RRT*. Jakarta: Bintang Terang, 1960.

Setiono, Benny G. *Tionghoa dalam Pusaran Politik*. Jakarta: Elkasa, 2003.

"Semangat Economie Baroe". *Liberty* 15, 182 (October 1946).

Sha Ping [Hu Yuzhi]. "Lessons from Indonesia". *China Digest* (Hong Kong) 5, 12 (1949): 5–6.

Shackford-Bradley, Julie. "Mao's Ghost in Golkar". *Inside Indonesia* (January–March 2000): 27–8.

Shi Ren. *Yindunixiya Zhendang* [Political parties in Indonesia]. Beijing: Shijie Zhishi Chubanshe, 1960.

Shils, Edwards. "Intellectuals in the Political Development of the New States". In his *The Intellectuals and the Powers and Other Essays*. Chicago: University of Chicago Press, 1972, pp. 386–423.

Siagian, Bachtiar. "Beberapa Segi Perfilman Tiongkok Sosialis". *Harian Rakjat*, 1–8 January 1962.

Siauw Giok Tjhan. *Lima Jaman: Perwujudan Integrasi Wajar*. Jakarta: Yayasan Teratai, 1981.

_____. *Siauw Giok Tjhan Remembers: A Chinese Peranakan in Independent Indonesia*. Book 2, Part 3. James Cook University, 1984.

Siauw Tiong Djin. "Siauw Giok Tjhan: The Making of a Peranakan Leader". In *Indonesian Political Bibliography: In Search of Cross-Cultural Understanding*, ed. Angus McIntyre. Clayton: Centre of Southeast Asian Studies, Monash University, 1993, pp. 123–60.

_____. *Siauw Giok Tjhan: Perjuangan Seorang Patriot Membangun Nasion Indonesia dan Masyarakat Bhineka Tunggal Ika*. Ph.D. dissertation, Monash University, 1998. [Chinese translation was published by Nandao Chubanshe in Hong Kong, 2001].

Simon, Sheldon W. *The Broken Triangle: Peking, Djakarta and the PKI*. Baltimore: Johns Hopkins University Press, 1969.

Sie Boen Liep. "Perasaan Ketuhanan di RRT". *Sin Tjun* 1 (1956): 83–4.

_____. "Perkembangan Kesenian di RRT". *Sin Tjun* 4 (1959): 13–5.

_____. "Tiongkok Susul … Diri Sendiri". *Sin Tjun* 4 (1959): 127–9.

Simatupang, Iwan. "Masalah Tionghoa di Indonesia". *Indonesia* 10, 10 (1959): 469–73.

*Sino-Indonesian Relations, 1950–1959 (Research Backgrounder)*. Hong Kong: Union Research Institute, 1960.

Sitompoel, Harris. "Sukses Besar bagi Chou En Lai". *Merdeka*, 27 April 1955.

Situ Zan. "Wo Dui Zhonghua Xiehui de Yuanwan" [My hope for the Chinese Association]. *Zhonghua Xiehui Tekan*. Jakarta, 1950, pp. 1–3.

Situmorang, Sitor. "Pengarang dan Intelektuil di Indonesia". *Mimbar Indonesia* 6, 50 (1953): 18, 26.

_____. "Pengaruh Luar terhadap Sastra Indonesia jang terbaru". *Seni* 1, 3 (1955): 113–21.

_____. *Zaman Baru: Sadjak-sadjak*. Jakarta: Madjalah Zaman Baru, 1961.

_____. "Suqing Xinzhiminzhuyi Sanbo de Dusu" [Eliminating the poison spread by neo-colonialism]. *Warta Bhakti* [*Zhong Cheng Bao*], 9 April 1964.

_____. "The Passion of the Sound and the Wanderer [interview with Situmorang]." *Tempo*, no. 46 (18–24 July 2006).

_____ et al. *Shiji*. [Selected poems]. Trans. Chen Xiaru *et al.* Beijing: Zuojia Chubanshe, 1963.

Sjahrir, Sutan. *Our Struggle*. Trans. Benedict R. Anderson. Ithaca: Cornell University Modern Indonesia Project, 1968.

Skinner, G. William. *Report on the Chinese in Southeast Asia*. Ithaca: Cornell University Southeast Asian Program, 1950.

———. "Java's Chinese Minority: Continuity and Change". *Journal of Asian Studies* 20, 3 (1961): 353–62.

———. *Communism and Chinese Culture in Indonesia: The Political Dynamics of Overseas Chinese Youth* (Unpublished manuscript written in 1962, deposited at the Kroch Library, Cornell University).

Soegito. "Demokrasi Baru". *Siasat* 4, 154 (1950): 10–1.

Soeharto. "Kesehatan Rakjat di RRT". *Suara Marhaenis* 6, 15 (1956): 24–8.

Soenarjo, H.A. "Sepintas tentang Agama Islam di Tiongkok". *Tiongkok Rakjat* 3 (1965): 49–51.

Soerjono. "Dari Komune Rakjat ke Pameran Expor Kanton". *Harian Rakjat*, 1–3 October 1964.

Soeroto. *Indonesia ditengah-tengah Dunia dari Abad Keabad* (Peladjaran Sedjarah untuk Sekolah Menengah), vol. 2. Jakarta: Djambatan, 1962.

Somers, Mary F. *Peranakan Chinese Politics in Indonesia*. Ithaca: Cornell University Southeast Asian Program, 1964.

———. "Peranakan Chinese Politics in Indonesia". Ph.D. dissertation, Cornell University, 1965.

Song Qingling [Soong Ching Ling]. "Zhongguo he Yindunixiya Zhijian Riyi Zhenzhan de Youyi" [The increasing friendship between China and Indonesia: A speech in Jakarta]. *Xinhua Yuebao* 8 (1956): 12–5; *Renmin Ribao*, 24 August 1956.

Song Zhi. "Yinni Zuojia Yishujia zai Zhandouzhong" [Indonesian writers and artists in fighting]. *Wenyibao* 5 (1958): 40–2.

Staf Umum Angkatan Darat-1. *Masalah Tionghoa di Indonesia*. N.p., 1961.

"Struktur Pemerintahan RRT". *Dunia Internasional* 2, 11 (1952): 416–9.

*Sujianuo Zongtong Furen Fanghuaji* [Records of Mrs Sukarno's visit to China]. Jakarta: Jajasan Kebudajaan Zamrud, 1962.

Suaidy, Hadji Saleh. "Kesan[2] Saja selama di RRT". Parts 1–5. *Abadi*, 16–20 June 1956.

Subandrio. *Indonesia on the March*. Jakarta: Djambatan, 1959.

Sudjono. "Tiongkok Baru Selajang Pandang". *Suara Guru* 3, 11/12 (1953): 4–7.

Sugardo. "Krisis=Kita sekarang". *Mimbar Indonesia* 5, 49 (1951): 3, 29.

———. *Si Djembel Mentjari Keadilan Sosial*. Jakarta: Dharma, 1952.

———. "Hak[2] Asasi di Tiongkok Baru". *Mimbar Indonesia* 6, 52 (1952): 9–10, 26.

———. *Tiongkok Sekarang: Terra Incognita (Tanah tak dikenal)*. Jakarta: Endang, 1953.

———. "Petani Tiongkok". *Mimbar Indonesia* 7, 7 (1953): 10–1.

———. "80,000 dollar untuk Membunuh Satu Komunis". *Mimbar Indonesia* 7, 17 (1953): 9–10.

———. "Bukan lagi Djamannja Tjina dibajar untuk Menjanji". *Mimbar Indonesia* 7, 27 (1953): 9–10.

———. "Apa Facet Komunisme di Asia?" *Mimbar Indonesia* 7, 31 (1953): 10–1.

Sugiono. "Masalah Cina di Indonesia dan Hubungan RI-RRC (1945–1977)". Skripsi. Yogyakarta: Gadjah Mada University, 1978.

Sukarno. "The Birth of Pantja Sila" (1945). In *Pantja Sila: The Basis of the State of the Republic of Indonesia*. Jakarta: Department of Information, 1964.

———. *Indonesia, Pilihlah Demokrasimu jang Sedjati*. Jakarta: Jajasan Prapantja, 1961 [1956].

———. *Marhaen and Proletarian*. Ithaca: Cornell University Modern Indonesian Project, 1960 [1957].

———. "My Concept". In *Guided Democracy: A Dynamic Approach to the Democratic Form for Indonesia: A Volume of Basic Speeches and Documents*. New Delhi: Unity Book Club of India, 1960, pp. 19–25.

———. *Toward Freedom and the Dignity of Man: A Collection of Five Speeches by President Sukarno of the Republic of Indonesia*. Jakarta: Department of Foreign Affairs, 1961.

———. *Dibawah Bendera Revolusi*. 2 volumes. Jakarta, 1965.

———. *Sukarno: An Autobiography as told to Cindy Adams*. Hong Kong: Gunung Agung, 1966.

*Sukarno: Leader of the Indonesian People, A Short Biography*. Beijing: Embassy of the Republic of Indonesia, 1956.

Sukma, Rizal. *Indonesia and China: The Politics of a Troubled Relationship*. London: Routledge, 1999.

———. "Indonesia's Perceptions of China: The Domestic Bases of Persistent Ambiguity". In *The China Threat: Perceptions, Myths and Reality*, ed. Herbert Yee and Ian Storey. London: RoutledgeCurzon, 2002, pp. 181–204.

Sukisman, W.D. *Masalah Cina di Indonesia*. 2nd printing. Jakarta: Yayasan Penelitian Masalah Asia, 1975.

Sulmi. "Tjatatan Perdjalanan ke Festival Bukares (II) dan (III)". *Zaman Baru* 4, 21 (1953): 31–5; 4, 22/23 (1953): 27–35.

Sumanang. "Perdamaian dan Persahabatan". In Sudhindra Pramanik *et al*., *Tiongkok Baru jang Kami Lihat*. Beijing: Pustaka Bahasa Asing, 1955, pp. 18–22.

Sumardjo, Trisno. "Tjatatan tentang Perutusan Kesenian Indonesia ke RRT". *Mimbar Indonesia* 5, 26 (1954): 7, 29–30.

———. "Kesan[2] Sastrawan Indonesia tentang Tiongkok". *Sin Min*, 3 December 1957.

———. "Sebulan di Tiongkok". *Budaya* 7, 1 (1958): 15–25.

Sunario. "Masjarakat: Politik Asimilasi". *Nasional*, 2 April 1963.

Sung Tjing-Ling [Song Qingling]. *Persahabatan jang Semakin Akrab antara Tiongkok dan Indonesia*. Beijing: Pustaka Bahasa Asing, 1957.

Suryadarma. "Zai Yin Zhong Youxie Chengli Shizhounian Jinianhui shang de Baogao, 16 December 1964". [Impressions of China: Speech at the conference commemorating the tenth anniversary of the Indonesia-China Friendship Association, 16 December 1964]. *Mingguan Seng Hwo Pao* (Jakarta), 1 January 1965.

Suryadinata, Leo. *Pribumi Indonesians, the Chinese Minority and China*. 3rd edition. Singapore: Heinemann Asia, 1992.

———. *Peranakan's Search for National Identity: Biographical Studies of Seven Indonesian Chinese*. Singapore: Times Academic Press, 1993.

———, ed. *Political Thinking of the Indonesian Chinese, 1900–1977: A Source Book*. Singapore: Singapore University Press, 1979.

Suwito. "Komune² Rakjat di Tiongkok". *Pesat* 15, 4 (1959): 9–10.

Tabrani, Mohamad. *Soal Minoriteit dalam Indonesia Merdeka*. Yogyakarta, 1950.

Tan Eng Tie. "Keadaan Makanan dan Agraris di Tiongkok". *Star Weekly*, no. 372 (February 1953), pp. 9–11.

———. "The Question of Minorities: A Hopeful View of a Present Problem". *The Atlantic Monthly* (Supplement, 1956), pp. 61–4.

Tan, Malaka. *From Jail to Jail*. 3 volumes, translated and introduced by Helen Jarvis. Athens: Ohio University Southeast Asian Series, 1991.

Tan Moh Goan. "Mao Bukan Tito". *Siasat* 3 (1949): 10.

Taylor, Carl. "Indonesian Views of China". *Asian Survey* 3, 3 (1963): 165–72.

Taylor, Jay. *China and Southeast Asia: Peking's Relations with Revolutionary Movements*. Revised ed. New York: Praeger, 1976.

*The Indonesian Revolution: Basic Documents and the Idea of Guided Democracy*. Issued by the Department of Information, Republic of Indonesia. Jakarta, 1960.

Teeuw, A. *Modern Indonesian Literature*. 2nd ed. 2 volumes. The Hague: Martinus Nijhoff, 1979.

Teng Ying Chao. "Mematahkan Belenggu Sistim Perkawinan Feodal". *Mimbar Indonesia* 7, 17 (1953): 11, 23.

Teng Yun, ed. *Dangdai Zhongwai Wenhua Jiaoliu Shiliao* [Historical materials on cultural exchanges between China and foreign countries in the contemporary era]. Beijing: Wenhua Yishu Chubanshe, 1990.

"Tentang Persahabatan Indonesia-RRT". *Republik* 1, 1 (1950): 10–3.

Thaib, Maisir. *Tiongkok Merah*. Bukittinggi: Nusantara, n.d.

Than Wei. "Masalah Kebangsaan dan Politik Kebangsaan". *Republik* 2, 4 (1951): 9–11.

Thio In Lok. "Interview dengan Prof. Dr. Tjan Tju Som: Perjakinan Sinologi dahulu dan sekarang". *Star Weekly*, no. 372 (February 1953), pp. 23–4, 95.

Thung Liang Lee. "The Unreality of Chinese Nationalism in Indonesia: An Apologia and a Reorientation". *Indonesian Review* 2, 1 (1954): 69–75.

*Tiansheng Ribao Shelun Xuanji*. [Selected editorials from the *Harian Thien Sung Yit Po*]. Jakarta: Harian Thien Sung Yit Po, 1951.

"Tiongkok". *Republik* 2, 5 (1951): 35–7.

*Tiongkok Baru*. Jakarta: Penerbit Kebudajaan Rakjat, 1950.

"Tiongkok Membangun Ekonomi Nasional". *Republik* 2, 5 (1951): 27–30.

"Tiongkok Merah". *Siasat* 3 (1949): 4–5.

Tjan Jang [Zhou Yang]. "Realisme Sosialis—Djalan kemadjuan bagi Kesusteraan Tiongkok". Trans. Pramoedya A. Toer. *Harian Rakjat*, 8 May 1954.

Tjiptodarsono. "Kawin dan Tjerai di Negara RRT". *Mimbar Indonesia* 6, 42 (1952): 8, 30.

Tjokrodirdjo, Ki. "Mao Tse Tung Pembina RRT". *Djiwa Baru* 3, 6 (1955): 19–21.

Tjokrosujoso, Abikusno. *Perkembangan Kooperasi dari India, Pakistan dan Tiongkok*. Jakarta: Widjaya, 1952.
Tjou Jang [Zhou Yang]. "Seni dan Sastera Sosialis". *Harian Rakjat*, 6 October 1956.
Tod Jones, "Indonesian Cultural Policy, 1950–2003: Culture, Institutions, Government". Ph.D. dissertation, Curtin University of Technology, 2005.
"Tonggak² Sedjarah Indonesia-RRT". *Nasional*, 17 April 1963.
Tsung Shan. "Indonesia's Anti-Imperialist Record". *Peking Review* 8, 3 (1965): 11–2.
Twang Peck-yang. *The Chinese Business Elite in Indonesia and the Transition to Independence, 1940–1950*. Kualu Lumpu: Oxford University Press, 1998.
Usmany, Hadi. "Surat dari Perdjalanan: Hari Pertama didaratan Tiongkok". *Minggu Merdeka*, 1 September 1957.
Utrecht, Ernst. "Sukarno's Populism Contributed Considerably to the Destruction of the Communist Party of Indonesia (PKI)". *Kabar Seberang* 16 (1985): 93–9.
Valk, Van der. "Revolusi dalam Keluarga Tiongkok". *Star Weekly*, no. 372 (14 February 1953), pp. 51–2.
Van Ness, Peter. "China as a Third World State: Foreign Policy and Official National Identity". In *China's Quest for National Identity*, ed. Lowell Dittmer and Samuel Kim. Ithaca: Cornell University Press, 1993, pp. 194–214.
Van Niel, Robert. *The Emergence of the Modern Indonesian Elite*. The Hague: Van Hoeve, 1960.
Vickers, Adrian. *A History of Modern Indonesia*. Cambridge: Cambridge University Press, 2005.
Vuyk, Beb. "Pengantar". In *Tjerita-tjerita Tiongkok*, ed. Bob Vuyk, Mochtar Lubis and S. Mundingsari. Jakarta: P.T. Pembangunan, 1953, pp. 7–19.
Wade, Geoff, ed. *China and Southeast Asia*. 6 volumes. London: Routledge, 2009.
Wang Enyuan. "President Sukarno in Peking". *People's China* 21 (1956): 8–12.
Wang Gungwu. "Political Chinese: An Aspect of Their Contribution to Modern Southeast Asian History". In *Southeast Asia in the Modern World*, ed. Bernard Grossman. Wiesbaden: Otto Harrassowitz, 1972, pp. 115–28.
_____. *The Chineseness of China: Selected Essays*. Hong Kong: Oxford University Press, 1991.
_____. *Community and Nation: China, Southeast Asia and Australia*. St Leonard, NSW: Allen & Unwin, for Asian Studies Association of Australia, 1992.
_____. *The Chinese Overseas: From Earthbound China to the Quest for Autonomy*. Cambridge, MA: Harvard University Press, 2000.
_____. ed. *Nation-Building: Five Southeast Asian Histories*. Singapore: Institute of Southeast Asian Studies, 2005.
Wang Hui. *The Politics of Imagining Asia*. Cambridge: Harvard University Press, 2011.
Wardhana, Wisnoe. "Tari dan Opera di RRT". *Budaya* 4, 4/5 (1955): 187–90.
Warner, Denis. "The Peking-Djakarta Axis". *Reporter* (23 September 1965): 25–7.
Weinstein, Franklin B. *Indonesian Foreign Policy and the Dilemma of Dependence: From Sukarno to Soeharto*. Ithaca: Cornell University Press, 1976.
Weng Xihuei. "Yinni Aiguo Huaqiao Weng Fulin" [Weng Fulin, a patriotic Indonesian Chinese]. *Huaqiao Huaren Lishi Yanjiu* 4 (1993): 77–9.

Wertheim, W.F. *Indonesian Society in Transition*. The Hague: W. Van Hoeve, 1964.
Wibowo, I. *Belajar dari Cina: Bagaimana Cina Merebut Peluang dalam Era Globalisasi*. Jakarta: Kompas, 2004.
Winichakul, Thongchai. "Writing at the Interstices: Southeast Asian Historians and Postnational Histories in Southeast Asia". In *New Terrains in Southeast Asian History*, ed. Abu Talib Ahmad and Tan Liok Ee. Athens: Ohio University Press, 2003, pp. 3–29.
Wispi, Agam, *et al. Dinasti 650 Djuta: Pilihan Sadjak-sadjak*. Jakarta: Lekra, 1961.
Wojowasito. *Tiongkok (Pembangoenan Politik)*. Yogyakarta: Badan Penerbit Nasional, [1947].
Wu Tsu-Min. "Kemadjuan Baru Kesusteraan Tiongkok". *Harian Rakjat*, 17 April 1963.
Wu Wenhua and Meifeng Gan. "Benshiji Sanshi-Wushi Niandai Huawen Tushu zai Yinni" [Chinese books and periodicals in Indonesia from the 1930s to the 1950s]. *Dongnanya Zongheng* 3 (1993): 41–6.
Yang Ming. "Zhuguo yu Huaqiao" [Motherland and the overseas Chinese]. *Seng Hwo Pao Xinnian Tekan*. Jakarta, 1955, p. 32.
Yang Qiguang. "Zhuming Yinni Huaren Minzu Zhuyizhe Guo Keming" [Kwee Kek Beng: A famous Indonesian Chinese nationalist]. *Guangdong Wenshi Ziliao* [Cultural and historical materials of Guangdong] 67 (1991): 148–70.
Yang Xuechun. "He Yindunixiya Guibin Zaiyiqi de Yitian" [One day with Indonesian guests]. *Shijie Zhishi* 70 (1954): 24–5.
Yao Zhongming, *et al. Jiangjun, Waijiaojia, Yishujia — Huang Zhen Jinian Wenji*. [General, diplomat and artist — Essays in commemorating Huang Zhen]. Beijing: Jiefangjun Chubanshe, 1992.
Yi Jiamin. *Huang Zhen Jiangjun de Dashi Shenya* [The Ambassador Career of General Huang Zhen]. Nanjing: Jiangsu Renmin Chubanshe, 1998.
Yi Kui. "Zhuguo Jinbu Dui Huaqiao de Yingxian" [Impact of motherland's progress upon the overseas Chinese]. *Seng Hwo Pao Xinnian Tekan*, Jakarta, 1954, p. 44.
Yin Yizu, ed. "Yinni Huayi Shaoshu Minzu Wenti Yiwen Zhuanji" [A special translation collection: The Chinese minority problem in Indonesia]. *Nanyang Wenti Ziliao Yicong* 3 (1963): 63–89.
Yogi, A. Rivai. "Sastera Seni Suara RRT". *Medan Bahasa* 7, 4 (1957): 19–22.
Yudhasiswa. "Mao Tse-Tung sebagai Pemikir Militer". *Star Weekly*, no. 733 (16 January 1960), pp. 11–2.
Yuti [Melik Sayuti]. "Satu-dua Peladjaran dari Negara Sosialis". *Suara Marhaenis* 6, 15 (1956): 8–13.
Zachri, A. "Menindjau Republik Rakjat Tiongkok: Kesan Seladjang Terbang pada bidang Pendidikan". *Suara Guru* 7, 11 (1957): 3–5.
Zhang Zhaoqiang. *Zhanhou Yindunixiya de Zhengzhi he Jingji* [Politics and economy of post-war Indonesia]. Beijing: Shijie Zhishi Chubanshe, 1956.
Zheng Zhenduo. "Jin Yibu Zhankai Yafei Guojia Zhijian de Wenhua Jiaoliu Gongzuo" [Carrying out further the work of cultural exchanges between China and Asian-African countries]. *Renmin Ribao*, 28 April 1955.

Zhongguo Xinwenshe Ziliaoshi [Resource Office of the New China News Agency], ed. *Yindunixiya Jiben Qingkuang Cankao Ziliao* [Materials on Indonesian conditions]. Beijing, for internal circulation, 1960.

*Zhonghua Renmin Gongheguo duiwai Guangxi Wenjianji* [Documents on foreign affairs of the People's Republic China], vol. 1 (1949–50), vol. 2 (1951–3), vol. 3 (1954–5), vol. 4 (1956–7), vol. 5 (1958), vol. 6 (1959), vol. 7 (1960), vol. 8 (1961), vol. 9 (1962), vol. 10 (1963), vol. 11 (1964), vol. 12 (1965). Beijing: Shijie Zhishi Chubanshe, 1957–65.

"Zhongyang Renmin Zhengfu yu Huaqiao" [The people's central government and the overseas Chinese]. *Chung Hua Hsies Hui Hui Khan* (Jakarta), no. 12 (1949).

Zhou Enlai. "Women de Waijiao Fangzhen he Renwu" (1949) [Our foreign policy principles and tasks]. In *Zhou Enlai Xuanji* [Selected writings of Zhou Enlai], vol. 2 (pp. 85–92). Beijing: Renmin Chubanshe, 1984.

———. "Guangyu Huaqiao de Shuangchong Guoji Wenti" [Issues concerning dual nationality of the overseas Chinese]. In *Zhou Enlai Waijiao Wenxuan* [Selected writings on foreign affairs by Zhou Enlai]. Beijing: Zhonggong Zhongyan Wenxian Chubanshe, 1990, pp. 135–9.

Zhou Erfu. "Zhongguo Wenhua Daibiaotuan zai Yindunixiya" [Chinese cultural delegation in Indonesia]. *Renmin Ribao*, 24 September 1955.

———. *Dongnanya Sanji* [Reflections on Southeast Asia]. Beijing: Zhongguo Qingnian Chubanshe, 1956.

Zhou Nanjing. "Lishishang Zhongguo he Yinduninxiya de Wenhua Jiaoliu" [Cultural exchanges between China and Indonesia during the historical era]. In *Zhongwai Wenhua Jiaoliushi* [A history of cultural exchange between China and foreign countries], ed. Zhou Yilian. Zhengzhou: Henan Renmin Chubanshe, 1987, pp. 190–238.

———, ed. *Baren yu Yindunixiya* [Ba Ren and Indonesia]. Hong Kong: Nandao Chubanshe, 2001.

Zhou Nanjing and Kong Yuanzhi, eds. *Sujianuo, Zhongguo, Yindunixiya Huaren* [Sukarno, China and Indonesian Chinese]. Hong Kong: Hong Kong Social Sciences Publisher, 2003.

Zhu Lin. *Dashi Furen Huiyilu: Xunyali, Yinni, Faguo, Meiguo* [Memoir of an ambassador's wife: Hungary, Indonesia, France and the USA]. Beijing: Shijie Zhishi Chubanshe, 1991.

Zhu Qi. *Zhongguo he Yindunixiya Renmin de Youyi Guangxi he Wenhua Jiaoliu* [Friendship and cultural exchange between the Chinese people and Indonesian people]. Beijing: Zhongguo Qingnian Chubanshe, 1956.

Zhuang Guotu. *Huaqiao Huaren yu Zhongguo de Guanxi* [Relations between Chinese overseas and China]. Guangzhou: Guangdong Remin Chubanshe, 2001.

Zou Fangjin. "Fan Yinni Guiqiao Laobaoren Zheng Manru" [Interview with Zheng Manru, a veteran journalist from Indonesia]. *Huaren Yuekan* (Hong Kong) 4 (1994): 34–6.

Zou Sheng, ed. *Sujianuo Zongtong zai Zhongguo* [President Sukarno in China]. Hong Kong: Zhonghua Shuju, 1957.

# INDEX

30 September Movement (1965), 2, 5, 132–3, 180, 275
1911 Revolution, 43, 49, 53, 55, *see also* Chinese revolution
1945 Constitution, 132, 226
1945 Generation, 259–60
1945–49 Revolution, *see* Indonesian revolution
1954 college-student delegation report, 101
1955 Bandung Conference, 177, 212, 221, 240, 284
1955 Sumatra People's Delegation, 81

Abdulgani, Roeslan, 19, 59, 68, 140, 174, 190, 199, 214, 217, 219, 275
Adinegoro, 20, 48, 71–2, 74, 87, 90
Adjitorop, Jusuf, 19, 68, 97, 275
Afro-Asian solidarity, 211
Agung, Ide Anak Agung Gde, 9, 231, 276
Ahmad, Zainal Abidin, 95, 276
Aidit, Dipa Nusantara, 19, 95, 192, 212, 276–7
All-China Federation of Literary and Art Circles (AFLAC), 242
Anantaguna, S., 20, 108, 277
Ang Goan Jan, 277
Arifin, Zainul, 74, 81, 120, 142, 215, 277
Assaat Movement, 170
Aziz, H.A., 100, 173, 277–8

*Badan Permusjawaratan Kewarganegaraan Indonesia*, *see* BAPERKI
Bafagih, Asa, 20, 69, 72, 122–3, 199
Bandaharo, H.R., 278
BAPERKI, 162, 167, 285
Barioen A.S., 20, 59, 65, 81, 84–6, 90, 106–7, 109–11, 116–7, 120, 145, 162, 199, 283
Batavia, 39–41, 291
Bey, Arifin, 20, 48, 65–6, 69, 74
Buru Quartet, 44, 253, *see also* Pramoedya Ananta Toer

Canton, 46, 82, *see also* Guangzhou
CCP, *see* Chinese Communist Party
Chen Xiaru, 26, 115, 243, 246, 250, 252–3, 256
Chen Yi, 174, 180–1, 186, 195, 221–2, 226–8
Chiang Kai-shek, 44, 50, 52, 56, 74, 103, 116, 128, 147, 169, 207
China
    fever, 3
    metaphor, 4–5, 22–4, 58, 101, 129, 153, 156, 167, 174, 206, 228, 233, 236, 260, 266, 270
China-image(s), 21, 23, 30, 34–5, 39–41, 43, 52–3, 60, 144, 155–6, 160, 183, 223
    -makers, 2, 17–8, 23, 28, 129, 136
Chinese
    anti-Chinese riots, 9, 170, 173

Communism/Communists, 52, 63–4
Communist Party (CCP), 50, 52, 55, 57, 61, 63–4, 69–72, 77, 84, 93, 97, 99, 103–4, 112–4, 128, 175, 185–7, 192, 211, 220, 232, 269
  identity, 9, 157–8, 162, 166
  intellectuals, 14, 42–3, 114
  local communities, 4, 6, 8–9, 12, 41, 44–5, 156, 168, 174, 176, 207, 277
  nationalism, 47, 62, 73, 166, 210, 268
  Red Army, 239–40
  revolution, 14, 22, 33, 41–2, 44, 48, 50, 57, 73, 107, 185, *see also* 1911 revolution
Cold War, 6, 12, 28, 61, 132, 155, 176, 188
collectivism, 84, 145, 147–8, 152, 171
colonialism, 146, 156, 196, 218, 228, 232, 251
  anti-, 46, 180, 187, 216
Communism, 11–2, 22, 50, 62, 70, 76–7, 95, 104–5, 122, 129, 143, 153, 174, 185, 210, 232, 241, 268
  Russian, 63
Communist Party of Indonesia (PKI), 6, 8, 19, 56, 68, 78, 87, 97, 130, 132–3, 135, 167, 170, 183, 192, 194, 212, 226–7, 242–3, 254–5, 260, 264, 266, 275–6, 282–4, 290
Confucius, 59, 64, 210
Confucian
  brother, 272
  times, 268
  tradition, 113
Cultural Congress
  First (Yogyakarta), 109
  Second (Bandung), 139
cultural radicalism, 24, 235, 250

democracy, 55, 91, 145, 160, 208, 221–2, 224
Dipanagara War, 40
divide-and-rule policy, 41
Djawoto, 191, 279
Dutch
  colonialism, 40, 142, 156, 169
  East Indies, 42, 44–5, 207
  Company (VOC), 39

East-West binary, 11
ethnicity, 11–2, 23, 274

First Five-Year Plan (1953–57), 89, 91, 97, 99

*gotong royong* (mutual assistance), 96, 152, 226
Great Leap Forward Movement, 89, 93, 96, 114, 165, 249, 251
Great Proletariat Cultural Revolution, 5
Guangzhou (Canton), 81, 198, 219, 245, 258, *see also* Canton
Guided Democracy, 5, 10, 132, 146, 184, 201, 206, 213, 222–4, 226–7, 230–1, 233, 254–7, 259–60, 266, 283, 288
Guomindang, *see* Kuomintang (KMT)

Hatta, Mohammad, 1, 3, 33, 42, 48–9, 53–4, 63, 71, 78, 91–2, 97, 99–100, 120–1, 128, 147, 149, 154, 169, 173, 175, 198–9, 232, 269, 278–9
Hong Kong, 81–2, 84, 103
*huaqiao*, 39, 43, 256

imperialism, 42, 54, 56, 142, 180, 184–5, 196, 232, 250–1
  anti-, 180, 183, 187, 211

China's, 57
Western, 39, 42, 46–7, 72, 209, 228
India, 35, 54, 89, 178
individualism, 84, 114, 147–8, 256
Indonesian
　archipelago, 4, 36, 156
　Catholic Party, 99
　-China Friendship Association, 173, 191, 229, 278, 283
　Communist Party, *see* PKI
　independence, 41, 48
　Journalists' Association (PWI), 94, 100
　nationalism, 45, 63, 208, 280
　nationalist movement, 19, 46
　Nationalist Party (PNI), 74, 90, 94, 130, 146, 169, 177, 208, 279–80, 284–5, 287–8, 291
　Conference, 225
　New Agency (PIA), 90
　revolution, 45–6, 54–5, 57, 137–8, 169, 175, 241, 277–8, 282–3, 285
　Socialist Party (PSI), 54, 70, 101, 150, 286
Institute of People's Culture, *see* Lekra
intellectuals, 3–5, 8, 14, 18–20, 22–5, 28, 42–3, 52, 57, 58, 63, 68–9, 78, 80, 85, 93, 95, 97, 103, 105–7, 109, 112–9, 123–4, 128–9, 134–47, 149–51, 164, 167, 181–2, 190–1, 196, 200–1, 210, 230, 235, 241, 243–5, 247–9, 251, 254–6, 258–60, 263, 266, 268–72, 282, 290
　political and cultural, 18–21, 23, 42, 77, 129, 136, 150, 183, 189, 202, 268, 270
Islam, 36–7, 56, 64, 107, 119–24, 209
　Islamization, 36

Jakarta, 2, 25, 37, 46, 91, 94–5, 103, 147, 158, 162, 175–7, 179–80, 182, 188–9, 191, 196, 200, 211–3, 227, 229, 242–4, 257, 276, 278–81, 285, 287, 289–90
　Greater, 86, 143, 146
Japan, 2, 11, 14, 29, 47, 90, 99, 131, 214, 271
Japanese occupation, 106, 109, 123, 164, 186, 237, 277, 281–2, 289–90
Java, 25, 35, 38–9, 132, 170, 179, 228, 276

Kang Youwei, 42
Karim, Abdul Daeng Patombong, 280
KNIL, *see* Royal Netherlands Indies Army
Koentjaraningrat, 95, 280
Korean War, 71
Kuomintang (KMT), 77, 114, 157, 209, 220, 287
Kussudiardjo, Bagong, 108, 110, 116, 198, 280
Kwee Kek Beng, 20, 64, 74, 79, 82, 87, 90, 100, 182, 280

Lekra (People's Institute of Culture), 20, 108, 141, 171, 235, 241–3, 255–6, 258–60, 263–4, 277–8, 280–2, 286, 291
*Lembaga Pembinaan Kesatuan Bangsa*, *see* LPKB
Li Peng, 2
Liang Qichao, 43
Liem Koen Hian, 19, 63, 70, 207, 281, 290
LPKB, 165, 167
Lu Xun, 210, 241–2, 244–6, 256, 258

Madiun Rebellion, 238, 276, 290
Majapahit empire, 38–9
Malacca, 36

Malay
   archipelago, 28, 36
   world, 44
Manikebu Affair, 260, 266
Mao Tse-tung, *see* Mao Zedong
Mao Zedong, 22, 44, 50, 52, 54–7,
   59–61, 63, 73–7, 89, 91, 108, 114,
   122–3, 127–8, 146–7, 160, 164,
   168, 175, 185, 189, 194, 207, 210,
   217–8, 220–2, 224, 233–4, 239–40,
   246–7, 250, 263, 266, 268–9
Marxism, 56, 64, 73, 121, 209
Marxist, 73
   historical analysis, 231
   ideology, 78, 104, 121, 128
   -Leninist teachings, 59, 64
   theory, 89
Masyumi Party, 76, 86, 95, 120, 123,
   128, 130, 134, 147–8, 183, 279,
   289
May 4th Movement, 116
Middle East, 35
Middle Kingdom, 29, 37
modernity, 2, 5, 12, 43, 267, 270–1
   alternative, 2, 5, 23, 28, 272, 274
modernization, 113, 271
Mohammad Natsir, 56, 134, 152, 176,
   278
Mononutu, Arnold, 71, 75, 121, 177,
   281

Nahdatul Ulama (NU), 81, 120, 122,
   130, 278
*Nanyang*, 14, 42, 58
Nasution, Abdul Haris, 56, 132, 140
nation-building, 3, 11, 20, 58, 73, 80,
   92, 107–8, 111–2, 114–6, 119,
   128, 142, 144, 153, 169, 183,
   213–4, 220, 224, 233–4, 248–9
nation-state, 6, 11–4, 16, 27, 34, 137,
   172
   narrative, 15

national identity, 20, 28, 53
nationalism, 11, 25, 33, 41, 44, 53,
   55–6, 63, 129, 137, 208–9, 231,
   237, 271
   Chinese, *see* Chinese nationalism
   Indonesian, *see* Indonesian
      nationalism
New Democracy, 22, 59–65, 68–70,
   77, 128, 145, 149, 164, 186, 210,
   233, 268
New Life Movement, 228–9
New Order government/regime, 7, 133
Ngantung, Henk, 146, 191, 255, 281
Nio Joe Lan, 281
Njoto, 19, 97, 106, 108–9, 243, 263,
   282


One Hundred Flowers movement, 118
Ong Hok Ham, 165, 282


pan-Asianism, 209, 215, 233, 270
*Panca Cinta*, 264, 266
Pancasila, 55, 208
Pane, Armijn, 20, 38, 50–1, 64–5, 67,
   73–4, 106–7, 110, 116, 168, 182,
   194, 199, 258, 282
parliamentary democracy
   Indonesian, 65, 132, 136, 140,
      224–5, 233
   Western-style, 12, 130, 139, 141,
      153, 206, 211, 213, 224
People's Institute of Culture, *see* Lekra
People's Republic of China (PRC),
   2–3, 5, 7, 9, 11, 26, 34, 56, 60–3,
   68–9, 72–4, 76–8, 80–2, 85, 87,
   90–2, 99, 103, 107, 111, 113,
   116–7, 119–20, 124, 127–8,
   142–3, 146–9, 151, 153–5, 157–8,
   160–5, 167–9, 171–3, 174–6, 179,
   182, 185–6, 188, 190–1, 197,
   199–200, 205–6, 210–2, 214–5,

219–20, 222–3, 225–30, 232–4, 236, 240–8, 253, 255, 257–8, 260, 263–4, 270, 275, 278, 281
*peranakan*, 156–7, 162–5, 169, 192, 281, 285
PKI, see Communist Party of Indonesia
PNI, see Indonesian Nationalist Party (PNI)
political populism, 24
Pramoedya Ananta Toer, 1, 3, 10, 20, 24, 44, 110–1, 115, 119, 139, 171, 192, 202, 230, 234–59, 263, 269, 282, see also Buru Quartet
PRC, see People's Republic of China
*pribumi*, 8, 167
Prijono, 20, 106, 109, 116, 143, 191, 244, 283–4
PSI, see Indonesian Socialist Party
*Pudjangga Baru*, 107

Ramadhan K.H., 20, 85, 92, 100, 115, 118–9, 121, 149–50, 199, 283
Royal Netherlands Indies Army (KNIL), 239

Said, Rasuna, 100, 161, 172, 279, 283
Sakirman, 19, 56, 97, 283
Saleh, Buyung, 20, 138, 171, 284
Sarikat Islam, 49, 290
Sartono, 19, 67, 74, 284
Sastroamidjojo, Ali, 75, 142, 187
Satya, Graha, 20, 94, 127, 146, 154, 173, 284–5
Sayuti, Melik, 20, 199, 285
Siauw Giok Tjhan, 19, 45, 162, 164, 207, 285
Sie Boen Lian, 165, 285
Shenzhen, 81, 103
Sino-Indonesian
Alliance/ties, 183–4
community, 156

conflict in 1959–60, 179, 197
cultural exchanges, 7
diplomatic relations/relationship, 6–7, 60, 155–6, 175, 181–2, 184, 201
exchanges, 26, 36, 41, 57
interactions, 2, 11, 14, 16, 29, 35
relations/relationship, 8, 28, 57, 176, 187, 201, 212, 216, 243, 277, 283
strategic partnership, 3
trade, 38
Treaty on Dual Nationality, 179, 212
Sino-Southeast Asian
relations, 37
trade, 41
Sino-Soviet alliance, 71–3
Siregar, Bakri, 286
Situmorang, Sitor, 20, 79, 82–3, 101, 149, 262–3, 286
Sjahrir, Sutan, 19, 42, 50, 54–5, 71, 286, 290
socialism, 55, 95, 185, 194, 208
Socialist Realism, 118, 246, 250, 253, 263, 282
Soeharto, R., 90, 287
Soemardjan, Selo, 95, 286
Soenarjo, Raden Haji Achmad, 120, 287
Soeto Meisen, 26, 65, 163, 210, 227, 287
Soong Ching Ling, 196, 225, 232
Southeast Asia, 25, 42–4, 46, 57, 70, 72, 173, 185–6, 188, 201, 268, 271, 273, 290
-China diplomatic relations, 13
postcolonial, 11
traditions, 15, 172
Soviet
model, 68, 70, 72, 114, 128
Union, 6, 52, 61, 64, 67, 70–2, 77, 89, 142, 175, 185, 212, 214–5, 223–5, 232, 246, 250, 256, 268

Srivijaya, 35, 38
Stalin, Joseph, 113, 122, 248
Suaidy, Hadji Muhammad Saleh, 104, 122, 287
Subandrio, 19, 90, 154, 174, 198, 288
Sudiro, Raden, 143–4, 288
Sugardo, 20, 52, 67, 69, 71, 74, 81–2, 84, 90, 148, 172, 288
Suharto, 7, 36, 133
  regime, 180, 272, 285
Sukarno, 9–10, 16–7, 19, 24, 26, 33, 42, 46–8, 53, 55, 65, 76–7, 90, 129, 131–4, 140, 145–6, 148, 150, 156, 165, 167–8, 170, 175–6, 179–82, 188–9, 195, 198–9, 201–2, 205–33, 235, 244, 254–6, 259–60, 266, 270, 275–6, 278–9, 283, 285–8, 290
  "Conception Speech", 224, 226, 254
  era, 2–3, 5, 7, 34, 42, 101, 130, 137, 151, 162, 201, 264, 272
  regime, 20, 184, 269
Sukiman, 86, 97, 148, 176, 189, 281, 289
Sumardjo, Trisno, 20, 104, 106, 117, 119, 150, 197, 199, 242, 289
Sumatra, 65, 81, 100, 175, 276, 290
Sun Yat-sen, 42–4, 48, 52, 55–6, 63, 73, 77, 90, 196, 207–9, 221, 225, 233, 268, *see also* Three People's Principles

Tabrani, M., 65, 106, 110, 116, 127, 142, 182, 199, 289
Tan Kah Kee, 163, 186
Tan Malaka, 19, 42, 46–8, 54, 285
Thaib, Maisir, 63, 71, 290

Three People's Principles, 55, 63, 208–10, 233, *see also* Sun Yat-sen
Thung Liang Lee, 166, 290
Tirtodiningrat, Djoko Marsaid, 90, 200, 290
tribute/tributary missions, 35, 37–8
transnational
  approach/enquiry, 6, 16
  perspective, 15–6, 28, 274

United States (USA), 30, 65, 90, 92, 96, 132, 162, 164, 176, 188, 197, 212, 214–5, 224–5
universal humanism, 237, 253, 257, 260, 264

Wang Jingwei, 56, 165
Wardhana, Wisnoe, 108, 110, 291
Wilopo, 19, 74, 142, 289, 291
Wirjopranoto, Sukardjo, 74, 94, 101, 147, 291
Wispi, Agam, 291
World War II, 13, 19, 120, 123, 208, 228, 258, 278–9, 281, 284, 286–8, 290

Yangtze River Bridge, 92, 219
Yogyakarta, 109, 127, 142, 283, 286, 291

Zheng He, 36–7
Zhou Enlai, 26, 75, 91, 155, 175–8, 185–7, 189, 195, 198, 211, 221, 239, 284
Zhu Rongji, 2